Niccolò Machiavelli, Christian Edward Detmold

The Historical, Political, and Diplomatic Writings of Niccolò Macchiavelli

Vol. I

Niccolò Machiavelli, Christian Edward Detmold

The Historical, Political, and Diplomatic Writings of Niccolò Macchiavelli
Vol. I

ISBN/EAN: 9783744641197

Printed in Europe, USA, Canada, Australia, Japan

Cover: Foto ©ninafisch / pixelio.de

More available books at **www.hansebooks.com**

OF

NICCOLO MACHIAVELLI

TRANSLATED FROM THE ITALIAN

BY

CHRISTIAN E. DETMOLD

IN FOUR VOLUMES

VOL. I.

BOSTON
JAMES R. OSGOOD AND COMPANY
1882

Copyright, 1882,
BY CHRISTIAN E. DETMOLD.

All rights reserved.

UNIVERSITY PRESS:
JOHN WILSON AND SON, CAMBRIDGE.

TRANSLATOR'S PREFACE.

In offering the present translation of Machiavelli's principal historical, political, and diplomatic writings, my original object was simply to afford to the general reader the opportunity of judging for himself of the character of the man, and of those of his works upon which his reputation for good or for evil mainly depends. I had no intention of entering the lists of the detractors and defenders of Machiavelli, or of adding to the number of his commentators. Enough of these have written in almost every European tongue, making volumes sufficient nearly to constitute a respectable library by themselves.

Nevertheless, as certain views and conclusions touching the more prominent of the seeming contradictions in Machiavelli's writings suggested themselves to me whilst engaged in this translation, I venture briefly to present them, although they may differ materially from those taken by leading critics and commentators. No writer perhaps has been more variously judged than Machiavelli; regarded by some as the very embodiment of the spirit of evil, especially by the earlier critics; and by others looked upon as a pure, unflinching patriot, misunderstood and misinterpreted. The manifest contradictions, real or apparent, in his writings, have naturally given rise to widely differing commentaries, aiming less to explain and reconcile these contradictions to each other, than to make the favorable or unfavorable estimate of the author prevail. None of Machiavelli's writings, except his treatise "On the Art of War," were printed during his lifetime. A few years after his death, however, the "Discourses on the First Ten Books of Titus Livius," the Florentine History, and "The Prince," were printed at Rome with the authorization of Pope Clement VII. But disregarding this previous papal permission, Pope Paul IV. ordered these works to be placed in the *Index Expurgatorius*, which order was confirmed by the Council of Trent in 1564. Eight years later, the commission on the Index proposed to the descendants of Machiavelli to publish an expurgated edition of his works, on condition that the author's name should be suppressed. This offer, however, was indignantly rejected by his grandsons, Giuliano de' Ricci, son of the daughter, and Niccolo Machiavelli, son of one of the sons; and thus for centuries his writings remained utterly discredited in Italy.

Bayle in his Dictionary observes that "Machiavellism" and the art of "governing tyrannically by violence and fraud are "terms of the same significance"; thus creating the word "Machiavellism," which has been generally adopted in European languages. Later, no less a personage than Frederick the Great, while Crown Prince of Prussia, published his "Anti Machiavelli," which, it is said, he somewhat regretted after having become king; and of which a Frenchman said, with as much wit perhaps as truth, that "the greatest homage "which any prince had ever paid to the doctrines of Machia-"velli was to have refuted him, so that he might follow his "precepts with the greater impunity."

The writings and reputation of Machiavelli became early known in England. Lord Bacon refers to him several times in his Essays, but makes no unfavorable reflections upon him. Shakespeare mentions him three times, and of course takes the then prevailing popular view of his character. First, in the Merry Wives of Windsor, Act III. Sc. 1, the host of the Garter inn exclaims: "Peace, I say! hear mine host of the Garter. Am I politic? am I subtle? am I a Machiavel?" Secondly, in the First Part of King Henry VI., Act V. Sc. 4, when the captive Maid of Orleans pleads for her life on the ground of being with child, and says, "It was Alençon that enjoyed my love," the Duke of York exclaims, "Alençon! that notorious Machiavel!" And thirdly, in the Third Part of King Henry VI., Act III. Sc. 2, when Richard, Duke of Gloster, resolves to make himself king of England, he ends his long soliloquy, in which he recounts his various qualifications for deceit and murder, by the following climax: —

> "I can add colors to the chameleon,
> Change shapes with Proteus for advantages,
> And set the murderous Machiavel to school.
> Can I do this, and cannot get a crown?
> Tut! were it farther off, I'll pluck it down!"

Upon one point the modern reviewers and commentators of Machiavelli are pretty much agreed; namely, that his morality must be judged of by that prevailing at the time of his writing, and that the principles of conduct laid down by him in "The Prince" are more the reflex of the perversity of the period in which he lived, than that of his own mind. It was the period of the Renaissance, a time of great interest and great troubles for Italy, and perhaps the most interesting period that any people ever passed through; and fruitful of the most important events, discoveries, and progress in nearly all human achievements. It was marked at the same time by contradictions similar to those noted in Machiavelli, — with the developments of human genius at their highest, and that of the moral sense, if not at its lowest, yet at a very low point. It was then that Alexander VI., the father of Cesare and Lucretia Borgia, was Pope, and shocked the world by his gross sensuality and licentiousness; and was succeeded in the Pontificate, after a brief interval of less than a month, by Julius II., who was more soldier than priest, and exceeded even the Borgia in the display of craft and violence in his efforts to recover and enlarge the possessions and temporal power of the Church.

In dedicating his little volume of "The Prince" to Lorenzo de' Medici, Machiavelli makes no pretence of offering a moral treatise; but simply, as the result of his reading and personal experience, a collection of the actions of great men, by which they succeeded in acquiring and preserving states. It is by the example of these that he attempts to instruct the Magnificent Lorenzo as to the qualities and conduct necessary for a prince to achieve similar success.

Modern English writers have judged Machiavelli differently, and some of them, perhaps, have gone to the other extreme; as may possibly be said of Byron in Childe Harold's Pilgrimage (Canto IV. St. 54, 55) :—

> "In Santa Croce's holy precincts lie
> Ashes which make it holier, dust which is
> Even in itself an immortality.
> . . . . . Here repose
> Angelo's, Alfieri's bones, and his,
> The starry Galileo, with his woes;
> Here Machiavelli's earth returned to whence it rose.
>
> "These are four minds, which, like the elements,
> Might furnish forth creation."

Prominent, however, amongst modern reviews of Machiavelli stands Macaulay's masterly, brilliant, though not always just essay, which appeared in the Edinburgh Review, March, 1827. This came like a revelation upon the reading public, and certainly did more than any other literary production to spread a more correct knowledge and juster views of Machiavelli in England and America.

I abstain from referring to the many most interesting and instructive works on Machiavelli, in Italian, French, and German, that have appeared within the last thirty years; but should be unjust were I not to mention specially that very able and exhaustive work, "Niccolo Machiavelli and his Times," by Professor Pasquale Villari of Florence. Two volumes of this have appeared simultaneously in Italian and in English (1877, 1881), and the third is looked for with eager interest.

The great experience in public affairs which Machiavelli had acquired during his many years' employment in the service of the state at home and in his various missions abroad, coupled with his natural gifts of quick perception and keen penetration, soon taught him that the constant resort to dissembling and treachery by the rulers and governments of the different states of Italy in their dealings with each other, as well as with their more powerful neighbors north of the Alps, was the consequence of their own weakness and fear. This weakness was the natural result of the subdivision of Italy into so many small principalities, forever warring against each other by means of mercenary soldiers of fortune.

Several of the more important of these principalities had in turn invoked the aid of their powerful Transalpine neighbors, France, Germany, and Spain, who in their turn had invaded, pillaged, and devastated Italy from one end to the other. The woes inflicted upon Italy by these foreign invasions were the cause of intense grief and mortification to Machiavelli; who, enthusiastic admirer of the ancient Romans that he was, could never forget the power wielded by Rome of old, when, exercising the concentrated sovereignty of all Italy, and with armies of her own, she had made herself the mistress of the world. He witnessed with shame and humiliation the degeneracy and helplessness of his country, and clearly saw the causes of it. It was this that made him the unceasing advocate of the union of all Italy, of the establishment of national armies, instead of the uncertain employment of the venal Condottieri, and of the expulsion of the detested foreigners from the soil of Italy. Machiavelli was a sincere republican and a true lover of liberty; but for the sake of a united Italy, with well-trained national armies, strong enough to protect her against the periodical inundations of Northern barbarians, he was willing to give up his cherished republican form of government, and accept the one man power of a prince, though he was a Medici. Thence that passionately eloquent appeal to Lorenzo de' Medici, to play the part of the long hoped for deliverer, with which Machiavelli thus closes his much debated treatise of "The Prince": —

"You must not, then, allow this opportunity to pass, so that
"Italy, after waiting so long, may at last see her deliverer ap-
"pear. Nor can I possibly express with what affection he
"would be received in all those provinces that have suffered so
"long from this inundation of foreign foes! — with what thirst
"for vengeance, with what persistent faith, with what devotion,

"and with what tears! What door would be closed to him?
"Who would refuse him obedience? What envy would dare
"oppose him? What Italian would refuse him homage? This
"barbarous dominion of the foreigner offends the very nostrils
"of everybody.

"Let your illustrious house, then, assume this task with that
"courage and hopefulness which every just enterprise inspires;
"so that under your banner our country may recover its an-
"cient fame, and under your auspices may be verified the
"words of Petrarca:—

>"'Virtù contro al furore
>Prenderà l'arme, e fia il combatter corto;
>Chè l'antico valore
>Negli Italici cuor non è ancor morto.'"

In fact, Machiavelli felt with regard to the union of Italy very much as President Lincoln did during the Secession war, when he said, with reference to the United States, "My para-"mount object is to save the Union, and not either to save "or to destroy slavery."

During his several missions to France Machiavelli had clearly observed that the power of France was the result of the unity of territory and of the government. This had been the work of Louis XI., who was indeed the recognized founder of the French monarchy. And the means which he had employed for the attainment of that end were precisely those which Machiavelli recommends for a similar purpose in his treatise of "The Prince"; namely, disregard of pledges, dissembling, perfidy, and violence. In fact, Louis XI. had anticipated these precepts, even to the extermination of a number of the great houses of France which, by their claims to sovereignty over any portion of the soil, could imperil in the slightest degree the absolute control of the king over the entire kingdom.

None of the states of Italy had at that time any regular armies of their own; thus their wars against each other were carried on, as already said, by hired soldiers of fortune, who, for stipulated sums of money, and for a fixed period of time, furnished a certain number of men, generally mounted. These captains, by an understanding amongst themselves, avoided killing or wounding each other's men, so that the battles of those days were rarely bloody. Military valor seems to have died out amongst the Italians, and cunning and perfidy had taken its place. It was a period of personal government, when despotism had supplanted the ancient liberties, which the people had not the courage to maintain or recover.

Machiavelli had also noticed, during his missions to France, the organization of the army, due to the efforts of Charles VII.; and made it the subject of especial notice in his despatches to the Florentine government. He succeeded subsequently in inducing the government of Florence to authorize the establishment of a national militia, and was himself employed to enlist and enroll the men of the Florentine dominion for that purpose. In this laborious duty he displayed the same zeal and devotion to his country, that he did in all his other public employments. Still later in life, after he had tasted the bitterness of degradation from office and the proverbial ingratitude of governments, he wrote and published his seven books on "The Art of War," a highly interesting and admirably written dissertation in the shape of a dialogue; but not comprised in this translation.

The famous eighteenth chapter of "The Prince" — "In what Manner Princes should keep their Faith" — has earned for Machiavelli the odious reputation of having originated and recommended a system of fraud and perfidy as one of the essential arts and practices of princes and governments in all public affairs. I think the unprejudiced reader will have no difficulty in coming to the conclusion that, like other wrongs imputed to Machiavelli, the charge is unjust. The chapter in question opens as follows: "It must be evident to every one that it is "more praiseworthy for a prince always to maintain good faith, "and practise integrity rather than craft and deceit. And yet "the experience of our own times has shown that those princes "have achieved great things who made small account of good "faith, and who understood by cunning to circumvent the in- "telligence of others; and that in the end they got the better "of those whose actions were dictated by loyalty and good "faith," etc.

Proceeding then to indulge in a fanciful and far-fetched allegory to sustain his argument, Machiavelli goes on to say: "A sagacious prince then cannot and should not fulfil his "pledges when their observance is contrary to his interest, "and when the causes that induced him to pledge his faith "no longer exist. If men were all good, then indeed this "precept would be bad; but as men are naturally bad, and "will not observe their faith towards you, you must, in the "same way, not observe yours to them."

In all this, Machiavelli merely states, with his accustomed unhesitating honesty, the practices of nearly all the sovereigns and governments of Europe at that time, — not only in Italy, but in Spain by Ferdinand the Catholic, by Henry VII. in England, and above all by Louis XI. in France, who did not hesitate to teach his son that "a prince who did not know how to dis-"semble was unfit to govern." In truth, this was the period of which it has been well said by one of the historians of France, "The princes of this century placed success before "honor."

To show further that Machiavelli, so far from being the originator of so vicious and reprehensible a practice, merely indicated it as one of the means generally employed by princes, and that it was sanctioned even in advance by the highest authority of the Church, the Popes themselves, I quote the following: "In virtue of the papal bulls of the latter part of the "fifteenth century,[*] the sovereigns of France had special im-"munities in all matters of conscience; for the king's confessor "had the power to absolve the king and his wife, his brothers, "and his children, from the greatest sins, and even crimes, "without being obliged to resort to pontifical authority. The "king was free to choose his own confessor, and to change him "at pleasure, if he found him too strict. The confessor had "also power to release the king from his vows and oaths; and

---

[*] Long prior, therefore, to Machiavelli's writing "The Prince," which was not until 1516, the early part of the sixteenth century.

"thus the king was raised by the Holy See above all the obli-
"gations of duty, law, and right." *

Another circumstance that has brought severe censure upon Machiavelli is his having held up Cesare Borgia as an example in "The Prince." But here he has also been misunderstood and misinterpreted; for after having pointed out wherein Cesare Borgia acted judiciously, and wherein he was at fault, Machiavelli says: "Whoever, then, in a newly acquired state, "finds it necessary to secure himself against his enemies, to "gain friends, to conquer by force or by cunning, to make him- "self feared or beloved by the people, to be followed and re- "vered by the soldiery, to destroy all who could or might injure "him, to substitute a new for the old order of things, to be "severe and yet gracious, magnanimous, and liberal, to disband "a disloyal army and create a new one, to preserve the friend- "ship of kings and princes, so that they may bestow benefits "upon him with grace, and fear to injure him,— such a one, "I say, cannot find more recent examples than those presented "by the conduct of the Duke Valentino." (Chapter VII.)

Machiavelli thus states most carefully in detail the particular cases in which the conduct of Cesare Borgia might serve as an example, but he does not by any means hold him up as a commendable model of general excellence. In fact, although Machiavelli cites many precedents in support of his theories, yet he never justifies crime. On the contrary, he almost invariably condemns it. For instance, in speaking of Agathocles the Sicilian, whom he cites as having achieved the sovereignty of Syracuse "by a thousand efforts and dangers," and maintained it "with great courage, and even temerity," he adds: "Yet we cannot call it valor to massacre one's fellow-citizens, "to betray one's friends, and to be devoid of good faith, mercy, "and religion; such means may enable a man to achieve em- "pire, but not glory."

In the "Discourses on the First Ten Books of Titus Livius" †

---

* See "Privilèges accordés à la Couronne de France par le Saint Siége," 1852, Imprimerie Impériale.

† Book III. Chap. XL. See Vol. II. p. 419.

Machiavelli speaks of stratagems, and of deceiving the enemy in time of war, as being laudable and honorable. But he is very careful to draw a distinction thus: "But I will say this, "that I do not confound such deceit with perfidy, which breaks "pledged faith and treaties; for although states and kingdoms "may at times be won by perfidy, yet will it ever bring dis- "honor with it."

As a further proof of the injustice of the aspersions of Machiavelli, I have included in these volumes a translation of a little book bearing the title of "Thoughts of a Statesman"; being a collection of maxims selected from the works of Machiavelli, and first published at Rome in 1771, and reprinted in the *Italia* edition of his works (1813).

In conclusion, I think it can with truth be said of Machiavelli, that he has been more abused than known, and that had he been better known he would have been less abused. For the reader of his works would have become satisfied that Machiavelli was neither devil nor saint, but simply a most gifted, honest man and patriot, who was not afraid to write, in the most terse and lucid manner, what he honestly thought calculated to advance the interests of his country, which he had so much at heart. If by the present translation I succeed in causing a more accurate acquaintance with the works of this remarkable man, I shall feel doubly rewarded, having already had ample compensation in the work itself, which, during several years of compulsory inactivity from impaired health, has afforded me constant, agreeable, and most instructive occupation.

C. E. DETMOLD.

Paris, March, 1882.

CONTENTS OF VOLUME I.

	PAGE
TRANSLATOR'S PREFACE	iii
LIFE OF NICCOLO MACHIAVELLI	xv

HISTORY OF FLORENCE.

DEDICATION	3
PREFACE	7
FIRST BOOK	11
SECOND BOOK	57
THIRD BOOK	118
FOURTH BOOK	166
FIFTH BOOK	212
SIXTH BOOK	266
SEVENTH BOOK	319
EIGHTH BOOK	367

LIFE

OF

NICCOLO MACHIAVELLI.

THE following sketch of the life of Machiavelli is, so far as the facts are concerned, translated almost verbatim from Luigi Passerini's article on Machiavelli, prefatory to the edition of his works by L. Passerini and G. Milanesi; that being the most concise and correct of the many biographies of the Florentine Secretary, and supported throughout by official documents.

The origin of the Machiavelli family dates from the old Marquis Hugo of Tuscany, who flourished in the middle of the ninth century. The family were lords proprietors of Monte Spertoli, in the Val di Pesa; but desirous of enjoying the right of citizenship of Florence, they moved into the city and established themselves in the quarter of Oltr' Arno. They became attached to the Guelf party, and a number of the ancestors of Niccolo were honored with the highest dignities in the government. Bernardo, the father of Niccolo, was a respectable jurisconsult, or, as it was then termed, judge, and treasurer of the Marches of Ancona. He had married Bartolomea Nelli, widow of Niccolo Benozzi, who was of an equally distinguished family, tracing their origin back to the old Counts of Borgo Nuovo di Fuecchio, known before the ninth century; and a number of the members of this family had also enjoyed the honors of some of the most important offices in the government of Florence. With all this the family were poor, receiving but a very scanty income from their landed possessions, and having to depend almost entirely upon the modest compensation which Bernardo derived from his profession.

Niccolo Machiavelli was born on the 3d of May, 1469; little or nothing is known of his early years, or who directed his first studies, though there is reason to believe that it was his mother, who was a great lover of poetry and had herself written some religious verses. Being desirous of devoting himself to the service of the government, he was placed about the year 1494 under the direction of Marcello Virgilio Adriani, in the Second Chancellery, whose business was mainly with the ambassadors and with all matters concerning war. It is probable that by way of beginning his political career he chose a moment when, in consequence of the expulsion of Piero de' Medici, there was an entire reform of the institutions of the republic, by establishing them upon a wider and more democratic basis. Fra Girolamo Savonarola had at that time a large share in the affairs of the government; but it cannot be truly said that Machiavelli was indebted to him for his admission to the public service, as has been asserted by some, misled probably by another of the family bearing the same name, and who was amongst the warmest supporters of Savonarola's faction, whilst the writings of our Niccolo show clearly that he was neither friend nor admirer of the terrible Dominican.

Machiavelli very soon gave proof of superior ability in the career which he had chosen; so that when the post of Secretary became vacant, in 1498, it was given to him by a decree of the Major Council on the 19th of June, 1498, although very able men, and more advanced in years than he, competed for the place. Amongst these was Francesco Baroni, who had but lately rendered valuable service to the state in the trial of Fra Girolamo Savonarola.

Machiavelli had scarcely held the office a few weeks, when, by another resolution of the Signoria, he was on the 14th of July chosen Secretary of the Ten of Liberty; at all times a most important office, inasmuch as he had to occupy himself with military matters, which had become much more important at that time, when Florence was engaged in war with Pisa for the purpose of bringing that revolted city back to her duty, and at the same time had to defend herself against the Venetians, who, at the instigation of the Medici, were moving against the Florentine republic. Although elected only for the month of August, Machiavelli remained nevertheless in charge for about fifteen years, an unquestionable proof that a person more capable of filling the post than he could not be found. And in fact the documents that remain to us of those times show the very large share he had in all the affairs of state, political as well as military; and the many records of external relations, as well as matters of war, written at the dictation of Niccolo Machiavelli, bear witness that nothing important was done whilst he was in office without his direction and counsel.

Besides the despatch of the ordinary business of his office, he was frequently employed by the Signoria, or more correctly speaking by the "Ten of Liberty and Peace," to whom this business belonged, in missions of the greatest interest. The series of these missions begins in November, 1498, with that to the Lord of Piombino, at that time in the military service of the republic, to request him to join the Florentine forces before the walls of Pisa. He was sent to him a second time on the 24th of March, 1499, whilst Jacopo d' Appiano was at Pontedera, to urge him to do his duty, and not to insist upon an increase of pay which he demanded. This mission was followed by another to the Lady Catharine Sforza Riario, at Furli, in July of the same year, in relation to the *condotta* of her son Ottaviano.

Machiavelli was several times sent as commissary to the army besieging Pisa, where he was exposed to very great fatigue and even danger of life. But in July, 1500, he was charged with the still more important duty of proceeding to the court of France, together with Francesco della Casa, ambassador to Louis XII., to explain to him the truth respecting the ill conduct of his troops, which he had sent against the Pisans at the request of the republic of Florence; and to vindicate the Florentine republic from the charges made by these rapacious mercenaries, for the purpose of exculpating themselves for their shameful conduct. Machiavelli, having been an eyewitness to the whole affair, was the soul of this embassy, from which he returned to Florence, after about six months' absence, on the 14th of January, 1501, when he immediately resumed his old office in the Chancellery of the Ten of Liberty; but for a very short time only, as by the end of the same month he had to proceed to Pistoja, which was all in confusion in consequence of the feud between the parties of the Panteatichi and the Cancellieri. After this he had to proceed in the summer to Cascina and Sienna, on business relating to the Pisan war. In August he went again to Pistoja, where he succeeded in making the opposing factions swear to keep the peace; which, however, was but ephemeral, for a peace imposed by menaces is not durable. After a little while the parties resumed their arms, and blood flowed in the streets; so that it became necessary for Machiavelli to return there in October, in company with Niccolo Valori.

Between the months of May and October he went several times to Arezzo; also to Vitellozzo Vitelli, Condottiere of the Duke Valentino, who had instigated that city to revolt; and also to the Florentine commissaries who were with the French army. On his return he presented to the Signoria a communication "On the Manner in which the revolted Population of the Val di Chiana should be treated," of which, however, only a fragment remains.

His mission to Cesare Borgia, whom he found at Imola in the early part of October, and whom he followed through the Romagna and Umbria until the 23d of January, 1503, is so well known as to make it unnecessary to enlarge upon its object here; particularly as it gave rise to Machiavelli's well-known " Description of the Manner in which the Duke Valentino pro- " ceeded to kill Vitellozzo Vitelli, Oliverotto da Fermo, the " Signor Paolo and the Duke Gravina Orsini." The Duke of Romagna, believing that this act, which he regarded as necessary for his own defence, did not displease the Florentine republic, induced his father, Pope Alexander VI., to request the government of the republic to contract an alliance with the Borgia family. This caused Piero Soderini to send Machiavelli to Sienna as ambassador to Pandolfo Petrucci on the 26th of April, 1503, to inform him of the fact, and to invite him to make common cause with the Florentines. But whilst the negotiations were pending, Pope Alexander VI. died, and Machiavelli was sent to Volterra to concert measures with Cardinal Francesco Soderini respecting the election of a new Pope. He accompanied this prelate as far as Val d'Arno, whilst on his way to Rome; and afterwards, on the 24th of October, he left himself for the Eternal City, where the conclave was assembled for the election of another new Pope in place of Pius III., who had died only twenty-six days after his election, and where Machiavelli remained until the 22d of December.

He was not permitted to enjoy a long repose, for on the 12th of January, 1504, we find him charged with a mission to Firenzuola; the object of which, however, is not known. A few days later he received instructions to proceed a second time to the court of France. He did not leave, however, until the 19th of January, and negotiated with King Louis XII. at Lyons, respecting the object of his mission; and on his return, which must have been near the close of February, he was glad to bring the Signoria the assurance that in the truce concluded between France and Spain it was stipulated that the republic of Florence should be comprised, and that the apprehensions excited by the success of the Spanish arms were groundless.

In April of the same year Machiavelli was at Piombino, with the apparent object of informing Jacopo IV. d' Alviano, lord of the place, of certain dangers that threatened him, and to counsel him; but with the real purpose of ascertaining exactly his disposition, and to bring him back to his good faith to the republic. Having returned to Florence, he had barely time to lift his foot from the stirrup, when he had, on the 8th of the same month, to proceed to Castiglione del Lago, to urge Gianpaolo Baglioni, then in the pay of the republic, to perform his duty, and to take the field with his troops against the Pisans, which he refused to do on the ground of his having to guard himself against enemies whom he had in Perugia, and by whom his power was menaced. As Baglioni persisted in his refusal, Machiavelli went to Mantua to conclude a *condotta* with the Marquis Giovan Francesco to enter the service of the republic. But he failed in his efforts, owing to the immoderate demands of the Gonzaga. After that he was sent in July to Sienna, to thank Pandolfo Petrucci for the information which he had secretly given to the Signoria of the hostile intentions of Bartolommeo d' Alviano, who was preparing to carry help to the Pisans, and to treat with Pandolfo about a *condotta* in the pay of the republic. But as the latter was cunningly playing a double part and contemplated treason, Machiavelli, who knew him well, and surpassed him in sagacity, drew from him the information which he wanted most; and then left him without concluding any engagement with him. Bartolommeo d' Alviano actually started for Pisa; but at Torre San Vincenzo he encountered Antonio Giacomini, and was completely defeated by him, so that he had to take to flight.

The Florentines thought that the favorable moment had arrived for capturing the revolted city, and for that purpose the Ten sent the Secretary to the besieging army to concert measures for the attempt. He fulfilled his duty, but the enterprise failed in consequence of the cowardly conduct of the mercenary soldiers.

This experience completely satisfied Machiavelli how little reliance could be placed upon hireling troops, and how necessary it was for every state to have an army of its own. Having convinced the Ten of the advantage of enrolling the subjects of the republic, he was intrusted with the charge of making a beginning of the work, and from the month of December, 1505, until towards the end of March of the following year, Machiavelli devoted himself to this business; and we have accounts of his presence in the Val di Sieve, in the Mugello, and in the Casentino.

Interrupting at this point the course of his missions, it seems opportune here to show how, from the time that he assumed office, the great mind of the Secretary became convinced that the military system of the Italians was false; for it had undermined valor and discipline, and had made that beautiful country the easy prey of every foreign robber.

He perceived, therefore, that it would be necessary to abolish the system of mercenary troops, and to constitute a national army. But as it requires time to eradicate inveterate prejudices, which can only be done gradually, he began by inducing the Ten to order the enrolment of one man for every hearth in the Florentine dominions. The first step was taken in 1500; meantime, however, it was ordered that all the men capable of bearing arms, in every family, should be registered; and when the opportune moment seemed to him to have come, he succeeded in having an order passed by the Ten, that there should always be ten thousand men kept under arms under the banner of the Lily, and that that number should be made up by selecting the most suitable men from amongst those that were already inscribed, in proportion to the number of the population of the different places.

As the burden of the business relating to war was increased, Machiavelli began to influence public opinion upon this point by pronouncing, in March, 1503, a discourse in the General Council exhorting the people to arm themselves for their own defence, rather than resort to mercenary troops, and endeavoring to stir them up to make the necessary sacrifices for supplying the means for this purpose. Afterwards he presented a written communication to the Ten, the manuscript of which is amongst the treasures transferred from the Royal to the National Library, by which he succeeded in inducing them to intrust the organization of the army to a magistracy of nine citizens, to be appointed by them, who should be called the "Nine of Ordinance and Militia," and should occupy themselves with the formation of the companies, the training and discipline of the soldiers, and should see that the prescribed number of men was always complete, armed, drilled, and ready to take the field; all other authority over the army, and the exclusive right to mobilize and send it into the field, remaining with the Ten. Machiavelli was secretary and the very soul of the magistracy of the Nine; and to him are due the celebrated decree of the 6th of December, 1506, by which this new magistracy was instituted, and the instructions for the infantry, as well as another decree of the 20th of March, 1512, which established the regulations for the mounted troops. With these institutions Machiavelli laid the foundation for the military system of the present time, and initiated that which was afterwards taken up by Emanuele Filiberto of Savoy, and was the glory of Piedmont, and later of Prussia, which imitated it, — making of the military profession a national institution, and not a trade. He introduced, moreover, a bold innovation in demonstrating the superiority of infantry over cavalry, which was highly praised by those contemporaries who were in position to appreciate its full importance. There exist several letters in the archives relating to it, amongst which are two full of patriotic enthusiasm, written by Cardinal Soderini in praise of this fact, — the one addressed to his brother Piero, and the other to Machiavelli.

In the autumn of 1504 Machiavelli wrote the *Decennali* in *terza rima*, and dedicated them to Alamanno Salviati; it is probable that he had the work printed about the end of that year, or in the beginning of the next, under the care of his colleague in the Chancellery, Ser Agostino di Matteo. The title of this extremely rare little volume is "Nicolai Malclavelli Flo-"rentini Compendium Rerum Decennii in Italiam Gestarum ad "Viros Florentinos, incipit feliciter." It bears neither the printer's name, nor the place or date.

Resuming now the interrupted series of Machiavelli's missions, it appears that, whilst he was occupied with the reorganization of the militia, he was sent a second time to the court of Rome, on the 25th of August, 1506. He did not return until the 1st of November, having accompanied Julius II. as far as Imola; the Pope's aim being the recovery of Bologna.

The particular object of this mission was to show to the irascible and suspicious Pontiff the good disposition of the Florentines, and their great desire to favor his attempt against Bologna. On the 14th of March, 1507, Machiavelli went to enroll and select infantry in the Val di Tevere, in the Val di Chiana, in Chianti, and in the vales of Elsa and Cecina, and was gone thirty-four days. In May he was charged again to proceed to the lord of Piombino; but he had hardly reached Volterra when he received orders to return, the motive of his mission having ceased to exist. The object for which the Ten sent Machiavelli to Sienna in August was not a serious one; for he was merely to ascertain the extent of the retinue of the Cardinal Legate Bernardino Caravajal, whose arrival was expected in Florence. But the mission to the Emperor Maximilian was of greater importance: he was sent to him in December, 1507, and remained until the 16th of June of the following year, the object being to arrive at some agreement respecting the pecuniary subsidy which the Emperor demanded of the republic on the occasion of his coming into Italy for the purpose of receiving the imperial crown from the Supreme Pontiff. Machiavelli, being a keen observer of the customs and conditions of the different peoples, made Germany a subject of special study; and to this period belong the two Reports "On the Affairs of Germany," and the "Discourse on the Affairs of Germany and on the Emperor."

In August he made an extraordinary levy of infantry and pioneers, and sent them into the Pisan territory to devastate the fields and to carry off the crops. The wretched inhabitants of the Vicariates of San Miniato and Pescia were subjected to similar injuries in October, because of the suspicion that they might possibly send supplies of provisions to Pisa. He spent all the following January and a couple of days of February in mustering corporals and soldiers in various provinces subject to the republic. On the 18th of February he went to inspect the army before Pisa, and had thence to proceed to Piombino in March, to negotiate an agreement with the Pisans through the mediation of Jacopo d'Appiano, which, however, was not concluded. Having afterwards returned to the camp before Pisa, he remained there until the 8th of June. During this time he was also occupied with other missions, all which had for their object the happy termination of this war, which ended with the surrender of the city.

Thence he went to Mantua, to pay into the hands of the Emperor's mandataries the second instalment of forty thousand ducats which the Florentines had agreed to pay him for the confirmation of the privileges conceded to the republic by his predecessors; and to obtain from the Emperor a full and explicit renunciation of all claims which he could possibly make upon the city or state of Florence, and particularly upon Pisa, which they had but so lately reconquered. This was done by an agreement in the preparation of which our Secretary had a large share. On this occasion he was also charged to proceed into Lombardy to watch personally the fierce war which the allies of Cambray were carrying on against Venice, and to report thereupon to the Signoria. This mission lasted from the 10th of November, 1509, until the 2d of January of the following year; and it was at that time that his enemies tried to ruin him, and presented a protest in December to the conservators of the laws demanding that he should be deprived of all office, as being the son of a bastard father; basing their demand upon an old law, that had fallen into desuetude. But if this storm raged for a few days, it had no evil consequences, mainly owing to the efforts of his friend and colleague, Biagio de Buonaccorsi. In March, Machiavelli was appointed arbiter to settle the dispute about the boundary between the men of the little commune of Gargonza, belonging to the republic of Florence, and those of Armaiuolo, subject to Sienna; and at the end of May he was sent into the Vicariates of San Miniato and of Pescia, to review certain companies of infantry, and to select other men to add to these companies.

The importance which the Signoria attached to having a confidential person near the king of France, who was the principal ally of the Florentines, and upon whom they relied more than upon any other, caused them, when the post of resident ambassador became vacant, to appoint Machiavelli to the place until a new one could be named. He therefore went to join the court of France, at Lyons, on the 24th of June, 1510, and followed it afterwards to Blois and Tours, returning to his own country on the 19th of October. To this third journey into France, it seems, we must refer his "Description of French Affairs," for he made a longer stay there this time than on the former occasions, so that he had better opportunity to investigate men and things.

From November, 1510, until the end of May, 1511, he was most active, for existing documents show that he remained but a few days quiet during that period, being at one moment ambassador at Sienna, afterwards engaged in enrolling men for the infantry and cavalry, and subsequently at Pisa, at Arezzo, and at Poggibonsi, to examine and put in a state of defence the fortresses of those places. After this he was at Monaco from the 11th of May to the 5th of June, to negotiate a treaty of friendship with Luciano Grimaldi, lord of that place; and from the 24th of August to the 7th of September he went rapidly through the upper Val d' Arno, the Val di Chiana, and the Casentino, to enroll one hundred men fit to serve on horseback.

He had hardly been back four days in Florence, when he was obliged to leave in haste for Lombardy, to have an interview at Milan with the lieutenant of King Louis XII., and to proceed immediately afterwards to Blois to treat directly with that monarch. The object of this mission was to prevent, if possible, the assembling in council at Pisa of the cardinals who were hostile to Pope Julius II., the republic having conceded to those cardinals the hospitality of Pisa, fully aware that by this act it would draw upon itself the vengeance of that implacable Pope. Machiavelli, however, did not succeed in this mission; so that, having returned to Florence on the 2d of November, he was ordered the next day to proceed to Pisa and persuade those prelates to leave that city. For this purpose a good body of soldiers was worth more than all arguments, and Machiavelli sent them into Pisa under pretext of protecting the cardinals; but these prelates were frightened by the troops; and better still, the lack of provisions subjected them to privations to which they were not accustomed. He rendered an account of this mission on the 11th of November, and left for the Romagna on the 2d of December, to register on his roll of ordinance the men suitable to serve in the infantry, and for the same purpose he went through the greater portion of the Florentine dominion from May until August, 1512.

Meantime the vengeance of Julius II. ripened, and fell terribly upon the Florentine republic. He began by summoning the Signoria to dissolve the alliance with the king of France, and to adhere to the league which he had formed against the French with Spain, England, and Venice, and which he was pleased to call "the holy league." After the refusal of Piero Soderini, the perpetual Gonfalonier, who wanted to remain faithful to the oaths which he had taken, the Pontiff sent a Spanish army into Tuscany, which was accompanied by his Legate, the Cardinal de' Medici, who sacked Prato so barbarously that she laments it to this day; and he encouraged the partisans of the Medici in Florence to set a conspiracy on foot to drive the Gonfalonier from the seat of government, and to replace the country under the yoke of the hated Medici family. If Soderini had had Machiavelli about him at that time, it is probable that he would have borne himself with more sagacity, and would have spared to himself and to Florence the injury and shame in which he found himself involved; although Machiavelli would probably not have advised him to detach himself entirely from France, for the Secretary remained friendly to that power even in after years, when he lived entirely removed from all public business, as his familiar letters show most clearly. But even if Machiavelli had been in Florence on that fatal day, he was nevertheless a stranger to the facts that afflicted her. The fall of Soderini actually occurred on the 30th of August, 1512, and it is proved by public documents that Machiavelli was on the 27th of August at Firenzuola, and that, with but rare and brief interruptions, he had been absent from Florence ever since the first week in May. So that it is evident that he could not have influenced the Gonfalonier in his councils, who was, however, in the habit of consulting him, but most probably could not do so on that occasion, because the demands of the Pope and the execution of his threat were an affair of but a very few days.

Speaking of this fact, it seems interesting to note that Machiavelli neither disapproved nor censured Soderini for his conduct, and the proof of this is a letter which he wrote shortly after the event to an unknown lady.* And as he preserved his esteem and friendship for the deposed Gonfalonier, and kept up a correspondence with him even during his own exile, we have the right to reject a biting epigram upon the death of Soderini attributed to Machiavelli, but which would have been an evidence of ingratitude and manifest contradiction on his part.†

Nevertheless, if Machiavelli did not influence Soderini in his determination, he had to experience the painful consequences of it. For so soon as the government was changed according to the will of the new masters, Machiavelli was formally dismissed, on the 8th of November, from the office of Secretary of the Second Chancellery of the Signoria, and at the same time from the secretaryship of the Magistracy of the Ten. By another decree of the 10th of November, he was confined for a whole year within the limits of the territory of the republic; and on the 17th, he was notified that for a whole year he was

---

* This lady is presumed to have been Alphonsina Orsini, the widow of Piero, and mother of Lorenzo de' Medici.

† "La notte che mori Pier Soderini
"L' alma n' ando dell' Inferno alla bocca.
"E Pluto la grido: Anima sciocca,
"Che Inferno? Va nel Limbo de Bambini."

The night when Peter Soderini died,
His soul for entrance into Hell applied.
But Pluto shouted: Hence, thou simple soul!
This is no place for you. Go to the infant's Limbo, fool!

not to enter the palace of the Signoria; which prohibition was, however, several times interrupted for special reasons, but always by particular authorization of the College of Priors.

But a much greater misfortune befell him in the following year, when the conspiracy of Pietropaolo Boscoli and Agostino Capponi against the lives of Giuliano and Lorenzo de' Medici was discovered. Being suspected of participation in this conspiracy, he was shut up in the prison of the Bargello, and had there to suffer the torture, the executioner having subjected him six times to the strappado. He was also kept for some days shackled, as we must presume from his writing that he had "jesses" on his legs; it being well known that that word signifies the leather straps that hold one of the claws of the falcons. There is no mention of his torture in the public documents, nor in the resolutions of the Eight, where the condemnation of the other conspirators is recorded. But there can be no doubt about it, as he mentions it himself in a letter written to his friend Francesco Vettori on the 13th of March.

Machiavelli was doubtless innocent of being a party to this conspiracy, which originated with Paolo Boscoli, a young man of one of the old and distinguished families of Florence, who had drawn Agostino Capponi into the plot. The latter committed the imprudence of letting fall a list of the conspirators, in going into the house of the Pucci; this list was picked up, and immediately communicated to the magistracy. Many of the most distinguished citizens were implicated, and Machiavelli amongst the rest. It is quite possible, however, that the list dropped by Capponi may have been merely a memorandum of those whom the originators of the conspiracy proposed amongst themselves to draw into the plot. For the firm denial of Machiavelli under the pangs of torture ought certainly, with so honest and fearless a mind as his, to be taken for the truth, and should acquit him, not only of an unpatriotic act, but also of an act of folly in being one of a numerous body of conspirators, which folly no writer has ever exposed with greater clearness and more conclusive force of argument than himself.

Whilst this process was going on, Pope Julius II. died, and the Cardinal Giovanni de' Medici was chosen as his successor, and assumed the title of Leo X. So soon as he heard of Machiavelli's imprisonment, he ordered his fetters to be struck off, and had him set free, as well as all the others who had been charged with being implicated in the Boscoli conspiracy. Unhappily Boscoli and Capponi, having been found guilty, were executed before the Pope's pardon arrived. It is very possible that Giuliano de' Medici was also active in Machiavelli's favor; for it was to him, and not to his namesake of another family, as some have supposed, that the two sonnets were addressed which Machiavelli wrote in prison; as is clearly shown by the title of "Magnificent Signore," and "Your Magnificence," which belonged only to the family of the Medici.

Released from prison, but disgusted with the ingratitude of the city which he had served so long and so well, Machiavelli withdrew to his little property in the Percussina, near San Casciano, where he spent the greater part of his time in rustic occupations and games; and in the evening he passed four hours at his desk, occupied with a little work which he intended to entitle "De Principatibus," in which he discusses "what a principality is, what kinds there are, how they are acquired, how maintained, and why they are lost." Thus he wrote in a letter to Francesco Vettori, on the 10th of December, 1513, that he felt somewhat uncertain whether or not to give it that title; and intimating his intention of dedicating it to the Magnificent Giuliano de' Medici. This fact ought to undeceive those who assert that he had prepared this book for Cesare Borgia; and that, having had no opportunity of presenting it to him, he afterwards used it as a homage to the Medici to gain their favor. This book is the famous treatise of "The Prince," which he presented to Lorenzo, son of Piero de' Medici, rather than to Giuliano, the uncle of Lorenzo, as he had at first intended. The reason of this was that Giuliano abandoned the government of Florence in 1514; having been called by his brother to Rome. Most probably Machiavelli did not wish to delay presenting his book to Lorenzo in 1516, when, after the death of Giuliano, Lorenzo began to spread his wings, in attempting the conquest of Urbino; which enterprise, according to Guicciardini, was the first step towards the dominion of all papal fiefs, and perhaps also of the kingdom of Naples.

Seeing that he was not employed by the new government, notwithstanding the unceasing efforts made in his behalf by Francesco Vettori, he lamented that he could not make himself useful to his country, whilst feeling himself capable of rendering the most valuable services, for he had not wasted his time during the fifteen years that he had studied the arts of statesmanship. Machiavelli, therefore, occupied his rare genius in benefiting his country by his writings, and by instructing the Florentine youth, who met together in the Rucellai Gardens, where the celebrated Platonic Academy, which had been instituted by the old Cosimo de' Medici after the disasters of his family in 1490, had found hospitality. We must also refer the "Discourses upon the First Ten Books of Titus Livius" to the period between 1516 and 1519; for this work is dedicated to Cosimo Rucellai and Zenobio Buondelmonti, both born in 1495; and it is evident from the character of the work that it was not written for boys, but for young men grown up. These "Discourses" seem like a continuation of "The Prince"; for after having shown the Medici by the latter work how to grasp the sovereignty, and how to expel the foreigners from Italy, he desired by the former to point out to them the necessity of new institutions for maintaining themselves and making a state happy, after having consolidated their dominion, by basing it upon three powers; namely, the prince, the nobles, and the people. He also read at the meetings of the Academy the "Dialogue upon Language"; and he undoubtedly prepared also for this Academy the "Seven Books of the Art of War." He did not begin this work before 1519, for he opens it with the praises of Cosimo Rucellai, who died in that year; and he certainly had finished it before November, 1520, as is proved by a letter of the 17th of that month, written by Filippo de' Nerli, who had just then read the book. In the following year he had it printed under the title "De Re Militari," and the edition, issued by the heirs of Filippo di Giunta, bears the date of the 16th of August. Unquestionably he was urged to this work by love of his country, seeing that he intended thereby to teach the Florentine people to defend their state with arms against whoever should, from within or without, plot against their liberty; showing at the same time by examples from antiquity the injury which results to republics from keeping mercenary armies, and explaining all things that seemed to him most suitable for instructing an army and leading it into the field.

If we are to believe two slanderous writers, Cardano and Bandello, Machiavelli was an able theoretician, but otherwise inexperienced in the practice of military affairs. And this was quite natural, for he was not accustomed to direct battalions in war, nor was this a matter that concerned him. The former of these two writers relates that, when asked by the Duke of Urbino to give a demonstration of his system, Machiavelli dared not attempt it; and the other relates that he tried in vain for two hours to put three thousand infantry in order of battle, which Giovanni de' Medici afterwards did with the greatest ease.

During his stay in Lucca, Machiavelli wrote the Life of Castruccio Castracani, in 1520; and Zanobi Buondelmonti, to whom he sent it, acknowledges the receipt of it in a letter of the 6th of December. At the same time, accurate observer that he was of what was passing under his eyes, he also wrote the "Summary of the Affairs of Lucca." Jacopo Nardi tells us, in the seventh book of his History, that Machiavelli did this work for Zanobi Buondelmonti, Luigi Alamanni, and Cosimo Rucellai, who loved him very much, and who, by way of courtesy, gave him some emolument, being infinitely delighted with his conversation, and holding all his works in the highest esteem.

Meanwhile the rulers of Florence, and especially the Cardinal

Giuliano de' Medici, began to have some consideration for Machiavelli, and to make use of him. In fact, he was sent to Lucca in June, 1520, to protect the interests of the Florentine merchants who were exposed to loss by the failure of Michele Guinigi; and whilst in that city he was charged by the Cardinal to ask the Signoria of Lucca to expel from their territory three Sicilians, formerly students at Pisa, but who had been banished from that university. It is very probable that the Medici decided to favor him after the "Discourse upon the Reorganization of the State of Florence"; to which he afterwards added another little treatise, without any title, relating to the same subject, (preserved amongst the manuscripts that came from the Royal to the National Library,) and which he had most probably presented to the Cardinal Giuliano de' Medici. Both of these may be referred to the year 1519, and were certainly written before December, 1521, Leo X., to whom the former was without doubt presented, having died on the first of that month. It cannot be ascertained whether Machiavelli's opinion was given spontaneously, or whether it had been requested; but it certainly did not displease the Pontiff. Although holding firmly to republican appearances, Machiavelli would have wished that, the powers being duly equilibrated, Leo X. should reserve the supreme arbitrament to himself, thinking perhaps that after Leo's death Florence might recover her liberty. Lorenzo de' Medici was already dead at that time, and therefore the hopes which Machiavelli had of making him Prince had vanished. It may also be that he had, during the lifetime of Lorenzo, tasted the bitterness of deception in having placed confidence in such a man; and unable therefore, for the moment at least, to think of the independence of Italy from foreigners, he tried to find a possible means for arriving at the necessary conciliation between the ambitious hopes of the Medici and the liberty of his country. But that was not what the Cardinal Giuliano de' Medici desired; he ruled over the republic more absolutely than his cousin, the Pope, and it seemed to him as though he had shown enough love of country and of liberty in inviting several citizens to prominent offices, with the hope of satisfying in that way the clamors of the malcontents. Having extinguished in blood a conspiracy set on foot amongst the young men of the Oricellari Gardens, he made that the pretext for casting aside all idea of reform; and continued to govern absolutely, with the forms of a republic, but with the magistrates devoted and subject to him personally.

Another benefit bestowed by the Medici on Machiavelli was the commission to write the Florentine History, which the Cardinal Giuliano gave him, although he did so through the officials of the University, who charged Machiavelli with it on the 8th of November, 1520. But that the person who really gave him this commission was the Cardinal, appears clearly from the author's dedication of his work to the Pope, in which Machiavelli expresses to him his gratitude in the most explicit manner. It must not, however, be passed over in silence, that public opinion had also designated him for this work; and a letter still exists from Zanobi Buondelmonti, written to Machiavelli on the 6th of September of the same year, in which he urges him, not only in his own name, but speaking also for Jacopo Nardi, Luigi Alamanni, and for all the most cultivated gentlemen of Florence, not to delay taking it in hand.

The friendship of Piero Soderini for Machiavelli continued uninterruptedly; and of the many proofs of the zeal with which he endeavored to relieve Machiavelli's misfortunes, there remains a letter written by Soderini in 1521, from which it appears that he was occupied in obtaining for Machiavelli the office of secretary of the republic of Ragusa, which, however, he declined to accept; and that in place of it he obtained for him the post of secretary to Prosper Colonna, with very liberal pay, which Machiavelli also refused, in the hope probably of a brighter future.

In May, 1521, he received from the Magistracy of the Eight of Practice the commission to go to Carpi, where the Chapter of the Minorite Brothers of San Francesco was assembled, and to request them to constitute the Florentine dominion a separate chapter; and also to select a good preacher for the church of Santa Maria del Fiore. He accepted and fulfilled this mission, but laughing all the while at the friars and the people of Carpi, as appears from his letters to his friend Francesco Guicciardini.

Fully four years elapsed before he was again actively employed; the cause of this was probably the conspiracy against the Medici, which was set on foot by some of the young men of the Oricellari Gardens, and which cost the lives of Jacopo Diacelto and Luigi Alamanni, who were beheaded on the 7th of June, 1522. According to the testimony of the historian Nardi, Machiavelli was not altogether free from blame for the thoughts and actions of the conspirators, although he was not subjected to any trouble on that account. In August, 1525, finally, he was sent as Ambassador to Venice, to claim before the Doge and the Senate the restitution of the money and objects taken by a certain Giovanbattista Donato from three young Florentines, who were coming from Ragusa; but the documents do not tell us what result this mission produced.

To this period must be referred the two very amusing and witty, but not over moral comedies, "The Mandragola" and "Clizia." Although there is evidence that the Mandragola was written in 1520, and studied to be performed before Pope Leo X. (as appears from a letter written by Machiavelli from Rome on the 26th of April of that year), yet it was performed for the first time in 1525, by the Academicians of the Cazzuola, in the house of Bernardino di Giordano; the scenery for it having been prepared by the painter Andrea del Sarto and the famous architect Bastiano Aristotele da San Gallo. Vasari relates that the Cardinal Silvio Passerini, with the young Alessandro and Ippolito de' Medici, was present at the performance. The familiar letters of Machiavelli tell us, moreover, that at the request of Francesco Guicciardini, governor of the Romagna, the Mandragola was repeated at Bologna during the Carnival of 1526; and in March of the same year it was performed with the greatest success at Rome. The Clizia followed soon after, and was also performed by the Academicians of the Cazzuola in the house of Jacopo, the furnace-man, near the gate of San Frediano; and Vasari tells us that the Cardinal of Cortona was so much pleased with the scenery made by San Gallo, that he took him under his protection from that day, and employed him in various magnificent works.

Machiavelli has been blamed for having written these comedies; he anticipated this himself, and in his prologue to the Mandragola, addressed to the public, he says: "And if this "play seems unworthy to occupy the leisure of a wise and grave "man, deign to excuse him, and bear in mind that he tries by "these distractions to soften the sorrows that pursue him. For "he can no longer turn his thoughts elsewhere, and has been "forbidden to show in any other way the qualities he may "possess," etc. These comedies, however, suited the taste of the period when they were written, as their popularity attests. They are certainly no worse than the tales of Boccaccio, and infinitely more spirited and witty.

Pope Clement VII., being free from all suspicion against Machiavelli, now wished to employ him in a matter for which he believed him better qualified than any one else; and therefore charged him, in March, 1526, to visit the fortifications of Florence in company with some military architects, for the purpose of examining their defects and needs; and to prepare a project for fortifying the whole city, so as to be able to resist the attacks of a hostile army. Machiavelli made a full report of this commission, which he sent to the Pope at Rome. It was probably in consequence of this that he was sent to the camp, to Francesco Guicciardini, commissary of the Pope, in the army of the allies against the Emperor Charles V.; and was sent by Guicciardini in August of the same year as envoy to the Venetian Proveditore, who was besieging Cremona, to hasten the capture of that place, or rather to persuade him to abandon this siege, and to unite all the forces for the more important acquisition of Genoa. About this time the Pope had, at the request of Jacopo Salviati, destined Machiavelli to an honorable office at court; but as he would not abandon his mission, this post was given to some one else. Machiavelli was sent, in November, a second time to the same Guicciardini, the Pope's lieutenant, and living at that time in Modena, with instructions that were most honorable for him, from the Cardinal Passerini, who governed Florence at that time as tutor of the young Ippolito and Alessandro de' Medici. The Cardinal, always timid, saw supreme danger imminent for Florence; for the Pope was almost a prisoner of the Colonnese at Rome, whilst a numerous German army was descending upon Italy; so that he would have preferred that Guicciardini had sent him substantial aid into the city, or rather that he should have managed to bring about some agreement with the enemy. The lieutenant, however, did nothing that was asked of him, for the simple reason that he could not do it, and therefore it became necessary to send Machiavelli to him once more, who went accordingly, in February, 1527. The negotiations of the ambassador were protracted, he having been charged to follow Guicciardini wherever the particular duties of his office might call him. They proved, nevertheless, to have no result; as the troops of the lieutenant were insufficient to restrain the violence of the German hordes that had invaded the Bolognese territory and were laying it waste.

Machiavelli returned to Florence on the 22d of April, but nothing is heard of him during the sedition against the Medici on the 26th of that month, which, however, was quickly put down; nor on the occasion of the subsequent events that led to the expulsion of the Cardinal Passerini with his pupils, and to the claim of the Florentines for the restoration of their liberties. Perhaps Machiavelli was not in Florence at the time, and had already returned to Guicciardini, by whom he was certainly sent to Andrea Doria, who was at Civita Vecchia, to obtain a brigantine from him. He was in this port on the 22d of May, as appears from one of his letters, and embarked the next day on a galley that escorted the Marchioness of Mantua, and a few days after landed with her at Livorno.

Being thus restored to his country, Machiavelli lived in obscurity the few days that were left him of life, until the 22d of June, 1527, when he died like a Christian, as is proved by a letter written by his son Piero to his relative Francesco Nelli.

Thus far the facts relating to Machiavelli's life have been, as before stated, mainly taken from L. Passerini's article, referred to at the beginning of this biography. For the subsequent remarks the author of these translations is alone responsible.

The story related by Benedetto Varchi, and believed by many, that Machiavelli died from disappointment because Donato Giannotti was preferred to him in the appointment to the office of Secretary to the Ten of Liberty and Peace, is manifestly incorrect, for Machiavelli died before Giannotti was elected to that office. His son Piero attests most positively that he died from pains in his stomach, resulting from a medicine which he had taken on the 20th of June. Equally unfounded is the story of his having lived unhappily with his wife, and that in his novel of "Belphegor," the Lady Onesta was intended to represent her; for although his frequent, nay, almost constant absences from Florence did not permit him to be a very devoted husband, which *rôle* was perhaps not entirely suited to Machiavelli's character, yet there is no evidence that he did not always treat his wife with every degree of respect; and the best proof of the good relations existing between them is the fact that in both his wills he speaks of his wife with esteem and affection, and intrusts her with the sole management of his property and the guardianship of his children.

Of Machiavelli's life little more can really be said than that, until the fall of Soderini and the return of the Medici in 1512, it was entirely devoted to the service of the state, either as Secretary of the Magistracy of the Ten, or in missions to foreign courts or to different states in Italy, in all of which he displayed as much zeal as capacity. These missions must often have been very distasteful and irksome to him, especially when sent as an envoy to the King of France or to the Emperor of Germany, to solicit the armed intervention of the one in the affairs of Italy, or to pay tribute to the other for a guaranty of the integrity of the republic. The eight years intervening between the time of his removal from office and the year 1521, when he was again employed by the government, were spent at his villa near Casciano in rural pastimes, and literary occupation, and in a highly interesting correspondence with various friends, chiefly with Francesco Vettori. He died poor, as he had lived, a good proof of his strict honesty, taking into consideration the opportunities he had to enrich himself in his many years' services to the state. During his frequent and important missions his pay never exceeded ten lire per day, out of which pittance he had to pay for his servants and horses, and frequently for the postage and express messengers to carry his despatches to the government of Florence, which often obliged him to borrow and to draw upon his own resources. And from this scanty pay of ten lire per day his salary as Secretary to the Ten was regularly deducted. We consequently find in his despatches frequent appeals, at times pathetic, at times humorous, but always urgent, to the government of Florence for increase of pay, or pecuniary assistance of some kind.

He was personally esteemed by the most distinguished men of Florence of his time, for he was of most cheerful social temper, and his conversation was full of learning and wit. He was a good Catholic, but no Papist; on the contrary, he attributed nearly all the miseries of Italy to the efforts of the Popes to maintain and increase the temporal power and possessions of the Church.* This brought upon him the enmity of the Church, the violent criticisms, perversions, and finally the condemnation of his writings, and their being placed in the *Index Expurgatorius.*

There are many editions of Machiavelli's works. The most

---

* See Discourses on Livy, Book I. Chap. XII.

perfect, so far as it goes, is the one printed at Florence in 1875, under the direction of L. Passerini and G. Milanesi, containing a large number of letters from the Florentine government and others to Machiavelli, which throw much light upon the various missions, the whole being carefully revised according to the original documents. Unfortunately, the untimely death of one of the editors put a stop to the completion of this edition. As early as 1772 an edition was published in London in three volumes, large quarto, containing all the works of Machiavelli then known, with a Preface by Baretti. Ten years later, however, in 1782, Lord Nassau Clavering, Earl Cowper, published at his own expense a handsome one in four volumes quarto, truly worthy of the Florentine Secretary. This edition is still greatly prized to this day, and has served as the standard for all subsequent to it. It was also due to the persistent efforts of the same generous Englishman, that the Grand Duke Leopold of Tuscany had a monument erected over the until then obscure tomb of Machiavelli, by the side of that of Michael Angelo in the church of Santa Croce at Florence, where the remains of Machiavelli had been buried in the family vault, and had remained unnoticed for two and a half centuries. This monument was designed by the Chevalier Alberto Rombotti, and executed in marble by the sculptor Spinazzi in the year 1787; it bears the following Latin inscription: —

TANTO NOMINI NULLUM PAR EULOGIUM
NICOLAUS MACHIAVELLUS.

Numerous portraits and busts exist, claiming to represent Niccolo Machiavelli; the greater part of them, however, — if not all save one, — are not portraits of the great Secretary. They are either fictitious, or they represent some other personage; in several instances they are portraits of Lorenzo, or some other of the Medici family. The marble bust in the museum of the Bargello at Florence, which bears the inscription "Niccolo Machiavelli," is certainly not the bust of our

Machiavelli. In the Palazzo Boutourlin at Florence there is a portrait by Andrea del Sarto, which represents an old man with a very sad expression; it is claimed to be the portrait of Machiavelli, but is not generally recognized as such, and certainly has not a single feature that suggests the character of Machiavelli. Mr. A. F. Artaud, who was for some years Chargé d'Affaires of France at Florence, and published in 1833 two most valuable and interesting volumes with the title of "Machiavel, son Génie et ses Erreurs," condemns all the engraved portraits, claims to have discovered the only true likeness of Machiavelli by Santi-Titi, and gives a small engraving of it by Rubière as the frontispiece to his first volume. The same picture has been admirably engraved on a much larger scale by P. Toschi and A. Isac; and certainly the face is most expressive of quick intelligence and penetration, and such as one might well imagine Machiavelli's countenance to have been. But unfortunately the picture is not authentic, for Santi-Titi was not born until 1538, eleven years after the death of Machiavelli, in June, 1527. It may have been painted by Santi-Titi from a sketch by some one else, or from a cast taken from Machiavelli's face; but an original portrait it cannot be called. It is this portrait that has been mainly consulted by the sculptor Bartolini in his admirable statue of Machiavelli, which, amongst the other great men of Florence, adorns the inner court of the Uffizii at Florence.

The portrait in profile prefixed to this volume of the present translation is presumed to be the only well authenticated portrait of Niccolo Machiavelli known to exist. The original was painted by Angelo Allori (Bronzino), and hangs in the Doria Gallery in Rome. It bears a striking resemblance to the colored plaster bust of Machiavelli belonging to the Marchioness Isabella Piccolellis, born Ricci, which was copied from a cast of Machiavelli's face, taken from his body after death. This bust has always been in possession of the Ricci family, the lineal descendants of Machiavelli, through his daughter.

The recent history of Italy has shown how correctly, and with almost prophetic vision, Machiavelli foresaw that her deliverance from all her ills could only be effected through the fusion of all the different Italian states into one, under the government of one man of courage, loyalty, and prudence, and with a national army. How nobly and completely this task was performed by the late King of Italy, Victor Emmanuel, aided by his great minister, Cavour, is familiar to all the world. No longer does any foreign power possess one foot of Italian soil, and Italy made one has taken her place amongst the great powers of the earth

The great merits of Machiavelli have been recognized by the Italian government. His bust in marble has been placed prominently amongst Italy's other great men in the Pincio Gardens at Rome; and the modest house in which he lived and died, in the Via Guicciardini at Florence, has two marble tablets above the door. The one records the fact of his having lived and died there; the other was placed there by order of the government, on the fourth centenary of his birth, and bears the following inscription: —

A NICCOLO MACHIAVELLI.

Dell' Unità Nazionale precursore audace e indovino
E d' armi proprie e non aventizie primo istitutore
E maestro, l' Italia una e armata pose il 3 maggio 1869
Il quarto di lui Centennario.

TO NICHOLAS MACHIAVELLI.

The intrepid and prophetic precursor of National Unity,
The first institutor and master of her own
In place of adventitious armies,
United and armed Italy placed this Tablet,
On his fourth Centenary, 3d May, 1869.

THE
HISTORY OF FLORENCE.

DEDICATION.

TO OUR MOST HOLY AND BLESSED FATHER AND LORD,

CLEMENT VII.

HIS HUMBLE SERVANT,

NICCOLO MACHIAVELLI.

MOST HOLY AND BLESSED FATHER, — Since your Holiness, before attaining your present exalted position, commissioned me to write an account of the things done by the Florentine people, I have used all the diligence and skill given me by nature and experience to satisfy your command. Having now in the course of my writing arrived at the period when the death of the Magnificent Lorenzo de' Medici caused a change in the government of Italy, and having to describe the events that followed with a greater and loftier spirit, they being of a greater and more elevated character, I have deemed it well to reduce all I have written up to that epoch into one volume, and to present it to your Holiness, so that you may begin in some measure to enjoy the fruits of your sowing and of my labors.

In reading this your Holiness will see first, after the beginning of the decline of the power of the Roman Empire in the West, how many changes the states of Italy underwent during several centuries, and how many disasters they experienced under so many princes. You will see how the Pope, the Venetians, the Kingdom of Naples, and the Dukedom of Milan took the first rank and power in that province. You will see how your country raised itself by its very division from subjection to the Emperors, and remained divided until it began to govern itself under the protecting shadow of your house.

And being particularly charged and commanded by your Holiness to write the doings of your ancestors in such manner that it might be seen that I was free from all adulation, (the true praises of men being agreeable to hear, whilst such as are feigned and written by favor are displeasing,) I have hesitated much in describing the goodness of Giovanni, the wisdom of Cosimo, the humanity of Piero, and the magnificence of Lorenzo; so that it might not seem to your Holiness that I had transgressed your commands. For this I excuse myself to you, and for any similar descriptions that might displease as being little faithful; for finding the recollections of those who have at various time written of them full of praise, it became me to write of them such as I found them, or to pass them over with invidious silence. And if under their distinguished acts there was concealed an ambition common to usefulness, or (as some say) contrary to it, I, who do not know it, am not bound to describe it; for in all my narrative I have never attempted to cover a dishonest act with honest reasons, nor have I ever dimmed a praiseworthy act by representing it as having been done for a contrary purpose. But it may be seen in all parts of my history how far I am from adulation, and especially in the private discourses and public speeches, direct or indirect, which I have preserved with the very sentences, order, manner, and disposition of the person that spoke them, and without any reserve. I avoid in all instances odious expressions, as being wholly unnecessary to the dignity and truth of history. No one, therefore, who considers my writings rightly, can charge me with being a flatterer, particularly seeing that I have not said much of the memory of the father of your Holiness, — the reason of which was the shortness of his life, during which he could not make himself known; nor could I by my writings have made him illustrious. Nevertheless the merit of having been the father of your Holiness is an ample equivalent of all those of his ancestors, and will insure him more centuries of fame than his evil fortune took years from his life.

I have endeavored then, Most Holy Father, in my descriptions, whilst not tarnishing the truth, to satisfy everybody; and yet I may have failed to satisfy any. Nor should I wonder if this were the case, for I judge it to be impossible to describe the events of one's own times without offending many. Nevertheless I enter the field cheerfully, hoping that inasmuch as I am honored and supported by the benevolence of your Holiness, so shall I be aided and defended by the armed legions of your most holy judgment; and with the same courage and confidence with which I have written till now, I shall continue my undertaking so long as life is left me, and your Holiness does not abandon me.

PREFACE.

It was my intention when I first resolved upon writing the things done by the Florentine people, within and without their city, to begin my narrative with the year 1434 of the Christian era, at which time the family of the Medici, by the merits of Cosimo and his father Giovanni, exercised more authority in Florence than any one else. For I thought to myself that Messer Lionardo d' Arezzo and Messer Poggio, two excellent historians, had related all the events that had occurred previous to that time. But having afterwards diligently read their writings to see in what order and manner they had proceeded, so that by imitating them our history might be the more approved by the reader, I found that in their descriptions of the wars carried on by the Florentines with foreign princes and peoples they had been most diligent; but of their civil discords and internal dissensions, and of the effects resulting therefrom, they had in part been silent, and in part had described them very briefly, which to the reader could be neither useful nor agreeable. I believe they did so because these facts seemed to them so unimportant that they judged them unworthy of being recorded in history, or because they feared to offend the descendants of those who took part in them, and who by the narration of these facts might have deemed themselves calumniated. These two reasons (be it said with their leave) seemed to me wholly unworthy of such great men; because if anything delights or instructs in history, it is that which is described in detail; and if any lesson is useful to the citizens who govern republics, it is that which demonstrates the causes of the hatreds and dissensions in the republic, so that, having learned wisdom from the perils experienced by others, they may maintain themselves united. And if the divisions of any republic were ever noteworthy, those of Florence certainly are most so, because the greater part of the other republics of which we have any knowledge were content with one division, by which, according to chance, they either increased or ruined their city. But Florence, not content with one division, had many. In Rome, as everybody knows, after the expulsion of the kings, a division arose between the nobles and the people, and with that she maintained herself until her downfall. So did Athens, and so all the republics that flourished in those times. But in Florence, the first division was amongst the nobles, afterwards between the nobles and the citizens, and finally between the citizens and the populace; and many times it happened that one of the parties that remained in power again divided in two. These divisions caused so many deaths, so many exiles, so much destruction of so many families, as never occurred in any other city of which we have any record. And truly no other circumstance so much illustrates the power of our city as that which resulted from these divisions, which would have been enough to destroy any other great and powerful republic.

Ours, nevertheless, seems always to have increased in power; such was the virtue of her citizens and the strength of their genius and courage to make themselves and their country great, that the many who remained untouched by so many evils could by their virtues exalt their city more than the malignity of those events that diminished her greatness could have oppressed her. And doubtless if Florence had had so much good fortune that, after having freed herself from the Empire, she could have adopted a form of government that would have kept her united, I know not what republic, modern or ancient, would have been her superior, such abundance of power of arms and industry would she in that case have possessed. For it will be seen that after she had expelled the Ghibellines in such numbers that Tuscany and Lombardy were full of them, the Guelfs, together with those who remained in Florence, drew from the city, and of her own citizens, twelve hundred mounted men and twelve thousand infantry for the war against Arezzo, one year before the battle of Campaldino.

Afterwards, in the war against Filippo Visconti, Duke of Milan, having to make trial of her own resources, but not of her own troops, (for they had exhausted them at that time,) it will be seen that she spent during the five years that this war lasted the sum of three and a half millions of florins; and after that war was finished they were not satisfied to remain at peace, but took the field against Lucca. I cannot see therefore what reasons there can be why these divisions should not be worthy of being particularly described. And if those most noble writers were withheld from doing so by the fear of offending the memory of those of whom they would have to speak, they deceive themselves in that respect, and show that they little know the ambition of men, and the desire they have to perpetuate the names of their ancestors and their own. And they do not remember that many, not having had the opportunity of acquiring fame by any praiseworthy acts, have endeavored to acquire it by disgraceful ones. Nor have they considered how the actions that have inherent greatness, such as those of governments and states, however they may have originated, or whatever their object may have been, always bring more honor than discredit to the actors. But I, having considered these things, have been induced thereby to change my purpose, and have resolved to begin my history from the origin of our city. And as it is not my intention to occupy the same ground as others, I shall describe particularly only those things up to the year 1434 that occurred within the city, and of the foreign relations I shall say no more than what may be necessary for a proper understanding of the internal affairs. From and after the year 1434, however, I shall fully describe both the one and the other. Beyond that, for the better understanding of each period, before I treat of Florence I shall relate by what means Italy came to be under the rule of those potentates who governed her at that time.

All of which things, Italian as well as Florentine, will be completed in four Books; the first of which will briefly relate all that befell Italy after the decline of the Roman Empire up to 1434; the second will go with its narrative from the beginning of the city of Florence up to the war which she carried on against the Pope after the expulsion of the Duke of Athens. The third will finish in 1414 with the death of King Ladislaus of Naples; and with the fourth we shall reach the year 1434, from which time forward will be described particularly the events that occurred, within Florence and without, up to our times.

HISTORY OF FLORENCE.

FIRST BOOK.

SUMMARY.

1. The Barbarians occupy the Roman Empire. — 2. The Franks and Burgundians give their names to France and Burgundy; the Huns, to Hungary; the Angles, to England. — 3. The Huns and Vandals overrun Italy. — 4. Theodoric and the Ostrogoths. — 5. The modern languages: great changes in the world. — 6. Death of Theodoric. Belisarius combats the Goths, who are afterwards defeated by Narsetes. — 7. Justinus reorganizes Italy. — 8. Kingdom of the Longobards. — 9. How the Popes became powerful. — 10. The Pope asks help of Pepin against the Longobards. — 11. Charlemagne and end of the Longobards. — 12. The Empire passes into Germany. 13. Organization and division of the Italian states. — 14. Nicholas II. devolves the election of the Popes upon the Cardinals. — 15. Alexander II. excommunicates Henry II. and releases his subjects from their oath of fidelity. Guelfs and Ghibellines. — 16. The Normans found the Kingdom of Naples. — 17. Urban II. goes to France and preaches the first Crusade. Orders of the Knights of Jerusalem, and of the Templars. End of the Crusades. — 18. The Countess Matilda dies, leaving her state to the Church. Frederick Barbarossa. His dissensions with Alexander III. Lombard League. — 19. Death of Thomas à Becket. Amends made by the King of England. Reconciliation of Frederick with the Pope. His death. — 20. The Kingdom of Naples passes into the hands of the House of Suabia. Orders of the Dominicans and Franciscans. — 21. Beginning of the greatness of the House of Este. Division of the cities and of the lords into Guelfs and Ghibellines. Frederick II. — 22. Death of Frederick II., who leaves the kingdom to his son Conrad. The kingdom falls under the tutelage of Manfred, bastard son of Frederick. Enmity between Manfred and the Church, in consequence of which the Pope calls Charles d'Anjou into Italy, and invests him with the Kingdom of Naples and Sicily. Battles of Benevento and of Tagliacozzo. — 23. Restless policy of the Popes to make themselves masters of Italy. — 24. Sicilian Vespers. — 25. The Emperor Rudolph sells their independence to many cities of Italy. — 26. Boniface VIII. institutes the Jubilee. Clement V. transfers the pontifical seat to Avignon. Henry of Luxemburg descends into Italy with the intention of uniting and pacifying it. He besieges Florence

in vain, and dies at Buonconvento, in the midst of his enterprise.—27. The Visconti make themselves masters of Milan and drive out the Torriani. Gio. Galeazzo first Duke of Milan.—28. Louis of Bavaria, and John, King of Bohemia, come into Italy. League of the Italian cities against John and the Pope.—29. Origin of Venice; its growth and decadence.—30. Discords between Benedict XII. and the Emperor Louis.—31. Cola di Rienzo, Tribune of Rome, attempts to restore the old form of republic.—32. The Jubilee is reduced to fifty years. Queen Joanna gives Avignón to the Church. The Cardinal Egidio d' Alborno restores the power of the Popes in Italy.—33. Turbulence in the Church, in Naples, and in Lombardy.—34. Companies of adventurers. Verona gives herself to Venice.—35. Dissensions between Pope Innocent VII. and the people of Rome, on account of the franchise. Council of Pisa.—36. Council of Constance, and end of the schism that has existed between the three Antipopes, Gregory XII., Benedict XIII., and John XXIII.—37. Filippo Visconti recovers his state.—38. Joanna II., Queen of Naples, and her wickedness.—39. Political condition of Italy at about the middle of the fifteenth century.

1. THE nations who inhabit the Northern regions beyond the rivers Rhine and Danube, being born in a healthful and prolific climate, often increase in such numbers that some of them are obliged to abandon their paternal lands and to seek new countries for their habitation. The order which they adopt when any one of these provinces desires to relieve itself of its surplus population is to divide themselves into three parts, apportioning to each an equal number of nobles and commons, rich and poor; after which that portion whom fate commands to leave, goes off to seek its fortune; and the two parts who have thus relieved themselves of the one third of their numbers remain to enjoy the paternal possessions. It was these nations that destroyed the Roman Empire, for which the Emperors afforded them the opportunity, who, having abandoned Rome, the ancient seat of their empire, went to reside at Constantinople, thereby enfeebling the western part of the Empire, because it was less watched over by them, and more exposed to the rapacity of their ministers and of their enemies. And truly, to ruin so great an empire, founded upon the blood of so many virtuous men, needed no less than the indolence of its princes, the faithlessness of its ministers, and the power and persistence of those who assailed it; for it was not only one people that assailed it, but many who conspired for its ruin.

The first who came from those Northern regions to assail the Empire, after the Cimbrians,—who were defeated by Marius, a Roman citizen,—were the Visigoths, which in their language signifies Western Goths. These, after some fighting on the confines of the Empire, were settled for a long time, upon a concession from the Emperor, above the river Danube; and although for various reasons and at different times they assailed the Roman provinces, they were nevertheless kept in check by the Emperors. And the last who gloriously overcame them was Theodosius, so that, being reduced to subjection, they did not re-establish any king over themselves, but, content with the stipend conceded to them, they lived and fought under his government and banner. But after the death of Theodosius, when Arcadius and Honorius, his sons, became heirs to the Empire, but not to their father's virtues and fortunes, the times became changed with the princes.

Theodosius had appointed three governors to the three parts of the Empire, — Rufinus to the Eastern, Stilicho to the Western, and Gildon to Africa; they all, after his death, thought no longer of how to govern those provinces, but only how to possess them as independent princes. Gildon and Rufinus were put down in their attempts; but Stilicho, knowing better how to conceal his intentions, sought to acquire the confidence of the new Emperors, and at the same time to disturb them in their state in such manner that it would be the easier afterwards for him to occupy it. And by way of making the Visigoths their enemies, he advised the Emperors not to give them their accustomed provision; and besides this, deeming that these enemies were not sufficient to disturb the Empire, he ordered that the Burgundians, Franks, Vandals, and Alans, likewise Northern tribes, and already on the move in search of new lands, should assail the Roman provinces. The Visigoths, consequently, deprived of their provision, for the sake of being better organized for revenge of their wrongs, created Alaric their king; — and having assailed the Empire, after many accidents, ravaged Italy, and took and sacked Rome. After this victory Alaric died, and Ataulf succeeded him, who took for wife Placidia, the sister of the Emperors; and by reason of this relationship he agreed with them to go to the assistance of Spain and Gaul, which provinces were being assailed by the Vandals, Burgundians, Alans, and Franks, for the reasons above stated. From this resulted that the Vandals, who had occupied that part of Spain called Betica, being powerfully assailed by the Visigoths, and seeing no relief, were called by Bonifacius, who governed Africa for the Empire, to come and occupy that province, which was in a state of revolt, hoping in this way to conceal his misgovernment from the Emperor. For the reasons above stated the Vandals readily undertook that enterprise, and under the lead of their king, Genseric, made themselves masters of Africa. In the midst of this Theodosius, son of Arcadius, had succeeded to the Empire, who, giving little attention to the West, caused those populations to think of securing to themselves the possession of the lands they had conquered.

2. Thus the Vandals ruled in Africa, the Alans and Visigoths in Spain; the Franks and the Burgundians not only took Gallia, but those parts that were occupied by them were named after them, — whence one part is called France, and the other Burgundy. The fortunate successes of these stirred up new nations to the destruction of the Empire: another people, called Huns, occupied Pannonia, a province situated on the other side along the shores of the Danube, which having taken its name from them was called Hungaria. Added to these disorders came that the Emperor, seeing himself assailed on so many sides, by way of reducing the number of his enemies, began to make treaties, now with the Vandals and now with the Franks, which caused the power and authority of the Barbarians to increase, and that of the Empire to decline. Nor was the island of Britain, now called England, secure from similar destruction; for the Britons, fearing the people that had occupied France, and not seeing how the Emperor could protect them, called to their aid the Angles, a people of Germany, who engaged in the enterprise under their king, Voltigern; at first they defended the Britons, but afterwards drove them from the island and remained themselves to inhabit it, and which was called after them Anglia. But the original inhabitants, being despoiled of their country, became from necessity aggressive, and thought that, although unable to defend their own country, yet they might be able to seize that of others. They therefore crossed the sea with their families, and occupied those places which they found near the ocean, and after their own name they called that country Brittany.

3. The Huns, who, as we have said above, had occupied Pannonia, united with other tribes called Zepidians, Erulians, Turingians, and Ostrogoths (which in their language signified Eastern Goths), and set out to find new lands; and not being

able to enter France, which was defended by the Barbarian forces, they went into Italy under their king, Attila, who shortly previous had killed his brother Bleda, so as to have the government all to himself; and having in this wise become very powerful, Andaric, king of the Zepidians, and Velamir, king of the Ostrogoths, became subject to him. When Attila got to Italy he besieged Aquileia, where he remained two years without any other hindrance; during this siege he ravaged the whole surrounding country and dispersed its inhabitants, which, as we shall see in its place, gave rise to the city of Venice. After the capture and destruction of Aquileia, and many other cities, Attila turned towards Rome, from the destruction of which he abstained in consequence of the entreaties of the Pope, whose venerableness had so much influence upon him that he left Italy and returned to Austria, where he died. After the death of Attila, Velamir, king of the Ostrogoths, and the chiefs of the other nations, took up arms against his two sons, Henry and Uric; they killed the one, and constrained the other to recross the Danube and return with the Huns to their own country; and the Ostrogoths and the Zepidians settled in Pannonia, and the Erulians and Turingians remained higher up on the other side of the Danube.

After the departure of Attila from Italy, Valentinian, the Western Emperor, thought of restoring the country; and by way of placing himself in better position to defend Italy against the Barbarians, he abandoned Rome and established his residence at Ravenna. The adversities which the Western Empire had suffered were the cause why the Emperor, who resided at Constantinople, had several times conceded it to others, on account of the danger and expense of its defence. And many times, even without his permission, the Romans, seeing themselves abandoned, created from their own midst an Emperor; or some one assumed the Empire of his own authority,— as happened at the time when, after the death of Valentinian, Rome was seized by Maximus, a Roman citizen, who constrained Eudoxia, widow of the former, to take him for her husband. But being of imperial blood and unable to bear her marriage to a private citizen, she resolved to revenge the insult, and for that purpose secretly agreed with Genseric, king of the Vandals and master of Africa, to come into Italy, pointing out to him the facility and advantage of such an enterprise. Genseric, attracted by such a prey, came promptly, and, finding Rome abandoned, sacked the city, where he remained two weeks. He also captured and sacked other places in Italy, loaded himself and his army with the plunder, and then returned to Africa. The Romans, having come back to the city after the death of Maximus, created Avitus Emperor. After many other events in Italy and elsewhere, and after the death of other Emperors, the Empire of Constantinople fell to Zeno, and that of Rome to Orestes, and Augustulus, his son, who obtained possession of the Empire by fraud. And whilst they attempted to hold it by force, the Erulians and Turingians, who, as I have said, had established themselves after the death of Attila beyond the Danube, leagued themselves together under their chief, Odoacer, and came into Italy. The settlements which they left vacant were occupied by the Longobards, a people also from the North, led by Godago, their king; and these were, as I shall show in its place, the worst plague of Italy. When Odoacer came into Italy he defeated and killed Orestes near Pavia, and Augustulus fled. After this victory (in order that Rome might change its title with its power) Odoacer abandoned the title of Emperor and had himself proclaimed King of Rome, and was the first of the chiefs of the Barbarian tribes that scoured the world at that time who undertook to reside in Italy. For the others, after having despoiled it, sought other countries where to establish their seats, influenced either by fear or inability to hold Italy, which could so easily be succored by the Emperor of the East, or from some other occult reason.

4. At this time, then, the ancient Roman Empire was reduced under the following princes: Zeno, ruling in Constantinople, commanded the whole of the Eastern Empire; the Ostrogoths were masters of Mœsia and Pannonia; the Visigoths, the Franks and Burgundians, held France; and the Erulians and Turingians, Italy. The government of the Ostrogoths had come to Theodoric, who, being on terms of friendship with Zeno, Emperor of the East, wrote to him that it seemed unjust to his Ostrogoths that, being superior to all the other tribes in power, they should be inferior in dominion, and that it was impossible for him to restrain them any longer within the limits of Pannonia; so that, seeing the necessity for allowing them to take up arms and go in search of new lands, he wished first to make it known to him,

so that he might provide for it by conceding them some country where, with his good grace, they might live honestly with more comfort and convenience to themselves. Whereupon, Zeno, partly from fear and partly from the desire to drive Odoacer out of Italy, conceded to Theodoric authority to move against Odoacer and to take possession of Italy. Theodoric promptly set out from Pannonia, which he left to the Zepidians, who were his friends, and having come into Italy he slew Odoacer and his son, and after his example he assumed the title of King of Italy, and established his seat at Ravenna, influenced by the same considerations that had induced the Emperor Valentinian to reside there.

Theodoric excelled both in war and in peace, whence he was always victorious in the one, and in the other greatly benefited his people and cities. He distributed the Ostrogoths through the country under their chiefs, so that in war he might be able to command, and in peace to supervise them. He increased Ravenna, restored Rome, and with the exception of military commands he gave back to her citizens all their former honors. He restrained within their limits all the Barbarian kings who were occupants of the Empire, without any warlike disturbance, but simply by the force of his authority. He built up the country, established fortresses between the Adriatic and the Alps, so as to impede more effectually the passage of fresh Barbarians, who might wish to assail Italy. And if so much virtue had not been stained at the end of his life by some cruelties practised towards certain suspected persons in his kingdom, such as the deaths of Simmaco and Boezio, two most saintly men, his memory would have been worthy of all honor; for by means of his valor and goodness Rome and all the other parts of the Western Empire, relieved of the constant shocks which it had borne during so many years from repeated Barbarian inundations, raised themselves again and brought themselves back to good order and happiness.

5. And truly, if ever there was a period of utter wretchedness in Italy and in those provinces that were overrun by the Barbarians, it was that from the time of Arcadius and Honorius to that of Theodoric. For when we consider how injurious a mere change of ruler or form of government is to any republic or kingdom, not from any extrinsic force, but merely from civil discords, — and when it is seen what inconsiderable changes

have caused the ruin of even the most powerful republics and kingdoms, — then it will be easy to imagine how much Italy and the other provinces of the Roman Empire must have suffered in those times, when they changed, not only their forms of government and their princes, but also their laws and customs, their mode of living, their religion, their language, dress, and even their names. Each one of such changes, to say nothing of all of them taken together, is enough to terrify any firm and constant mind by merely thinking of it, and without witnessing or being himself obliged to undergo it. This state of things caused the ruin, but also the birth and growth, of many cities. Amongst those that were ruined were Aquileia, Luni, Chiusi, Popolonia, Fiesole, and many others; and amongst those that sprung into existence were Venice, Sienna, Ferrara, Aquila, and other considerable places and castles, the names of which I omit for the sake of brevity. Those which from small cities grew into large ones were Florence, Genoa, Pisa, Milan, Naples, and Bologna; to all these must be added the destruction and rebuilding of Rome and other cities that were at various times destroyed and rebuilt. From these ruins and these new peoples sprang new languages, as appears from those which obtained in France, Spain, and Italy, where the mixture of the native tongues of these nations with the ancient Roman tongue produced the new language. Besides this, not only were the names of the provinces changed, but also those of lakes, rivers, seas, and of men; for France and Italy are full of new names, altogether different from the old ones; for without noting many others we see that the names of Po, Garda, Archipelago, &c. are entirely dissimilar from the ancient names of those localities. Men also changed their names, and from Cæsar and Pompey became Pieri, Giovanni, and Mattei. But amongst all these changes not the least one was that of religion; for combating the habit of the ancient faith with the miracles of the new, gave rise to the gravest tumults and discords amongst men, — and even if the Christian religion had been a united one, its introduction would nevertheless have been followed by minor discords; but the Greek Church, opposing those of Rome and Ravenna together, and the heretical sects being in conflict with the Catholics, caused infinite misery in the world: of which Africa furnishes us proof, for she had to endure far more troubles from the sect of the Arians, to which the Vandals adhered, than she suffered from their cruelty and rapacity. Men thus living in the midst of so many persecutions bore the terror of their souls written in their eyes; for, besides the infinite evils which they had to endure, they were deprived in great measure of the ability to seek a refuge in the help of God, which is the hope of the wretched; for the greater portion of them, being uncertain as to what God they should fly to for refuge, died miserably, bereft of all help and all hope.

6. Theodoric therefore merited no mean praise as having been the first to put an end to so many evils, so that for the thirty-eight years during which he reigned in Italy he restored her to such greatness that the former miseries were in great part forgotten. But when he came to die and the kingdom fell to Atalaric, son of his daughter Amalasiunta, the measure of Italy's ill fortune not being yet exhausted, she relapsed into her former wretchedness; for Atalaric died shortly after his grandfather, and, the government remaining in the hands of his mother, she was betrayed by Teodatus, whom she had called to her aid in the government of the kingdom. Having killed the queen and declared himself king, he became very odious to the Ostrogoths, which encouraged the Emperor Justinian to believe himself able to drive Teodatus out of Italy. Justinian appointed Belisarius as captain of this undertaking, who had already conquered Africa, expelled the Vandals from it, and brought that province back to subjection to the Empire. Thereupon Belisarius took possession of Sicily, and, passing thence into Italy, took Naples and Rome. The Goths seeing their impending ruin, killed King Teodatus as being the cause of it, and elected in his stead Vitigites, who after some fighting was besieged by Belisarius in Ravenna, and taken; but before his victory was completed Belisarius was recalled by Justinian, and Giovanni and Vitales put in his place, who were in no way his equals in valor and experience. This caused the Goths to take courage again, and they created Ildovado their king, who at that time was governor of Verona. He was killed, and after him the kingdom fell to Totilas, who routed the troops of the Emperor and reoccupied Tuscany and Naples, and drove his captains back almost to the extreme limits of the states which Belisarius had recovered. Justinian therefore deemed it advisable to send Belisarius back to Italy, who, having returned there with a small force, rather lost the reputation which his

first victories had given him, but which he had to achieve anew. For whilst Belisarius was at Ostia with his troops, Totilas took Rome under his very eyes, and, finding that he could neither hold nor leave it, he destroyed it in great part, and drove the people out, who carried their Senators away with them; and paying but slight heed to Belisarius, he went with his army into Calabria to meet the troops that had come from Greece to aid that general. Belisarius, seeing Rome abandoned, resolved upon an undertaking worthy of him; for, having entered the ruins of Rome, he rebuilt the walls of the city with the utmost celerity, and recalled its inhabitants. Fortune, however, did not favor this praiseworthy attempt, for Justinian, being at that time attacked by the Parthians, recalled Belisarius, who, in obedience to his master, abandoned Italy to the mercy of Totilas, who retook Rome, but did not treat the city with the same cruelty as at first, because of the entreaties of St. Benedict, who had a reputation of great sanctity, and induced Totilas to apply himself rather to the rebuilding of the city. Justinian meantime made terms with the Parthians, and, attempting to send fresh troops to the succor of Italy, was prevented by the Sclaves, a new Northern people who had passed the Danube and assailed Illyria and Thracia, so that Totilas was enabled to occupy almost the whole of Italy.

But after Justinian had defeated the Sclaves he sent the eunuch Narsetes with an army into Italy, who, being eminent in the art of war, defeated and killed Totilas immediately upon reaching Italy. And the rest of the Goths that remained after this defeat retreated to Pavia, where they made Teja their king. Narsetes, on the other hand, after his victory, took Rome, and finally came to battle with Teja near Nocera, and killed him and scattered his army. In consequence of this victory the name of the Goths disappeared from Italy entirely, where they had ruled for seventy years, from the time of their King Theodoric to that of Teja.

7. But no sooner was Italy liberated from the Goths than Justinian died, and was succeeded by his son Justinus, who by the advice of his wife Sophia recalled Narsetes from Italy and sent Longinus in his place. Following the practice of others, Longinus established his residence at Ravenna, and moreover gave a new form of government to Italy; for he did not establish governors of provinces, as the Goths had done,

but created chiefs in all the cities and places of moment, with the title of Duke. And in this distribution he did not honor Rome more than the other places, for having abolished the Consuls and the Senate, which dignities had until that time been maintained there, he put Rome under a duke, who was sent there every year from Ravenna, so that it was thence called the Dukedom of Rome; and to him who remained in place of the Emperor at Ravenna he gave the title of Exarch. These divisions made the ruin of Italy still more easy, and gave more ready opportunity to the Longobards to take possession of it.

8. Narsetes was very indignant against the Emperor for being deprived of the government of that province, which he had conquered by his valor and with his blood; for Sophia, not content with injuring him by having him recalled, added insulting words, saying that she wanted him to return to spin with the other eunuchs; so that Narsetes, full of indignation, persuaded Alboin, king of the Longobards, who then ruled over Pannonia, to come and seize Italy. The Longobards, as we have seen above, had taken possession of the places near the Danube that had been abandoned by the Erulians and Turingians, when they were led into Italy by their king, Odoacer. Having remained there some time, and Alboin, a cruel and daring man, having become their king, they passed the Danube, and fought with Commundo, king of the Zepidi, who held Pannonia, and defeated him. Amongst the booty taken was the daughter of Commundo, named Rosamunda, whom Alboin took for his wife, and made himself master of Pannonia. Prompted by his cruel nature, he had a cup made out of the skull of Commundo, from which he drank in memory of that victory. But when called into Italy by Narsetes, with whom he had formed a friendship during his war with the Goths, he left Pannonia to the Huns, who, as we have said, had returned to their country after the death of Attila, and thence came into Italy. Finding that country divided into so many parts, Alboin occupied in one move Pavia, Milan, Verona, Vicenza, all Tuscany, and the greater part of Flaminia, now called the Romagna. So that it seemed to him that, after so many and such rapid victories, he had already conquered all Italy, and celebrated it by a grand banquet at Verona. Having become excited by much drink, he filled the skull of Commundo with wine, and had it presented to Rosamunda, his queen, who

sat opposite to him at table; saying in a loud voice, so that she might hear it, that on an occasion of so much gladness he wished her to drink with her father. This speech was like a sword thrust into the breast of the lady, who resolved upon revenge; and knowing that Almachilde, a noble and savage Longobard youth, was in love with one of her maids, arranged with her that she should secretly cause Almachilde to pass a night with the queen instead of herself. Almachilde, having according to appointment met the queen in a dark place, and believing himself to be with the maid, lay with Rosamunda, who, after having discovered herself to him, told him that it was at his option either to kill Alboin, and always to enjoy her and the kingdom, or to be himself killed by Alboin as the ravisher of his wife. Almachilde consented to kill Alboin; but, after having put him to death, seeing that he could not hold the kingdom, and fearing to be killed himself by the Longobards, who were greatly attached to Alboin, he fled, taking with him the queen and all the royal treasure, to Longinus, in Ravenna, who received him honorably. During these troubles, the Emperor Justinus had died, and Tiberius had been made Emperor in his place, who, being engaged in a war with the Parthians, could not go to the assistance of Italy. This seemed, therefore, a favorable opportunity to Longinus to make himself king of the Longobards and of all Italy by means of Rosamunda and her treasures; and having conferred with her on the subject, he persuaded her to kill Almachilde, and to take him for her husband. Rosamunda having agreed to this, she ordered a cup of poisoned wine, which she carried with her own hand to Almachilde, who, being thirsty as he came out of his bath, drank the half of it; and feeling immediately after an internal commotion, he concluded that he had been poisoned, and forced Rosamunda to drink the rest, and thus in a few hours they both died, and Longinus was deprived of the hope of becoming king.

Meantime the Longobards met together at Pavia, which they had made the principal seat of their kingdom, and made Clefi their king, who rebuilt Imola, which had been destroyed by Narsetes, and occupied Rimini, and almost every other place down to Rome; but in the course of his victories death overtook him. This Clefi was cruel in his ways, not only to strangers, but also to his Longobards, who, being alarmed by the royal power, resolved to have no more kings, but created from amongst themselves thirty dukes, who should govern them. This was the reason why the Longobards never obtained possession of all Italy, and why their kingdom never extended beyond Benevento; and also why Rome, Ravenna, Cremona, Mantua, Padua, Monselice, Parma, Bologna, Faenza, Furli, and Cesena partly defended themselves for a time, and partly were never occupied by the Longobards. For the fact of their having no kings had made them more disposed for war; but afterwards having again established royalty, they became, from having for a time enjoyed freedom from control, less inclined to obedience, and more ready for discord amongst themselves, which circumstance first retarded their success, and in the end caused their being driven entirely out of Italy. The Longobards then being established within the above indicated limits, the Romans and Longinus made a treaty with them that each should retain their arms, and keep and enjoy what they possessed.

9. About that time the Popes began to acquire greater authority than they had hitherto enjoyed. The first successors of St. Peter had secured the respect and reverence of men by the sanctity of their lives and the miracles which they performed. The example of their virtues extended the Christian religion to that degree that the princes were obliged to submit to it for the sake of putting an end to the great confusion that prevailed in the world. The Emperor then having become a Christian, and having left Rome and established himself at Constantinople, it followed, as we have said at the beginning, that the Roman Empire fell more rapidly into decadence, whilst the Church of Rome increased in power and influence. Nevertheless, until the coming of the Longobards, all Italy being subject to the authority of the Emperors or kings, the Popes at that time never assumed more authority than what the reverence of their characters and their learning gave them. In all other respects they obeyed either the Emperors or the kings, and on several occasions were put to death by them, or were employed by them as ministers. But he who caused the pontiffs to become more influential in the affairs of Italy was Theodoric, king of the Goths, when he established his residence at Ravenna; because Rome, having been left without a prince, the Romans had reason for yielding more obedience to the pontiffs, for the sake of their protection. Their actual authority, however, was not much increased by this; it only caused the church of Rome to have

precedence of that of Ravenna. But when the Longobards came and reduced Italy to many parts, they afforded the Popes the opportunity to become more active; for being, as it were, the chief power in Rome, the Emperor of Constantinople and the Longobards held them in such respect that the Romans, through the Pope, not as subjects but as equals, confederated with the Longobards and with Longinus. And thus the pontiffs, continuing to be at one time the friends of the Longobards and then again of the Greeks, materially increased their consideration and influence.

It was at this epoch, and under the Emperor Heraclius, that the ruin of the Eastern Empire began. The Sclaves, of whom we have made mention above, having again attacked Illyria, made themselves masters of it, and gave it their own name, Sclavonia. The other parts of that empire were assailed, first by the Persians and after that by the Saracens, who came from Arabia under Mahomet, and finally by the Turks, who, having taken Syria, Africa, and Egypt, the impotence of that empire no longer afforded the Pope any refuge there in his oppressions; and, on the other hand, as the power of the Longobards increased, he thought it necessary for him to seek new friends, and therefore had recourse to the king of France. So that all the wars that were made by the barbarians in Italy after that time were caused by the pontiffs, and all the Barbarians that overran that country were, in most instances, called there by them. This course of proceeding is continued even in our times, and has ever kept, and still keeps, Italy disunited and weak. And therefore the history of the events from that time until the present will not show any more the progress of the decline of the Empire, which was general, but the growth of the power of the pontiffs, and of those other princes that ruled Italy after that time until the coming of Charles VIII. And it will be seen how the Popes, first by means of the Censure, and afterwards by the Censure and force of arms together and combined with indulgences, became at the same time both terrible and venerable, and how, having misused both the one and the other of those means, the Censure lost its terrors entirely and the indulgences were no longer valued.

10. But to return to the order of our history, I say that when Gregory III. had become Pope, and Aistolfo king of the Longobards, the latter occupied Ravenna, in contravention of the

treaties he had made, and set on foot a war against the Pope. Gregory thereupon, for the reasons above given, having no confidence in the Emperor of Constantinople on account of his weakness, and unwilling to trust the Longobards, who had repeatedly broken their faith, had recourse to Pepin II., who from being lord of Austrasia and Brabant, had become king of France, not so much by his own power and merits as by those of Charles Martel, his father, and of Pepin, his grandfather. It was Charles Martel who, when governor of that country, gained that memorable victory over the Saracens at Torsi, on the river Loire, where more than two hundred thousand of them were slain; whereupon Pepin II., through the influence of his father's reputation and his own valor, became king of that realm. Pope Gregory, as has been said, sent to him for assistance against the Longobards, which Pepin promised him, but desired first to see him personally and to honor his presence. Gregory, therefore, went to France, and, after having been honored by the king, was sent back to Italy accompanied by an army, who besieged the Longobards in Pavia. Whereupon Aistolfo, constrained by necessity, made terms with the French, who concluded the agreement at the request of the Pope, who did not wish his enemy killed, but desired that he should live and be converted to the Christian faith. Aistolfo bound himself by this treaty to restore to the Church all the lands which he had occupied; but after the return of Pepin with his troops to France, Aistolfo disregarded his obligations under the treaty, and Gregory had again recourse to Pepin, who once more sent his troops into Italy, defeated the Longobards, and took Ravenna; which, contrary to the will of the Greek Emperor, he gave to the Pope, together with all the other lands that were comprised under the Exarchate, adding thereto the lands of Urbino and La Marca. During the transfer of these lands, Aistolfo died, and Desiderius, a Longobard, who was Duke of Tuscany, took up arms to seize that kingdom, and demanded assistance from the Pope, promising him his friendship in return, which Gregory conceded to him, so that the other princes submitted to him. At first, Desiderius kept his pledges, and transferred the lands to the pontiff according to the agreement made with Pepin; after which no more exarchs came from Constantinople to Ravenna, which remained subject to the rule of the Pope. After that Pepin died, and was succeeded by his son Charles, who, from the greatness of his deeds, was called the Great.

11. Meantime Theodore I. had been elevated to the papal chair; he soon became involved in difficulties with Desiderius, and was besieged by him in Rome; so that he was obliged to have recourse to Charles, who, having passed the Alps, besieged Desiderius in Pavia, took him and his sons prisoners and sent them to France, and then went to visit the Pope at Rome, where he decided that the Pope, as Vicar of God, could not be judged by men, and in turn the Pope and the Roman people declared Charles Emperor. And thus Rome again began to have Emperors in the West, and whilst formerly the Pope had to be confirmed by the Emperor, the Emperor now on his election had need of the Pope; and thus the Empire began to lose its dignity, and that of the pontiff was increased; and by these means the papal authority steadily grew beyond that of the temporal princes.

The Longobards had now been two hundred and thirty-two years in Italy, and only remained foreigners in name; and when King Charles wanted to reorganize Italy during the papacy of Leo III., he consented to the Longobards inhabiting the places where they had been born and bred, and that that country should be called after them Lombardy. And as they held the name of Rome in great reverence, they desired that that entire portion of Italy adjacent to their possessions, and which was subject to the Exarch of Ravenna, should be called the Romagna. Besides this Charles created his son Pepin King of Italy, whose jurisdiction extended as far as Benevento, and all the rest was held by the Greek Emperor, with whom Charles had concluded a treaty.

At that time Pascal I. was chosen supreme pontiff, and the parochians of the churches of Rome, from being near the Pope and present at his election, assumed the name of Cardinals for the purpose of sustaining their power with a splendid title, and they arrogated to themselves so much influence, particularly after they had excluded the Roman people from the elections of the Popes, that the choice of pontiffs rarely passed outside of their number.

After the death of Pascal, Eugene II. was created Pope under the title of St. Sabina; and Italy, since being under the control of the French, changed in part the form and organization of its government, by the Pope's having assumed more authority in temporal matters, and by the introduction into Italy of the titles of Count and Marquis, in the same way as the title of Duke was first established by Longinus, the Exarch of Ravenna. After Eugene II. a Roman priest called Osporco came to be Pope; the ugliness of his name caused him on his election to assume that of Sergio, and it was this circumstance that gave rise to the practice of changing their names which the Popes adopt on their election.

12. Meanwhile the Emperor Charles had died, and was succeeded by his son Louis; after whose death there occurred such dissensions amongst his sons, that at the time of his grandsons the Empire was taken from France and transferred to Germany; and the first German Emperor was called Arnolfo. The discords amongst the descendants of Charles lost them not only the Empire, but also the kingdom of Italy; for the Longobards, having recovered their strength, attacked the Pope and the Romans, so that, not knowing where to seek assistance, the Pope, from necessity, made Berengarius, Duke of Friuli, king of Italy. These events encouraged the Huns who were in Pannonia to assail Italy; but having encountered Berengarius in battle, they were forced to return to Pannonia, or rather to Hungary, as that province was then called. At that period Romano was Emperor in Greece, having taken the Empire from Constantine, whose armies he had commanded. This usurpation had stirred up a rebellion against him in Puglia and Calabria, which provinces owed obedience to the Empire; this made Romano so indignant that he permitted the Saracens to enter those provinces, of which they made themselves masters, and then also attempted to take Rome. But the Romans, seeing Berengarius occupied in defending himself against the Huns, put Alberic, Duke of Tuscany, at their head, and his valor saved Rome from the Saracens; who, after raising the siege of Rome, built a fortress on Mount Galgano, whence they dominated Puglia and Calabria and threatened the rest of Italy. It was thus that Italy suffered terrible afflictions in those days, being assailed towards the Alps by the Huns, and towards Naples by the Saracens.

This unhappy state of things lasted many years in Italy under the three Berengarii, who succeeded one another. The Pope and the Church were constantly disturbed by these troubles, there being no one to whom they could resort for help, owing to the dissensions of the Western princes and the impotence of the Eastern. The city of Genoa and its adjacent shores were ravaged by the Saracens, which gave rise to the greatness of the city of Pisa, which afforded a refuge to many unfortunate people who had been driven from their own homes. These events occurred in the year 931 of the Christian era. But now, when Otho, Duke of Saxony and son of Henry and Mathilda, a man of great prudence and reputation, had become Emperor, the Pope Agapites appealed to him to come into Italy and to deliver her from the tyranny of the Berengarii.

13. The states of Italy were at that time distributed as follows: Lombardy was under Berengarius III. and his son Albert; Tuscany was governed by a minister of the Western Emperor; Puglia and Calabria obeyed in part the Greek Emperor, and in part the Saracens. Rome chose every year two Consuls from amongst her nobles, who governed it according to ancient customs; to these was added a Prefect, who represented the people. There was also a Council of Twelve, who distributed every year the rectors for the different places subject to Rome. The Popes had more or less authority throughout Italy, according as they were in favor with the Emperors or with the other princes that were most powerful in the country. The Emperor Otho then came into Italy and took the government from the Berengarii, who had held it for fifty-five years, and restored to the Pope all his dignities. Otho had a son and a grandson bearing the same name as himself, who one after the other succeeded him in the Empire. At the time of Otho III., Pope Gregory V. was expelled by the Romans, whereupon Otho came into Italy and restored the Pope in Rome; who, by way of revenging himself upon the Romans, took from them the power of creating the Emperors, and bestowed it upon six princes of Germany, namely, the Bishops of Mayence, Treves, and Cologne, and the princes of Brandenburg, the Palatinate, and of Saxony. This occurred in the year 1002.

After the death of Otho III., Henry, Duke of Bavaria, was created Emperor by the Electors, and was crowned twelve years afterwards by Pope Stephen VIII. Henry and his wife, Simeonda, led a most holy life, as may be seen from the many churches endowed and built by them; amongst others, the Church of San Miniato, near the city of Florence. Henry died in the year 1024, and was succeeded by Conrad of Suabia; and after him came Henry II., who came to Rome, and, there being a schism in the Church and three Popes, he displaced them all and had Clement II. elected, by whom he was crowned Emperor.

14. At this time Italy was governed in part by the people and in part by princes, and partly by envoys of the Emperors, the most prominent of which, and to whom the others deferred, were called Chancellors. Amongst the most powerful princes was Gottfried, and the Countess Mathilda, his wife, who was the daughter of Beatrice, sister of Henry II. She and her husband possessed Lucca, Parma, Reggio, and Mantua, together with all the lands that are now called " Il Patrimonio." The pontiffs experienced at this time great difficulties from the ambition of the Roman people, who at first availed of the authority of the Popes to free themselves from the Emperors; and, after having taken the government of the city into their own hands and remodelled it according to their own seeming, suddenly became hostile to the Popes, who received more ill-treatment from the people of Rome than from any other Christian prince. And in the days when the Popes by means of the Censure caused all the West to tremble, the Roman people revolted, none of them having any other intention than to deprive each other of influence and authority.

As Gregory V. had taken from the Romans the power to create the Emperors, so Nicholas II., when he came to the pontificate, deprived the people of Rome of the privilege of concurring in the creation of the Popes, and established that the election of the Popes should belong exclusively to the Cardinals. Nor was he content with this, but having come to an agreement with the princes that governed Calabria and Puglia (for reasons which we shall presently state), he constrained all the officials sent there by the Romans for the administration of justice to render obedience to the Popes, and some of them he deprived of their offices entirely.

15. After the death of Nicholas II. there was a schism in the Church, because the clergy of Lombardy would not yield obedience to Alexander II., who had been elected Pope at Rome; and they created Cadolo of Parma Antipope. The Emperor Henry, who hated the power of the Popes, gave Pope Alexander to understand that he must resign the pontificate,

and the Cardinals that they must go into Germany to create a new Pope. This caused Henry to be the first prince who was made to feel the power of spiritual weapons; for the Pope called a council at Rome, and deprived Henry of the Empire and of his kingdom. Some of the Italian people followed Henry and some the Pope, which was the seed of the feuds between the Guelfs and the Ghibellines (Waiblingen); so that Italy, after the invasions of the Barbarians had ceased, became torn by intestine wars. Henry thereupon, being excommunicated, was constrained by his people to go to Italy and kneel barefoot to the Pope and ask his forgiveness, which occurred in the year 1080. Nevertheless, soon after, other differences arose between the Pope and Henry, so that the Pope excommunicated him anew, whereupon the Emperor sent his son, who was also called Henry, to Rome; and he, assisted by the Romans, who hated the Pope, besieged him in his castle; but Robert Guiscard having come from Puglia to relieve the Pope, Henry did not wait to encounter him, but returned alone to Germany. The Romans, however, persisted obstinately in the siege, so that the city of Rome was again sacked by Robert, and thrown back into its former ruined condition, from which it had been restored by several successive Popes. As this Robert Guiscard was the founder of the kingdom of Naples, it seems to me not superfluous to give some particular account of his origin and his deeds.

16. The dissensions amongst the heirs of Charlemagne, of which we have spoken above, afforded the opportunity to a new Northern people, called the Normans, to come and assail France, and to take possession of that portion which is called Normandy. A part of this people came into Italy at the time when that country was infested by the Berengarii, the Saracens, and the Huns, and took possession of some lands in the Romagna, where they maintained themselves bravely during the subsequent wars. Tancred, who was one of these Norman princes, had numerous sons, amongst whom were William, called Ferabar, and Robert, called Guiscard. The principality had now come to William, and the disturbances of Italy had ceased in that part of the country. Nevertheless, the Saracens held Sicily, and constantly plundered the shores of Italy. William therefore agreed with the Princes of Capua and Salerno, and with Melorco, the Greek, who governed Puglia and Calabria

for the Greek Emperor, to attack the Saracens in Sicily; and it was agreed between them that, in case of success, they should divide the booty and the lands equally, one fourth to each. The enterprise proved fortunate, and after driving out the Saracens they took possession of Sicily. But after this victory Melorco secretly caused troops to be sent over from Greece, by the aid of whom he seized the whole island in the name of the Emperor, and only divided the booty with the others. William was ill content with this, but awaited a more convenient time to manifest it, and left the island, accompanied by the Princes of Salerno and Capua. When these had parted from him to return to their homes, William, instead of returning to the Romagna, turned with his troops towards Puglia, and promptly seized Melfi, and thence in a short time, despite of the resistance of the troops of the Greek Emperor, made himself master of almost the whole of Puglia and Calabria, which provinces had been subject to his brother, Robert Guiscard, at the time of Pope Nicholas II. Having had great differences with his nephews about the inheritance of these provinces, Robert availed of the influence of the Pope to compose them, which the latter did most readily, being desirous of securing the friendship of Robert, so that he might defend him against the German Emperor and the insolence of the Roman people. This indeed happened, as we have related above, when at the instance of Gregory VII. he drove Henry from Rome, and reduced the people of that city to subjection. Robert was succeeded by his sons Ruggieri and William, who added to their possessions Naples, and all the country between Naples and Rome, as also Sicily, of which Ruggieri had made himself master. But William afterwards, whilst on his way to Constantinople to espouse the daughter of the Emperor, was attacked by Ruggieri, and deprived by him of his state. Ruggieri, elated by this acquisition, had himself proclaimed King of Italy, but afterwards contented himself with the title of King of Puglia and Sicily, and was the first to give a name and organization to that kingdom, which has maintained itself in its ancient limits, although it has several times changed not only its dynasty, but also its nationality. For when the Norman line became extinct, the kingdom was transferred to the Germans, and from them to the French; from these it passed to the Aragonese, and is now possessed by the Flemish.

17. Urban II. had now come to the supreme Pontificate; he was hated by the Romans, and believing that he could not remain securely in Rome on account of the disturbances in Italy, he turned his attention to a grand and noble enterprise. He went to France with all his clergy, and having gathered a large assemblage of people at Antwerp, he addressed them a discourse against the infidels, by which he inflamed their minds to that degree that they resolved to undertake a war against the Saracens in Asia. This enterprise and similar subsequent ones were called the Crusades, because all who joined in them wore a red cross on their arms or on their clothes. The chiefs in this enterprise were Godfrey, Eustace, and Baldwin, Counts of Bouillon, and a certain Peter the Hermit, who was celebrated for his sanctity and wisdom. Many kings and nations aided this undertaking with money, and many individuals served as soldiers without any pay; such was the power and influence of religion upon the minds of men in those days, stimulated by the example of those who were the leaders in this enterprise. At first the results were glorious, for all Asia Minor, Syria, and part of Egypt, fell under the power of the Christians. It gave rise to the order of the Knights of Jerusalem, which exists to this day and holds the island of Rhodes, and has remained the chief obstacle to the power of the Mahometans. It also gave birth to the order of the Knight Templars, which became extinguished, however, soon after, in consequence of their bad habits. Various events occurred in connection with this undertaking by which at different times many individuals and nations became famous. The kings of England and France lent it their aid and support; and the people of Pisa, Venice, and Genoa acquired great renown, and fought with varying fortunes in this expedition, up to the time of Saladin the Saracen, whose valor, together with the dissensions of the Christians, deprived them in the end of all the glory they had acquired in the beginning; and after ninety years they were driven out of the places which they had at first recovered with so much honor.

18. After the death of Urban, Pascal II. was made Pope, and the Empire fell to Henry IV., who went to Rome feigning friendship for the Pope; but afterwards he imprisoned him, together with all his clergy, and did not liberate them again until they conceded to him the power of disposing of the Church in Ger-

many as seemed to him proper. At this time occurred the death of the Countess Mathilda, who left all her estates to the Church. After the death of Pascal and of the Emperor Henry, more Popes and Emperors succeeded, until the Pontificate came to Alexander III., and the Empire to Frederick of Suabia, called Barbarossa. At that period the Popes had had many difficulties with the Roman people and the Emperors, which increased very much at the time of Barbarossa. Frederick excelled in war, but his pride was such that he could not bear to yield to the Popes; nevertheless, after his election, he came to Rome to be crowned, and then returned peacefully to Germany. But he did not remain long in that frame of mind, for he returned to Italy to reduce to subjection some towns of Lombardy that had refused him obedience. At this time the Cardinal St. Clement, a Roman by birth, separated himself from the Pope, and was himself made Pope by some of the cardinals. The Emperor Frederick was at that time encamped before Crema, and when Pope Alexander complained to him of the Antipope, Clement, he replied that they should both come before him, and that then he would decide which of them was the true Pope. This answer displeased Alexander, and seeing Frederick inclined to favor the Antipope, he excommunicated him, and fled to Philip, king of France. Frederick meanwhile continued the war in Lombardy, and took and destroyed Milan; in consequence of which Verona, Padua, and Vicenza united against him for their common defence.

In the midst of these occurrences the Antipope died, whereupon Frederick created Guido of Cremona Antipope in his place. The Romans at this time, partly in consequence of the absence of the Pope and partly in consequence of the obstacles which the Emperor met with in Lombardy, had resumed considerable authority in Rome, and claimed obedience from those places that used to be subject to them. And as the Tusculanians refused to concede any authority to them, they went in mass to attack them; but the Tusculanians, being supported by Frederick, routed the Roman army with such slaughter that Rome never afterwards was either populous or rich. Pope Alexander meantime had returned to Rome, deeming himself safe now in remaining there because of the enmity between Frederick and the Romans, as also on account of the enemies which Frederick had in Lombardy. But, regardless of all such considerations,

Frederick took the field and marched upon Rome, where Alexander, however, did not await him, but fled to William, king of Puglia, who had become heir to that kingdom after the death of Ruggieri. But Frederick gave up the siege of Rome in consequence of the pest, and returned to Germany; and the towns of Lombardy that had conspired against him, by way of enabling them to subdue Pavia and Tortona, which were held by the Imperialists, built a city that should serve them as a stronghold, and which they called Alexandria, in honor of Pope Alexander, and in derision of Frederick. Guido the Antipope also died, and his place was filled by Giovanni da Fermo, who, favored by the Imperial party, remained at Montefiascone.

19. In the midst of these events Alexander had gone to Tusculum, called there by the people to protect them with his authority against the Romans. Whilst there, envoys came to him from the king of England to explain to him that their king had no share in the guilt of the murder of the blessed Thomas, Bishop of Canterbury, of which he had been publicly accused. On account of which the Pope sent two cardinals to England to investigate the truth of the matter; who, although they could discover no manifest proof of the king's being guilty, yet, on account of the infamy of the crime and for not having honored Thomas as he deserved, ordered that the king, by way of penance, should convene all the barons of his realm, and by a solemn oath should excuse himself in their presence; and that, furthermore, he should at once send two hundred soldiers to Jerusalem, and pay them for one year; and that the king should also be obliged personally to go to Jerusalem within three years, with as great an army as he could bring together; and to annul all the acts passed during his reign that were adverse to ecclesiastical liberty; and to consent that every one of his subjects should have the right to appeal to Rome; all which conditions were accepted by King Henry. And so great a king submitted to such a judgment, to which any private individual of the present day would disdain to submit. And yet, whilst the Pope had so much authority with princes at so great a distance, he could not make himself obeyed by the Romans, whom he could not induce, even by entreaties, to allow him to stay in Rome; although he promised them, moreover, that he would not interfere in any but ecclesiastical matters. So much more are appearances dreaded at a distance than when seen near by.

At that time Frederick had returned to Italy, and whilst he was preparing to renew hostilities against the Pope all the prelates and barons gave him to understand that they would abandon him if he did not reconcile himself with the Church; so that Frederick was obliged to go to Venice to render homage to the Pope. A pacification was there effected between them; and in the treaty the Pope withdrew from the Emperor all authority over Rome, and named William, king of Sicily and of Puglia, his coadjutor. Frederick, unable to live without being engaged in some war, undertook to go to Asia, there to give vent to his ambition against Mahomet, which he had not been able to do against the Vicar of Christ. But having reached the river Cydnus, and being attracted by the clearness of its waters, he bathed in it, and died in consequence; and thus the water rendered greater service to the Mahometans than the excommunications had rendered to the Christians; for these only checked the pride of the Emperor, whilst the former extinguished it.

20. After the death of Frederick, it only remained for the Pope to subdue the contumacy of the Romans; and after much disputing about the creation of consuls, it was agreed that the people of Rome should elect them according to custom, but that they could not enter upon their functions until after having first sworn fidelity to the Church. This agreement caused the Antipope Giovanni to fly to Monte Albano, where he died soon after. William, king of Naples, died also about this time, and the Pope proposed to take possession of that kingdom, as the king had left no son but Tancred, who was an illegitimate child. The barons, however, did not concur in the Pope's intentions, and wanted Tancred for their king. Celestin III. was Pope at that time, who, being desirous to get the kingdom out of the hands of Tancred, managed to have Henry, son of Frederick, made Emperor, and promised him the kingdom of Naples on condition of his restoring to the Church all the lands that had belonged to her. And, by way of facilitating this matter, he withdrew from the convent Costanza, a daughter of William's and no longer very young, and gave her to Henry for his wife. And thus did the kingdom of Naples pass from the Normans, who were the founders of it, to the Germans. After having settled matters in Germany, Henry came to Italy with his wife, Costanza, and a son four years of age, called Frederick, and

took possession of the kingdom of Naples without much difficulty; for Tancred had already died, leaving only a small boy, called Ruggiero. After a time Henry died in Sicily, and Frederick succeeded to the kingdom of Naples, and Otho, Duke of Saxony, to the Empire, through the favorable influence of Pope Innocent III. But no sooner had Otho taken the crown than, contrary to all expectation, he turned against the Pope, seized the Romagna, and ordered an attack upon the kingdom, in consequence of which the Pope excommunicated him, so that he was abandoned by everybody; whereupon the Electors chose Frederick, king of Naples, Emperor. Frederick came to Rome for his coronation, but the Pope would not crown him, for he feared his power, and therefore sought to get him out of Italy, the same as he had done with Otho. Frederick became so indignant at this that he returned to Germany, and, after a protracted war, defeated Otho.

In the midst of these events Pope Innocent died, who, besides many other excellent works, built the Hospital of Santo Spirito at Rome. He was succeeded by Honorius III., during whose Pontificate the orders of St. Dominic and St. Francis were established, in the year 1218. It was this Pope who crowned Frederick, to whom John, a descendant of Baldwin, king of Jerusalem, who was with the remnant of the Christians in Asia, gave one of his daughters for wife, and with her dower he conceded to Frederick the title to that kingdom; and this gave rise to the custom that whoever is king of Naples also bears the title of king of Jerusalem.

21. The state of things in Italy at that time was as follows. The Romans made no more Consuls, and in their stead they created, by the same authority, first only one Senator, and afterwards more. The league that had been formed amongst the cities of Lombardy against Frederick Barbarossa was still in existence, and was composed of the cities of Milan, Brescia, Mantua, with the greater part of the cities of the Romagna, and in addition Verona, Vicenza, Padua, and Trevisi. On the side of the Emperor were Cremona, Bergamo, Parma, Reggio, Modena, and Trent. The other cities and castles of Lombardy and the Trevisian Marches, according to necessity, favored either the one or the other party.

At the time of Otho III. there had come into Italy one Ezzelino, of whom there remained a son born in Italy, who became father to another Ezzelino. The latter, being rich and powerful, united with Frederick II., who, as we have said, had become hostile to the Pope; and having come into Italy through the favor and means of Ezzelino, he took Verona and Mantua, destroyed Vicenza, seized Padua, and routed the army of the leagued cities, and then marched upon Tuscany. Meantime Ezzelino had subjugated the entire Trevisian Marches; but failed to take Ferrara, which was being defended by Azone d' Este and by the troops which the Pope had in Lombardy. When the siege was raised, the Pope gave that city in fief to Azone d' Este, from whom those are descended who rule over the city at the present day. Frederick, desirous of making himself master of Tuscany, stopped at Pisa; and in scanning his friends and his enemies in that province, he sowed so much discord that it was the ruin of all Italy, because the factions of the Guelfs and Ghibellines multiplied everywhere, those being called Guelfs who adhered to the Church, and Ghibellines those who followed the Emperor. These appellations were first applied at Pistoja. After departing from Pisa Frederick attacked and wasted the lands of the Church in every direction, so that the Pope, seeing no other remedy, proclaimed a crusade against him, the same as his predecessors had done against the Saracens. And Frederick, to prevent being suddenly abandoned by his troops, as in the case of Frederick Barbarossa, and others more powerful than himself, took a number of Saracens into his pay; and by way of fixing them as a permanent obstacle to the Church in Italy, who would not fear the papal maledictions, he gave them Nocera in the kingdom of Naples, so that, having a place of refuge of their own, they might serve him with a greater sense of security.

22. The Pontificate had now come to Innocent IV., who, fearing lest Frederick should go to Genoa and thence into France, ordered a council to be held at Lyons; to which Frederick resolved to go, but was prevented by a rebellion of the city of Parma; and being repulsed in his attack upon that city, he went into Tuscany, and thence to Sicily, where he died, leaving his son Conrad in Suabia, and his natural son Manfred he left in Puglia, having made him Duke of Benevento. Conrad came to take possession of the kingdom, but died after having reached Naples; he left one son, named Conradin, who was still young, and was at that time in Germany. Meantime

Manfred seized the government, first as the guardian of Conradin; and afterwards, having started a report of Conradin's death, he made himself king, contrary to the will of the Pope and of the Neapolitans, whom he forced to yield their consent. Whilst these things were going on in the kingdom of Naples, many disturbances occurred between the factions of the Guelfs and the Ghibellines. At the head of the Guelf party was a Legate of the Pope; and the Ghibellines were led by Ezzelino, who possessed nearly all Lombardy beyond the Po. And as the city of Padua revolted during the progress of the war, Ezzelino had twelve thousand Paduans put to death, but died himself at the age of thirty before the war had been brought to a close; after his death all his possessions became free. Manfred, king of Naples, continued in hostility towards the Church the same as his ancestors, and kept the then Pope Urban IV. in continual anxiety; so that the Pope, by way of reducing him to subjection, proclaimed a crusade against him, and went himself to Perugia there to await the gathering of troops. And as it seemed to him that but a few came, feebly and tardily, he bethought himself that, to enable him to conquer Manfred, he would need to have assistance; and therefore he turned for aid and favor to France, and created Charles of Anjou, brother of Louis, king of France, king of Sicily and Naples, and urged him to come into Italy to take possession of that kingdom. But the Pope died before Charles came to Rome, and Clement IV. was elected in his place. During his Pontificate Charles came with thirty galleys to Ostia, having ordered the other portion of his troops to come by land. During his stay in Rome the Romans, by way of gratifying him, made him Senator; and the Pope invested him with the kingdom, with the obligation, however, that he should pay every year to the Church the sum of fifty thousand florins; and he issued a decree that in future neither Charles nor any one else that held the kingdom of Naples should be Emperor. And Charles, having taken the field against Manfred, routed and killed him near Benevento, and made himself master of Sicily and of the kingdom. But Conradin, to whom the state belonged according to his father's will, gathered a large force in Germany and came into Italy against Charles, whom he encountered and fought at Tagliacozzo, but was routed, and whilst flying in disguise was taken and put to death.

28. Italy remained quiet until the accession of Adrian V. to the Pontificate. Whilst Charles was at Rome governing it by virtue of his office of Senator, the Pope could not brook his power, and went to live at Viterbo, and solicited the Emperor Rudolph to come to his aid against Charles into Italy. And thus did the Popes, influenced either by the love of their religion, or by their personal ambition, continue to call into Italy new people, and to stir up new wars; and after having made one prince powerful they repented of it and sought his ruin, and would not permit that that province which they were themselves too weak to hold should be possessed by any one else. And the princes feared the Popes, because these always carried the day, whether fighting or flying, unless they were overpowered by some fraud, as was Boniface VIII. and some others, who were taken prisoners by the Emperor under the pretence of friendship.

Rudolph did not come into Italy, being detained by the war in which he was engaged against the king of Bohemia. In the midst of this Adrian died and was succeeded in the Pontificate by Nicholas III. of the house of Orsini, an ambitious and audacious man. Resolved by every means to diminish the power of Charles, he directed that Rudolph should complain because Charles kept a governor in Tuscany on account of the Guelf party, which had been re-established by him in that province after the death of Manfred. Charles yielded to the Emperor, and withdrew his governor, and the Pope sent his cardinal nephew there as governor of the Empire; so that the Emperor, in return for the honor shown him, restored the Romagna to the Church, which had been taken from her by his ancestors, and the Pope made Bartoldo Orsini Duke of the Romagna. The Pope, thinking that he had become sufficiently powerful to be able to contend against Charles, deprived him of the office of Senator, and issued a decree that henceforth no one of royal lineage should be able to be a Senator in Rome. He had it in his mind also to take Sicily from Charles, and for this purpose set secret negotiations on foot with Pedro, king of Aragon, which were carried into effect afterwards under his successor. He contemplated furthermore to create from amongst his family two kings, one in Lombardy and the other in Tuscany, so that they might defend the Church against the Germans whenever they might attempt to come into Italy, and against the French who were in the kingdom of Naples. But before putting these designs into execution he died, having been the first Pope who openly manifested his selfish ambition, and who designed, under color of aggrandizing the Church, to bestow honors and benefits upon his own family. Previous to that time no mention had ever been made of nephews or relatives of any of the Popes; but henceforth history is full of them, so that even their children are seen to figure in it. And after having attempted to make their children princes, there really seemed to remain nothing more for the Popes to do than to leave them the Papacy as an hereditary right. It is very true that the principalities established by the Popes until then have been but short-lived, because in many instances the Popes themselves did not live long; so that either they could not finish planting their seeds, or, if they did, they left them whilst their roots were yet so feeble and few that they were destroyed by the first storm after the power that sustained them had ceased to exist.

24. The next Pope was Martin IV., who, being French by birth, favored the party of Charles; in return for which Charles sent his troops into the Romagna, which had revolted against the Holy See; and whilst besieging Furli, Guido Bonatti, an astrologer, directed the people to assail Charles at a particular point indicated by him, so that all the French were either taken or slain.

At that time also was carried into effect the plot that had been arranged between the Pope Nicholas and Pedro, king of Aragon, according to which the Sicilians killed all the French that were found on the island. Pedro made himself master of Sicily, claiming it as belonging to him by right of his wife, Costanza, daughter of Manfred. But Charles died whilst organizing the campaign for the recovery of Sicily, leaving a son, Charles II., who was taken prisoner during the war in Sicily. For the sake of gaining his liberty he promised to return to prison provided he should not have succeeded within three years in inducing the Pope to invest the royal house of Aragon with the crown of Sicily.

25. The Emperor Rudolph, instead of coming into Italy to restore the influence of the Empire there, sent an ambassador with authority to concede their freedom to all the cities that were willing to purchase it; in consequence of which many

cities purchased their liberties and changed their form of government. Adolf of Saxony succeeded to the Empire, and Pietro del Murone to the Pontificate; the latter took the name of Celestin, but being a hermit of great sanctity he renounced the Pontificate, and Boniface VIII. was elected Pope in his stead. Heaven, knowing that the time was to come when the French and the Germans should leave Italy, and that country should remain wholly in the hands of the Italians, so that the Pope deprived of foreign aid should neither be able to confirm nor enjoy his power, raised up two powerful families in Rome, the Colonna and the Orsini, who by their proximity would keep the Pope impotent. Boniface, aware of this, resolved to crush the Colonna; and after having excommunicated them, he proclaimed a crusade against them, which although it did them some harm yet injured the Church more. For the same weapon which had been most valiantly and successfully employed in defence of the faith, failed of effect when for purposes of personal ambition it was turned against Christians. And thus their very lust of power caused the Popes little by little to be enfeebled. Besides the above extreme measures, Boniface deprived two of the family of the Colonna who were cardinals of this dignity. Sciarra, the head of the house, which before him had been unknown, having fled, was taken by Catalan corsairs and put to the oars; but being afterwards recognized at Marseilles he was sent to Philip of France, who had also been excommunicated and deprived of his kingdom by Boniface. Philip considering himself as in open war against the Pope, in which he might remain either a loser or be exposed to great risks, had recourse to deceit, and, feigning a desire to make peace with the pontiff, sent Sciarra secretly into Italy. Upon arriving at Anagni, where the Pope was, he gathered his friends in the night and took the Pope prisoner. And although Boniface was soon after liberated by the people of Anagni, yet the mortification caused by that insult drove him mad, and he died.

26. It was this Boniface who organized the Jubilee of the Church in the year 1300, and ordered that it should be celebrated every hundred years. In these days there occurred many troubles between the Guelfs and the Ghibellines; and Italy, having been abandoned by the Emperors, many cities became free, and many fell under the control of despots. Pope

Benedict restored the hat to Cardinal Colonna, and readmitted King Philip of France to the blessings and privileges of the Church. Benedict was succeeded by Clement V., who, being a Frenchman, transferred the pontifical seat to France in the year 1305. In the midst of these events Charles II., king of Naples, died, and was succeeded by his son, Robert; and Henry of Luxemburg had become Emperor, who came to Rome to be crowned, although the Pope was not there. His coming caused great disturbances in Lombardy; for he restored all the banished, whether Guelfs or Ghibellines, to their country, whence it resulted that, each party endeavoring to drive out the other, the province was torn by warlike dissensions, which the Emperor with all his power could not obviate. Having departed from Lombardy, the Emperor Henry went by way of Genoa to Pisa, where he attempted to take Tuscany from King Robert; but failing in this, he went on to Rome, where he remained but a few days, being driven out by the Orsini, with the help of King Robert; whereupon he returned to Pisa, and by way of carrying on the war more securely against Tuscany, and taking that state from King Robert, he caused it to be attacked by Frederick, king of Sicily. But whilst he hoped at the same time to obtain possession of Tuscany and to deprive King Robert of his state, he died, and was succeeded in the Empire by Louis of Bavaria. In the midst of these events John XXII. was elected Pope. Under his Pontificate the Emperor did not cease his persecutions against the Guelfs and the Church, which was defended in great part by King Robert and the Florentines. This gave rise to the many wars in Lombardy on the part of the Visconti against the Guelfs, and on the part of Castruccio of Lucca against the Florentines in Tuscany. But as it was the family of the Visconti that created the Dukedom of Milan, — one of the five principalities that subsequently governed Italy, — it seems to me proper here to give some account of their condition.

27. After the establishment in Lombardy of the league of the cities, already mentioned, for the purpose of mutual defence against Frederick Barbarossa, the city of Milan, having been rebuilt after its destruction, for the purpose of revenging herself for the wrongs endured, joined the league, which checked Barbarossa, and kept the Church party alive for some time in Lombardy. And in the disorders of the wars that followed

thereupon the family of the Della Torres became most powerful in that city; so that their influence increased steadily, whilst the Emperors possessed but little authority in that province. But when Frederick II. came into Italy, and the Ghibelline party had become powerful by the acts of Ezzelino, there occurred in all the cities Ghibelline disturbances, whilst in Milan the Visconti were amongst the adherents of the Ghibellines, and drove the Della Torres from Milan. These had been absent, however, but a little while, before they were restored to their country by the treaties made between the Pope and the Emperor.

But the Pope, having gone with his court to France, and Henry of Luxemburg having come into Italy to be crowned at Rome, he was received at Milan by Maffeo Visconti and Guido della Torre, who were the heads of those families. Maffeo conceived the idea to avail of the presence of the Emperor to drive out Guido, believing the undertaking easy, because Guido belonged to the faction opposed to the Emperor. He therefore profited by the complaints of the people of the oppressive conduct of the Germans, and cautiously encouraged and persuaded the people to take up arms, and to arise and shake off the yoke of these barbarians. And when he supposed that he had arranged everything for his purpose, he caused some of his devoted adherents to create a tumult, whereupon the people rose in arms against the Germans. No sooner was this disturbance begun than Maffeo, with his sons and his partisans all in arms, rushed to Henry, and represented to him that the tumult had been created by the Della Torres, who, not content to remain quiet in Milan, had taken that opportunity to try and plunder him, for the purpose of ingratiating themselves with the Guelfs in Italy, and to make themselves masters of that city. But he bade Henry to be of good cheer; that he would stand by him, and that he and his party were ready to aid and defend him with all the means in their power. Henry, believing all that Maffeo told him to be the truth, united his forces to those of the Visconti, and attacked the Della Torres, who had run to all parts of the city for the purpose of staying the tumult; and those who were not taken prisoners were killed, the others were deprived of their property and sent into exile. Thus Maffeo Visconti remained Prince of Milan, and after him came Galeazzo and Azzo, and then Luchino and Giovanni; the latter became Archbishop of Milan, and Luchino, who died before him, left two sons, Bernabo and Galeazzo. But soon after, Galeazzo also died, leaving a son, Giovanni Galeazzo, called Conte di Virtu. After the death of the Archbishop, Giovanni Galeazzo murdered his uncle, Bernabo, in a treacherous manner, and remained sole Prince of Milan, and was the first who took the title of Duke. He left two sons, Philip and Giovanni Maria Angelo; the latter was killed by the people of Milan, and the government remained in the hands of Philip, who left no male children; whence the state was transferred from the house of Visconti to that of the Sforzas, in the manner and for the reasons which we shall relate at the proper time.

28. Returning now to the point from which I digressed, the Emperor Louis, for the purpose of reviving the power and influence of the imperial party, and to assume the crown, came into Italy; and being at Milan, as a pretext for obtaining money from the Milanese, he made show of leaving them their liberty and put the Visconti in prison. Afterwards he liberated them by means of Castruccio da Lucca; and having gone to Rome for the purpose of more easily disturbing Italy, he created Piero della Corvara Antipope, intending by his influence and the power of the Visconti to keep the opposing parties of Lombardy and Tuscany in a condition of weakness. But Castruccio died, which was the beginning of the Emperor's failure; for Pisa and Lucca revolted against him, and the Pisans sent the Antipope as prisoner to the Pope in France; so that Louis, despairing of affairs in Italy, returned to Germany. No sooner had he left than John, king of Bohemia, came into Italy, called there by the Ghibellines of Brescia, and made himself master of that city and of Bergamo. And as he had come into Italy with the consent of the Pope, who however feigned the contrary, he was supported by the Legate of Bologna, who judged that that would be a good means of preventing the return of the Emperor into Italy. It was in this way that the condition of Italy became changed; for the Florentines and King Robert, seeing that the Legate supported the project of the Ghibellines, became hostile to all who were friends of the Legate and of the king of Bohemia. And many princes united with them without having any regard to either Guelf or Ghibelline party; amongst these were the Visconti, the Della Scalas, Philip Gonzago of Mantua, and the Princes of

Carrara and of Este. Whereupon the Pope excommunicated them all; and the king, fearing this league, returned home to collect more forces. But having afterwards returned with these into Italy, he nevertheless found the enterprise so difficult for him that he returned to Bohemia disheartened, to the great displeasure of the Legate; leaving only Reggio and Modena guarded, and recommending Parma to Marsiglio and Piero de Rossi, who were most powerful in that city. After his departure, Bologna joined the league, and the confederates divided the four cities that yet remained to the party of the Church amongst themselves, and agreed that Parma should belong to the Della Scalas, Reggio to Gonzaga, Modena to the D' Estes, and Lucca to the Florentines. The taking of these places occasioned many wars, which however were afterwards composed in great part by the Venetians. Some persons perhaps may wonder that, in narrating so many events that have occurred in Italy, we have deferred so long to speak of the Venetians, their state being a republic, which on account of its organization and power should be noted above every other principality in Italy. But the wonder will cease when they understand the reason of it, and therefore I shall resume the history of Venice so far back that the reader may understand her origin, and why the Venetians delayed so long taking an active part in the affairs of Italy.

29. When Attila, king of the Huns, besieged Aquileia, its inhabitants, after defending themselves a long time, despaired of their safety, and took refuge as best they could, with their movables, upon those rocky shoals that lay unoccupied near the head of the Adriatic Sea. The Paduans, also, seeing the conflagration approach, and fearing that, after Aquileia should have been taken, Attila would attack them, carried all their movables of greatest value to a point on the same sea called Rivo Alto, where they also sent their women and children and old men, keeping the young men in Padua for its defence. Besides these, the people of Monselice, together with the inhabitants of the hills in the rear, impelled by the same fears, took refuge also on the same rocky shoals of the Adriatic. But after Aquileia was taken and after Attila had destroyed Padua, Monselice, Vicenza, and Verona, the inhabitants of Padua and the most influential of the other cities remained to inhabit the swamps around Rivo Alto. And all the people of

the vicinity of that province, which was anciently called Venezia, driven from their homes by the same circumstances, in like manner took refuge in those marshes. Thus constrained by necessity, they left the most agreeable and fertile places to dwell in sterile and unsettled ones, deprived of all comforts. A great many people being thus suddenly brought together there, they made those places in a very short space of time, not only fertile, but most delightful; and having established order and laws amongst themselves, they lived securely whilst there was so much ruin and distress throughout Italy, and in a little while they grew in reputation and power. For, besides the above-mentioned inhabitants, many others took refuge there from the cities of Lombardy, mostly driven away by the cruelties of Clefi, king of the Longobards; and which caused the new city to increase so considerably, that at the time when Pepin, king of France, came at the Pope's request to drive the Longobards from Italy, in the conventions that were made between Pepin and the Emperor of the Greeks, the Duke of Benevento and the Venetians obeyed neither the one nor the other, but enjoyed their independence and liberty in the midst of them. Besides this, as necessity had obliged them to live as it were in the water, so, unable to avail of the land, they were forced to see how they could gain an honest living by sea; and going with their vessels to all parts of the world, they filled their city with various kinds of merchandise, of which other people being in need caused them frequently to resort there for their supplies. Nor did the Venetians for many years think of any other dominion than that which facilitated the transport of their merchandise; and therefore they acquired many ports in Greece and in Syria. And as the French in their voyages to Asia availed of the vessels of the Venetians, they assigned to them the island of Candia as a reward. And so long as they lived in this wise their name became feared on the seas, whilst in Italy it was venerated, so that in most of the controversies that arose the Venetians for the most part became the arbiters; as was the case in the differences between the confederated princes on account of the places which they divided amongst themselves, which dispute being referred to the Venetians, the Visconti received Bergamo and Brescia.

But as the Venetians, urged on by the lust of conquest, had in the course of time obtained possession of Padua, Vicenza, and Trevisi, and afterwards of Verona, Bergamo, and Brescia, and of a number of places in the kingdom and in the Romagna, they acquired such a reputation for power that they became a terror not only to the princes of Italy, but also to the Ultramontane kings. In consequence of which these combined against the Venetians, who thereupon lost in one day that state and power which they had achieved in so many years and at such infinite expense. And although they subsequently reacquired it in part, yet not having recovered their former reputation or power, they exist, like all the other Italian states, at the discretion of others.

30. Benedict XII. having become Pope, it seemed to him that he had lost all control of Italy, and, fearing lest the Emperor Louis should make himself master of it, he bethought himself to secure the friendship of all those who had usurped the places that used to be subject to the Emperor, so that, having reason to fear the Empire, they might ally themselves to him for the defence of Italy. He therefore issued a decree that all the tyrants of Lombardy should by a just title continue to hold the places they had usurped. But after having made this concession Benedict died, and was succeeded in the Pontificate by Clement VI. The Emperor, seeing with what liberality the Pope had donated the possessions of the Empire, resolved to be not less liberal with the goods of others, and so he gave to all those who had usurped the lands of the Church full imperial authority to retain them as their own property. In consequence of which Galeotto Malatesta and his brother became lords of Rimini, Pesaro, and Fano; Antonio da Montefeltro became lord of Marca and Urbino; Guido da Polenta, of Ravenna; Sinibaldo Ordelaffi, of Furli and Cesena; Giovanni Manfredi, of Faenza; and Lodovico Alidosi, of Imola. Besides these, many others became lords of other cities; so that of the many towns that belonged to the Church but a few remained without princes. This kept the Church weak until Alexander VI., in our day, restored her to her former authority by the ruin of those princes.

At the time of granting the above concession the Emperor was at Trent, and gave out that he intended to pass into Italy, which occasioned many wars in Lombardy, whereby the Visconti made themselves masters of Parma. Robert, king of Naples, died about this time, leaving only two granddaughters, children of his son Charles, who had died some time before him. By his will he constituted the elder, Joanna, heiress of the kingdom, and that she should take for her husband Andreas, king of Hungary, his nephew. Andreas had not lived long with Joanna before she had him killed, and married another cousin the Prince of Taranto, called Lodovico. But Louis, then king of Hungary and brother to Andreas, for the purpose of avenging the death of his brother, came with troops into Italy and drove Queen Joanna and her husband from the kingdom.

31. At this time there occurred a memorable affair at Rome; namely, a certain Niccolo di Lorenzo, Chancellor of the Campidoglio, expelled the Senators from Rome and proclaimed himself chief of the Roman republic, with the title of Tribune; and re-established that ancient form of government, with so much reputation of justice and virtue that not only the neighboring states, but all Italy, sent ambassadors to him; so that the ancient provinces, seeing the regeneration of Rome, also began to raise their heads; and some from fear, and others influenced by hope, did him honor. But despite of this great reputation, Niccolo became discouraged almost at the very outset; for borne down by the weight of responsibility he fled secretly of his own accord, and went to Charles of Bohemia, who had been elected Emperor by order of the Pope, and in disregard of Louis of Bavaria. Charles, by way of making himself acceptable to the Pope, sent him Niccolo as prisoner. Not long after this, however, it occurred that one Francesco Baroncelli, in imitation of Niccolo, seized the Tribunate of Rome and expelled the Senators. The Pope, as the promptest means for repressing this attempt, had Niccolo liberated and sent to Rome, and restored him to the office of Tribune; and when Niccolo had resumed the government he had Francesco put to death. But the Colonnese having become his enemies, Niccolo was also killed a short time afterwards, and the Senators restored to their offices.

32. In the midst of these events the king of Hungary, after having driven the Queen Joanna from the kingdom of Naples, returned to his own dominions. But the Pope, who preferred to have the queen near Rome rather than the king, managed in such manner as to have the king of Hungary consent to restore the kingdom to Joanna, provided that her husband, Lodovico, should content himself with the title of Prince of Taranto, and

not claim that of king. It was now the year 1350, and it seeming to the Pope that the Jubilee, which Boniface VIII. had ordained for every hundred years, might be celebrated every fifty years, and having proclaimed this by a decree, the Roman people in return for this benefit agreed that the Pope should send four cardinals to Rome to reform the government of the city, and to create Senators according to his pleasure. The Pope also pronounced Lodovico di Taranto king of Naples; whereupon the queen out of gratitude gave her patrimony of Avignon to the Church. About this time Luchino Visconti was killed, whereupon the Archbishop Giovanni remained sole lord of Milan. He frequently engaged in war against Tuscany and his other neighbors, so that he became very powerful. After his death there remained his nephews, Bernabo and Galeazzo; the latter, however, died soon after, leaving a son, Giovanni Galeazzo, who shared the government with Bernabo. At this period Charles, king of Bohemia, was Emperor, and Innocent VI. was Pope; the latter sent the Cardinal Egidius, a Spaniard, into Italy, who by his ability and valor restored the reputation of the Church, not only in the Romagna and in Rome, but in all Italy. He recovered Bologna, which had been occupied by the Archbishop of Milan; compelled the Romans to accept a foreign Senator, who should be sent there every year by the Pope; made honorable treaties with the Visconti; defeated and took prisoner Giovanni Aguto, an Englishman (John Sharpe) who was carrying on a war with four thousand English in Tuscany in aid of the Ghibellines. Whereupon Urban V., having become Pope and having heard of all these victories, resolved to visit Italy and Rome, where the Emperor Charles also came; after a few months, however, the Emperor returned home, and the Pope went back to Avignon.

After the death of Urban, Gregory XI. became pontiff; and the Cardinal Egidius also having died, Italy relapsed into its former condition of discord, caused by the peoples having combined against the Visconti. So that the Pope first sent a Legate into Italy with six thousand Bretons, and afterwards came in person and re-established his court at Rome in the year 1376, after its having been seventy-one years in France. After the death of Gregory, Urban VI. was made Pope, but shortly afterwards Clement VII. was created Pope by ten cardinals at Fondi, who declared Urban VI. improperly elected.

At this time the Genoese, who had lived many years under the government of the Visconti, revolted, and an important war broke out between them and the Venetians, on account of the island of Tenedos, in which all Italy took sides. It was in this war that the first cannons were seen, a new instrument of war invented by the Germans. And although the Genoese were for a time superior and held Venice besieged for some months, yet at the end of the war the Venetians remained victors, and through the intervention of the Pope made peace in the year 1381.

33. A schism having been created in the Church, as has been stated, the Queen Joanna of Naples supported the schismatic Pope, whereupon Urban induced Charles of Durazzo, who was descended from the royal family of Naples, to attack Joanna in her kingdom. He deprived her of the government and made himself master of the kingdom. Joanna fled to France, and the king of France, irritated by the conduct of Charles, sent Louis of Anjou into Italy to recover the kingdom for the queen, and to drive Urban out of Rome and to establish the Antipope Clement there. But in the midst of this enterprise Louis died; and his troops, having been defeated, returned into France. During these events the Pope went to Naples, where he imprisoned nine cardinals for having adhered to France and to the Antipope. Afterwards he became dissatisfied with the king for having refused to make one of his nephews Prince of Capua; but feigning not to care about it, he asked the king to grant him Nocera for his residence, where he afterwards fortified himself and prepared to deprive the king of his realm. The king thereupon took the field, and the Pope fled to Genoa, where he caused the cardinals whom he had imprisoned to be put to death. Thence he went to Rome, and for the purpose of recovering his influence he created twenty-nine cardinals.

Meanwhile, Charles of Durazzo went to Hungary, and was made king of that country, where he died soon after, having left his wife and his children, Ladislas and Joanna, at Naples. At this same time, Giovanni Galeazzo, after having had his uncle, Bernabo, put to death, seized the entire government of Milan for himself. Not satisfied, however, with having become Duke of all Lombardy, he wanted also to possess Tuscany; but at the very moment when he thought that he had gained his object, **and that he would now be able to have himself crowned** king of Italy, death carried him off. Boniface IX. had succeeded to Urban VI.; and the Antipope Clement VII. had also died at Avignon, and Benedict XIII. was elected in his place.

34. Italy at this time was overrun by soldiers of every nationality, — English, Germans, and Bretons, — brought there in part by those princes who at various times had come into Italy, and in part sent there by the Popes whilst at Avignon. It was with these soldiers that the princes of Italy carried on their wars, until one Lodovico da Cento, a native of the Romagna, formed a company of Italian soldiers, called the San Giorgio, whose bravery and discipline very soon transferred the high reputation of the foreign soldiers to those of Italy, and of which the Italian princes afterwards availed themselves in their wars against each other. The Pope, on account of the difference which he had had with the Romans, went to Scesi, where he remained until the year of jubilee, 1400; when the Romans, to induce him to return, on account of the benefit which it would be to the city, agreed anew to accept a foreign Senator to be sent by the Pope, and allowed him to fortify the castle of San Angelo. Having returned on these conditions, the Pope, by way of enriching the Church, ordered that during a vacancy of any benefice, one year's income of it was to be paid over to the Apostolic Chamber.

After the death of Giovanni Galeazzo, Duke of Milan, this state fell a prey to many divisions, notwithstanding his having left two sons, Giovanni Maria Angelo and Philip. In the troubles that resulted, the former was killed, and Philip remained for a time shut up in the castle of Pavia, whence he escaped by the courage and fidelity of its castellan. Amongst others who seized the places that had been possessed by their father, was Guglielmo della Scala, who during his banishment had taken refuge with Francesco da Carrara, lord of Padua, with whose assistance he retook the city of Verona, where, however, he lived but a short time, having been poisoned by order of Francesco, and the city taken from him; in consequence of which the people of Vicenza, who had lived securely under the banner of the Visconti, fearing the power of the lord of Padua, gave themselves to the Venetians, who, with their aid, made war against Francesco, and took from him first Verona and afterwards Padua.

35. In the midst of these events Pope Boniface died, and

Innocent VII. was elected to succeed him. The people of Rome besought him to restore to them the fortresses and their liberty, and upon the Pope's refusal they called King Ladislas of Naples to their aid. Afterwards, when harmony had been restored between them, the Pope returned to Rome, whence he had fled to Viterbo, where he made his nephew, Lodovico, Count della Marca. After this he died, and Gregory XII. was made Pope, with the understanding that he should resign the papacy whenever the Antipope should resign. And by the persuasion of the cardinals, and as proof that the Church could be united, Antipope Benedict came to Porto Venere, and Gregory to Lucca, where they negotiated in relation to many matters, but concluded nothing; so that the cardinals of the respective popes left them, and Benedict went to Spain and Gregory to Rimini. The cardinals, on the other hand, with the aid of Baldassar Cossa, Cardinal and Legate of Bologna, ordered a council at Pisa, where they created Alexander V. Pope, who promptly excommunicated King Ladislas, and invested Louis of Anjou with the kingdom; and, in conjunction with the Florentines, the Genoese, and the Venetians, they attacked Ladislas and took Rome from him. But in the very height of this war Alexander died, and Baldassar Cossa was created Pope, who took the name of John XXIII. He left Bologna, where he had been made Pope, and went to Rome. There he found Louis of Anjou, who had come with the army from Provence, and, having encountered Ladislas, had defeated him. But owing to the desertion of the Condottieri he could not follow up his victory, so that the king in a short time recovered his forces and recaptured Rome; whence the Pope fled to Bologna, and Louis returned to Provence. The Pope, thinking in what manner he might reduce the power of Ladislas, managed to have Sigismund, king of Hungary, elected Emperor, and persuaded him to come into Italy, where he met him at Mantua. They agreed to convene a general council, at which the Church should be reunited, so that she might be able to resist the power of her enemies.

36. At this period there were three Popes, — Gregory, Benedict, and John, — who kept the Church weak and without authority. The city of Constance, in Germany, was chosen as the place for the meeting of the general council, which, however, was not in accordance with the intentions of Pope John.

And although the death of Ladislas had removed the reason which had induced the Pope to propose this general council, yet, having accepted the obligation, he could not now refuse to be present at its meeting. Having come to Constance a few months after the opening of the council, he discovered his error too late, and in attempting to fly he was arrested, imprisoned, and obliged to resign the papacy. Gregory, one of the Antipopes, resigned through an envoy sent by him to the council; and the other Antipope, Benedict, who refused to resign, was condemned as a heretic. Finally, however, being abandoned by his cardinals, he too was obliged to resign, and the council created Oddo, of the house of Colonna, Pope, who was thereafter called Martin V.; and thus the Church became united again under one Pope, after having been divided during forty years into several Pontificates.

37. At that time, as we have said, Philip Visconti was shut up in the castle of Pavia. But Fazino Cane who, during the troubles of Lombardy had made himself master of Vercelli, Alexandria, Novara, and Tortona, and had amassed great wealth, died without issue, and leaving his wife, Beatrice, heir to his estates. He had by his testament engaged his friends to make his widow marry Philip, who, having become powerful by this marriage, recovered possession of Milan and of all Lombardy; after which, by way of showing his gratitude for the great benefits received, in the ordinary manner of princes, he accused Beatrice of infidelity, and had her put to death. Having now become very powerful, Philip began to meditate war against Tuscany, in accordance with the designs of his father, Giovanni Galeozzo.

38. King Ladislas of Naples, in dying, left to his sister, Joanna, the kingdom, together with a large army, headed by the principal Condottieri of Italy. Chief amongst these was Sforza da Contignuola, who was reputed very valiant, according to the mode of fighting then in use. The queen, to escape the infamous suspicion of keeping one Pandolfo, whom she had brought up, took for her husband Giacopo della Marcia, a Frenchman of royal blood, upon condition that he should content himself with the title of Prince of Taranto, leaving to her that of queen, and the government of the kingdom. But so soon as he arrived in Naples the soldiers proclaimed him king, so that great differences arose between husband and wife, with

alternate advantages to each; but in the end the queen retained control of the government, and soon after manifested her hostility to the Pope. Thereupon Sforza, for the purpose of placing her in the necessity of invoking his support, withdrew from her service. Thus the queen suddenly found herself disarmed, and, having no other resource, she appealed for aid to Alfonso, king of Aragon and Sicily, and adopted him as her son, and took into her pay Braccio da Montone, who was as well reputed in arms as Sforza, and an enemy of the Pope, from whom he had taken Perugia and some other places belonging to the Church. Subsequently, peace was made between them and the Pope; but King Alfonso, fearing lest the queen should treat him as she had done her husband, sought cautiously to make himself master of the fortresses; but Queen Joanna, being astute, prevented him, and fortified herself in the castle of Naples. This increased their mutual suspicions, so that they came to arms, and the queen, with the assistance of Sforza, who had returned to her pay, overcame Alfonso, drove him from Naples, and cancelled her adoption, and in his stead adopted Louis of Anjou, which occasioned fresh wars between Braccio, who adhered to the party of Alfonso, and Sforza, who supported the queen. In the course of this war, Sforza was drowned in crossing the river at Pescara; so that the queen, being again left without a commander, would have been driven from the kingdom had not Philip Visconti, Duke of Milan, come to her aid, in consequence of which Alfonso was obliged to return to Aragon. But Braccio, undaunted by having been abandoned by Alfonso, continued to make war against the queen. Having besieged Aquila, the Pope, deeming the greatness of Braccio inopportune for the Church, took into his pay Francesco, the son of Sforza, who went to encounter Braccio at Aquila, where he defeated and killed him. Braccio left a son, Oddo, from whom the Pope took Perugia, leaving him in possession of Montone. But Oddo was killed soon after that, whilst fighting in the Romagna for the Florentines; so that of those who had been fighting under Braccio there remained, as the most renowned, Niccolo Piccinino.

39. Having now brought our narrative down to near that period which I had designed for this First Book, there remains but little of consequence to relate except the wars of the Florentines and Venetians with Duke Philip of Milan, which will

be related when we come specially to treat of Florence. I will therefore proceed no further, and will only briefly recall the condition of Italy at the period at which we have arrived with our history, and what princes and what armies she then possessed. Of the principal states, Queen Joanna II. held the kingdom of Naples; La Marca, the Patrimony, and some of the places in the Romagna, in part obeyed the Church and in part were possessed by their vicars or usurpers, — Ferrara, Modena, and Reggio by the family of Este, Faenza by the Manfredi, Imola by the Alidosi, Furli by the Ordelaffi, Rimini and Pesaro by the Malatesti, and Camerino by the Varanos. A portion of Lombardy obeyed the Duke Philip, and a portion the Venetians; for all the families that had possessed particular states in that province were extinguished, except the house of Gonzaga, which ruled over Mantua. The Florentines were masters of the greater part of Tuscany; only Lucca and Sienna had laws of their own, — Lucca under the government of the Guinigi, whilst Sienna was entirely free. The Genoese, at one time free and at another time subject to the kings of France, enjoyed no consideration, and were counted amongst the smaller powers. All these principal potentates had no troops of their own. Duke Philip, shut up in his palace, and not allowing himself to be seen, carried on his wars by commissaries. The Venetians, when they turned their attention to the land, dispensed with those forces that had won them so much glory on the seas, and, following the custom of the other Italian states, intrusted the control and direction of their armies to others. The Pope, being a priest and therefore unsuited to the profession of arms, and Queen Joanna, being a woman, did from necessity what the others had done from an evil choice. The Florentines also obeyed the same necessity; for having by their constant dissensions extinguished the nobility, and the republic being controlled by men brought up in commercial pursuits, followed the practice and fortunes of the others.

The armies of Italy then were in the hands either of the smaller princes, or of men who possessed no state; for the smaller princes adopted the profession of arms, not from any love of glory, but for the sake of wealth and security. The others, from having been reared to it from childhood, and having no other calling, sought in the profession of arms the means of achieving wealth, power, and honor. Amongst these the most famous were the Carmagnola, Francesco Sforza, Niccolo Piccinino, pupil of Braccio, Agnolo della Pergola, Lorenzo and Micheletto Attenduli, the Tartaglia, Giacopaccio, Accolino da Perugia, Niccolo da Tolentino, Guido Torello, Antonio dal Ponte ad Era, and many others of the same kind. Added to these were those smaller princes or lords of whom we have spoken above, and who were joined by the barons of Rome, the Orsini and the Colonna, together with other lords and gentlemen of the kingdom of Naples and of Lombardy. Being constantly in arms, these men had formed a league, or a sort of understanding amongst themselves, and had reduced the profession of arms to an art by which they protracted the wars, so that generally both parties for whom they were carried on were losers. And at last they reduced it to so low a standard that any captain of the most ordinary capacity, who had but a spark of the ancient valor, would have put them to shame, and would have been admired and honored by all Italy for his courage. Of such idle and indolent princes, therefore, and of these most cowardly armies, my history will be full; but before I descend to these, I shall, in accordance with my promise in the beginning, relate the origin of Florence, to explain fully to the understanding of every one what the condition of that city was in those days, and how she arrived at it in the midst of all the troubles that had befallen Italy for a thousand years.

SECOND BOOK.

SUMMARY.

1. Custom of the ancient republics to plant colonies, and its advantages. — 2. Origin of Florence and of its name. Destroyed by Totilas and rebuilt by Charlemagne. The Florentines take Fiesole. — 3. First intestine dissensions in Florence, occasioned by Messer Buondelmonte Buondelmonti, who, having engaged himself to a lady of the family of the Amidei, broke his faith and married one of the Donati (1215); in consequence of which Buondelmonte is killed, and in consequence of the enmity caused thereby between his family and that of the Uberti, relatives of the Amidei, great disturbances and slaughter occur in Florence. — 4. Frederick II. of Suabia favors the Uberti, and the Buondelmonti are supported by the Church. These factions in Florence also take the names of the Ghibelline party and of that of the Guelfs. Families of the Ghibelline party. Families of the Guelf party. The Guelfs are driven out of Florence, but after the death of Frederick they make terms with the Ghibellines and return to Florence, and then jointly attempt to reorganize the government of the city (1250). — 5. Florence is divided into wards, with two Ancients per ward. Captain of the People and Podesta taken from amongst strangers. Order of the militia by banners, twenty in the city and seventy-six in the country. — 6. Greatness to which Florence attained under the new government. Fresh movements of the Ghibellines, on account of which they are driven out of Florence. The Guelfs are routed at the battle of Arbia by the troops of Manfred, king of Naples (1260). — 7. Council of Ghibellines at Empoli. Farinata degli Uberti opposes the proposition to level Florence with the ground. — 8. Pope Clement IV. favors the banished Guelfs, and gives them his banner. The Guelfs, with the help of Charles d'Anjou, grow in power (1266), in consequence of which the Ghibellines of Florence attempt by new enactments to win the good will of the people. They divide the citizens into twelve Trades, seven major and five minor ones (the minor ones were afterwards increased to fourteen); and each Trade has a magistrate and banner. — 9. The Count Guido Novello, deputy of King Manfred at Florence, is expelled in consequence of his attempting to impose a tax upon the Florentines. — 10. The Guelfs return to Florence and reorganize the government. They create twelve chiefs called Buonomini, a Council of eighty citizens, and a College of one hundred and eighty of the people, who together should compose the General Council. They also create a Council of one hundred and twenty, composed of men of the people and nobles, to supervise the deliberations and the

distribution of the public offices of the Republic. Gregory X. attempts to reestablish the Ghibellines in Florence. Nicholas III. seeks to lower the power of Charles d'Anjou. — 11. Messer Latino, the Imperial Legate, restores the Ghibellines in Florence, and gives them a share in the government (1280). At first three Priors are created from the trades or guilds, and afterwards six, for the government of the city. Battle of Campaldino (1289). — 12. Gonfaloniers of Justice are created, with one thousand men under twenty banners (1293). — 13. Giano della Bella remodels the government in favor of the people. His enmity with Corso Donati, and his voluntary exile from Florence. — 14. Disturbances between the people and the nobles. — 15. New reorganization of the state. Arnolfo di Lasso builds the Palace of the Signoria and the prisons (1298). — 16. Fresh dissensions between the Cerchi and the Donati. Origin of the factions of the Bianchi (Whites) and the Neri (Blacks) in Pistoja. Messer Corso Donati places himself at the head of the Neri party in Florence, and Messer Vieri de' Cerchi at the head of the Bianchi party. — 17. The Pope's Legate in Florence increases the fusion by an interdict. — 18. The Donati and others of the Neri party are exiled by the advice of Dante Alighieri. — 19. They go to the Pope, who sends Charles de Valois to Florence; under his protection the Donati return to Florence, and the Cerchi are obliged to fly. Matteo d' Acquasparta, the Papal Legate, tries in vain to compose these discords, and being angered he leaves Florence after having again placed the city under an interdict. — 20. Dante Alighieri is exiled with the Bianchi party (1302). — 21. Great pride of Corso Donati. Nicholas de Prato is sent as Legate of the Pope to Florence. Riots. Conflagration of Orto San Michele and of the New Market. — 22. Fresh reforms in Florence. Capture of the Stinche castle. Corso Donati returns from Rome. — 23. He is accused and condemned. He resists the sentence with arms in hand; but is taken near San Salvi and is there slain. — 24. Henry of Luxemburg besieges Florence in vain; and afterwards dies at Buonconvento (1313). — 25. Florence gives herself for five years to Robert, king of Naples; he makes unsuccessful war upon Uguccione della Faggiuola. Florence withdraws her obedience to the king of Naples, and takes Lando d' Agobbio for her Bargello, who is expelled in consequence of his tyranny and dishonest proceedings. Fresh reforms. — 26. War between the Florentines and the Lucchese under the lead of Castruccio Castracani. The Buonomini. — 27. The nobles within Florence, and the exiles, attempt to recover control of Florence. — 28. New political measures. — 29. The Florentines are routed by Castruccio at Altopascio. — 30. Gauthier, Duke of Athens, comes to Florence as deputy of Charles, Duke of Calabria. New reforms in the state. Two councils are created: one consisting of three hundred of the people, and the other composed of two hundred and fifty nobles and citizens of the people. The first is called the "Council of the People," and the other "Council of the Commune." — 31. Louis of Bavaria. The Germans sell Lucca. Castruccio dies. Inundation of Florence. — 32. A conspiracy of the Bardi and the Frescobaldi is discovered and crushed. — 33. Lucca is purchased by the Florentines, but is taken by the Pisans. — 34. Efforts of the Duke of Athens to gain the lordship of Florence. — 35. The Duke of Athens is proclaimed Prince of Florence by the people, for life (1342). — 36. His misgovernment. — 37. He is expelled from Florence (1343). — 38. Many cities and towns of the Florentine dominion rebel, but the Florentines by their prudent conduct preserve their lordship over them. — 39. The city is divided into quarters, with three Signori per quarter; and in place of the twelve Buonomini they create eight Counsellors, four from the people and four from the nobles. Disturbances between the people and the nobles, in consequence of which the nobles are driven out of the palace, and the government remains in the hands of the people. — 40. Riot created by Andrea Strozzi in favor of the nobles. — 41. After great disturbances the nobles are entirely subdued by the people. Fresh reforms of the government. — 42. The people divide themselves into the rich, the middle, and the lower class. They take two Signori from the rich, three from the middle, and three from the lower class; and the Gonfalonier is taken alternately from the different classes. Dreadful pestilence in Florence, described by Boccaccio (1348).

1. Amongst other great and admirable institutions of the ancient republics and principalities that are now extinct, we must note the practice of constantly building new towns and cities. In fact, nothing is so worthy of a good prince, or of a well-organized republic, nor more useful to any province, than to build up new cities, where men may establish themselves with the conveniences for defence and habitation. It was easy for the ancients to do this, being accustomed to send new inhabitants to occupy conquered territories and vacant lands; such settlements were called colonies. This practice, besides causing new towns to be built up, rendered the conquered territory more secure to the conqueror, filled the vacant lands with inhabitants, and maintained the population well distributed in the provinces. Whence it came that, living more securely in a province, the people multiplied there more rapidly, and were more prompt in offence, and in defence more secure. The discontinuance of this practice, because of the vicious administration of republics and princes, has resulted in the ruin and weakness of the provinces; for it was the only system that insured an abundant population to the country and rendered empires more secure. This greater security is due to the fact that a colony which is established by a prince in a newly acquired country is like a fortress and garrison, which keeps the other inhabitants in allegiance. Moreover, without such a system, a province would not become fully inhabited, nor keep her population well distributed; for all the places in it are not equally fertile and salubrious. This causes a superabundance of inhabitants in one place, and an insufficiency in another. And if there be not some means for remedying this unequal distribution, the province will in a

little while be ruined; for one portion of it will become deserted from want of inhabitants, whilst the other portion will be impoverished from having too many. And as nature cannot correct this defect, we have to resort to art to do it; for unwholesome countries are made salubrious by being settled at once by a large population, who by cultivation make the land fertile, and by fires purify the air; which nature unaided could not do. This is demonstrated by the city of Venice, situated in a marshy and unwholesome place; nevertheless, the large number of inhabitants that flocked there at once made it healthy. Pisa also, in consequence of its insalubrious air, never was fully inhabited until Genoa and its shores were ravaged by the Saracens, which caused those people who were thus driven from their homes to move at once in great numbers to Pisa, which thus became populous and powerful.

Without the system of sending out colonies, conquered territories are held with greater difficulty; vacant lands never become inhabited, and such as are overpopulated will not be relieved. Whence many parts of the world, and more especially portions of Italy, have become deserted as compared with ancient times. And all this comes from the fact that her princes are destitute of the love of true glory, and her republics lack institutions that are worthy of praise. In ancient times, then, the system of colonies often caused new cities to spring up, or such as had already a beginning were largely increased thereby. Of the latter was the city of Florence, which owed its origin to Fiesole, and its increase to colonies.

2. It is undoubtedly true, as has been shown by Dante and Villani, that the city of Fiesole, being situated on the summit of a mountain, and wishing to make its markets more frequented and accessible to those who desired to come there with their merchandise, established a place for this purpose in the plain between the foot of the mountain and the river Arno. This market,' I judge, caused the first buildings to be erected at that place, owing to the desire of the merchants to have convenient places for receiving and delivering their goods, and these buildings in the course of time became permanent structures. Afterwards, when the Romans, by the conquest of the Carthaginians, had rendered Italy secure from foreign attacks, these buildings were multiplied in great numbers; for men do not select inconvenient places to dwell in, except from necessity; so that if the

fear of attack constrains them to live in rude and inaccessible places, they will naturally be attracted to inhabit agreeable and convenient localities whenever that fear of attack ceases. Security, then, which sprang from the reputation of the Roman Republic, caused the increase of those habitations (which were already commenced in the manner above stated) in such numbers that they assumed the form of a settlement, which at first was called Villa Arnina. Afterwards civil wars arose in Rome, first between Marius and Sylla, subsequently between Cæsar and Pompey, and then between the murderers of Cæsar and those who wished to avenge his death. Sylla first, and after him those other three Roman citizens, who, after having avenged Cæsar, divided the Empire between them, sent colonies to Fiesole, and these established their dwellings, in whole or in part, in the plain, near the settlement which had already been commenced. And thus by this increase that place became filled with habitations and men, which by its civil organization could soon be counted amongst the cities of Italy. As to the origin of the name of Florentia, however, there are various opinions. Some claim that it was so called after Florino, one of the chiefs of the colony; others maintain that it was at first called, not Florentia, but Fluentia, from being situated near the river Arno, and they adduce the testimony of Pliny, who says: "The Fluentines dwell near the river Arno." This opinion may, however, be erroneous; for the text quoted from Pliny tells where the Florentines dwelt, not how they were called. And most probably the word "Fluentines" is a corruption; for both Frontinus and Cornelius Tacitus, who wrote in the times of Pliny, call the place Florentia and the people Florentines. At the time of Tiberius, already (in the year 17 after Christ) the Florentines governed themselves, according to the custom of the other cities of Italy. And Cornelius Tacitus refers to the coming of Florentine ambassadors to the Emperor to request that the waters of the river Chiana might not be discharged into the Arno above their settlement. It is not reasonable to suppose that that city should in those days have had two names, and I am inclined to believe that it was always called Florentia, whatever the reason may have been why it was so named. And to whatever cause its origin may be due, it came into existence under the Roman Empire, and began to be mentioned by writers at the time of the first Emperors. When that Empire became a prey to the incursions of the Barbarians, Florence was also destroyed by Totilas, king of the Ostrogoths, and was rebuilt two hundred and fifty years afterwards by Charlemagne, from which time until the year of Christ 1215 it shared the fortunes of those who ruled over Italy. At that period, Italy was governed by the descendants of Charlemagne, afterwards by the Berengarii, and lastly by the German Emperors, as we have shown in our general remarks. During this interval, the Florentines, restrained by the power of their rulers, could neither increase nor do anything memorable. Nevertheless, in the year 1010, on the day of St. Romulus, a day of solemn festival for the Fiesolans, their city was captured and destroyed, either with the consent of the Emperor, or in the interval between the death of one Emperor and the creation of another, during which a general license prevailed. But afterwards, when the authority of the Popes increased in Italy, whilst that of the German Emperors had diminished, all the cities of that province governed themselves with less respect for their princes. Thus, in the year 1053, at the time of the Emperor Henry, Italy was openly divided between him and the Church; notwithstanding which the Florentines maintained themselves united until the year 1215, yielding obedience to the victorious party, and having no other ambition than their own security. But as the infirmities of our bodies are dangerous in proportion as their progress is slow, so Florence, being slower in following the factions of Italy, was also afterwards the more sorely afflicted by them. The cause of the first division is most noteworthy; and although having been mentioned by Dante and many other writers, it seems to me proper briefly to relate it here.

3. Amongst the other powerful families of Florence were the Buondelmonti and the Uberti; next to these were the Amidei and the Donati. In the latter family there was a rich widow having a most beautiful daughter, whom the mother in her own mind had designed to marry to Messer Buondelmonte, a young cavalier and head of the house of Buondelmonti. But as she had not made this design known to any one, either from neglect or perhaps because she thought it would always be time enough, it happened that Messer Buondelmonte engaged himself to marry a young lady of the Amidei family, which contravened the Lady Donati very much. And hoping that she might yet, ere the nuptials were actually celebrated, interrupt the engage-

ment by the beauty of her daughter, and seeing Messer Buondelmonte coming alone towards her house, she descended to the lower floor, making her daughter follow her. And as the gentleman passed, she said: "I am truly glad that you have chosen "a wife, although I had kept my daughter for you"; and, pushing open the door, she enabled him to see her. The gentleman, on beholding the beauty of the young lady, which was indeed remarkable, and considering that her family and dowry were not inferior to that of the one he had chosen, became so inflamed by the desire to have her, that, unmindful of his plighted faith and of the evils that might result from his breaking his engagement, he replied: "Since you have kept her for "me, I should be an ingrate to refuse her, it being still time"; and without delay he solemnized his marriage with her. When this became known to the families of the Amidei and the Uberti, who were nearly related to them, it filled them with deep indignation; and having convened a number of the other relatives of the families they concluded that this insult could not be tolerated without shame, nor avenged except by the death of Messer Buondelmonte. And although some spoke of the evils that might result from this course, yet Mosca Lamberti said that "he who thought of too many things never did "anything," and quoted the old proverb, "A thing done must "have a beginning." The execution of the murder was therefore confided to Mosca, Stiatta Uberti, Lambertuccio Amidei, and Oderigo Fifanti. These met on Easter morning at the house of the Amidei, between the Ponte Vecchio and Santo Stefano; and as Messer Buondelmonte was crossing the bridge on a white horse, thinking it to be as easy to forget an insult as to renounce an alliance, they attacked and killed him at the foot of the bridge, by the statue of Mars. This homicide divided the whole city of Florence, — the one party supporting the Buondelmonti, and the other the Uberti. And as these families had strong houses and towers, with plenty of men, they fought for many years without the one being able to drive out the other. Their enmity, however, though not terminated by a formal peace, yet was at different times composed by truces, and in this way, according to new accidents, it was at one time quieted and then again rekindled.

4. Florence remained involved in these troubles until the time of Frederick II. (1246), who, being king of Naples, thought

of strengthening himself against the Church; and, by way of
establishing his power more firmly in Tuscany, he supported
the Uberti and their followers, who with his aid drove the
Buondelmonti out of the city. And thus Florence, the same
as all Italy had been before, became divided into Guelfs and
Ghibellines. And here it seems to me not superfluous to make
a record of the families who adhered to the one and the other
party. Those, then, who sided with the Guelfs were the
Buondelmonti, Nerli, Rossi, Frescobaldi, Mozzi, Bardi, Pulci,
Gherardini, Foraboschi, Bagnesi, Guidalotti, Sachetti, Manieri,
Luccardesi, Chiaramontesi, Compiobessi, Cavalcanti, Giando-
nati, Gianfigliazzi, Scali, Gualterotti, Importuni, Bostichi, Tor-
naquinci, Vecchietti, Tosinghi, Arrigucci, Agli, Sizi, Adimari,
Visdomini, Donati, Pazzi, Della Bella, Ardinghi, Tebaldi, and
Cerchi. To the Ghibelline party belonged the Uberti, Mannelli,
Ubriachi, Fifanti, Amidei, Infangati, Malespini, Scolari, Guidi,
Galli, Cappiardi, Lamberti, Soldanieri, Cipriani, Toschi, Amieri,
Palermini, Migliorelli, Pigli, Barucci, Cattani, Agolanti, Brunelleschi, Caponsacchi, Elisei, Abati, Tedaldini, Giuochi, and the
Galigai. Besides this, many of the people attached themselves
to one or the other of these families, so that the whole city, as it
were, was infected with this division. The Guelfs then, expelled
from Florence, established themselves in the country above, in
the Val d' Arno, where they had most of their strongholds, so
that they might the better defend themselves against their
enemies. But after the death of Frederick the moderate men
of Florence, who had most influence with the people, deemed it
advisable to restore union amongst the inhabitants of the city,
rather than to have it ruined by continued divisions. They
therefore managed that the Guelfs, forgetting their former
griefs, should return; and that the Ghibellines, laying aside
their suspicions, should receive them (1250); and being thus
reunited, the time seemed to them favorable for the adoption of
a form of government that should insure them liberty and the
means of defending themselves before the new Emperor should
have acquired too much power.

5. They therefore divided the city into six wards, and elected
twelve citizens, two for each ward, who should govern it:
these were called *Ancients*, and were changed every year. And
to remove all cause for enmities that might result from their
judicial functions, two foreign judges were appointed, one of

whom was called *Captain of the People*, and the other the *Podesta*, who were to decide all civil and criminal cases that should occur amongst the people. And inasmuch as no civil organization is stable unless its defence is provided for, they constituted twenty banners in the city and seventy-five in the country, under which all the young men were enrolled; and it was ordained that, whenever called by the Captain or the Ancients, every one was to appear promptly and well armed, under his banner. And they varied the devices of these banners according to the different arms, so that the crossbowmen had different ensigns from the shield-bearers. And every year, at Pentecost, they distributed with great pomp their ensigns to the new soldiers, and assigned new captains to all the companies. And to render their army more imposing, and to assign to each a rallying-point in case of being hard pressed in battle, whence they might make head anew against the enemy, they had a great car made, to be drawn by two oxen, all covered with scarlet, above which floated a white and red flag. And when they wanted to call the army out, this car was drawn to the New Market, and consigned with great pomp to the chiefs of the people. They had also, by way of giving more *éclat* to their military enterprises, a bell called *Martinella*, which was sounded continually during one month before they moved their troops out of the city, so as to afford the enemy time to prepare for defence. Such was the valor of those men, and such their magnanimity, that they deemed it shameful and wrong to attack an enemy unawares, whilst nowadays this is considered a proof of courage and of prudence. This bell was also carried into the field with their armies, and by means of it they communicated their commands to the guards and sentinels.

6. By means of these civil and military institutions the Florentines established their liberty; and it is not easy to imagine how much power and influence Florence acquired in a short time, so that she became not only the chief city of Tuscany, but was counted amongst the first cities of Italy; and would have risen to almost any height had she not been afflicted by frequent new dissensions. The Florentines lived ten years under this government, during which period they constrained the Pistojans, the Aretines, and the Siennese to form a league with them. Returning with their army from Sienna they took Volterra, destroyed several castles, and carried their inhabit-

ants to Florence. These enterprises were all conducted under the direction of the Guelfs, who had much more power with the people than the Ghibellines; either from the fact that the latter had made themselves odious by their haughty conduct when they ruled Florence at the time of Frederick, or because the former, being the party of the Church, were more beloved than the party of the Emperor; for with the help of the Church they hoped to preserve their liberty, which they feared to lose under the Emperor. The Ghibellines, however, seeing their authority diminish, could not remain quiet, and only awaited an opportunity to seize the state again; this they thought had arrived when Manfred, son of Frederick, had made himself master of the kingdom of Naples and had materially lowered the power of the Church (1257). They therefore engaged in secret intrigues with Manfred for the recovery of their power, but did not manage them with sufficient prudence to prevent their being discovered by the Ancients. Whereupon these cited the Uberti before them, who, however, not only did not obey the summons, but took to arms and fortified themselves in their houses. Whereat the people became indignant and armed themselves, and with the aid of the Guelfs forced them to leave Florence and go with the Ghibelline party to Sienna (1258). From there this faction called in the help of Manfred, king of Naples, whose troops, under the skilful direction of Messer Farinata of the Uberti, defeated the Guelfs on the river Arbia with such slaughter (1260) that those who escaped took refuge in Lucca, and not in Florence, fearing that their city would certainly be lost.

7. Manfred had sent to the Ghibellines the Count Giordano as commander of his troops, he being a man of high military reputation in those days. After the above victory Giordano went with the Ghibellines to Florence, and subjected that city entirely to Manfred, abolishing the magistrates and all the other institutions that gave any evidence of their former liberty. This outrage, committed with great want of prudence, excited the greatest indignation amongst the people of Florence; so that, from being regarded as friendly to the Ghibellines, they became their greatest enemy, which in time caused their total ruin. Count Giordano, having to return to Naples on account of the troubles in that kingdom, left the Count Guido Novello, lord of Casentino, as viceroy in Naples. He called a council

of Ghibellines at Empoli, where it was unanimously resolved that to preserve the power of their party in Tuscany it would be necessary to destroy Florence, which city, from its people being Guelfs, was alone able to restore the Church party to power. Not one citizen or friend objected to this cruel sentence against so noble a city, except Messer Farinata degli Uberti, who openly opposed it and defended the city regardless of consequences, saying, "that he had exposed himself to "much fatigue and danger for no other purpose than to be able "to inhabit his native city, and that he did not intend now to "forego the object he had so earnestly sought, nor to refuse the "favors of fortune, and that he would be no less the enemy "of those who intended differently, than he had been of the "Guelfs; and that if any one from fear of his country wished "to destroy it, he yet hoped to defend it with the same valor with "which he had driven the Guelfs from it." Messer Farinata was a man of great courage, and excelling in the art of war; he was chief of the Ghibellines, and greatly esteemed by Manfred. His influence put the proposition to destroy Florence at rest, and the council thought of other means of preserving the control of the state to the Ghibellines.

8. The Guelfs who had taken refuge in Lucca, and who had been sent away from there by the people of that city because of the threats of the Church, went to Bologna. From there they were called by the Guelfs of Parma to aid them against the Ghibellines, and, having succeeded in defeating them, all their possessions were given to them. Having thus grown in riches and honor, and knowing that Pope Clement had called Charles of Anjou to take the kingdom of Naples from Manfred, they sent envoys to the Pope to offer him their forces (1266). The Pope not only received them as friends, but gave them his banner, which was ever after borne by the Guelfs in all their wars. After this Manfred was despoiled of his kingdom by Charles, and was killed. The Guelfs of Florence having aided in this, their party gained strength, whilst that of the Ghibellines became weaker. Whereupon those who governed Florence, together with the Count Guido Novello, judged that it would be well by some benefits to try and win over to their side the same people, whom before they had aggravated by every kind of wrong. And had they employed these means of conciliation before necessity forced them to it, they would

have been of service to them; but now, being employed reluctantly and too late, they proved of no use, but actually hastened their ruin. They thought, nevertheless, that they would make the people their friends and partisans if they restored to them a share of the honors and authority of the government which they had taken from them; they therefore selected thirty-six citizens from the people, who, together with two nobles, whom they had caused to come from Bologna, should reform the government of the city. These, according to what had been previously agreed upon, divided the whole city into trades or guilds, and placed a magistrate over each guild, who should be the means of communication between the guilds and themselves. They moreover assigned to each guild a banner, under which to assemble in arms whenever the city might have need of them. At first there were twelve of such guilds, seven major and five minor ones; the latter were afterwards increased to fourteen; so that there were in all twenty-one, the same as at the present day. The thirty-six reformers introduced also other measures for the general benefit.

9. For the support of the army, the Count Guido ordered a tax to be laid upon the citizens, which, however, caused so much difficulty that he did not venture to have it collected by force. Seeing that he had lost the control of the government, he held a council with the chiefs of the Ghibellines, and they resolved together to take from the people by force what they had conceded to them with such want of prudence. And when the moment seemed to him to have come for taking to arms, the Thirty-six being assembled in council, the Count Guido and the Ghibellines raised a tumult, whereupon the Thirty-six retreated to their houses and gave the alarm; and promptly the banners of the guilds made their appearance, followed by many armed men. When these heard that the Count Guido and his party were at San Giovanni, they made a stand at the Santa Trinita, giving the command to Messer Giovanni Solderani. The Count, on the other hand, learning where the people were, started to meet them. Nor did the people shrink from the conflict, but, facing the enemy, they encountered him where now the Loggia of the Tornaquinci stands. The Count Guido was repulsed, with the loss and death of a number of his men; which so frightened him that he became afraid the enemy would again attack him in the night, and, finding his men beaten and dis-

heartened, would kill him. And this fear obtained such mastery over him that, without thinking of any other remedy, he concluded to save himself by flight rather than fight; and, contrary to the advice of the Rectors of the party, he marched off with all his men to Prato. But so soon as he found himself in safety he perceived his error, and, wishing to make it good, in the morning, when day had come, he returned with his men to Florence, for the purpose of entering by force into the city, which he had abandoned from cowardice. But he did not succeed in his design; for the people, who would not have been able to drive him out without great difficulty, easily kept him out; so that he went off to Cascentino filled with grief and shame, whilst the Ghibellines retreated to their villas.

The victorious citizens thereupon resolved, by the advice of those who had the good of the republic at heart, to reunite the city, and to recall all its citizens, Ghibellines as well as Guelfs, who might be in exile. Thereupon the Guelfs, who had been expelled six years before, returned, and the Ghibellines were pardoned their recent offences, and were also restored to their country (1276). They were nevertheless very odious to the people and to the Guelfs; for the latter could not forget their banishment, and the former remembered too well the tyranny they had endured under their government, which prevented both the one and the other from remaining quiet. Whilst this was the state of things in Florence, the report spread that Conradin, nephew of Manfred, was coming with an armed force from Germany to take possession of Naples. This filled the Ghibellines with hopes of being able to recover their power and authority; and the Guelfs began to think of the means to secure themselves against their enemies, and applied to King Charles for aid in defending themselves during the passage of Conradin. When therefore the troops of Charles came, it made the Guelfs insolent, and so alarmed the Ghibellines that they fled two days before their arrival, without being driven away.

10. The Ghibellines having departed, the Florentines reorganized the government of the city, and elected twelve chiefs, who should hold the magistracies for two months. These were not called Ancients, but Buonomini (Goodmen). Next to these came a council of eighty citizens, called the Credenza; after these there were one hundred and eighty of the people, thirty for every sixth, who, together with the Credenza and the twelve

Buonomini, were called the Council General. They also established another council of one hundred and twenty citizens and nobles, which should give final force to all the acts resolved upon in the other councils, and whose duty it should also be to distribute the public offices. Having established this government, the Guelf party strengthened themselves also with magistrates and other institutions, so as to be able more effectually to defend themselves against the Ghibellines, whose possessions they divided into three parts; one of which they devoted to public uses, another was assigned to the magistrates of the party, called the Captains, and the third part was given to the Guelfs in compensation for the losses they had suffered. And, by way of keeping the Guelf faction dominant in Tuscany, the Pope appointed King Charles Imperial Vicar of Tuscany.

Whilst the Florentines, by virtue of this government, maintained their authority at home by laws and abroad by arms, the Pope died; and after a long dispute, which lasted two years, Gregory X. was chosen pontiff (1271). Gregory had resided a long time in Syria, and was still there at the time of his election, and was consequently a stranger to the intrigues and strife of the factions, to which he did not attach so much importance as his predecessor had done. When therefore he came to Florence for the purpose of going into France, he deemed it the duty of a good pastor to restore harmony to the city, and labored so effectually to that end that the Florentines agreed to receive the syndics of the Ghibellines in Florence to negotiate as to the mode of their return (1273). And although the negotiations were concluded, yet the Ghibellines were afraid to return. The Pope blamed the city of Florence for this, and in his indignation launched an interdict against her. She remained in this state of contumacy during the lifetime of the Pope; but after his death, the interdict was removed by his successor, Pope Innocent V. (1275). The Pontificate had now come to Nicholas III. of the house of Orsini; and as the Popes always feared any one who had attained great power in Italy, even though he had acquired it by the support of the Church, so they fought again to abate that power, which gave rise to frequent disturbances and consequent changes; for the fear of a powerful state or individual made the pontiffs raise up a weak one to keep the other in check; and when the one had become powerful in turn, they again feared him, and sought to put him down. It was this policy that caused the kingdom of Naples to be taken from Manfred, and to be given to Charles; and when the latter afterwards occasioned them apprehension, they sought to ruin him. Pope Nicholas, influenced by these considerations, labored so effectually that Charles was deprived of the government of Tuscany by means of the Emperor; and he sent Messer Latino as his Legate into that province in the name of the Emperor (1279).

11. The condition of Florence was at that time most deplorable; for the Guelf nobility had become insolent, and had lost all fear of the magistrates; so that almost daily murders and other acts of violence were committed, without their authors being punished, as they were protected by some one of the nobility. The chiefs of the people thought that the recall of the banished would be a good means for curbing this insolence; and this gave the Legate opportunity to restore union to the city. The Ghibellines returned to Florence (1280), and, instead of twelve chiefs, it was resolved to have fourteen, — seven for each party, — who should govern for one year, and should be chosen by the Pope. Florence continued under this system during two years, when Martin, a Frenchman, came to the Pontificate, who restored to Charles all the authority that had been taken from him by Nicholas. This immediately revived the parties in Tuscany. The Florentines armed against the imperial governor, and, by way of depriving the Ghibellines of the government and restraining the license of the nobles, they instituted a new form of government. This was in the year 1282. Since the bodies of the guilds had received the magistracies and the banners, they had become so influential that of their own authority they ordained that, in place of fourteen governors, there should be chosen three citizens, who should be called *Priors*, and should remain two months in the government of the republic, and might either be taken from amongst the nobles or the people, provided that they were merchants, or exercised some branch of industry. They then reduced the number of the first magistrates to six, so as to have one for each sixth of the city, which number was maintained until the year 1382; when the city was divided into four quarters, and the number of the priors increased to eight, although it happened several times that they made twelve priors. This organization of the government was the cause, as will be seen, of the ruin of the nobles; for they were, from various circumstances, excluded by the people from

all participation in the government. At first the nobles submitted to this, owing to their divisions amongst themselves; for, being too eager to take the government from each other, they lost it entirely. To this new magistracy a palace was assigned for their residence; it having until then been customary for the magistrates and councils to hold their meetings in some of the churches. This palace was supplied with sergeants and other necessary officers. And although in the beginning these magistrates only called themselves priors, yet, by way of greater magnificence, they soon added to it the title of Signori (Lords). For some time the Florentines remained at peace amongst themselves, during which period they carried on the war against the Aretine, because these had expelled the Guelfs, and they achieved a complete victory over them at Campaldino (1289). As the city increased in population and wealth, it became necessary to extend the walls; and the circumference of Florence was enlarged, as it is seen at the present day, — the city having originally occupied only the space from the Ponte Vecchio to the church of San Lorenzo.

12. The wars abroad and the peace at home had pretty much extinguished the factions of the Guelfs and the Ghibellines; there remained only some jealousies between the nobles and the people, which is natural in every city; for the people desiring the observance of the laws, and the nobles wishing to command the people, it is not possible for a good understanding to exist between them. This ill feeling did not manifest itself so long as the Ghibellines inspired them with fear; but so soon as these were subdued it showed its strength, and every day some of the people were insulted, and the laws and the magistrates were insufficient to protect them; for each noble with his relatives and adherents defended himself against the forces of the priors and the captains. The chiefs of the guilds, nevertheless, desirous of remedying this state of things, provided that every Signoria, upon first assuming office, should appoint a Gonfalonier (Standard-bearer) of Justice, and who should be of the people, and to whom were given one thousand men, enrolled under twenty banners, and who with his standard and his armed force should promptly enforce justice, whenever he should be called upon by them or by the captains. The first one chosen to this office was Ubaldo Ruffoli (1293); he displayed his standard and pulled down the houses of the Galletti

because one of that family had killed one of the Florentine people in France. It was easy for the guilds to establish such an institution, owing to the grave dissensions that prevailed amongst the nobles, who at first gave little heed to the provision thus made against them, until they saw the harshness of this execution against the Galletti. This caused them much consternation; but they soon resumed their former insolence, for, as some of the nobility always belonged to the Signoria, they could easily impede the Gonfalonier in the execution of his office. Besides, the accuser who had received an injury was obliged to have a witness, and none could be found willing to testify against the nobility. Thus Florence soon relapsed into the same disorders as before, and the people were again subjected to the same insults and injuries from the nobles; for the judgments were slow, and the sentences failed to be executed.

13. The people did not know what course to pursue in this state of things, when Giano della Bella, a noble of most ancient lineage, but at the same time also a true lover of the liberty of his city, encouraged the chiefs of the guilds to reform the government of the city. And by his advice it was ordained that the Gonfalonier should reside in the palace with the Priors, and should have four thousand men under his command. They also deprived the nobles of all right to sit in the Signoria, and subjected the abettors of any crime to the same penalty as the principal; and ordained that public report should suffice to warrant judgment. By these laws, which were called *the Ordinances of Justice*, the people gained much influence and Giano much odium; for he was in the worst possible odor with the nobles, who looked upon him as the destroyer of their power; and the wealthy citizens were jealous of him, thinking that he had too much influence. These feelings manifested themselves on the first occasion that presented itself. It so happened that one of the people was killed in a fight in which many nobles had intervened. Amongst these was Messer Corso Donati, who, being more audacious than the others, was charged with the murder. He was therefore arrested by the captain of the people, but whether it was that Messer Corso was not guilty, or that the captain was afraid to condemn him, he was entirely acquitted. This decision so displeased the people that they took to arms and rushed to the house of Giano della Bella to ask him to see to it that the laws which he had originated should

be executed. Giano, who desired that Messer Corso should be punished, did not cause the people to disarm, as many thought he should have done, but he advised them to go to the Signoria to lay the case before them, and to ask them to take the matter in hand. The people thereupon, full of indignation, feeling themselves wronged by their captain and abandoned by Giano, went, not to the Signoria, but to the palace of the captain, took and sacked it. This act gave great offence to all the citizens, and those who desired Giano's ruin charged him with being the cause of it. And some of his enemies being amongst the Signoria, he was accused by them before the captain as an instigator of the people; and whilst his case was being discussed, the people took to arms and rushed to his house, offering to defend him against the Signoria and his enemies. Giano wished neither to put this popular favor to the test, nor to commit his life to the hands of the magistrates, for he feared the malignity of the latter, and the instability of the former; and therefore, by way of depriving his enemies of the opportunity of injuring him, and his friends of the occasion to offend his country, he determined to go away to escape envy, and to relieve the citizens of the fear they had of him, and to leave the city which by his efforts and dangers he had freed from the tyranny of the nobles; and therefore he chose voluntary exile (1295).

14. After the departure of Giano the nobles hoped again to recover their power; and judging that their troubles were the result of their own discords, they united together and sent two of their number to the Signoria, whom they judged to be favorably disposed towards them, to request that they would in some measure temper the harshness of the laws against them. The people upon learning this demand became greatly excited, fearing lest the Signoria might concede it; and thus, what with the demands of the nobles and the suspicions of the people, they came to arms between them. The nobles made head in three places, at San Giovanni, the Mercato Nuovo, and the Piazza de' Mozzi, and under three chiefs, Messer Forese Adimari, Messer Vanni de' Mozzi, and Messer Geri Spini; and the people assembled in great numbers under their banners at the palace of the Signori, who lived at that time near the church of San Procolo. And as the people mistrusted this Signoria, they deputed six citizens who should govern with them. Whilst both parties were preparing for a conflict, some of them, both citizens

and nobles, as also certain priests of good repute, set to work to pacify them, reminding the nobles "that it was their own "haughtiness and bad government that had caused them to be "deprived of certain dignities, and the enactment of the laws "against them; and that their attempt now to recover by force "of arms what they had allowed to be taken from them by their "dissensions amongst themselves, and by their evil conduct, "could only lead to the ruin of their country, and to an aggra- "vation of their own condition; and that the people in regard "to wealth, numbers, and violence of resentment were greatly "their superiors; and that that nobility by which they con- "sidered themselves superior to others was but a vain word "when it came to a conflict of arms, and would prove of little "service in defending them against so many enemies."

On the other hand, they reminded the people "that it was "not wisdom always to desire the last victory, and that it was "never prudent to drive men to desperation, for he who had no "hope of good also had no fear of evil; and that they must "bear in mind that it was the nobility who had brought honor "to the city in war, and that therefore it was neither just nor "well to persecute them with so much rancor; that the nobles "bore very well their being deprived of a share in the supreme "magistracies, but that they could not bear that it should be "in the power of any one by means of these new ordinances to "drive them from their country; and therefore it was well to "mitigate these, and by such concessions to induce the nobles "to lay aside their arms, and not to tempt the fortune of a "fight by confiding too much in their numbers, for it had often "been seen that the few have overcome the many." The people differed in opinion; many wished it to come to a fight, to which it would have to come anyhow some day, and therefore it was better to have it now rather than wait until the enemy should become more powerful. And, said these, if it were believed that the nobles would remain content if the laws against them were mitigated, then it were well that this should be done; but they thought that the arrogance of the nobles was such that nothing but force would ever keep them quiet. Many others, who were more prudent and of less violent disposition, thought that a modification of the laws was a matter of little consequence, whilst it would be a very grave matter to come to a conflict of arms. And this opinion prevailed, so that it was provided that, in all accusations against nobles, witnesses should be required.

15. Although both parties laid aside their arms, yet they remained very mistrustful of each other, and fortified themselves by raising towers and providing arms. The people reorganized the government, and reduced the Signoria in numbers because they had been favorable to the nobles; and the chiefs of those that remained were the Mancini, Magalotti, Altoviti, Peruzzi, and Cerretani. The state being thus constituted, they built a palace, in 1298, for the purpose of lodging the Signori with greater magnificence and security; and adjoining to it they formed an open square or piazza by removing the houses that had formerly belonged to the Uberti. At the same time they began also to build the public prisons, and in a few years these edifices were completed. Our city, abounding in wealth and population and influence, never enjoyed a state of greater prosperity and contentment than at that time. The citizens capable of bearing arms numbered thirty thousand, and the country belonging to Florence was able to furnish seventy thousand more. All Tuscany recognized her authority, either as subjects or as allies. And although some angry feeling still remained between the nobles and the people, yet no ill effects resulted from it, and all lived in peace and union. This peace, had it not been disturbed by fresh intestine discords, would never have been troubled from without; for Florence had attained that condition that she feared neither the Empire nor those whom she had banished; and with her own forces she could have held her ground against all the other states of Italy. But the evil which no foreign power could have caused to the city was produced by her own inhabitants.

16. (1300.) Amongst the most powerful families of Florence, by their riches, their nobility, and the number of their followers, were the Cerchi and the Donati. Being neighbors in Florence as well as in the country, some differences had arisen between them, but not sufficiently grave to provoke a resort to arms, and which would perhaps never have had any serious consequences had not some fresh causes increased the ill feeling between them. The family of the Cancellieri was one of the principal families of Pistoja. It happened that Lore, son of Messer Guglielmo, and Geri, son of Messer Bertaccio, all of that family, whilst playing together, fell to disputing, and Geri

was slightly wounded by Lore. Messer Guglielmo was greatly pained at this; but in the belief that humility would remove the offence, he thereby increased it. He ordered his son to go to the house of the father of the boy whom he had wounded, and ask his forgiveness. Lore obeyed his father; but this act of humiliation did not assuage the harsh, vindictive temper of Messer Bertaccio, who caused Lore to be seized by his servants by way of aggravating the insult, and had his hand cut off over a manger, saying to him: "Return to your father and tell "him that wounds are cured with iron, and not with words." The cruelty of this act so enraged Messer Guglielmo that he armed his followers for the purpose of avenging it; and Messer Bertaccio also armed himself for defence. This feud divided not only the family of the Cancellieri, but all Pistoja. And as this family were descended from a Messer Cancellieri who had had two wives, one of whom had borne the name of Bianca, the party who were descended from her adopted her name of "Bianchi"; and the other party, by way of having a name the very opposite of that of the others, called themselves the "Neri." These two factions continued their warfare against each other for many years, causing the death of many men and the destruction of many families. Unable to restore peace amongst themselves, and weary of the evil, and determined either to put an end to their dissensions or to increase them by drawing others into their quarrel, they came to Florence. The Neri, from old relations of friendship with the Donati, were supported by Messer Corso, head of that family; whereupon the Bianchi, for the sake of also having a powerful support that would sustain them against the Donati, had recourse to Messer Veri de' Cerchi, a man in all respects not the least inferior to Messer Corso.

17. This Pistoja quarrel increased the ancient hatred between the Cerchi and the Donati, and had already become so public that the Priors and other good citizens thought that they might at any moment come to an armed conflict, which might involve the whole city in the difficulty. And therefore they resorted to the Pope, praying him to employ his authority in putting an end to this quarrel, which they themselves had been unable to compose. The Pope sent for Messer Veri, and charged him to make peace with the Donati; at which Messer Veri professed to be astonished, saying that he had no enmity against them,

and as the making of peace presupposed a state of war, which did not exist, he could not see the necessity of making peace. When Messer Veri returned from Rome without having accomplished anything, the quarrel increased to that degree that the most trifling accident might at any moment have provoked the factions to violent excesses, which in fact occurred. It was in the month of May, at the time when the public festivals are being celebrated in Florence, that some young gentlemen of the Donati, being on horseback with some of their friends, had stopped to see some women dance at the Santa Trinita. Some of the Cerchi, accompanied by a number of young nobles, came there also, and wished to see the dancing, and, not knowing the Donati who were before them, pushed their horses right in amongst them. Whereupon the Donati considered themselves insulted, and drew their swords, to which the Cerchi bravely responded; and after many on both sides were wounded, the parties separated. This encounter was the beginning of much evil; for the whole city became divided, the people as well as the nobles, and the parties took the names of Bianchi and Neri. The chiefs of the Bianchi party were the Cerchi, who had been joined by the Adimari, the Abati, a portion of the Tosinghi, of the Bardi, of the Rossi, of the Frescobaldi, of the Nerli, and of the Mannelli, and all the Mozzi, the Scali, the Gherardini, the Cavalcanti, the Malespini, Bostichi, Giandonati, Vecchietti, and the Arrigucci. These were joined by many families of the people, together with all the Ghibellines that were in Florence; so that within the great number of their adherents were comprised nearly the entire government of the city. On the other hand, the Donati were chiefs of the party of the Neri. With these were those portions of the abovenamed families who had not attached themselves to the Bianchi; and furthermore all the Pazzi, the Visdomini, the Manieri, the Bagnesi, the Tornaquinci, Spini, Buondelmonti, Gianfigliazzi, and the Brunelleschi. And not only was the whole city affected by this feud, but the whole country was also divided by it; so that the captains of the parties, and all the adherents of the Guelfs and lovers of the republic, began to be very apprehensive lest this new division would cause the ruin of the city and the resuscitation of the Ghibelline party. They therefore sent anew to Pope Boniface so that he might devise some remedy for this state of things, unless he desired to see the city of Florence, which had ever been the shield of the Church, become either ruined or Ghibelline. The Pope therefore sent Matteo d' Acquasparta, a Portuguese cardinal, as his Legate, to Florence; but he found such difficulty with the Bianchi party, who, from supposing themselves to be the most powerful, were the most audacious, that he became indignant and departed, placing the city, however, under an interdict, so that she remained in still greater confusion than before his arrival.

18. It happened in the midst of this general fermentation, that a number of the Cerchi and the Donati met at a funeral and began to quarrel. From words they came to blows, although it caused for the moment only a slight disturbance. But when each had returned home, the Cerchi resolved to attack the Donati, and started with a number of men to find them. They were repulsed, however, by the bravery of Messer Corso, and a number of their men were wounded. All Florence was quickly in arms; the Signoria and the laws were overpowered by the nobles, and the best and wisest citizens were filled with fears and misgivings. The Donati and their party, being the weaker, were the most apprehensive; and by way of providing for their safety Messer Corso met with the other chiefs of the Neri and the leaders of the party, and agreed to ask the Pope for some one of royal blood to come to Florence and reorganize the government, hoping in that way to be able to put down the Cerchi. This meeting and resolution was made known to the Priors, and was represented by the opposite faction as a conspiracy against the liberty of the city. Both factions being in arms, the Signoria, of which Dante was a member at that time, encouraged by his advice and prudence, caused the people to arm; they were joined by many of the people of the country, and thus they forced the chiefs of the factions to lay down their arms; whereupon they banished Messer Corso Donati and many others of the Neri party. And to show that they had been impartial in that judgment, they banished also several of the Bianchi party, who, however, soon after were permitted, under color of good reasons, to return to their homes.

19. Messer Corso and his adherents, believing the Pope to be favorable to their side, went to Rome, and by their personal efforts persuaded him to do what they had already asked of him by letters. There happened to be at that moment at the papal court Charles de Valois, brother of the king of France,

who had been called to Italy by the king of Naples to go to Sicily. Being very much urged thereto by the banished Florentines, the Pope concluded to send Charles to Florence so soon as the weather should be favorable for the voyage. Charles thereupon went to Florence, and although the Bianchi, who at that time held the government, mistrusted him, yet, as he was chief of the Guelfs and sent by the Pope, they did not venture to impede his coming; and by way of securing his good will they gave him authority to dispose of the city according to his pleasure. Having received this authority, Charles caused all his friends and partisans to arm themselves. This so filled the minds of the people with mistrust of him, that they all took up arms and remained in their houses, so as to be ready in case Charles should attempt any movement.

The Cerchi and the chiefs of the Bianchi party, from having been for some time at the head of the republic, and having borne themselves very proudly, had made themselves universally odious. This encouraged Messer Corso and the other banished Neri to come to Florence, well knowing that Charles and the captains of the party were favorably disposed towards them. And whilst the city, from mistrust of Charles, was in arms, Messer Corso, with all the banished, and many others who had followed him, entered Florence without hindrance from any one. Although Messer Veri de' Cerchi was urged to move against them, yet he refused, saying that he wanted the people of Florence to chastise them, as it was against them that they had come. But the very contrary happened; for instead of being chastised by the people, Corso and his followers were well received by them, and Messer Veri was obliged to seek safety in flight. Corso, after having forced the gate of the Pinti, made a stand at the church of San Pietro Maggiore, a place near his own house; and having been joined by many of his friends and the people, who, eager for something new, had collected there, he first of all liberated from prison all who were confined either for reasons of state or private causes; and then he compelled the Signori to return to their own houses as private citizens, and elected others from the people and of the Neri party; and continued during five days to pillage the houses of the foremost of the Bianchi party. The Cerchi and the other chiefs of the faction, seeing that Charles was adverse to them and the people hostile, had left the city and withdrawn to their strongholds. And whereas formerly they were never willing to follow the counsels of the Pope, they found themselves now obliged to recur to him for help, showing him how Charles, instead of uniting, had only come to make the divisions of Florence greater. Whereupon the Pope again sent his Legate, Messer Matteo d' Acquasparta, to Florence, who succeeded in bringing about a peace between the Cerchi and the Donati, and fortified it by fresh intermarriages amongst them. But wishing that the Bianchi should also participate in the public offices, the Neri who held the government refused their consent; so that the Legate departed no better satisfied nor less angry than he had been the first time, and left the city under an interdict for her disobedience.

20. Both parties then remained in Florence dissatisfied; the Neri, because, seeing the opposite party near them, they feared that they might ruin them and repossess themselves of the power they had lost; and the Bianchi, because they felt themselves deprived of all power and honors. To these natural aversions and suspicions new injuries supervened (1302). Messer Niccolo de' Cerchi, being on his way to his estates accompanied by a number of his friends, and having arrived at the bridge over the Affrico, was assailed by Simone, son of Messer Corso Donati. The conflict was severe and ended unhappily for both parties; for Messer Niccolo was killed, and Simone so seriously wounded that he died the following night. This affair disturbed the whole city anew, and although the Neri party was chiefly to blame, yet it was defended by those in the government. And before any judgment had been rendered in this matter, a conspiracy was discovered of the Bianchi and Messer Piero Ferrante, one of the barons of Charles, with whom they were negotiating to be reinstated in the government. The discovery of this conspiracy was made from certain letters written by Cerchi to Ferrante. And although it was generally believed that these letters were forged, and suggested by the Donati for the purpose of covering up the infamy they had acquired by the murder of Messer Niccolo, yet the Cerchi, together with their adherents of the Bianchi party, amongst whom was the poet Dante, were banished, their property confiscated, and their houses pulled down. These, together with a number of Ghibellines who had joined them, scattered in many places, seeking by fresh labors to gain new fortunes. Charles, having accom-

plished the object for which he had come to Florence, returned to the Pope to follow out his enterprise against Sicily, in which he proved himself neither better nor wiser than he had done in Florence, so that he returned to France with the loss of reputation and of many of his men (1304).

21. After the departure of Charles things remained tolerably quiet in Florence. Only Messer Corso was restless, because he thought that he did not hold that rank in the city to which he considered himself entitled. The government being in the hands of the people, he saw the republic administered by men much inferior to himself. Influenced therefore by his restless and ambitious spirit, he sought to cloak his dishonest intentions with an honest pretext, and falsely charged a number of citizens who had administered the public funds with having misappropriated them to private purposes, and demanded their trial and punishment. This demand was supported by many whose desires were similar to his own; others, who in their ignorance believed Messer Corso to be actuated by patriotic feelings, also united with him. The calumniated citizens, on the other hand, who were supported by the people, defended themselves against this accusation. This difference increased to such a degree that, according to the customary fashion, the parties came to arms. On the one side were Messer Corso and Messer Lottieri, Bishop of Florence, with many nobles and some of the people; on the other were the Signori, with the greater part of the people; and the quarrel grew to that point that in many parts of the city they actually came to fighting. The Signori, seeing the great danger in which they were, sent to the people of Lucca for assistance; these quickly came to Florence, and by their intervention matters for the time were settled and the disturbances stopped, and the people of Florence retained their government and their liberties without otherwise punishing the authors of this trouble. The Pope, having heard of the disturbances in Florence, sent his Legate, Messer Niccolo da Prato, to put a stop to them, who, being a man of great repute by his office, his learning and exemplary mode of life, very soon obtained such influence with the people of Florence that they gave him authority to establish a government according to his own views. Being by birth a Ghibelline, Messer Niccolo contemplated the recall of the banished; but wished first to win the people entirely over to him, and for that purpose he

re-established the old companies of the people, whereby the power of the people was greatly increased, whilst that of the nobles was diminished. When the Legate, therefore, thought that he had thoroughly secured the good will of the multitude, he attempted to carry out the recall of the banished. But he failed in his various efforts, and became thereby so mistrusted by those who governed the city that he was obliged to depart and return to Rome filled with anger, and leaving Florence in much confusion and under an interdict.

The city was perturbed not only by this, but also by many other troubles in consequence of the enmities between the people and the nobles, the Guelfs and the Ghibellines, and the Bianchi and the Neri. The whole city was therefore in arms, and conflicts were of daily occurrence; for many were greatly discontented at the departure of the Legate, being themselves desirous for the return of the banished. The first who started these troubles were the Medici and the Giugni, who had made themselves known to the Legate as being in favor of the rebels. There was fighting then in most parts of Florence, and to these troubles was added a great conflagration, which broke out first in the Orto San Michele and in the houses of the Abati, whence it spread to those of the Caponsachi, burning them, together with the houses of the Macci, the Amieri, Toschi, Cipriani, Lamberti, and Cavalcanti, and the entire Mercato Nuovo. Thence the fire passed to the Porta San Maria, burning the whole of it; then, turning from the Ponte Vecchio, it burned the houses of the Gherardini, Pulci, Amidei, Lucardesi, and many others; so that the number of houses destroyed amounted to over seventeen hundred. According to the opinion of many the fire originated by accident in the very midst of a fight; others affirmed that it had been kindled by Neri Abati, Prior of San Pietro Scheraggio, a dissolute and evil-minded man, who, seeing the people engaged in fighting, committed this villanous act, knowing that it could not be checked by the people who were occupied by the fight; and by way of insuring its success he set fire to the houses of his associates, where he had a better opportunity of doing it. It was in the month of July, of the year 1304, that Florence was thus visited by fire and sword. Messer Corso Donati was the only one who in the midst of all these tumults did not arm, for he judged it would be easier for him to become the arbiter between the two parties when, weary of fighting, they should wish to come to terms. The parties however deposed their arms more from satiety of evil than from a desire for union; and the only result was that the banished did not return, and that the party who favored them failed to gain control of the government.

22. The Legate, having returned to Rome, and hearing of the fresh disturbances that had taken place in Florence, persuaded the Pope that the only means of restoring peace and union to Florence would be for him to cause twelve of the first citizens of that city to come to him, and that thus by taking away the food of the evil he would be able to quench it. The Pope acted upon this advice; and the citizens whom he called obeyed and came to Rome, and Messer Corso Donati was one of them. No sooner had these left Florence than the Legate gave the banished to understand that now was the time for them to return, as the city was at that moment without any of its chiefs. The banished therefore made the attempt, and came to Florence and entered the walls, which had not been prepared for defence, and advanced as far as San Giovanni. It was a notable fact that the very men who a short time before had fought for the return of the banished, when these had begged unarmed to be allowed to return to their country, took up arms against them when they saw them come armed, with the intent to seize the city by force. So much more did these citizens esteem the public good than their private friendships; and having called all the people to their assistance, they forced the banished to return whence they had come. The failure of the banished in their attempt was caused by their having left a part of their men at Lastra, and by their not having waited for Messer Tolosetto Uberti, who was to have come with three hundred mounted men from Pistoja; they had vainly imagined that celerity of movement would more surely give them the victory than strength. And thus it often happens in such enterprises that celerity robs you of strength, whilst tardiness deprives you of the opportunity. The rebels having withdrawn, Florence relapsed into its old dissensions. The people, wishing to abate the power of the family of Cavalcanti, forcibly took from them the castle of Stinche, situated in the Val di Greve, and which had from time immemorial been their residence. And as those who were captured in it were the first to be confined in the new prisons that had been built in Florence, these were thence-

forth called after the castle whence the prisoners had been taken, and to this day these prisons are called the *Stinche* (1307).

Those who were at the head of the government of the republic re-established the companies of the people, and gave them the banners under which the guilds had formerly assembled. The captains of these assumed the title of Gonfalonieri of the companies and colleagues of the Signori, and claimed the right to aid the Signori with their counsels in all armed conflicts or other disturbances. To the ancient Rectors they added an officer called Executor of Justice, whose duty it was to aid the Gonfalonieri in repressing the insolence of the nobles. In the midst of all this the Pope died, and Messer Corso and the other citizens returned from Rome; and all would have been tranquil if the turbulent spirit of Messer Corso had not disturbed Florence anew. For the purpose of gaining influence he opposed the nobles on every occasion, and to whatever side he saw the people inclined, to that he inclined also; so that he became the head and front of all differences and innovations, and all who wished to obtain anything extraordinary had recourse to him. Thus many of the best reputed citizens came to hate him, which increased to such a degree that the party of the Neri broke out into open division. Messer Corso relied upon his private power and influence, his adversaries upon that of the government; but such was his personal authority that everybody feared him. And therefore for the purpose of depriving him of this popular favor his opponents adopted a plan by which it was easily destroyed, for they spread the report that he wanted to seize the government and make himself tyrant of Florence. It was easy to make the people believe this, for his way of life exceeded all civil bounds, and his marriage with a daughter of Uguccione della Faggiuola, head of the Ghibellines and of the Bianchi party, and a man of greatest power in Tuscany, gave still greater consistency to this report.

23. So soon as this alliance became known, his adversaries took courage, and armed against him. The same considerations caused the people not to defend him, but the greater part rather joined his enemies. The principal of these were Messer Rosso della Tosa, Messer Pazzino de' Pazzi, Messer Geri Spini, and Messer Berto Brunelleschi. These, with their followers and the greater part of the people, met, armed, at the palace of the Sig-

noria, by whose order an accusation against Messer Corso had been placed in the hands of Messer Piero Branca, captain of the people, charging Messer Corso with an attempt, by the aid of Messer Uguccione, to make himself tyrant of the city. Thereupon he was cited to appear, and condemned for contumacy as a rebel (1308), — not more than two hours having been allowed to elapse between the accusation and the sentence. After this judgment, the Signori, with the companies of the people under their banners, went to seek Messer Corso. He, on the other hand, undaunted at seeing himself abandoned by many of his adherents, nor by the sentence pronounced against him, nor by the authority of the Signori or the multitude of his enemies, fortified himself in his palace, hoping to be able to defend himself until Uguccione, for whom he had sent, should come to his assistance. He barred his palace and the streets around it, which were occupied by his partisans, who defended them so well that the people, though very numerous, could not dislodge them. The combat, however, was very severe, and many were killed and wounded on both sides; and the people, seeing that they could not get at Messer Corso from the open streets, occupied the adjoining houses, and, breaking through the walls, they succeeded in entering his palace. Messer Corso, finding himself surrounded by enemies, and relying no longer upon the expected aid of Uguccione, resolved, after despairing of victory, to find a means of safety; and, together with Gherardo Bordoni and a number of his stoutest and stanchest friends, he charged so impetuously upon his enemies that they opened their ranks, and allowed him to pass through, fighting, and to escape from the city through the Porta alla Croce. They were, however, pursued by a number of their enemies, and Gherardo was killed on the Affrico by Boccaccio Cavicciuli. Messer Corso was also overtaken and captured at Rovezzano by some Catalan horsemen in the service of the Signoria. But on approaching Florence, he threw himself off his horse, so as to avoid meeting his enemies face to face and being torn in pieces by them; and, being down on the ground, one of the men charged with conducting him to Florence cut his throat. His body was picked up by the monks of San Salvi, and was buried without any honors. Such was the end of Messer Corso, who had done both much good and much evil to his country and to the party of the Neri; and his memory would have been more glorious if his spirit had been less turbulent. Nevertheless, he deserves to be numbered amongst the great citizens which Florence has produced. It is true that his turbulence caused his country and his party to forget the obligations they owed him, and in the end brought many ills upon both the one and the other, and death upon himself. Uguccione, whilst coming to the support of his son-in-law, heard, at Remole, how Messer Corso had been defeated by the people; and, seeing that he could be of no possible service to him, and not wishing uselessly to expose himself to harm, returned to his estates.

24. After the death of Messer Corso, which occurred in the year 1308, the disturbances ceased in Florence, and the people lived in peace until it became known that the Emperor Henry had passed into Italy, together with all the banished Florentines, whom he had promised to restore to their country. The chiefs of the government, judging it to be desirable to diminish the number of their enemies by diminishing that of the banished, resolved that these should all return, excepting those who had been specially forbidden by law to come back. The greater part of the Ghibellines were obliged, therefore, to remain in exile, as also some of the Bianchi party; amongst these were Dante Alighieri, the sons of Messer Veri de' Cerchi, and those of Giano della Bella. They, moreover, sent to implore the assistance of Robert, king of Naples; and as they could not obtain this aid from him as an ally, they gave him the control over the city for five years, so that he might defend them as his subjects. The Emperor, in coming into Italy, took the road by way of Pisa, and passed through the low country (Maremme) on to Rome, where he was crowned in the year 1312. After that, having resolved to subjugate the Florentines, he went by way of Perugia and Arezzo to Florence, and encamped with his army at the monastery of San Salvi, within a mile of the city, where he remained fifty days without any results. Despairing of being able to disturb the government of that city, he marched to Pisa, where he agreed with Frederick, king of Sicily, to undertake the conquest of the kingdom of Naples. Having started with his army, confident of victory, whilst King Robert was already trembling with fear of losing his kingdom, death overtook Henry, at Buonconvento, in the year 1313.

25. Shortly after that, Uguccione della Fagginola became lord of Pisa, and soon after also of Lucca, where he was placed by the

Ghibelline party; and, with the aid of these cities, he did much serious damage to the neighboring country. To save themselves from this, the Florentines applied to King Robert for his brother Piero to take command of their armies. Uguccione, on the other hand, continued to strengthen himself, and had seized by force and by fraud a number of castles in the Val d' Arno and in the Val di Nievole. He then went to besiege Monte Catini, which the Florentines deemed it necessary to succor, so as to put a stop to this conflagration, and prevent it from spreading over the whole country. Having assembled a large force, the Florentines went over into the Val di Nievole, where they encountered Uguccione, but were routed after a bloody battle. Piero, brother of King Robert, was killed, and his body never found; with him over two thousand men lost their lives. Nor was this victory a joyous one for Uguccione, for it cost the lives of one of his sons and of many other captains of his army. After this defeat, the Florentines fortified the places in the vicinity of their city, and King Robert sent them as captain of their forces Conte d' Andria, called the Count Novello. Whether it was the bad conduct of this general, or whether it was owing to the natural disposition of the Florentines to get tired of every government, and to differ amongst themselves on every occasion, the city, notwithstanding the war with Uguccione, divided into two factions, the one friendly and the other hostile to the king. The leaders of the hostile faction were Messer Simone della Tosa and the Magalotti, with certain others of the people who had the preponderance in the government. These managed to induce the government to send to France and to Germany to obtain men and commanders, with whose aid they might drive out the Count governor of the king. But fortune would have it that they could not obtain any. They did not, however, give up the attempt; and, seeking for some one to whom they could look up, and unable to find such either in France or in Germany, they took one from Agobbio. Having first expelled the Count Novello, they made a certain Lando of Agobbio Executor, that is to say, Bargello, and gave him absolute power over all the citizens. This Lando was a cruel and rapacious man. He went through the city, followed by a number of armed men, and took the lives of this or the other one, according to the dictation of those who had elected him. And he carried his audacity to that point that he coined base money with the Florentine dies, without any one's daring to oppose him (1316). To this condition had Florence been reduced by her discords! Truly great and wretched city! whom neither the memory of her past dissensions, nor the fear of Uguccione, nor the authority of a king, had been able to keep united and stable; so that she was brought to the most wretched state, being assailed from without by Uguccione, and plundered within by Lando d' Agobbio.

The noble families, and the most considerable amongst the people, and all the Guelfs, supported the king and opposed Lando and his followers. But as the king's adversaries had control of the government, the former could not openly declare themselves without great danger. Still, having resolved to rid themselves of this infamous tyranny, they sent secret letters to King Robert, requesting him to appoint the Count Guido da Battifolle his vicar in Florence. The king complied with this request, and the opposite party, notwithstanding that the Signori were hostile to the king, dared not oppose the Count, because of his excellent qualities. With all this, however, his authority was but limited, as the Signori and the Gonfalonieri favored Lando and his party. Whilst Florence was in this troubled condition, the daughter of King Albert of Bohemia passed through the city, on her way to join her husband, Charles, son of King Robert of Naples. She was received with great honors by the friends of the king, who complained to her of the condition of the city and of the tyranny of Lando and his followers. Her influence and efforts, together with that of the representatives of the king, restored union and peace amongst the citizens before she departed from Florence; and Lando was deprived of all authority, and sent back to Agobbio, laden with plunder and stained with blood.

In the reorganization of the government, the king's lordship over Florence was extended for three years; and inasmuch as seven Signori had already been elected by the party of Lando, six were now chosen by the adherents of the king; so that there were several Signoria consisting of thirteen in number, although they were afterwards reduced again to seven, according to ancient custom.

26. At this time the lordship of Lucca and Pisa was taken from Uguccione, and Castruccio Castracani, a citizen of Lucca, was made lord of these cities in his stead (1322); and being an ardent and courageous youth, and fortunate in his undertakings,

he became in a short time chief of the Ghibellines in Tuscany. The civil discords of Florence having been quieted for some years, the Florentines thought at first that they had nothing to fear from the power of Castruccio; but when it afterwards increased beyond their expectations, they began to consider as to the best means of protecting themselves against it. And to enable the Signori to deliberate with greater wisdom and execute their resolves with greater authority, they chose twelve citizens, whom they called Buonomini, and whose advice and concurrence should be required for every important act of the Signori.

In the midst of this the term of King Robert's lordship over Florence expired, and the city, having thus regained its independence, restored the former organization of the government, with the customary rectors and magistrates; and the fear which Castruccio inspired kept them united. After several attempts against the lords of Lunigiana, Castruccio assailed Prato (1323); whereupon the Florentines, having resolved to succor that place, closed their shops and marched there in a body, being twenty thousand foot and fifteen hundred mounted men. And by way of diminishing the forces of Castruccio and increasing their own, the Signoria published a proclamation to the effect that every banished Guelf who came to the rescue of Prato should afterwards be reinstated in his country; which caused four thousand banished to flock to their standard. The bringing of so great a force so promptly to Prato alarmed Castruccio, so that he retired to Lucca, unwilling to tempt fortune in a battle. This occasioned a difference of opinion in the Florentine camp between the nobles and the people; the latter wishing to follow Castruccio and to engage him in battle and to destroy him, whilst the former wanted to return home, saying that it was enough to have exposed Florence to danger for the sake of relieving Prato, which was very well when necessity constrained them to it; but that now, such being no longer the case, and when the risk of loss was great and the chance of gain small, it would be tempting fortune to pursue Castruccio. And as they could not agree, the question was submitted to the Signori, who were as much divided in opinion as the people and the nobles had been. When this became known in the city, the people collected in great numbers in the Piazza, and used threatening language against the nobles, so that these yielded from fear. But the resolve being taken so late, and so unwillingly by a large portion, it afforded time to Castruccio to retreat in safety to Lucca.

27. This disappointment excited great indignation amongst the people against the nobles; so that the Signori refused to observe the promise which they had made to the four thousand banished, by the advice and order of the nobles. These rebels, anticipating this refusal, resolved to forestall it; and, leaving the camp in advance of the army, they presented themselves at the gates of Florence for the purpose of entering the city first. This movement, however, having been foreseen, did not succeed, and they were repulsed by those who had remained in the city. They thereupon attempted to obtain by negotiation what they had failed to obtain by force, and sent eight envoys to the Signori to remind them of the pledge given to them, and of the dangers to which they had exposed themselves in the hope of the promised reward. And although the nobles made great efforts in behalf of the banished, regarding the promise of the Signori as a sacred obligation, for the fulfilment of which they had made themselves responsible, yet they did not succeed, owing to the universal indignation against them in consequence of their failure in the attempt against Castruccio, in which they might have succeeded. This was a dishonor and a shame for the city, and caused great irritation amongst the nobles, some of whom in consequence endeavored to obtain by force what had been denied to their entreaties. They engaged the banished, therefore, to come armed to the city, whilst they would take up arms in their behalf within Florence. This plot, however, was discovered the day before that set for its execution, so that the banished found the citizens armed and prepared to repel those outside; whilst they filled the nobles within with alarm to that degree that they dared not take up arms. And thus the banished had to desist from their attempt without having obtained any result. After the withdrawal of the banished the Signori wanted to punish those who had invited them to come; and although every one knew who the guilty parties were, yet no one dared to name and accuse them. To get at the truth of the matter, therefore, regardless of any one, it was provided that in a general council each one should write a list of the names of the guilty parties, and that these written lists should be secretly presented to the captain of the people. Whereupon there appeared as accused Messer Amerigo Donati,

Messer Thegiao Frescobaldi, and Messer Lotteringo Gherardini. But the judge was more lenient to them than what their offence merited, and they were condemned merely to a fine in money.

28. The disturbances created in Florence by the coming of the banished to the very gates of the city proved that a single chief did not suffice for the command of the companies of the people. And therefore it was ordained that in future every company should have three or four captains; and they gave to each Gonfalonier two or three adjuncts, who were called Pennonieri; so that in cases of necessity, where the whole company was not required to be present, a portion of them might act together under one head. And as it happens in all republics that after a disturbance of any kind some old laws are annulled and some new ones enacted, so it happened in this case. Instead of, as heretofore, creating a Signoria at stated intervals, the Signori and such of their colleagues as were then in charge, relying upon their strength, obtained from the people the authority themselves to choose the Signoria, who should in future hold this office for a term of forty months. The names of these were to be put into a bag or purse, whence they were to be drawn every two months. But before the period of forty months had expired, they recommenced placing the names in the purse, because many citizens suspected that their names had been omitted to be put in. This gave rise to the practice of placing in a purse, a long time in advance of the drawing, the names of all the magistrates within as well as without the city; whilst according to the former system, at the expiration of the term of a magistracy, the successors were elected by the councils. This method of drawing the names of the magistrates from purses (imborsations) was called the *Squittini;* and as it occurred only once in every three, or at most five years, the city was relieved of much trouble and disturbance that had previously accompanied the creation of magistrates, owing to the great number of competitors for the several offices. The Florentines adopted this system as the best means of correcting the troubles attending the old method; but they did not perceive the defects that were concealed under these unimportant advantages.

29. It was now the year 1325. Castruccio, having made himself master of Pistoja, became so powerful that the Florentines, fearing his greatness, resolved to attack him and to

rescue that city from his rule before he should have fairly established his dominion over it. They raised from amongst their own citizens and allies twenty thousand infantry and three thousand mounted men, and with this force they took the field at Altopascio, intending to seize that city, and thus to prevent assistance being sent from there to Pistoja. They succeeded in taking the place; and from there they marched upon Lucca, wasting the country as they went. But owing to their want of prudence and the bad faith of their captain they made but little progress. The name of this captain was Raimondo di Cardona. Having seen how readily the Florentines had disposed of their liberties, yielding them first to the king of Naples, then to the Pope's legates, and then again to others of lesser grade, he thought that, by involving them in some difficulties, it might easily happen that they would appoint him their prince. He did not fail repeatedly to suggest this, asking them to give him the same authority over their city as they had given him over their army, adding that without this he could not enforce the obedience essential to a general. And as the Florentines did not concede to him his demands, he went on losing time, of which Castruccio promptly took advantage. For the assistance which had been promised him by the Visconti and the other tyrants of Lombardy arrived, and, having been strengthened by this accession, Castruccio attacked Messer Raimondo, who, having in the first instance lost the victory from want of good faith, knew not how to save himself after defeat from want of prudence. For advancing slowly with his army he was met and attacked by Castruccio near Altopascio (1325), and after severe fighting was completely routed. In this battle many citizens were made prisoners, and many were slain; amongst the latter was Messer Raimondo himself, who thus received from fortune that punishment for his bad faith and evil counsels which he had deserved at the hands of the Florentines. The damage done by Castruccio to the Florentines after this victory, in the way of plunder, prisoners, destruction, and burnings, could not be told; for the Florentines having no troops to oppose him, he rode and roved over the country when and where he pleased during several months; and the Florentines after such an overwhelming defeat deemed themselves fortunate in being able to save their city.

80. And yet they were not so much disheartened but what they raised large sums of money for the payment of troops and to send to their allies for help. But all this did not suffice to keep their powerful enemy in check; so that they applied to Charles, Duke of Calabria, and son of King Robert of Naples, to come to their defence; but by way of inducing him to come they were obliged again to make him lord of the city; for being accustomed to rule in Florence, he preferred her subjection rather than her alliance. But as Charles was at that time occupied with the war against Sicily, and could not come in person to assume the sovereignty over Florence, he sent in his stead Gauthier, a Frenchman by birth and Duke of Athens, who as vicar of the sovereign took possession of the city and organized the government according to his own will. Nevertheless he made himself generally beloved by the modesty of his bearing, by which he concealed in a measure his real nature.

When Charles had terminated the war with Sicily, he came with one thousand horsemen to Florence, and made his entry in July, 1326. His arrival put a stop to Castruccio's further devastations of the Florentine territory. But the reputation which Charles gained outside of the city he lost within, and the injuries which the enemy did not do had to be borne when done by friends; for the Signoria could do nothing without the concurrence of the Duke, who within the period of one year extorted from the city four hundred thousand florins, although according to the convention made with him he had no right to go beyond two hundred thousand florins. Such were the charges with which he or his father burdened the city daily. Fresh suspicions and enmities were added to these losses; for the Ghibellines of Lombardy took such umbrage at the coming of Charles into Tuscany, that Galeazzo Visconti and the other Lombard tyrants, by means of money and promises, caused Louis of Bavaria, who had been elected Emperor contrary to the will of the Pope, to come into Italy. Louis came into Lombardy and thence into Tuscany, and with the help of Castruccio made himself master of Pisa (1327), and, having been supplied with money there, he moved on towards Rome. This caused Charles to depart from Florence, as he had become apprehensive for the safety of the kingdom of Naples; he left Messer Filippo da Saginetto as his vicar in Florence. After the departure of the Emperor, Castruccio made himself master ordinca; but the Florentines took Pistoja from him by means of secret intelligence with some of its inhabitants. Castruccio thereupon besieged it with such valor and obstinacy, that all the efforts of the Florentines to relieve Pistoja were fruitless. In vain did they attack his army and his possessions, but neither force nor perseverance on their part could drive him off, such was his determination to chastise the inhabitants, and to triumph over the Florentines. The Pistojans were obliged therefore to accept him as their lord; and although he achieved this with so much glory to himself, yet it also cost him such efforts and fatigue that he died from the effects of it on his return to Lucca, in 1328. And as fortune rarely fails to accompany any good or evil with another good or evil, so it happened in this case; for Charles, Duke of Calabria and lord of Florence, also died at Naples; so that the Florentines, without any effort of their own, were relieved from the fear of the one and the lordship of the other. Thus they remained free to remodel the government of their city; and they consequently annulled the organization of the old councils entirely, and created two others, the one composed of three hundred citizens of the people, and the other of two hundred and fifty nobles and citizens; the first being called *the Council of the People*, and the other *the Council of the Commons*.

31. When the Emperor arrived at Rome he created an Antipope, ordered many things adverse to the Church, and attempted many other things unsuccessfully; so that in the end he departed with shame and went to Pisa (1329), where, either from disgust or from not having received their pay, eight hundred German cavaliers rebelled against him and fortified themselves at Montechiaro, above Ceruglio. After the Emperor had left Pisa to go into Lombardy, these seized Lucca and expelled Francesco Castracani, who had been left there in command by the Emperor. And thinking to derive some advantage from the capture of this city, they offered it to the Florentines for the sum of eighty thousand florins, which offer, however, was declined, by the advice of Messer Simone della Tosa. This course would have been most advantageous for the Florentines if they had remained of the same mind; but very soon after a number of them changed their views, which proved most injurious to the city. For whilst they declined it at the time when they might have had Lucca peaceably for so small a sum, they

afterwards wanted it when they could no longer have it, though they now would willingly have paid a much larger sum. This caused the Florentines to alter their government several times, to the great injury of their city. Lucca, having been refused by the Florentines, was purchased by Messer Gherardino Spinoli, a Genoese, for the sum of thirty thousand florins. And as men are apt to be less eager to take what they can get easily than they are in desiring what they cannot get, so the people of Florence, when they became cognizant of the sale of Lucca and the small price at which Messer Gherardino had obtained it, became seized with an eager desire to possess it, and blamed themselves and Messer Simone, who had advised them to decline the purchase. And in the hope of obtaining it by force, after having refused to purchase it, they sent their troops to ravage and plunder the Lucchese territory. Meantime the Emperor had left Italy, and the Pisans had sent the Antipope a prisoner to France.

From the death of Castruccio, in 1328, until the year 1340, Florence enjoyed internal tranquillity, and occupied herself wholly with the foreign relations of the state. She was involved in several wars; in Lombardy in consequence of the coming of King John of Bohemia, and in Tuscany on account of Lucca. The city was embellished with many new edifices: amongst others they built the Campanile (Bell Tower) of the Santa Reparata under the direction of Messer Giotto, a most celebrated painter in those days. In 1333 the waters of the Arno had risen throughout Florence more than twelve braccia, and by its overflow had destroyed some of the bridges and many buildings, all of which, however, were restored, with the greatest care and at much expense.

32. The year 1340, however, brought with it fresh causes for discord. The citizens holding power had two means of increasing and maintaining their control; the one was to restrict the number of names put into the purses for the election of magistrates, so that only their own names or those of their friends should be drawn; and the other was always to keep in their own hands the control of the election of the Rectors, so as to insure to themselves favorable judgments at their hands. And so highly did they value this second means, that on several occasions when the ordinary Rectors did not suffice them, they brought in a third one. It was in this extra-

ordinary way that they had introduced Messer Jacopo Gabrielli of Agobbio, under the title of Captain of the Guard, giving him plenary authority over the people. He committed daily acts of injustice to oblige and please those who held the government; and amongst those whom he had thus wronged were Messer Piero de' Bardi and Messer Bardo Frescobaldi. These, being nobles and naturally proud, could not bear that a stranger should thus wrong them to gratify a few men in power. To revenge themselves upon him and those who held the government, they formed a conspiracy, in which many noble families became engaged, and also some of the people who were dissatisfied with the tyranny of the chiefs of the government. The plan agreed upon amongst these conspirators was that they should collect a number of armed men in their houses, and on the morning of the feast of All Saints, when all the people were in the churches praying for their dead, they should all take up arms, kill the captain and the chiefs of the government; and that then they should reorganize the government by creating new Signori and by establishing an entirely new order of things.

But the more dangerous enterprises are reflected upon, the more reluctantly do men enter upon them; and thus it happens (almost always) that those conspiracies which fix upon a certain time in advance for their execution are generally discovered. Amongst the conspirators was Messer Andrea de' Bardi; in thinking over the matter, the fear of punishment overcame in him the desire of revenge; and therefore he disclosed the whole plot to Jacopo Alberti, his brother-in-law, who made it known to the Priors, and these communicated it to the Signori. As the danger was pressing, All Saints' day being near at hand, a number of people assembled in the palace; and deeming delay dangerous, they wanted the Signori to have the tocsin sounded, and the people called to arms. Taldo Valori was Gonfalonier at that time, and Francesco Salviati was one of the Signori; these, being relatives of the Bardi, objected to having the alarm sounded, alleging that it was not well to cause the people to arm for every slight cause, as power given to the multitude, and not controlled by any check, never resulted in good; that it was easy to start tumults, but difficult to check them; and therefore it would be better first to hear the truth of the matter, and then to punish it legally, rather than to chastise it in a tumultuary manner at the risk of the ruin of Florence and upon a simple denunciation. This advice was not listened to, but, with vile and insulting words and manner, the people forced the Signori to have the alarm-bell sounded; and when this was heard, the whole people of Florence rushed armed to the Piazza. On the other hand, the Bardi and Frescobaldi, seeing their plot discovered, took to arms, resolved either to conquer with glory or to die without shame; and hoping to be able to defend that part of the city on the opposite side of the river where they had their palaces, they fortified the bridges, trusting in the aid which they expected from the nobles of the country and from their other friends. But their plans were thwarted by the people who inhabited the same side of the city, and who armed in support of the Signori; so that, finding themselves hemmed in, they abandoned the bridges and retreated to the street in which the Bardi lived, that being a stronger position than any other, and there they defended themselves most gallantly. Messer Jacopo, knowing that this conspiracy was aimed mainly against him, being afraid of death and stupefied with terror, placed himself in the midst of his armed men near the palace of the Signori. But the other Rectors, being less conscious of guilt, were more courageous, especially the Podesta, Messer Maffeo da Marradi. He showed himself fearlessly in the thickest of the fight; and having passed the bridge of Rubaconte, he rushed into the midst of the Bardi, and made signs to them for a parley. The respect which his conduct inspired, and his other well-known great qualities, put a stop to the fighting, and caused the conspirators quietly to listen to him. In a modest but grave manner he blamed the conspiracy, and pointed out the danger in which they were if they did not yield to the popular impulse, and held out to them the hope that they should afterwards be heard and judged with leniency, and promised to exert himself to have their reasonable dissatisfaction treated with proper consideration. He then returned to the Signori, and persuaded them not to desire a victory at the expense of the blood of their fellow-citizens, nor to condemn the conspirators without first giving them a fair hearing. His efforts succeeded, so that, by consent of the Signori, the Bardi and the Frescobaldi, with their friends, were permitted to leave the city, and retire unmolested to their castles. After their departure the people disarmed, and the Signori proceeded only against such of the families of the Bardi and Frescobaldi as were taken with arms in hand. And by way of depriving them of power they purchased from the Bardi the castles of Mangona and Vernia; and provided by law that thenceforth no citizen should be allowed to possess any castle within twenty miles of the city. A few months afterwards Stiatta Frescobaldi was beheaded, and many others of the family were exiled. It was not enough for those who governed to have overcome and subdued the Bardi and Frescobaldi, but as is always the case with men clothed with authority, that the more power they have the more they abuse it, so where previously there was but one captain of the guard who harassed the city, they appointed another for the country, giving him very extensive authority, so that those who incurred the suspicion of these captains could neither live within the city of Florence nor outside of it. And they irritated the nobles to that degree against themselves, that these were ready to sell the city and themselves for the sake of revenge. The opportunity they had waited for soon presented itself, and they made good use of it.

33. During all the troubles that had prevailed in Tuscany and Lombardy the city of Lucca fell under the control of Mastino della Scala, lord of Verona (1341). Although according to his engagements he should have handed that city over to the Florentines, yet he did not do so; for as lord of Parma he thought himself able to hold it regardless of his pledges. The Florentines therefore, by way of revenging themselves, united with the Venetians and attacked him so fiercely that he came near losing his whole state. They however derived no other advantage from all this than the small gratification to their pride of having defeated Mastino; for the Venetians, according to the fashion of all who ally themselves with others less powerful, after having won Trevisa and Vicenza, made terms with Mastino, regardless of the Florentines. But the Visconti, lords of Milan, having soon after taken Parma from Mastino, he judged that he would in consequence no longer be able to hold Lucca, and therefore he resolved to sell it. The Florentines and the Pisans were equally competitors for it; and the latter, whilst pressing the negotiations for it, perceiving that the Florentines, being the richer, were about to obtain it, resorted to force, and aided by Visconti they laid siege to the city. The Florentines, however, did not in conse-

quence of this withdraw from the purchase, but concluded the
bargain with Mastino, paying part of the money down and
giving hostages for the payment of the other part; and sent
Naddo Rucellai, Giovanni di Bernardino de' Medici, and Rosso
di Ricciardo de' Ricci to take possession of Lucca. They entered the city by force, and it was handed over to them by the
troops of Mastino. The Pisans nevertheless pursued their
enterprise, and made every effort to make themselves masters
of Lucca. The Florentines, on the other hand, endeavored to
make the Pisans raise the siege; and after a long war the Florentines were driven off with loss of their money and their
glory, and the Pisans became masters of Lucca. The loss of
that city, as usually happens in such cases, made the people
indignant against those who held the government, and they
openly denounced them in all the public places and piazzas,
charging them with avarice and blaming them for the evil
counsels they had given. At the beginning of this war its
conduct had been confided to twenty citizens, who had chosen
Malatesta da Rimini as captain of the enterprise. He had
conducted it with little courage and still less prudence, and
therefore the Council of Twenty sent to ask the assistance
of Robert, king of Naples, who sent to them Gauthier, Duke of
Athens; who, according to the decrees of Heaven, whose hand
always prepares the evils to come, arrived at Florence at the
moment when the attempt upon Lucca had just failed so completely (1342). Whereupon the Twenty, seeing the people indignant, sought to inspire them with fresh hopes by appointing
a new captain, and thereby either to check them or to deprive
them of all further pretext for denouncing them. And to
constrain them also by fear, and to enable the Duke of Athens
to defend them with more authority, they appointed him first
as Conservator and afterwards as Commander of their armed
forces.

The nobles — who for the reasons above given were malcon-
tent, and many of them having known Gauthier at the time
when he had on a previous occasion governed Florence in the
name of Charles, Duke of Calabria — thought that the moment
had come when they might, with the ruin of the city, avert
their own destruction. They thought that there was no other
means of subduing the people who had inflicted so many
wrongs upon them than to subject themselves to a prince who,

knowing the merits of the one party and the insolence of the other, might reward the one and curb the other. To these considerations was added the hope of advantages which they would derive from it, if by their efforts he should be made Prince of the city. They therefore had several secret conferences with Gauthier, and persuaded him to assume the sovereignty over all, offering him all the support in their power. Some of the burgher families united their influence to the authority and advice of the nobles. These were the Peruzzi, Acciaiuoli, Antellesi, and Buonaccorsi, who, being weighed down by debts which they were unable to pay with their own means, wished to acquit themselves of them with the property of others, and counted upon liberating themselves from the servitude to their creditors by the enslavement of their country. These persuasions fired the ambitious spirit of the Duke with the greatest desire of domination; and by way of obtaining the reputation of being severe and just, and thereby to gain the good will and support of the people, he prosecuted those who had conducted the war against Lucca, and inflicted the penalty of death upon Messer Giovanni de' Medici, Naddo Rucellai, and Guglielmo Altoviti; many others he condemned to exile or to heavy pecuniary fines.

34. These executions greatly alarmed the middle class of citizens, and gave satisfaction only to the nobles and the populace; to the latter because it is their nature to rejoice in evil, and to the former because they saw themselves avenged of the many injuries received at the hands of the citizens. When the Duke passed through the streets, the people loudly praised his frankness of spirit, and he was urged on all sides to inquire into the frauds of the citizens and to punish them. The authority of the Twenty had declined, and the influence of the Duke had become great, and the fear of him still greater; and everybody by way of displaying their devotion to him had his arms painted over their doors; so that he really lacked nothing of being a prince except the title. Believing that he might now attempt anything with safety, he gave the Signori to understand that he deemed it necessary for the good of the state that they should freely concede to him the sovereignty over it, and that, inasmuch as the whole city seemingly consented to it, he desired that they also should give their concurrence. Although the Signori had for a long time foreseen the

ruin of their country, yet they were greatly troubled by this demand; and though they well knew their danger, still, so as not to fail of their duty to their country, they refused his demand in a spirited manner. By way of making greater show of religion and humanity the Duke had chosen for his residence the convent of the Minorite Brothers of Santa Croce; and desiring to put his evil intentions into execution, he published a proclamation commanding all the people to assemble before him in the Piazza of Santa Croce. This proclamation frightened the Signori much more than the previous words of the Duke had done; and they united themselves closely with such of the citizens as were regarded as true lovers of their country and of liberty. And knowing the power of the Duke, they did not think of any other means of resistance than by petition; and to try, as their forces were insufficient, whether prayers and supplications would not make him renounce his attempt, or alleviate the yoke which he was about to impose upon them. A portion of the Signori therefore went to see him, and one of them addressed him as follows:—

"We have been induced, O Signor, to appear before you, "first by your demand to have the lordship over our city con- "ferred upon you, and next by your order for an assembly of "the people; for it appears certain to us that you aim to obtain "by extraordinary means that to which by ordinary means you "have been unable to obtain our consent. It is not our inten- "tion to oppose your designs in any way by force, but only to "point out to you the weight of the burden which you are "about to take upon yourself, and the greatness of the danger "of the course which you are pursuing, so that you may always "remember our counsels, and those of the persons who advise "you differently, for the gratification of their revenge, and not "for your good. You seek to enslave a city that has always "lived in the enjoyment of liberty; for the authority which "on a former occasion we accorded to the king of Naples was "an alliance, and not servitude. Have you considered the im- "portance of this in a city like ours, and how powerful the "mere name of Liberty is, which no force can subdue, nor time "consume, and for which nothing else can compensate? Think, "O Signor, what power would be requisite to keep such a city "in subjection! The foreign troops which you may always "keep there will not suffice, and those of the city you will not

"be able to trust; for those who are your friends to-day, and
"counsel you to your present attempt, will no sooner have
"profited by your power to defeat their own enemies, than
"they will seek your overthrow for the purpose of making
"themselves masters. The people, in whom you trust, will
"turn against you at the first mischance, however small; so
"that you may expect in a little while to have the whole city
"hostile to you, which would involve her ruin and your own.
"Nor can you hope to find a remedy for this evil, for those
"princes only can assure their sovereignty who have but few
"enemies, of whom they can easily rid themselves by death or
"by exile. But against a universal hatred there can never be
"any security, for you can never know where the evil has its
"origin; and he who fears every man can never make sure of
"any one. And if yet you attempt it, you will only aggravate
"your danger, for the hatred of those who remain will become
"more inflamed, and they will be the more ready for revenge.
"Nothing is more certain than that time will not efface the
"love of liberty; for we often hear of its being reasserted in
"cities by those who have never tasted its sweets, and who
"loved liberty only from the memory of it transmitted to them
"by their fathers. And once recovered they have defended it
"with the utmost obstinacy and through every danger. And
"even if the fathers left no record of the liberties they enjoyed,
"yet the public palaces, the dwellings of the magistrates, the
"banners of the free orders, all bear witness to them; and
"the memory of all these things is fondly cherished by the
"citizens. What acts of yours could you offer as an equiva-
"lent for the happiness of living in the enjoyment of liberty,
"or that could extinguish in men's minds the desire for their
"present condition? In vain would you add all Tuscany to
"the possessions of the city! In vain would you return daily
"crowned with victory over our enemies, for that would not
"redound to the glory of Florence, but only to yours, and her
"citizens would thereby not gain subjects, but merely fellow-
"slaves, whereby their own servitude would be aggravated.
"And if your life were that of a saint, your manners benevo-
"lent, and your judgments just, all this would not suffice to
"secure their affection. And if you were to believe that it
"would suffice, you only deceive yourself; for every chain
"is heavy and every fetter irksome to him who has been accus-

"tomed to live unconstrained. A turbulent state and a benign "prince are incompatible, for of necessity they must either "become assimilated, or the one will quickly destroy the other. "You must expect therefore either to hold this city by vio- "lence, for which the citadels and their garrisons and foreign "allies are generally insufficient, or you must be content with "the authority which we have conferred upon you, and to this "we would advise you, reminding you that that dominion only "is desirable which is borne willingly. Do not attempt then, "under the promptings of your ambition to place yourself "where you can neither remain nor rise higher, and whence "you would of necessity fall, with equal injury to yourself and "ourselves!"

35. The obdurate soul of the Duke was in no way moved by this address. He replied, "that it was not his intention to "deprive Florence of her liberty, but rather to restore it to "her; that cities were enslaved only by discord, whilst union "insured them freedom; and if Florence by her factions, "ambitions, and enmities deprived herself of liberty, and he "restored her to union, he could not be charged with an "attempt to enslave her. And as he had been induced to take "this task upon himself, not from any ambition of his own, but "at the urgent instance of many citizens, it would be well for "them to be content with what would satisfy the others. And, "as for the dangers to which he would expose himself by this "step, he did not regard them, for it was not the practice of "a good man to be deterred by fear from doing a good act, and "only a coward desisted from a glorious enterprise because its "issue was involved in doubt. And that he believed his con- "duct would be such that in a short time they would find out "that they had trusted him too little and feared him too "much."

The Signori, seeing therefore that they could effect no good, agreed that the people should assemble the following morning, and with their concurrence to give the Duke the sovereignty over Florence for one year, with the same conditions as those given on a former occasion to Charles, Duke of Calabria. It was on the 8th of September, of the year 1342, that the Duke, accompanied by Messer Giovanni della Tosa and all his adherents, and many other citizens, came into the Piazza, and together with the Signoria mounted the *Ringhiera*, as the people of Florence called those steps which were at the foot of the palace of the Signoria. From there the terms of agreement were read to the people that had been concluded between the Signoria and the Duke; and when they came to that passage by which they accorded to the Duke the lordship over Florence for one year, there arose cries from the people, "*For life!*" And when Messer Francesco Rustichelli, one of the Signori, arose to speak for the purpose of allaying the tumult, he was interrupted by cries; so that the Duke was elected by the people sovereign of Florence, not for one year, but in perpetuity; and he was taken and carried by the people around the Piazza, who shouted his name aloud. It was customary for the captain of the guard of the palace, in the absence of the Signoria, to keep the gates of the palace locked inside. This office was held at the time by Rinieri de Giotto, who, having been bribed by the friends of the Duke, admitted him inside of the palace without awaiting any attempt at force. The Signori, frightened and covered with shame, retired to their own houses; the palace was sacked by the Duke's adherents, the gonfalon of the people was torn down, and the Duke's standard raised instead. All of which caused immeasurable grief and regret to all the good citizens, and much joy to those who had consented to it from malice or ignorance.

36. No sooner had the Duke obtained the sovereignty of Florence than, for the purpose of depriving those of power who had been the customary defenders of liberty, he prohibited the Signori from assembling in the palace, and assigned to them a private house. He took the standards from the Gonfalonieri of the companies of the people, suspended the ordinances of justice against the nobles, liberated the prisoners, recalled the Bardi and the Frescobaldi from exile, and forbade everybody from bearing arms. And, by way of being the better able to defend himself against those within Florence, he formed alliances with those outside of the city. He favored and bestowed great advantages upon the people of Arezzo, and upon all others that were subject to the Florentines, and made peace with the Pisans, although one of the conditions on which he was placed at the head of the state was that he should make war upon Pisa. He withheld the interest from those merchants who had loaned money to the city during the war with Lucca, increased the old taxes and laid new ones, and deprived the Signori of all author-

ity. His Rectors were Baglione da Perugia and Messer Guglielmo d' Ascesi; with these, and Messer Ceretticri Bisdomini, he consulted. The taxes which he imposed upon the citizens were heavy, and his judgments unjust. He threw off the cloak of religion and of humanity, which he had assumed, and abandoned himself to pride and cruelty. Many noble and prominent citizens were condemned to heavy fines or death, or subjected to all sorts of newly contrived torments. And so that his government outside of the city should not be better than that within, he created six Rectors for the country, who plundered and maltreated the inhabitants. Although the nobles had supported and aided him in obtaining the sovereignty, and he had recalled many from exile, yet he held them in suspicion; for he could not believe that the generous spirit that belongs to true nobility could be content to live under his rule. He therefore turned to favor and conciliate the common people, thinking that with their support, and with foreign troops, he would be able to maintain his tyranny. When, however, the month of May had come, at which time the people are accustomed to hold their festivals, he had the common people and the small citizens formed into several companies, on whom he bestowed splendid titles, and gave them banners and money; and whilst a part of these went through the city with festive rejoicings, the others received them with the greatest pomp.

As the fame of the new sovereignty of the Duke spread, many Frenchmen flocked to him, and he gave employment to them all as men worthy of all trust; so that, in a short time, Florence became subject, not only to Frenchmen, but also to their manners and customs and fashions in dress; for all men and women imitated them, regardless of all decencies of life and without shame. But what gave the greatest offence were the outrages committed by the Duke and his followers upon the women, regardless of everything. The citizens, therefore, were filled with indignation at seeing the majesty of their state ruined, all order disregarded, the laws annulled, all honesty corrupted, and all modesty extinguished; for those who were not accustomed to see royal pomp could not meet the Duke, surrounded by armed satellites on foot and on horseback, without being deeply pained. And they were made to feel their shame more keenly by being obliged to do honor to him whom they hated most. All this was aggravated still more by the apprehension caused by the many deaths and heavy taxes with which he exhausted and impoverished the city. The Duke was aware of this general feeling of hatred and apprehension, and he feared it, although he tried to make it appear that he was beloved by everybody.

Thus it happened that when Matteo di Morozzo, either for the purpose of ingratiating himself or to save himself from danger, revealed to the Duke that the family of the Medici and some others were conspiring against him, he not only caused no investigation of the matter, but had the informer miserably put to death. By this course the Duke discouraged those who desired to advise him for his safety, and encouraged those who sought his destruction. He also subjected Bettone Cini to the cruel torture of having his tongue cut out, causing his death thereby, for having dared to speak against the taxes imposed upon the citizens (1343). This act incensed the citizens still more, and increased their hatred of the Duke; for the city, which had been accustomed in all matters to act and speak with the utmost degree of freedom, could no longer endure to have her hands fettered and her mouth gagged. This indignation and hatred, therefore, increased to such a point, that it would have stirred not only the Florentines, who were alike incapable of maintaining their liberty or of supporting their servitude, but any other enslaved people, to make an effort for the recovery of their liberty. Accordingly, many citizens of all conditions resolved either to sacrifice their lives or to recover their liberty. They formed three separate conspiracies, composed of three different classes of citizens, — nobles, people, and artificers, — who, besides the general causes of discontent, were influenced thereto by the opinion that, although the people had lost the control of the government, yet the nobles had not gained it; and that the artificers were deprived of their customary gains. Messer Agnolo Acciaiuoli was Archbishop of Florence at that time. In his preaching he had magnified the doings of the Duke, and had won for him great favor with the people. But when he afterwards saw him as lord of Florence, and perceived his tyrannical conduct, he became convinced that he had misled his country; and to make good the error which he had committed, he could think of no other remedy than that the same hand that had inflicted the wound should also heal it; and therefore he placed himself at the head of the first and most powerful conspiracy, in which there were also the Bardi, the Rossi, the Fres-

cobaldi, Scali, Altoviti, Magalotti, Strozzi, and the Mancini. One
of the other conspiracies was headed by Manno and Corso Donati, and with them the Pazzi, Cavicciulli, Cerchi, and the Albizzi. The chiefs of the third conspiracy were Antonio Adimari,
and with him the Medici, Bordoni, Rucellai, and Aldobrandini.
They resolved upon killing the Duke in the house of the Albizzi,
where they supposed he would go on the day of San Giovanni to
see the horses run. But as he did not go there, they could not
carry out that plan. They then thought of attacking him as he
made his promenade through the city; but they saw that that
would be difficult, as he went always accompanied and well
armed, and always varied his promenade, so that they could not
with any certainty lie in wait for him in any particular place.
They also talked about killing him in the council chamber, but
feared that, even if they succeeded, they would be at the mercy
of the Duke's guard. Whilst the conspirators were discussing
these different plans, Antonio Adimari communicated the matter
to some of his Siennese friends, for the purpose of obtaining
their assistance. He made known to them a part of the conspirators, and assured them that the whole city was ready to
strike for liberty. One of these mentioned the subject to Messer
Francesco Brunelleschi, not by way of denouncing it, but merely
to ascertain whether he too was one of the conspirators. Messer
Francesco, either from fear for himself or from hatred of the
other conspirators, revealed the whole to the Duke, who immediately had Pagolo della Mazzacca and Simone de Montcrappoli
arrested; and when the Duke learned from them the character
and extent of the conspiracy, he became frightened, and was
advised to have the conspirators summoned for examination,
rather than arrested as prisoners, because, if they should escape
by flight, he could easily and without any disturbance rid himself of them by declaring them exiles. The Duke therefore had
Antonio Adimari summoned, who, confiding in his companions,
promptly appeared. He was kept prisoner, and the Duke was
advised by Messer Francesco Brunelleschi and Messer Uguccione
Buondelmonti to have the country scoured, and to have all the
conspirators that were captured put to death. But the Duke did
not consider himself strong enough to act according to this advice in the midst of so many enemies; he therefore adopted a
different plan, by which, if it had succeeded, he would have made
sure of his enemies and provided new forces for himself. The

Duke was in the habit of convoking some of the citizens for the purpose of consulting with them upon cases that occurred. Having thereupon taken the precaution to send outside of the city for troops, the Duke prepared a list of three hundred citizens, and had them summoned by his sergeants under pretence that he wished to consult with them; it being his intention when they were assembled to have them either killed or imprisoned. The imprisonment of Antonio Adimari and the sending for troops, which could not be done secretly, frightened the citizens, and especially those implicated in the conspiracy, so that the most daring refused to obey the summons of the Duke. And, as every one had read the list, they met and encouraged each other to take up arms, and to resolve rather to die like men than to be led like calves to the shambles. Thus in a few hours all the conspirators became known to each other; and resolved on the following day, which was the 26th of July, 1343, to cause a tumult in the old market, and then to arm themselves and call upon the people to arise and assert their liberty.

37. On the following morning, therefore, according to the order agreed upon, at the hour of nine, the conspirators took up arms, and at the cry of "Liberty," the people armed themselves and threw up barricades, and raised the banner that had been secretly provided by the conspirators. All the heads of families, nobles as well as citizens, united and swore to defend themselves and to kill the Duke; the only exceptions were some of the Buondelmonti and Cavalcanti, and those four families of the people who had aided the Duke in making himself sovereign of the city; these, together with the butchers and others of the lowest class of the people, came together armed in the Piazza, in support of the Duke. At this disturbance the Duke armed the palace, and his people who were lodged in various parts of the city mounted their horses to go into the Piazza; but on the way they were attacked in several places, and many of them killed. Nevertheless some three hundred horsemen reached the Piazza. The Duke was in doubt whether to go to encounter his enemies, or to defend himself within the palace. On the other hand, the Medici, Cavicciulli, Rucellai, and other families who had been most wronged by him, doubted lest, in case the Duke should come out, many who had taken up arms against him might not declare in his favor; desirous therefore to prevent his coming out of the palace and

increasing his forces, they made head and assailed the Piazza. Upon their arrival those families of the people who had declared for the Duke, seeing themselves boldly attacked, changed their resolve as the Duke's fortune had changed, and all joined the citizens, excepting Messer Uguccione Buondelmonte, who went into the palace, and Messer Gianozzo Cavalcanti, who retreated with a portion of his companions to the New Market; there he mounted upon a bench and entreated the people who were going armed to the Piazza to go there in support of the Duke. And for the purpose of alarming them he magnified the forces of the Duke, and threatened the people that they would all be killed if they persisted obstinately in their attempt against their lord. Finding not a man to follow him, nor any one to chastise him for his insolence, and seeing that he was exerting himself in vain, he resolved to tempt fortune no more and retired to his own house. Meantime the fight between the people and the Duke's forces was hotly contested, and although the Duke aided them from the palace yet his men were beaten; a part of them surrendered to the people, and a part, abandoning their horses, took refuge in the palace. Whilst the fighting was going on in the Piazza, Corso and Messer Amerigo Donati with a portion of the people broke open the prison of the Stinche, burned the papers of the Podesta and of the chancelry, sacked the houses of the Rectors, and killed all the officers of the Duke they could get hold of. The Duke, on the other hand, seeing that he had lost the Piazza and that the whole city was against him, and himself without help of any kind, made an attempt to win the people over to his side by some act of signal humanity; and having the prisoners brought before him, he liberated them with kind and condescending words, and made Antonio Adimari a noble against his own wishes. He removed his own standards from the palace, and had them replaced by the gonfalons of the people. But all these things being done too late and out of season, being evidently done unwillingly and by constraint, proved of no advantage to him. He remained therefore, ill content, besieged in the palace, and saw how from having attempted to grasp too much he had lost all; and began to fear that in a few days he would have to die either from hunger or the sword. The citizens went to Santa Reparata to reorganize the government, and chose fourteen citizens, half nobles and half of the people, who together with the Bishop should be invested with full powers to remodel the government of Florence. They also elected six others who should exercise the powers of the Podesta until one could be chosen for that post.

A good many strangers had come to Florence to aid the people in their struggle, amongst others some citizens of Pisa together with six ambassadors, men who were held in high honor in their own city. These attempted to negotiate an arrangement between the Duke and the people; but the people refused any agreement unless Messer Guglielmo d' Ascesi and his son, together with Messer Cerettieri Bisdomini should first be delivered into their hands. The Duke would not consent to this, yet, on being threatened by the people who were shut up with him in the palace, he allowed himself to be forced to it. Certainly the resentments seem fiercer and the wounds more deadly when a people struggle to recover their liberty than when they defend it. Messer Guglielmo and his son were given up to the thousands of their enemies, although the son was not yet eighteen years of age. But neither his tender years nor graceful form, nor his innocence, could save him from the fury of the multitude; and those who could not wound him whilst alive, did so after his death. Nor did it satisfy them to hack him with their swords, but they tore him with their hands and teeth. And so that all senses should be satisfied by revenge, having first heard his lamentations, and seen his wounds, and touched his torn and palpitating flesh, they wanted also to have their palates taste it; so that after having satisfied all their outer senses, they might also glut those within. The more these unhappy victims were subjected to this rabid frenzy, the better was it for Messer Cerettieri; for the multitude, tired by their cruelty upon the two Ascesi, did not think of Messer Cerettieri, who, not being otherwise demanded, remained in the palace, whence he was taken and carried away during the night by some of his friends and relatives. When the multitude had assuaged their fury upon the blood of the two Ascesi, an agreement was concluded by which the Duke was to renounce all the claims he had upon Florence, and be allowed to depart in safety with all his people and his goods; and according to which he was to ratify this renunciation at Casentino, outside of the Florentine dominions. After signing the agreement the Duke departed from Florence accompanied by many citizens; and on arriving at Casentino he ratified his renunciation, though most reluctantly; nor would he have kept his faith had he not been threatened by the Count Simone to carry him back to Florence. The Duke, as is proved by his conduct, was cruel and avaricious, difficult of access, and haughty in his demeanor. He wanted the servility of the people, and not their good will; and for that reason he desired more to be feared than to be loved. Nor was his appearance less odious than his conduct; for he was of low stature and swarthy, with a long and coarse beard. He was equally hated by all parties, so that within a period of ten months he lost by his own bad conduct that sovereignty which the evil counsels of others had bestowed on him.

38. These events in the city of Florence encouraged all the other places that were subject to the Florentines also to assert their liberties; so that Arezzo, Castiglione, Pistoja, Volterra, Colle, and San Gimignano revolted. Thus Florence at one blow got rid of her tyrant and lost her dominions; and in recovering her own liberty she taught her subject cities how they could recover their own. After the expulsion of the Duke and the loss of the subject cities, the fourteen citizens and the Bishop thought it better to placate their subjects by peace than to make them enemies by war, and to prove to them that they were willing that they should enjoy their liberties the same as the Florentines did their own. They therefore sent ambassadors to Arezzo to renounce the sovereignty which they held over that city, and to conclude a treaty with her citizens to the effect that, since they could not hold them as subjects, they would value them as allies. With the other places they also agreed as best they could to keep them as friends, so that they might aid them in maintaining the independence of Florence. This course, so wisely taken, had the happiest results; for a few years after Arezzo returned voluntarily under the government of Florence; and the other places also came back within a few months to their former obedience. And thus the things we desire are often obtained with more ease and less danger by seemingly renouncing them, than by pursuing them with the greatest energy and perseverance.

39. Having settled outside matters the Florentines now turned their attention to those within the city; and after some disputes

between the nobles and the people, it was agreed to concede to the nobles one third of the Signoria, and one half of the other public offices. The city, as stated above, was divided into sixths, whence there were always six Signori, that is one for each sixth; except that on several special occasions twelve or thirteen Signori were created; though the number was soon after again reduced to six. Still some reform seemed necessary in this respect; whether it was that the sixths were badly distributed, or whether it was that they wished to give a greater part to the nobles, it was deemed advisable to increase the number of the Signori. The city was therefore divided into fourths, and for each fourth they created three Signori. They left the Gonfalonier of Justice and those of the companies of the people; and in place of the twelve Buonomini they created eight Counsellors, four nobles and four citizens. Having established the government with this organization, the city would have been quiet, if the nobles had been content to live with that degree of modesty which is suitable for a republic. But their conduct was just the reverse; for in private life they wanted no equals, and in the magistracies they wanted to be masters, and every day gave birth to some fresh display of their insolence and pride. This displeased the people, who complained that in place of one tyrant, whom they had crushed, a thousand others had sprung up. The insolence on the one hand, and the dissatisfaction on the other, increased to that degree that the chiefs of the people complained to the Bishop of the shameless conduct of the nobles, and of the bad fellowship which they manifested towards them, and persuaded him to bring it about that the nobles should content themselves with having a share of only the other offices, and leave the magistracy of the Signoria exclusively to the people. The Bishop was naturally good, but easily swayed first in one direction and then in another. It was this weakness which had caused him, at the instance of his associates, first to give his support to the Duke of Athens, and afterwards to conspire against him by the advice of some of the citizens. In the reorganization of the state he had favored the nobles, and now he seemed to favor the people; and for that reason the chiefs of the people addressed themselves to him with their request. Believing that he would find in others as little stability of purpose as he himself possessed, he hoped to carry the matter through by agreement, and convoked the Fourteen, who still held their authority; and with the best words he knew how to employ, he advised them to consent to yield the office of the Signoria wholly to the people, promising them that in that case the city should remain quiet, but otherwise they might expect disorder and their own destruction. These words greatly excited the nobles, and Messer Ridolfo dei Bardi replied sharply, calling the Bishop a man of little faith, and reproving his friendship for the Duke as inconsiderate, and the Duke's expulsion as treason; and concluded by telling him that they would defend at all hazards the honors they had acquired at their own peril. And having departed with the others indignant at the Bishop, they communicated the matter to their associates and all the noble families. The representatives of the people also made their views known to the people. And as the nobles organized themselves with such aid as they could get for the defence of their Signori, the people thought best not to wait until the nobles should be prepared, but rushed armed to the palace, crying that they wanted the nobles to resign from the magistracy. The noise and tumult were great. The Signori saw themselves abandoned; for the nobles, seeing the people armed, dared not take to arms themselves, and all remained in their houses. The Signori of the people, having first endeavored to quiet the people by assuring them that their associates were good and modest men, and having failed in that, as the least objectionable course, sent the Signori of the nobles home to their houses, whither they were safely conducted with much difficulty. The nobles having thus left the palace, the four Counsellors were also deprived of their offices, and instead of them twelve of the people were appointed; and to the eight Signori that remained they gave one Gonfalonier of Justice and sixteen Gonfaloniers of the companies of the people, and they reorganized the councils so that the whole government depended upon the will of the people.

40. At the time when these events occurred there was a great scarcity in the city, so that the nobles as well as the small people were both ill content; the latter from hunger, and the former from having lost their offices and dignities. This encouraged Messer Andrea Strozzi to think that he might make himself master of the liberties of the city. He therefore sold his grain at a less price than others, in consequence of which

many people used to collect at his palace. Thereupon he ventured one morning to mount his horse, and with a few followers to call the people to arms. In a few hours he gathered more than four thousand men, with whom he proceeded to the palace of the Signoria, and demanded to have the palace opened to them. But the Signori drove them from the Piazza by threats and force of arms, and afterwards frightened them so much with the ban, that little by little they all returned to their homes; so that Messer Andrea, finding himself left alone, could only save himself with difficulty from the hands of the magistrates. This attempt, though reckless, and ending as such attempts are apt to do, yet gave hopes to the nobles that they might still compel the people to terms, seeing that the lower class was in discord with the better classes. And so as not to lose this opportunity they resolved to arm and recover by force that which by force had been taken from them. And their confidence of success increased to that point that they provided themselves openly with arms, fortified their houses, and sent to their friends and into Lombardy for assistance. The people and the Signori, on the other hand, provided themselves with arms, and called upon the people of Sienna and Perugia for assistance. Help for both parties had already appeared, and the whole city was in arms. The nobles made head in three places on this side of the Arno; at the houses of the Cavicciulli near San Giovanni, at the houses of the Pazzi and the Donati at San Pier Maggiore, and at those of the Cavalcanti in the New Market. Those on the other side of the Arno had fortified themselves at the bridges and in the streets near their houses; the Nerli at the Ponte alla Carraja, the Frescobaldi at the Santa Trinita, and the Rossi and Bardi defended the Ponte Vecchio and that of the Rubaconte. The people, on the other hand, gathered under the Gonfalonier of Justice and under the banners of the companies of the people.

41. Matters being thus, the people thought best not to defer the contest. The first that moved were the Medici and the Rondinelli, who attacked the Cavicciulli from the street that leads towards their houses by the Piazza di San Giovanni. Here the fighting was severe, for the people were struck by stones thrown from the towers, and wounded by crossbows from below. The battle here had lasted three hours, and the number of the people steadily increased; so that the Cavicciulli, seeing

themselves overpowered by the multitude and receiving no assistance, became frightened and surrendered to the people, who spared their houses and goods, only taking from them their arms, and ordering them to distribute themselves and their relations and friends amongst the houses of the people. The first attack having been victorious, the Donati and the Pazzi were also easily overcome, being less powerful than the others. There only remained on this side of the Arno the Cavalcanti, who were strong in numbers and in position; but on seeing all the banners coming against themselves, whilst only three had sufficed to overcome the others, they surrendered without making much resistance. Three parts of the city were already in the hands of the people, and only one remained in possession of the nobles; but this was the most difficult, both on account of the strength of its defenders as well as from its position, being protected by the river Arno, so that it was necessary to take the bridges, which were guarded in the manner above stated. The Ponte Vecchio was therefore the first to be attacked. This was gallantly defended, for the towers were armed, the streets barricaded, and the barricades were held by the most desperate men, so that the people were repulsed with great loss. Finding their exertions here to be in vain, they tried to pass the Rubaconte bridge, and meeting there the same desperate resistance, they left four companies to guard these two bridges, and all the others went to assail the Ponte alla Carraja. And although the Neri defended it most manfully, yet they could not resist the furious onslaught of the people, partly because this bridge was less strong, not having any towers for defence, and partly because the Capponi and other families of the people also assailed them. Being thus attacked on all sides, they abandoned the barricades, and gave way to the people, who after this also overcame the Rossi and the Frescobaldi, for all the people on the other side of the Arno joined the victors. There were therefore only the Bardi left, who were neither daunted by the defeat of the others, nor by the union of all the people against them, nor by the hopelessness of all succor; preferring rather to die fighting and to see their houses sacked and burnt, than to yield voluntarily to the power of their enemies. They defended themselves therefore so well that the people were unsuccessful in their several attempts to drive them either from the Ponte Vecchio or the Ponte dal Rubaconte, being each time repulsed, with the loss of many killed and wounded. In olden times there had been a road made by which one could pass from the Via Romana, between the houses of the Pitti, to the walls above the hill of San Giorgio. The people sent six companies by this road, with orders to attack the houses of the Bardi from the rear. This caused the Bardi to lose courage, and insured the victory to the people; for when those who guarded the barricades became aware that their houses were being attacked, they abandoned the fight, and ran to protect their homes. This enabled the people to take the barricade of the Ponte Vecchio, whilst the Bardi, who were everywhere put to flight, were sheltered by the Quaratesi, Panzanesi, and the Mozzi. The people thereupon, — that is, the lowest and most ignoble of them, — thirsting for booty, plundered and sacked all their houses, pulled down their palaces and towers, and burnt them with such fury that everybody, even the most cruel enemy of the Florentine name, would have been ashamed at such wanton destruction.

42. The nobles being vanquished, the people reorganized the government so as to be composed of three classes of the people, — the rich, the middle, and the lower class. It was ordained that the rich should have two Signori, and the middle and lower classes each three, and that the Gonfalonier should alternately be taken from each class. Furthermore, all the old ordinances against the nobles were re-established, and, by way of weakening them still more, many of them were reduced from their rank and mixed with the people. The ruin of the nobles was so great, and so overwhelmed their party, that they never again ventured to take up arms against the people, and thus they became continually more humble and abject; and thus Florence deprived herself not only of all military valor, but also of all sentiment of generosity. After this destruction of the nobles, Florence enjoyed tranquillity until the year 1353; in the course of which period occurred that memorable pestilence, described by Messer Giovanni Boccaccio with so much eloquence, and by which Florence lost ninety-six thousand inhabitants (1348). The Florentines also made war for the first time against the Visconti, in consequence of the ambition of the Archbishop, then Prince of Milan. So soon as this war was terminated, the factions within the city revived; and, although the nobility was destroyed, yet fortune soon found new ways of causing fresh troubles to arise from fresh dissensions.

THIRD BOOK.

SUMMARY.

1. Reflections upon the domestic discords of the republic. Parallel between the discords of Rome and those of Florence. — 2. Enmity between the two families of the Albizzi and Ricci. — 3. Origin of the system of *admonishing;* scandals resulting from it (1357). — 4. Checks put upon the captains of the Guelf party. — 5. Many citizens, moved by the disorders of the city, meet in San Pietro Scheraggio, and from there go to the Signori to urge them to provide for the peace of the city. The Signori commit the welfare of the republic to fifty-six citizens, who, by showing more favor to the Guelf faction than to the other, leave the field to be overrun by the evil weeds of discord with increased exuberance. — 7. War of the Florentines against the Legate of Pope Gregory IX., who attacks them at a time of scarcity, hoping to subdue them (1375). League of the Florentines against the Pope with Messer Bernabo and all the cities that were hostile to the Church. — 8. Florence divides into two factions, the captains of the Guelf party against the Eight of the War (1378). — 9. Salvestro de' Medici is made Gonfaloniere. His laws against the captains of the parties, and in favor of the *Admonished* (1378). The colleges disapprove of them. — 10. Afterwards, constrained by popular tumults, they approve them. — 11. The magistrates and the Gonfaloniere Guicciardini strive in vain to allay these tumults. — 12. Origin of the corporations of the trades. — 13. The wool trade or *guild*, being the most powerful amongst the trades, invites the people to fresh disturbances; more ruin, burning, and sacking of houses. — 14. The people demand that the Signoria shall leave the palace. — 15. They constrain them by force to come out of it. — 16. Michele di Lando, wool-carder, is made Gonfaloniere by the clamor of the people. He abolishes the Syndics of the Guilds, the Signoria, and the Colleges; also the Eight of the War. The people, thinking that Michele is too favorable to the rich, rise against him, but he encounters and compels them to submission. Disposition of Lando. — 18. Fresh regulations for the election of Signori, by which the common people are deprived of any share in the Signoria, but the minor trades or guilds are left more powerful than the noble citizens, whence after a short time the city is again thrown into confusion. — 19. Piero degli Albizzi and other citizens, suspected of holding secret relations with Charles of Durazzo, pretender to the kingdom of Naples, and with the Florentine exiles, are taken and condemned to death (1379). — 20. Insolence of Giorgio Scali and of Tommaso Strozzi

against the authority of the magistrates. Scali is decapitated and Strozzi obliged to fly (1331). — 21. Reform of the magistracy unfavorable to the people (1332). — 22. Michele di Lando and other chiefs of the people are imprisoned. The Florentines purchase Arezzo (1384). — 23. Benedetto degli Alberti becomes suspect to the Signoria by his magnificence and popularity; he is confined, and his family admonished. — 24. Many other citizens are admonished and confined. — 25. War of the Florentines with Gio. Galeazzo Visconti, Duke of Milan, called Conte di Virtu (1390). The people, irritated by the violence of Maso degli Albizzi, intrust themselves to Messer Veri de' Medici, who refuses to make himself Prince of the city, and appeases the people (1393). — 26. The Signoria attempt by violent means to prevent insurrections, and Donato Acciaiuoli, who opposes them, is confined. — 27. The banished attempt to return to Florence; they enter by stealth and excite a riot in the city; but are taken in the Santa Reparata and put to death (1397). — 28. Supported by the Duke of Milan they conspire anew, but without success (1400). — 29. The Florentines take Pisa (1406). They make war against Ladislas, king of Naples, and having defeated him they take Cortona (1414). State of Florence at this time.

1. THE causes of nearly all the evils that afflict republics are to be found in the great and natural enmities that exist between the people and the nobles, and which result from the disposition of the one to command, and the indisposition of the other to obey. It is this diversity of disposition that supplies nourishment to all the troubles that disturb these states. This was the cause of the divisions in Rome, and it is this that kept Florence divided, if I may compare small things with great ones, although different effects were produced by it in these two republics; for the dissensions that arose in the beginning in Rome were marked by disputes, those of Florence by combats. Those of Rome were terminated by a law, those of Florence by the death and exile of many citizens. Those of Rome ever increased military valor, whilst those of Florence destroyed it entirely. Those of Rome led from an equality of citizens to the greatest inequality, and those of Florence from inequality to the most wonderful equality. This diversity of effects must have been caused by the different character of the aims which these two peoples had in view. For the people of Rome desired to enjoy the highest honors of the state equally with the nobles; the people of Florence fought for the exclusive control of the government, without any participation in it by the nobles. And as the object of the Roman people was more reasonable, so the nobles bore the wrongs inflicted upon them more readily, and yielded without coming to arms. And, after some disputes, they agreed to

a law that should satisfy the people, and yet leave the nobles in possession of their dignities. On the other hand, the demands of the Florentine people were injurious and unjust, and therefore did the nobility prepare itself for defence with greater energy; and thus the people resorted to bloodshed and exile. And the laws which were afterwards made were not for the common benefit, but were wholly in favor of the victor. From this resulted also that the victories of the people over the nobles made Rome more virtuous, because the plebeians, in sharing with the nobles the civil, military, and judicial administration, became inspired with the same virtues that distinguished the nobles; so that Rome grew at the same time in power and in virtue. But in Florence, when the people were victors, the nobles, excluded from the magistracies, found it necessary not only to be, but also to appear, similar to the people, in their conduct, in their opinions, and in their habits of life. Thence arose the changes in their armorial bearings, and the mutations in the titles of families, to which the nobles resorted for the sake of appearing to belong to the people. So that the valor in arms and magnanimity of spirit which had existed amongst the nobles became extinguished, and could not be kindled amongst the people, who had never possessed it. Florence thus became steadily more debased and abject; and whilst Rome, whose valor had degenerated into pride, was reduced to that condition that she could not maintain herself without a prince, Florence came to that condition that any wise legislator might easily have remodelled her government in any form he pleased. All these things may in part be clearly known by the reading of the preceding Book. And having shown the origin of Florence, the commencement of her liberty, and the causes of her dissensions, and how the party struggles between the nobles and the people ended in the tyranny of the Duke of Athens and the ruin of the nobility, it remains for us now to narrate the enmities between the citizens and the common people, and the various incidents which these produced.

2. The power of the nobles being broken, and the war with the Archbishop of Milan terminated (1353), there seemingly remained no cause for trouble in Florence. But the evil fortune of our city, and its imperfect organization, caused difficulties to arise between the families of the Albizzi and the Ricci, which divided Florence the same as the feud between the Buon-

delmonti and the Uberti had done, and afterwards that of the Donati and the Cerchi. The Popes, who resided at that time in France, and the Emperors, who were in Germany, for the purpose of preserving their influence in Italy, had sent there, at different times, a large number of soldiers of various nationalities; so that there were at this time English, German, and Breton troops there. When the wars were over, these remained without any pay, and levied contributions, under some chance flag, from this or the other prince. Thus there came, in the year 1353, one of these companies, under the captaincy of Monseigneur Reale, a Provençal, into Tuscany. His arrival alarmed all the cities of that province, and the Florentines not only levied troops for the defence of the city, but many private citizens — amongst others, the Albizzi and the Ricci — armed themselves for their own safety. An old feud had divided these two families, and each strove to oppress the other, with the view to gaining the control of the government of the republic. They had, however, not yet come to arms, but opposed each other on every occasion in the magistracies and councils. Whilst the whole city was armed, a quarrel occurred in the old market, and at once a great many people flocked together there, as is usual under such circumstances. As the tumult spread, a report came to the Ricci that the Albizzi were about to attack them, and, in like manner, to the Albizzi that the Ricci were coming to assail them. This roused the whole city; and the magistrates had great difficulty in restraining the two families, and to prevent a conflict, which accidentally and without the fault of either had been reported. This incident, though slight, yet inflamed the hostile spirit of both still more; and each strove with greater diligence than ever to secure partisans for themselves. As the ruin of the nobles had established such equality amongst the citizens that the magistrates were more respected than they had ever been before, they attempted by ordinary legal means, and without any private violence, to turn this occurrence to their own advantage.

3. We have narrated before how, after the victory of Charles, the magistracy was appointed from the party of the Guelfs, and that great authority was given them over the Ghibellines. But time, various events, and the new dissensions, had caused these regulations to fall into oblivion, so that many descendants of the Ghibellines filled the offices of some of the highest magis-

tratures. Uguccione de' Ricci, chief of that family, managed therefore to have the law against the Ghibellines revived, as it was generally believed that the Albizzi were descendants of that party, they having come, many years since, from their native town, Arezzo, to inhabit Florence (1354). Uguccione expected that, by the revival of these laws, the Albizzi would be deprived of the magistracies, as the old law provided that any descendant of a Ghibelline should be condemned if found exercising the functions of a magistrate. This design of Uguccione was made known to Piero di Filippo degli Albizzi, who resolved to favor it, fearing that, if he opposed it, he would thereby declare himself a Ghibelline. This law, therefore, renewed by the ambition of Uguccione de' Ricci, did not deprive Piero of his influence, but rather increased it, and was the beginning of many calamities; for no laws can be made more prejudicial to a republic than such as are very far retrospective in their action. Piero then, having supported the law which had been contrived by his enemies to serve as an obstacle to him, found in it the very road to greatness for himself; for, by placing himself at the head of this new organization, his authority and influence steadily increased, being more favored than any one else by this new faction of the Guelfs (1357). And, as there were no magistrates to investigate who were Ghibellines, and the law which had been revived being therefore of little value, it was provided that authority should be given to the captains to denounce the Ghibellines; and being so denounced, to signify to them and to admonish them that they must accept no magistracy; and that whoever failed to heed this admonition should be condemned. This gave rise subsequently to the custom in Florence of designating all such as had been deprived of the right to sit in the magistracies as *Admonished*. The captains, whose audacity increased with time, " admonished " without regard, not only such as deserved it, but all such as suited them, according to the promptings of avarice or ambition. Thus, from the year 1357, when this practice began, until the year 1366, more than two hundred citizens were admonished. Thus the captains and the faction of the Guelfs became very powerful; for every one, from fear of being admonished, did honor to them, and especially to the chiefs of the faction, who were Piero degli Albizzi, Messer Lapo Castiglionchio, and Carlo Strozzi. And, although the insolence of their proceedings gave offence to many, yet the Ricci were more dissatisfied by it than any others, for they felt that they themselves had been the cause of this abuse, by which they saw the republic ruined, and their enemies, the Albizzi, greatly increased in power, contrary to their design.

4. Uguccione de' Ricci, therefore, finding himself a member of the Signoria (1366), and wishing to put an end to this evil, of which himself and his family had been the originators, caused a new law to be enacted, that to the six captains of the quarters three more should be added, two of whom should be from the minor guilds, and that the denunciation of Ghibellines should have to be confirmed by twenty-four Guelf citizens, appointed for the purpose. This checked for a time the power of the captains in a measure, so that the admonishing ceased in great part; and, although some were yet admonished, still they were but few. The factions of the Albizzi and Ricci, however, continued to watch each other, and opposed all laws, enterprises, and resolves from mutual hatred and jealousy. Thus things went on with these dissensions from 1366 until 1371, when the Guelf faction recovered power. Amongst the family of the Buondelmonti there was a cavalier named Benchi, who, by his merits in a war against the Pisans, had been made a citizen, and in consequence had become qualified to be made one of the Signoria. But when he expected to take his seat in that magistracy, they made a new law, by which any noble who had been made a citizen was prohibited from exercising that function. This greatly irritated Messer Benchi, and, having allied himself with Piero degli Albizzi, they resolved by admonitions to reduce the power of the smaller citizens, and to make themselves sole masters of the government. And by the credit Messer Benchi had with the old nobility, and by that of Messer Piero with the majority of the more influential citizens, they succeeded in depriving the Guelf party of power again; and, by new reforms, they arranged matters so that they could dispose of the captains and of the twenty-four citizens. Thereupon the practice of admonishing was resumed with even more audacity than before, and the house of the Albizzi, as chiefs of the Guelfs, steadily increased in power. The Ricci, on the other hand, together with their friends, did all in their power to check that proceeding, and thus the two parties lived in the greatest mutual suspicion, each fearing every kind of wrong and violence from the other.

5. In consequence of this a number of citizens, influenced by their love of country, assembled in San Pietro Scheraggio (1372), and, having conferred amongst themselves in relation to these disorders, they went to the Signori, to whom the one who enjoyed most consideration addressed the following words: —

"Many of us, O magnificent Signori, doubted the propriety "of assembling privately, although it was for public reasons, "fearing lest we might be regarded as presumptuous or con- "demned as ambitious. But seeing that many citizens assem- "ble daily in the Loggie and in their houses, without any "consideration, not for any purposes of general interest, but "merely to serve their private ambition, we have thought that, "inasmuch as these do not hesitate to meet for the destruction "of the republic, we need have no apprehension in assembling "for the public good and advantage. Nor do we care about "the judgment which the others may form of us, for we know "that they are indifferent as to our opinion of them. The "same love of country, O Signori, which caused us to assemble "in the first instance, now induces us to appear before you, to "discuss the evils which already are so great, and which are "daily increasing in our republic, and to proffer to you our "aid in destroying them. Although the task may seem diffi- "cult, yet you will succeed in accomplishing it whenever you "choose to disregard all private considerations, and employ "your authority supported by the public force. The general "corruption of the other Italian cities, O magnificent Signori, "has spread to Florence and infects our city daily more and "more. For ever since Italy has ceased to be subject to the "Imperial authority, her cities, being without any powerful "check to control them, have organized their states and gov- "ernments, not according to the principles of liberty, but ac- "cording to the spirit of the factions that divided them. From "this have sprung all the disorders and misfortunes that have "afflicted this province. There is neither union nor friendship "amongst the citizens, unless it be amongst such as are bound "together by some villanous crime, committed either against "the state or some private individual. And as all religion "and the fear of God is dead in all their hearts, they value an "oath or a pledge only so far as it may be useful to them- "selves. Men employ them, not for the purpose of observing

"them, but solely as means to enable them more easily to
"deceive; and just as this deceit succeeds more easily and
"securely, so much greater is the praise and glory derived
"from it; and therefore are dangerous men praised as being
"ingenious, and good men derided for being dupes. And thus
"do we see in fact all who can be corrupted, and all who can
"corrupt others, gather together in the cities of Italy. The
"young men are idle, and the old men lascivious, and every
"age and sex give themselves up to unbridled habits; and
"good laws are no remedy for this, being made useless by evil
"usages. Thence comes that avarice which we see so common
"amongst the citizens, and that craving, not for true glory, but
"for those false honors from which flow hatreds, enmities,
"dissensions, and factions, which, in turn, produce murders,
"exiles, and the afflictions of the good and the elevation of
"the wicked. For the good, confiding in their innocence, do
"not, like the wicked, seek extraordinary means for their de-
"fence, and to obtain honors; and thus are they ruined unde-
"fended and unhonored. From this example spring the love
"of factions and their power; for the wicked adhere to them
"from avarice and ambition, and the good from necessity.
"And what is most pernicious is to see the promoters and
"chiefs of these factions cloak their aims and designs with
"honest pretexts; for on pretence of defending Liberty, either
"against the nobles or the people, they only seek to destroy
"her, for they all hate the very word Liberty. The reward
"which they desire to obtain by their victory is not the glory
"of having liberated the city, but the satisfaction of having
"overcome the others, and of having usurped the public au-
"thority. And having achieved that, there is nothing so unjust,
"cruel, or avaricious but they will dare do it. Hence the laws
"and ordinances are not made for the public, but for private
"benefit; and hence wars and peace are resolved upon, not for
"the common glory, but for the satisfaction of a few. And
"if the other cities are full of such disorders, ours is more
"tainted by them than any of them; for here the laws and
"civil ordinances are always made, not according to the prin-
"ciples of liberty, but according to the ambition of that party
"which for the time has the ascendency. Hence it comes that,
"so soon as one party is expelled and one division extinguished,
"another one springs up in its place; for in a city which pre-

"fers to maintain itself by factions rather than by laws, if one
"faction remains without opposition, it must of necessity divide
"against itself; for the very private measures which it had
"previously originated for its own promotion will now prove
"insufficient for its defence. And the truth of this is demon-
"strated by the former and the present divisions of our city.
"Every one believed that, when the Ghibellines were crushed,
"the Guelfs would for a long time after live happy and hon-
"ored. But in a little while they divided into Bianchi and Neri;
"and since the Bianchi have been put down, our city has never
"been without factions that were always fighting, now for the
"sake of the banished, and then again on account of the jeal-
"ousies between the people and the nobles. And by way of
"giving to others that which by agreement amongst ourselves
"we could not or would not possess, we surrendered our liber-
"ties first to King Robert, then to his brother, afterwards to
"his son, and finally to the Duke of Athens. And with all
"this we did not remain content in any condition, like men
"who are unable to agree to live in freedom, nor content to
"exist in servitude. Nor did we hesitate, (so much do our
"institutions favor dissensions,) whilst still under the govern-
"ment of a king, to prefer a low-born man of Agobbio to his
"majesty. For the honor of our city we must not recall the
"memory of the Duke of Athens, for his harsh and tyrannical
"spirit ought to have made us wise, and should have taught
"us how to live. And yet, no sooner was he driven out, than,
"being still armed, we fought amongst ourselves with more
"bitterness of hatred and fury than we ever displayed when
"combating him together; so that our old nobility remained
"vanquished and subject to the will of the people. Nor would
"it ever have been believed that after that any further cause
"for dissensions or disturbance would have arisen in Florence;
"for an effectual check had been put to those who by their
"pride and insupportable ambition seemed to have been the
"cause of all preceding troubles. But experience shows us
"now how fallacious men's opinions are, and how erroneous
"their judgment; for the pride and ambition of the nobles is
"not extinguished, but has only been taken from them to be
"assumed by our citizens, who now, according to the fashion
"of ambitious men, strive themselves to obtain the first rank
"in our republic. And having no other means of attaining it,

"they have anew divided the city, and have revived the names
"of Guelfs and Ghibellines, which had been extinguished,
"and which it would have been well never to have resus-
"citated. As there is nothing permanent and stable in hu-
"man affairs, so Heaven has ordained that in all republics
"there are some fatal families who seem born to cause the
"ruin of the state. Of such our republic has been more pro-
"lific than any other, for it is not only one, but many, who
"have afflicted her. At first it was the Buondelmonti and
"the Uberti; afterwards the Donati and the Cerchi; and now,
"O shameful and ridiculous fact! the Ricci and Albizzi per-
"turb and divide the city.

"We have not reminded you of the corrupt habits and of
"these ancient and constant dissensions for the purpose of
"alarming you, but only to recall to your memories the causes
"of the same; and to show you that, if you do not remem-
"ber them, they are at least fresh in our memories. And to
"tell you that these examples should not make you distrust
"your ability to arrest the present evils. For the power of
"those ancient families was so great, and the favors of the
"princes which they enjoyed were so important, that civil
"ordinances and regulations did not suffice to keep them in
"check. But now that the Empire has no forces here, so
"that the Pope has nothing to fear, and that all Italy and
"our republic have attained that degree of independence that
"they can govern themselves, there is no longer any difficulty.
"And our city above all, despite of the old examples to the
"contrary, can maintain itself not only united, but can reform
"its manners and institutions, provided you, O Signori, are
"resolved to have it so. And to this we advise you, moved
"by pity for our country, and not by any private passions.
"Although the corruption of the city is great, yet we implore
"you at once to destroy the evil that afflicts her, the madness
"that consumes her, and the passions that kill her. You must
"not attribute the ancient disorders to the nature of men, but
"rather to the times; and as these are changed, you may hope
"for our city a happier state of things, by establishing a better
"government. Wisdom will triumph over the malignity of
"fortune, by putting a curb upon the ambition of those indi-
"viduals, and by annulling those ordinances that foster fac-
"tions, and by adopting such as are in harmony with liberty

"and civil institutions. And be you content now rather to
"make such laws in the spirit of kindness, which, if delayed,
"men will be necessitated to make by force of arms!"

6. The Signori were moved by this statement of facts, of which they had been already cognizant; also by the authority and advice of the deputation of citizens; and therefore they confided to fifty-six citizens authority to provide for the safety of the state. Certainly it is most true that the majority of men are more capable of preserving an existing good order of things, than of devising a new one themselves. And so it was with these citizens, who thought more of destroying the present factions than of removing the causes of future ones; so that they neither accomplished the one nor the other. For they did not destroy the causes of new factions, and by increasing the power of one of those that existed over the other one, they exposed the republic to increased danger. They, however, excluded all the factions for three years from the magistracies, excepting those that had been created for the Guelf party; of these they gave three places to the members of the Albizzi family, and three to those of the Ricci; amongst these were Piero degli Albizzi and Uguccione de' Ricci. They prohibited all citizens from entering the palace except during the sessions of the magistrates; and provided that every citizen who was personally maltreated or deprived of his goods might bring an accusation before the councils, and call upon the nobles to give testimony in the case, and if the accused was convicted he was to be subjected to fines. This provision diminished the boldness of the Ricci faction, and increased that of the Albizzi; and although the council had both factions equally in view when making this regulation, yet the Ricci suffered by far the most from it. For if the palace of the Signori was closed to Piero Albizzi, yet that of the Guelfs was open to him, and it was there where he enjoyed the most influence and authority. And if at first he and his followers were active in "admonishing," they became still more so after this affront. Other fresh causes aided to increase this evil disposition.

7. The pontifical chair was occupied at this time by Gregory IX. (1375), who, being at Avignon, governed Italy as his predecessor had done, by legates, who by their avarice and pride had afflicted many cities. One of these legates, who at that time was at Bologna, availed of the occasion of the scarcity

which existed that year in Florence, and attempted to make himself master of Tuscany. Not only did he not supply Florence with provisions, but by way of depriving them of future harvests he attacked the Florentines with a large force so soon as spring appeared, hoping to find them unarmed and distressed by want, and therefore he counted upon an easy victory. And perhaps he would have succeeded, if the army with which he attacked them had not proved faithless and venal. For the Florentines, having no other resource, gave to his soldiers one hundred and thirty thousand florins, and thus induced them to abandon the enterprise. Wars are often begun by the will of others, but rarely are they terminated at their pleasure. This war, commenced by the ambition of the legate, was continued by the indignation of the Florentines. They formed an alliance with Messer Bernabo Visconti, and with all the cities that were hostile to the Church, and appointed eight citizens to direct the war, with authority to act without appeal, and to spend without rendering any accounts. Although Uguccione was dead, yet this war against the Pope reanimated the adherents of the Ricci faction, who had always supported Messer Bernabo against the Albizzi, and opposed the Church; and they were the more encouraged as the Eight were all hostile to the Guelf faction. This caused Piero degli Albizzi, Messer Lapo di Castiglionchio, Carlo Strozzi, and the others, to unite more closely against their adversaries. And whilst the Eight carried on the war these "admonished." The war lasted three years, and was terminated only by the death of the Pope; it had been conducted with so much ability, and gave such general satisfaction, that the Eight were continued in office from year to year. They were called "Saints," although they had paid but little regard to the Censure, despoiled the churches of their goods, and forced the clergy to perform the holy offices. Thus did those citizens at that time value their country more than their souls; and demonstrated to the Church, that as much as they had at first, as her friends, defended her, so they could now, as her enemies, injure her; for they caused all the Romagna, the Marca, and Perugia to revolt.

8. Nevertheless, whilst they carried on so vigorous a war against the Pope, they could not defend themselves against the captains of the sections and their factions; for the hatred of the Guelfs against the Eight increased their audacity to that degree,

that they insulted not only some of the most distinguished citizens, but even the Eight themselves. And the arrogance of the captains of the sections rose to that point, that they were actually more feared than the Signori; so that no ambassador came to Florence who had not also some commission to the captains. Pope Gregory being dead now, and Florence having no longer any foreign war on hand, the internal discord and confusion were very great; for whilst on the one hand the audacity of the Guelfs was insupportable, on the other hand there seemed to be no means of abating it. And therefore it was thought that they would of necessity have to come to arms, and thus to decide which of the factions should prevail. The Guelf party comprised all the old nobles and the greater part of the most powerful citizens, of whom, as we have said, Messer Lapo, Piero, and Carlo Strozzi were the heads. The other party was composed of all the lesser citizens, and their chiefs were the committee of Eight on the war, Messer Giorgio Scali and Tommaso Strozzi; and with these were united the Ricci, Alberti, and the Medici. The remainder of the populace, as almost always happens, attached themselves to the party of the malcontents. The chiefs of the Guelfs found the forces of their adversaries very formidable; and felt that they were in great danger whenever an adverse Signoria should be disposed to put them down. Deeming it well, therefore, to forestall this, they met together and examined the condition of the city and their own. They concluded that the large increase in the number of the admonished, which was laid entirely to their charge, had caused the whole city to be hostile to them; which left them no other remedy than, having already deprived the other party of the honors of office, to take the city from them also, by seizing the palace of the Signori and transferring the whole government to their own faction. It was in this way that the old Guelfs had secured to themselves the mastery over the city, by driving out all their adversaries. All agreed to this course, but differed as to the time of its execution. Messer Lapo was of opinion not to defer action, affirming that nothing was so dangerous to success as time itself, and especially so in their case, as in the next Signoria Salvestro de' Medici could easily be made Gonfaloniere, whom they all knew to be opposed to their faction. Piero degli Albizzi, on the other hand, was of opinion that delay was advisable, because he thought they would need troops, and that

these could not be got together without exposing themselves to
a discovery of their designs, which would involve them in manifest danger. He judged it necessary, therefore, that they should
at least await San Giovanni, which was near at hand, as, that
being a solemn festival day in the city, a great multitude would
assemble, amongst whom they could easily conceal as many
troops as they needed. And by way of preventing what was
feared with regard to Salvestro de' Medici, he proposed to have
him admonished; and if they thought that this would not
do, then they should admonish some member of the college of
his quarter; so that when they should come to draw a new
Signoria, the election purses being empty, it might easily chance
that this one or some one of his colleagues might be drawn,
which would disqualify him from becoming Gonfaloniere. They
resolved upon this course, although Messer Lapo consented to
it most unwillingly, judging the delay to be injurious; and that
the time to do a thing is never in all respects convenient,
so that he who waits until everything suits will either never
attempt it, or if he does he will in most cases do it to his disadvantage. However, they admonished the college, but did
not succeed in disqualifying Salvestro; for the object having
been discovered by the Eight, they managed so that a change
of Signori should not take place.

9. Salvestro, son of Messer Alemanno de' Medici, was thereupon drawn as Gonfaloniere. Being descended from a most
distinguished citizen family, he would not tolerate seeing the
people oppressed by a few powerful nobles. Having resolved
to put an end to this insolence, and seeing the people well disposed towards himself, and being supported by many prominent
citizens, he communicated his designs to Benedetto Alberti,
Tommaso Strozzi, and to Messer Giorgio Scali, who promised to
render him whatever aid he required. They therefore secretly
prepared a law which renewed the Ordinances of Justice against
the nobles, and reduced the authority of the captains of the
sections, and afforded to the admonished the means of being
restored to the privilege of holding office. This law had to be
acted upon first in the colleges and afterwards in the councils;
and Salvestro being Gonfaloniere, which gave him almost sovereign power over the city, they attempted at the same time to
make as it were the experiment, and to obtain a result, and induced Salvestro to assemble the colleges and the councils on

the same morning. The law was then proposed to the colleges separately; but being regarded as an innovation, it met with such opposition from a few that it was not adopted. Salvestro, finding himself thwarted at the first step, feigned a necessity of being obliged to go out, and, without the others being aware of it, he went into the councils; and there, mounting upon a high place where he could be seen and heard by every one, he said: "That he believed he had been made Gonfaloniere, not to adjudi-
"cate private matters for which there were the ordinary judges,
"but to guard the welfare of the state, to repress the insolence
"of the nobles, and to temper the rigor of those laws which
"were destroying the republic; and that, having diligently de-
"voted himself to these objects, he had, as far as it was possible
"for him, provided for the same. But the malignity of men op-
"posed his just efforts to that degree that they impeded the way
"for him to effect any good, and for them to resolve upon any-
"thing and even to hear him. Seeing, therefore, that he could
"be of no further use to the state or the public good, he did
"not know why he should continue to hold an office, which
"either he did not deserve, or which others thought him un-
"worthy of. And therefore he desired to retire to his home,
"so that the people might replace him by some one who had
"more merit or better fortune." Having spoken thus, he withdrew from the council and returned to his house.

10. Those of the council who were cognizant of the matter, and such others as desired the change, sounded the alarm; whereupon the Signori and the colleges came running to them, and, seeing their Gonfaloniere depart, they retained him by entreaties, and by their authority made him return to the council, which was in the greatest confusion, and where many distinguished citizens were menaced in most insulting terms. Amongst these, Carlo Strozzi was seized by the breast by an artisan, who would have killed him but that he was with difficulty protected by those who were near him. But the one who made most noise, and caused the whole city to arm, was Messer Benedetto degli Alberti, who, from the window of the palace, called the people to arms with a loud voice, so that the Piazza was quickly filled with armed men. Thereupon the colleges accorded to menaces what before they had refused to simple requests. The captains of the sections had meantime assembled a great many people in their palace to consult how to de-

fend themselves against the ordinances of the Signori. But when they heard the tumult that had been raised, and understood what the councils had resolved, they all fled to their homes.

Let no one who introduces a change in the government of a city believe that he can stop it at his pleasure, or regulate it in his own way. It was the intention of Salvestro to have this law passed, and then to settle the government of the city; but the thing turned out otherwise, for the discords stirred up by it had alarmed everybody to that degree that the shops were closed, the citizens fortified themselves in their houses, many concealed their valuables in monasteries and churches, and every one seemed to apprehend some impending catastrophe. The guilds of the trades assembled, and each created a syndic. Thereupon the Priors called together their colleges and these syndics, and they conferred a whole day as to the best means of tranquillizing the city to everybody's satisfaction; but as they differed in opinion, they came to no conclusion. On the following day the guilds brought out their banners; and when the Signori heard this, they became alarmed at the consequences, and assembled the council to devise a remedy. Scarcely had they met when a tumult was started, and in a moment the banners of the guilds, with a great many armed followers, were seen in the Piazza. Whereupon the council, for the purpose of giving the guilds and the people the hope of contenting them, and to deprive them of all occasion for violence, invested the Signori, the Colleges, the Eight of the War, the Captains of the Sections, and the Syndics with a general power (called a "Balia" in Florence) to reorganize the government of the city for the common benefit. Whilst these things were being done, some banners of the minor guilds, instigated by those who desired to revenge themselves for the recent injuries received at the hands of the Guelfs, separated themselves from the others, and sacked and burnt the house of Messer Lapo da Castiglionchio. When he had heard that the Signoria were proceeding against the Guelfs, and saw the people in arms, he thought of no other means of safety than flight or concealment. At first he hid himself in Santa Croce, and afterwards he fled, in the disguise of a friar, to Casentino, where he was often heard to blame himself for having joined Piero degli Albizzi, and to blame Piero for having insisted upon delaying until San

Giovanni their attempt to seize the government. Piero and Carlo Strozzi concealed themselves at the first outbreak, believing that, after it should have ceased, their numerous friends and relatives would enable them to remain securely in Florence. After the house of Messer Lapo had been burnt, many others were likewise sacked and burnt, either from the general hatred, or from private enmities; for disorders increase easily after having once been started. The authors of these outrages, by way of having accomplices who were impelled by even a greater thirst for the goods of others, broke open the prisons and liberated the prisoners; and then they sacked the monastery Degli Agnoli and the convent of San Spirito, where a number of citizens had concealed their valuables. Nor would the public treasury have escaped from the hands of these miscreants had it not been for the respect with which they were inspired by one of the Signori, who, mounted on horseback and followed by a number of armed men, resisted the fury of the multitude. This popular fury was in a measure appeased by the authority of the Signori and by the coming on of night. On the following morning the Balia pardoned the "admonished," with the condition, however, that they should remain disqualified from holding office for a period of three years. The laws that had been made by the Guelfs to the prejudice of the citizens were annulled, and Messer Lapo da Castiglionchio and his consorts were declared rebels, as well as such others as had incurred the general hatred. After these acts, the names of the new Signori were published, of whom Luigi Guicciardini was named Gonfaloniere, which inspired the public with the hope that the disturbances would be arrested, as they were universally regarded as men of peace and lovers of public tranquillity.

11. The shops, however, were not reopened, and the citizens did not disarm, and numerous guards patrolled throughout the city all night. The Signori therefore did not assume their office outside of the palace with the customary pomp, but did so indoors, and without any further ceremonies. These magistrates thought that there was nothing more essential for them to do at the outset of their holding office than to pacify the city. They therefore caused the citizens to disarm, the shops to be opened, and sent back from Florence a number of men who had been called from the country by the citizens for their support. They also established guards in many parts of the city; so that,

if the " admonished " had remained quiet, the city would have been at peace. These, however, were not content to wait three years to regain their privileges; so that, to satisfy their desires, the guilds reassembled anew, and demanded of the Signori that, for the good and tranquillity of the city, they should ordain that no citizen should at any time be liable to be " admonished " as a Ghibelline who was either one of the Signori or of the colleges, or any captain of a section, or council of any of the guilds. They demanded, further, that new election purses should be made up in the Guelf party, and that the existing ones should be burnt. These demands were promptly adopted, not only by the Signori, but also by the councils; in consequence of which the disturbances, which had already recommenced, were stopped. But, as men are never satisfied with merely recovering their own, but wish also to have that which belongs to others and to satisfy their revenge, so those who hoped to profit by disorders pointed out to the artisans that they would never be secure unless a number of their enemies were expelled and crushed. When this became known to the Signori, they caused the officers of the guilds to appear before them with their syndics, whom Luigi Guicciardini addressed as follows: —

" Were it not that these Signori and myself have known
" for a long while back that it is the fate of this city to be
" torn by internal dissensions the moment that foreign wars
" are ended, we should have been more surprised at the dis-
" turbances that have taken place, and should have looked
" upon them with greater displeasure. But as the evils to
" which one is accustomed produce less pain, we have borne
" the past disturbances patiently, they having been originated
" wholly without any fault of ours; and in the hope that, like
" former troubles, they would soon come to an end, we have
" conceded your many and important demands. But foreseeing
" that, so far from being satisfied, you are disposed rather to
" inflict fresh injuries upon your fellow-citizens, and to demand
" fresh proscriptions, our displeasure has increased with evil and
" unjust designs. And truly, if we could have believed that,
" during the time of our magistracy, we should have seen our
" city involved in ruin, either by our opposing you, or by our
" conceding your demands, we should have tried to escape these
" honors, either by flight or exile. But hoping to have to deal
" with men who had some humanity in them, and some love of

"country, we accepted the magistracy cheerfully, hoping with
"our humility and spirit of concession to overcome your ambi-
"tion. But we now see from experience that the more humbly
"we bear ourselves, and the more we concede to you, the more
"arrogant you become, and the more unreasonable and unjust
"your demands. In speaking to you thus, our object is not to
"offend you, but to make you reflect; for we wish to tell you only
"that which will be of advantage to you, leaving to others to tell
"you what may be agreeable. But in good faith tell us what it
"is that in fairness you could still demand of us. You wanted
"to have the power taken from the captains of the sections; it
"was taken from them. You wanted the lists of their election
"purses burnt, and that new ones should be made instead, and
"we conceded it. You wanted that the 'admonished' should
"be restored to their privileges; and that too was permitted.
"At your request we have pardoned those who burnt houses and
"robbed churches; and ever so many prominent and honored citi-
"zens have been sent into exile to satisfy you; and to please you,
"the nobles have been subjected to new restraints. Where is to
"be the end of your exactions, and for how long will you abuse
"our liberality? Do you not see that we bear defeat with more
"patience than you do victory? What will your discords bring
"our city to? Have you forgotten that, when on a former occa-
"sion she was torn by dissensions, a low-born citizen of Lucca,
"Castruccio, defeated her? A Duke of Athens, originally a pri-
"vate Condottiere of yours, subjugated her when she was thus
"divided. But when she was united, an Archbishop of Milan
"and a Pope himself failed to subdue her, and after many years
"of war gained nothing but shame. Why do you now wish by
"your discords to bring this city, which is at peace, to servitude,
"when so many powerful enemies failed to deprive her of her
"liberty? What else but servitude will you achieve by your
"dissensions? What else but poverty will you gain by the rob-
"beries you have committed, or still design to commit? For
"the very property you take sustains the industries that feed our
"city, which without it could not be supported. And the prop-
"erty you have unlawfully taken, like any ill-acquired thing,
"you will neither know how to employ nor how to preserve, and
"indigence and famine will be the consequence for our city.
"The Signori and myself command you, and, if propriety admits,
"we entreat you, that for once you will stay your demands, and

"rest quiet and content with the ordinances we have established.
"And if nevertheless at any time you desire further changes,
"ask for it in a lawful manner, and not by tumults and with
"arms in hand. For if your demands are just, they will always
"be conceded; and thus you will not afford to evil-minded per-
"sons the opportunity, at your charge and to your injury, to
"ruin your country."

These words, so full of truth, made a deep impression upon those citizens. They thanked the Gonfaloniere humbly for having performed his duty to them as a good magistrate, and to the city as a good citizen, promising always promptly to obey whatever commands might be given them. And the Signori, by way of satisfying them, deputed two citizens for each of the greater magistracies, who should confer with the syndics of the guilds about such points as needed reform, and who should then report to the Signori.

12. Whilst this was being arranged another disturbance broke out, which proved much more injurious to the republic than the first. The greater part of the burnings and robberies that had taken place in the previous days had been committed by the lowest people of the city; and those amongst them who had been the most audacious feared that, when the more important differences should be quieted and composed, then they would be punished for their crimes; and that, as it always happens, they would be abandoned by those who had instigated them to these outrages. To this apprehension was added the hatred which the populace felt towards the rich citizens and the chiefs of the guilds, by whom they conceived themselves insufficiently compensated for their labor, according to their own ideas of what they justly merited. For in the time of Charles I., when Florence was first divided into guilds, a chief and a form of government were given to each; and it was provided that the members of each guild should in all civil matters be judged by their chiefs. The number of these guilds, as has already been said, was at first twelve; afterwards they were increased to twenty-one, and their power grew to that extent that they soon controlled the government of the whole city. And as there were amongst them some more or less honorable, they divided themselves into major and minor guilds, seven being called major and fourteen minor. From this division, and from other causes which we have narrated above, sprung

the arrogance of the captains of the sections; for those citizens who of old had been Guelfs, under whose government the office of captain was always held in rotation, favored the citizens of the major guilds, and persecuted those of the minor ones, together with their defenders. Thence it came that so many tumults arose against them, as we have narrated above. In organizing the guilds there were found to be many trades at which the small citizens and the low people worked, and which were not constituted into separate guilds; and as these placed themselves under the different guilds, according to the nature of their trades, it occurred that, when they were either not satisfied with their wages, or were in any way oppressed by their employers, they had no other recourse except the magistrate of that guild to which they had attached themselves, but who they believed had never rendered them the justice to which they felt themselves entitled. And of all the guilds that which always had and still has the greatest number of members is that of the manufacturers of wool; which from being the most powerful was also the first in authority, and has always fed and still feeds with its industry the greater part of the common people and the small citizens.

13. The men of this lower class of the people then, those as well who had placed themselves under the wool guild as those who had joined other guilds, were greatly irritated for the above given reasons. To this came their fears on account of the burnings and robberies committed by them, and therefore they held several meetings at night and discussed the events that had taken place, as well as the danger to which they were exposed. Hereupon some one who was bolder and more experienced than the rest addressed them in the following words:—

"If we had to determine now whether to take up arms and "burn and rob the houses of citizens and plunder churches, "I should be one of those who would deem it dangerous to "think of it; and perhaps I should approve the idea that tran- "quil poverty is preferable to hazardous gain. But inasmuch "as we are in arms and much evil has already been done, it "seems to me that we should not think of laying down the "former, but how to secure ourselves against the consequences "of the evils committed. I certainly believe that, if nothing "else were to compel us to that course, necessity would. You "see the whole city is full of hatred and resentment against us.

"The citizens draw closer together; and the Signoria holds in "all things with the magistrates. Believe me, they are laying "snares for us, and new dangers are menacing our heads. We "should therefore seek two things and have two aims in our "deliberations; the one to prevent our being chastised within "the next few days for the acts we have committed, and the "other to be able in the future to enjoy more liberty and to "live with more satisfaction than hitherto. In my opinion, "therefore, if we wish to be pardoned for our past errors, we "must commit new ones, doubling the evils and multiplying "the burnings and robberies, and in that way strive to have "numerous accomplices. For where the guilty are many, none "will be punished; little faults are chastised, great and grave "ones are rewarded. And when many suffer, few will seek to "revenge themselves, for general injuries are borne with more "patience than individual ones. The multiplying of our crimes, "therefore, will make it easier for us to obtain pardon, and will "open the way to our having those things which we desire. It "seems to me that our success is certain, for those who could "oppose us are rich and divided. Their disunion, therefore, will "give us victory, and their riches, when they shall have become "ours, will enable us to maintain it. Do not be alarmed by "the antiquity of the blood for the shedding of which they "reproach us; for all men, having sprung from the same be-
"ginning, have equally ancient blood, and are by nature all "made alike. Strip yourselves naked, and you will see that "you are the same; dress yourselves in their garments and "them in yours, and doubtless you will appear noble and they "ignoble; for it is only poverty and riches that make men "unequal. It really grieves me that many of you should from "mere conscience repent of your past acts, and be resolved to "abstain from new ones. Certainly, if this be true, then you "are not the men I took you to be; for neither conscience nor "infamy should frighten you; victory never brings shame, no "matter how obtained. Of conscience you should make no "account at all; for where there is, as in your case, the fear of "hunger and prisons, you cannot and should not be restrained "by the fear of hell. And if you note the conduct of men, you "will see that all who achieve great riches and power obtain "them either by force or by fraud; and then they conceal the "abomination of their acquisitions by falsely calling them gain,

"so as to make it appear that they have come by them honestly.
"And those who from too little prudence, or too great stupidity,
"avoid these modes of gain, will always grovel in servitude and
"poverty; for the faithful servants always remain servants,
"and the good men ever remain poor. None ever escape from
"servitude except the unfaithful and the audacious, and none
"from poverty except the fraudulent and the rapacious. For
"God and nature have placed the fortunes of men in their
"midst, where they are more easily got by rapine than by in-
"dustry, and are more accessible to evil practices than to good
"ones. Thence it comes that men devour each other, and the
"weakest always fare the worst. We must then use force
"whenever occasion is given us; and fortune can never offer
"us this to greater advantage than now. The citizens are still
"divided, the Signori full of doubts, and the magistrates are
"frightened; thus we can easily overpower them before they
"become united and take courage. Thus we shall either re-
"main masters of the city, or we shall have such part of the
"government of it that our errors will be pardoned, and we
"shall have the power to threaten them with fresh injuries.
"I confess that this course is audacious and dangerous; but
"where necessity presses, audacity is accounted prudence, and
"in great matters brave men never take note of danger. For
"those enterprises that begin with danger always end with
"reward, and there is no escape from danger except by danger.
"And moreover, I believe that where we see prisons, tortures,
"and death being prepared for us, there is more to be appre-
"hended from our remaining here than from any attempt to
"place ourselves in security; for in the first case the evil is
"certain, and in the other doubtful. How often have I heard
"you complain of the avarice of your employers and of the in-
"justice of your magistrates! Now is the moment, not only to
"rid ourselves of them, but to make ourselves entirely their
"masters, so that they will have more cause to complain of
"you, and fear you more, than you do them. The opportunity
"which present circumstances offers flies, and when it is lost
"you will strive in vain to recover it. You see the prepara-
"tions of your adversaries; let us anticipate their designs, and
"whichever of us resumes arms first will assuredly be the
"victor; his enemies will be destroyed, and he will be advanced.
"From such a course many of us will derive honor, and all of
"us security!"

This address inflamed their already excited spirits still more violently for evil, and they resolved to resume arms after they should have secured more accomplices to act with them; and they bound themselves by an oath mutually to succor and stand by each other whenever any one of them should be oppressed by the magistrates.

14. Whilst these men were preparing to seize the state, the Signori became informed of their designs through one Simone, whom they had arrested on the Piazza, and who revealed to them the whole conspiracy, and that it was intended on the following day to begin the disturbances. Seeing the danger upon them, they at once assembled the colleges, and those citizens who together with the syndics of the guilds were laboring for the re-establishment of union in the city. It was already evening before they had all assembled; they advised the Signori also to call in the consuls of the guilds, who all advised the immediate collecting of all the troops in Florence, and that the Gonfalonieri should appear the next morning with their companies fully armed in the Piazza. At the time when Simone was being put to the torture and the citizens were already assembling in the Piazza, one Niccolo da San Friano was engaged in regulating the clock of the palace; and having noticed what was going on, he returned home and stirred up his whole neighborhood with alarm; so that in an instant more than a thousand armed men collected in the Piazza di San Spirito. The noise of this reached the other conspirators and almost immediately the Piazzas of San Pier Maggiore and San Lorenzo, which had been appointed as meeting-places, became filled with armed men. The next morning, which was the 21st of July, not over eighty men at arms had appeared in the Piazza in support of the Signori, and not one of the Gonfalonieri had come; for, having heard that the whole city was in arms, they were afraid to leave their houses. The first body of the populace that appeared in the Piazza was that which had assembled at San Pier Maggiore; and on their arrival the men at arms made no movement. The other crowd, from San Lorenzo, also came and joined them; and having encountered no opposition, they demanded with terrible shouts that the Signoria should release the prisoners. Seeing that they were not given up at their threats, they determined to resort to violence, and burnt the palace of Luigi Guicciardini;

so that the Signori for fear of worse gave them up the prisoners. No sooner was this done than they took the Gonfalon of Justice from the Executor, and proceeded under that banner to burn the houses of a number of citizens, especially of such as were hated by them from public or private reasons. And many citizens to avenge private wrongs led the crowd to the houses of their enemies; for it merely needed one voice from the multitude to cry out, "To this, *or* To that house!" for him who bore the Gonfalon to turn in that direction. Amongst other things they burnt all the records of the wool guild. Having done much damage, and wishing to accompany their evil acts with some laudable ones, they created Salvestro de' Medici and a number of other citizens Cavaliers, making altogether sixty-four in number. Amongst these were Benedetto and Antonio degli Alberti, Tommaso Strozzi, and others of their friends; although some of them accepted the title with great reluctance. What is most remarkable in these occurrences is the circumstance that, on the same day after having burnt the houses of many persons, the rabble conferred upon the same individuals the title of Cavalier (so near are benefits at times to injuries): this happened to Luigi Guicciardini, the Gonfaloniere of Justice. The Signori, seeing themselves abandoned in the midst of all these tumults by their armed force, by the chiefs of the guilds, and by their Gonfalonieri, were confounded, for no one had come to their support according to the orders given; and out of sixteen gonfalons only two made their appearance, namely, that of the Golden Lion and that of the Squirrel, under the command of Giovenco della Stufa and Giovanni Cambi. And even these remained but a little while in the Piazza; for when they perceived that they were not followed by any of the others, they withdrew again. On the other hand, some of the citizens, seeing the fury of this enraged multitude, and that the palace was abandoned, stayed within their houses; some followed the armed crowd, so that being amongst them they might be the better able to protect their own houses and those of their friends. And thus the force of the rabble was increased, whilst that of the Signori was diminished. The rioting continued all day, and when night came the crowd stopped at the palace of Messer Stefano behind the church of San Barnabas. Their number amounted to over six thousand; and before day appeared they forced the guilds by threats to send them their banners. And when morning came they marched, with the Gonfalon of Justice and the ensigns of the guilds at their head, to the palace of the Podesta; and upon his refusal to give them possession of it, they attacked and seized it by force.

15. The Signori, desirous of giving proof of their willingness to make terms with the rioters, seeing their own inability to control them by force, sent four members of their colleges to proceed to the palace of the Podesta and state their wishes to the rioters. This deputation found that the leaders of the populace, together with the syndics of the guilds and some citizens, had already prepared the demands which they intended to make of the Signori. They therefore returned to the Signoria accompanied by four deputies from the populace, who made the following demands: — That the wool guild should no longer have any foreign judge; — that three new guilds should be created, one for the carders and dyers, another for the barbers, doublet-makers, tailors, and similar crafts, and a third for the smaller trades; and that two of the Signori should be taken from these new guilds, and three from the fourteen minor guilds; — that the Signoria should provide houses for the meetings of these new guilds; — that none of the members of these guilds should be constrained during the next two years to pay any debt of less than fifty ducats; — that the Monte de Pietà (public pawn house) should charge no interest, and receive back only the principal sum loaned; — that those who were confined in prison and condemned should be set free and acquitted; — and that the admonished should be reinstated in all their privileges. They demanded many more things for the benefit of their particular supporters; and, by way of the reverse, they wanted a number of their enemies banished and admonished. These demands, though dishonorable and injurious to the republic, were yet promptly conceded by the Signori, the colleges, and the council of the people, for fear of still worse. But to give full validity to their action it was necessary that it should also be approved by the Council of the Commune. And as both councils could not be called together on the same day, it was agreed to defer the matter until the day following. The guilds and the populace nevertheless seemed satisfied for the moment, and promised that all rioting should cease so soon as these new laws should be perfected.

The following morning, whilst the Council of the Commune were deliberating, the impatient and inconstant multitude came with their customary banners into the Piazza with such loud and frightful shouting that the whole council and the Signori became frightened. Whereupon Guerriante Marignuoli, one of the Signori, moved more by fear than any other personal motive, went down stairs on pretence of guarding the door of the palace below, and fled to his house. Unable to conceal himself as he went out, he was recognized by the crowd, but no harm was done him. When the multitude saw him, however, they called out that all the Signori should leave the palace, and if they did not, that they would kill their children and burn their houses. In the midst of this the law was ratified, and the Signori had gone back to their chambers, and the council having descended below, without going out, remained in the Loggia and in the court, despairing of the safety of the city at seeing so much villany in the multitude, and such indisposition or cowardice in those who could have controlled or put it down. The Signori also were confused and doubtful of the safety of the country, seeing themselves abandoned by their adherents, and unsupported by either counsel or assistance from any citizen. In their uncertainty as to what they could or should do, Messer Tommaso Strozzi and Messer Benedetto Alberti, influenced either by selfish ambition, desiring to remain masters of the palace, or perhaps because they believed it best, persuaded the Signori to yield to the popular clamor, and to return as private individuals to their houses. This advice, given by those who had been the prime cause of the disturbances, caused Alamanno Acciaiuoli and Niccolo del Bene to become indignant, although the other members of the Signoria yielded. And having recovered a little vigor, they said, "that, if others wished to go away, they could not prevent "them; but that they themselves would not before the expi-"ration of their term of office give up their authority, even if it "cost them their lives." This difference of opinion redoubled the fears of the Signori and the fury of the populace; so that the Gonfaloniere, willing rather to end his magistracy with shame than with danger, committed himself to the care of Messer Tommaso Strozzi, who conducted him from the palace to his house. The other Signori in like manner departed one after the other; whereupon Alamanno and Niccolo, seeing themselves left alone, and not wishing to be regarded more brave than wise, went away also. Thus the palace remained in the hands of the mob, and the committee of the Eight on the War, who had not yet laid down their office.

16. When the mob entered the palace, one Michele di Lando, a wool-carder by trade, was carrying the standard of the Gonfaloniere. He took off his shoes, and, not being encumbered with much clothing on his back, leaped upstairs; and on reaching the audience hall of the Signori, he stopped, and turning to the multitude, he said: "You see this palace is yours, and the city "is in your hands. What do you think should be done now?" To which all replied, "that they wanted him to be Gonfaloniere "and Signore, and that he should govern the city and themselves "as seemed to him best." Michele accepted the office; and being a sagacious and prudent man, and more favored by nature than by fortune, he resolved to restore the city to tranquillity, and put a stop to the riots. And by way of keeping the people occupied and giving himself time to arrange his plans, he directed them to go and find a certain Nuto, who had been designated by Messer Lapo da Castiglionchio as Bargello. The greater part of those around him started upon this errand. And by way of beginning with an act of justice the exercise of that authority which he had obtained by favor, he published an order forbidding all further plundering and burning; and for the purpose of inspiring terror, he had a gibbet erected in the Piazza. And, as a beginning of a reform of the government of the city, he annulled the syndics of the guilds, and appointed new ones; deprived the Signori and the colleges of their magistratures, and burnt the election purses containing the names of those to be drawn for offices. Meantime Ser Nuto was brought into the Piazza by the multitude, and hanged by one foot on the gibbet erected there; and the bystanders having each torn a piece from his body, there was in a few minutes nothing left of him but the foot by which he had been suspended. The Eight of the War, on the other hand, believing that by the withdrawal of the Signori they had become the chiefs of the city, had already nominated the new Signori. When this became known to Michele, he sent them word immediately to leave the palace, for he wanted to show to everybody that he knew how to govern Florence without their advice. Thereupon he assembled the syndics of the guilds, and created a Signoria, — four of the

common people, two of the major, and two of the minor guilds. Besides this, he appointed a new election, and divided the government into three parts, one of which was to belong to the new guilds, one to the minor, and the third to the major guilds. He gave to Messer Salvestro de' Medici the income from the shops on the Ponte Vecchio, and took for himself the Podesteria of Empoli, and bestowed other benefits upon numerous other citizens who had favored the people, not so much as rewards for their exertions as for the purpose of protecting himself for all time against their envy.

17. The common people thought that Michele, in his reforms of the state, had been too partial to the greater citizens; and that they themselves had not such part in the government as was necessary for their own protection. Urged on, therefore, by their habitual audacity, they again took to arms, and came tumultuously with their banners into the Piazza, and demanded that the Signoria should come down on to the Ringhiera, for the purpose of deciding upon new measures for their safety and advantage. Michele, seeing their insolence and not wishing to excite their anger, without fully understanding what they wanted, blamed their manner of demanding it, and advised them to lay down their arms, and that then their demands should be considered; to which the Signoria could not yield with dignity under the pressure of force. The crowd, incensed by this against the palace, went to the Santa Maria Novella, where they chose from amongst themselves eight chiefs, with ministers and such other appointments as they thought would insure them authority and public respect. Thus the city had two sets of officers, and was controlled by two different governments. These new chiefs decided amongst themselves that eight members, chosen from the bodies of their guilds, should always reside with the Signoria in the palace, who should confirm all the resolves of the Signoria. They took from Messer Salvestro de' Medici and from Michele di Lando all that they had conceded to them by their former resolutions, and assigned to many amongst themselves offices and subventions wherewith to support their positions with dignity. By way of giving validity to these resolutions, they deputed two of their number to the Signoria to demand that their acts should be confirmed by the councils; suggesting at the same time that, if not conceded by consent, they would have it by force. These deputies laid their commission

before the Signori with great audacity and presumption; they reminded the Gonfaloniere of the rank which they had conferred upon him and of the honor done him, and reproached him for the ingratitude with which he had borne himself towards them. Having closed their address with menaces, Michele could not brook so much insolence; and thinking more of his rank than of the low condition from which he had sprung, it seemed to him that such extraordinary insolence should be checked by extraordinary means, and drew the sword which he had at his side, and, after first inflicting severe wounds upon these deputies, had them bound and imprisoned. When this became known to the crowd, it excited them to fury; and believing that they would be able to obtain by force of arms what had been refused to them unarmed, they seized their arms with tumultuous frenzy, and started to compel the Signori by violence. Michele, on the other hand, fearful of what might happen, resolved to forestall them, thinking that it would be more to his glory to attack the enemy rather than to await him between four walls, and, like his predecessor, be obliged to fly from the palace with dishonor and shame. Having therefore collected a number of citizens, who had already begun to see their previous error and to repent it, he mounted a horse, and, followed by many armed men, he went forth to Santa Maria Novella to encounter the multitude. These, as we have said before, had formed a similar resolution, and had started to go to the Piazza just about the same time that Michele set out from the palace. Chance would have it that they took different roads, so that they did not meet on the way. When Michele returned, therefore, he found the Piazza in possession of the multitude, who had already begun to attack the palace. He at once attacked and defeated the rabble, and drove a portion of them out of the city, compelling others to throw down their arms and to conceal themselves. Having accomplished this victory, the city was restored to quiet by the mere valor of the Gonfaloniere, who excelled at that time all other citizens in courage, prudence, and goodness, and deserves to be counted amongst the few men who have really benefited their country. For had he been of an evil or ambitious disposition, the republic would have lost all her liberties, and would have fallen under a greater tyranny than that of the Duke of Athens. But his natural goodness never permitted a single thought to enter his mind that was contrary to the general good, and his prudence caused him to conduct matters in such a way that many of his own party gave him their confidence and yielded to him, and those who did not he was enabled to control by force of arms. This caused the common people to fear him, and the better class of artisans to reflect, and to think what a shame it was for them now to be obliged to bear with the vile rabble, after having humbled the pride of the nobles.

18. At the time when Michele obtained this victory over the common people, the new Signoria had already been drawn, amongst whom were two of such vile and infamous condition that everybody was desirous to free themselves of such disgrace. When, therefore, on the 1st of September, the new Signori assumed office, the Piazza was full of armed people; and before the old Signori were out of the palace, a tumultuous cry arose amongst the armed men that they did not want any of the low people to be Signori. The Signoria therefore, by way of satisfying this demand, deprived those two of the magistracy. One of these men was called Tira, and the other Baroccio; and in their stead they appointed Messer Giorgio Scali and Francesco di Michele. They also cancelled the guild of the small trades, and deprived all the members of that guild of the offices they held, excepting Michele di Lando and Lorenzo di Puccio, and some others of better quality. They divided the public offices into two parts, one of which was given to the major and the other to the minor guilds. Only of the Signori they required five always to be taken from minor and four from the major guilds, and the Gonfaloniere should alternately be from the one and the other.

This organization of the government for the time restored quiet to the city. But although the government of the republic had been rescued from the hands of the populace, yet the smaller trades retained more power than the noble citizens, who had to yield to this state of things so as to prevent the smaller tradesmen from being dissatisfied at being deprived of the privilege of the guild. This arrangement was also favored by those who desired to keep that party down which under the name of Guelf had maltreated the citizens with so much violence. Messer Giorgio Scali, Messer Benedetto Alberti, Messer Salvestro de' Medici, and Messer Tommaso Strozzi were amongst those who favored this organization of the government, as it left them, as it were, the chiefs of the city. The regulation of things in this wise confirmed the division between the noble citizens and the smaller tradesmen, which had been started by the ambition of the Ricci and the Albizzi. And as this gave rise at various times to the gravest consequences, which we shall have occasion frequently to mention, we shall call one of these parties the citizens' party, and the other that of the populace. This state of things lasted three years, during which banishments and death were abundant; for those who governed lived in the greatest apprehension because of the many malcontents within and without the city. The malcontents within attempted, or were suspected of attempting, every day, some innovations. Those without, being entirely unrestrained, and being encouraged now by some prince, now by some republic, originated various dissensions, first in one place and then in another.

19. At this time there happened to be at Bologna Giannozzo da Salerno, captain of Charles of Durazzo, a descendant of the kings of Naples. This prince, designing an attempt upon the kingdom against Queen Joanna, kept his Captain Giannozzo in that city through the favor of Pope Urban, who was hostile to the queen. There were also at Bologna many banished Florentines who kept up intimate relations with Charles. These intrigues caused the governing magistrates of Florence much uneasiness, and made them give ready ear to the evil reports against the suspected citizens. In this state of things the magistrates received information that Giannozzo was about to appear before Florence with the banished, and that many within were ready to arm and to surrender the city to him. Upon this report many were accused; the first were Piero degli Albizzi and Carlo Strozzi; and next, Cipriano Mangioni, Messer Giacopo Sacchetti, Messer Donato Barbadori, Filippo Strozzi, and Giovanni Anselmi; who were all arrested with the single exception of Carlo Strozzi, who fled. To prevent an armed rising in favor of these men, the Signori deputed Messer Tommaso Strozzi and Messer Benedetto Alberti, with a large armed force, to guard the city. The citizens who had been arrested underwent an examination; but no guilt was proved upon them, either by the accusations or by confrontations, so that the Captain declined to condemn them; but their enemies excited the people to such fury against them, that they were by force condemned to death. Neither the

greatness of his family, nor his ancient reputation of having been honored and feared above all other citizens, could save Piero degli Albizzi from his fate. On a former occasion, at a great feast, either some friend, for the purpose of making him more humble in his prosperity, or some enemy who wished to threaten him with the fickleness of fortune, sent to Piero a silver bowl filled with sweetmeats, amongst which a nail was concealed. When this was discovered and seen by all the guests, it was interpreted as intending to remind him that he should nail fast the wheel of fortune, which, having carried him to the summit, would otherwise, if permitted to complete its turn, drag him to the bottom. This interpretation was verified first by his ruin and afterwards by his death (1380).

After this execution the city remained in a great state of confusion, owing to the mutual fears of the victors and the vanquished. But still worse effects resulted from the apprehensions of the chiefs of the government, because the slightest incident caused them to inflict fresh injuries upon the party, either by condemning or "admonishing" their citizens, or by sending them into exile. To this were added the frequent new laws and ordinances made to strengthen the government. All these things caused great wrongs to those who were suspect to the ruling faction, which appointed forty-six individuals, who, together with the Signoria, should purge the republic of those who were suspected by the government. These admonished thirty-nine citizens, made a number of citizens noble, and reduced many nobles to the rank of citizens. And to enable them to resist any attacks from without, they employed Giovanni Aguto (John Sharpe) an Englishman, greatly reputed as a soldier, and who had for a long time conducted wars for the Pope and others. Their apprehensions of danger from without arose from their having heard that Charles of Durazzo was preparing for an attack upon the kingdom of Naples with a large armed force, amongst which were many of the banished Florentines. In consequence of this danger they provided, in addition to the troops, a considerable sum of money; so that when Charles had reached Arezzo the Florentines paid him forty thousand ducats on condition that he should not molest them. Thence he went to attack the kingdom of Naples, of which he succeeded in making himself master, and sent the queen captive to Hungary. This victory revived and increased the fears of those who held the government of Florence, for they could not persuade themselves to believe that their money would have more influence with the king than the ancient friendship that had existed between his house and the Guelfs, whom they had oppressed with so many wrongs.

20. These increased fears produced an increase of injuries, which in turn did not extinguish, but rather augmented, the suspicions, so as to cause a general discontentment amongst the people. To this came in addition the insolence of Messer Giorgio Scali and Messer Tommaso Strozzi, who overpowered with their authority that of the magistrates, so that everybody lived in terror of being in turn maltreated by them, as they were supported by the populace. Thus the government appeared equally tyrannical to the well-disposed and the seditious. But as the arrogance of Messer Giorgio had at one time or another to come to an end, it happened that one of his familiars accused Giovanni di Cambio of having intrigued against the state, who was however acquitted as not guilty by the Captain. The judge therefore wished to inflict upon the accuser the same penalty with which the guilty would have been punished had he been convicted. And as Messer Giorgio had in vain employed entreaties and his authority to save this man, he went, accompanied by Messer Tommaso Strozzi and a number of armed followers, to liberate him by force; and they sacked the palace of the Captain, who only saved himself by concealment. This act so irritated all the citizens against Messer Giorgio that his enemies thought they could crush him; and relieve the city not only of his tyranny, but also of that of the populace who had kept it in subjection for three years by their insolence. The Captain's conduct also afforded an excellent opportunity for this; for after the tumult had subsided he went to the Signori and told them "that he "had willingly accepted the office to which their lordships had "elected him, because he thought that he would have to serve "just men, and that they would have taken up arms to support "justice, and not to impede it. But having seen and experi- "enced the government of the city and its manner of conduct, "he desired, for the sake of avoiding peril and injury, volun- "tarily to surrender that dignity which he had voluntarily "accepted for the purpose of making himself useful, and on "account of the honor which it conferred." The Signori com-

forted the Captain, and reanimated his courage, promising him indemnity for past injuries and security for the future. And a portion of them having united with some citizens whom they regarded as lovers of the public good, and less suspect to the government, concluded to profit by this opportunity for liberating the city from the power of Messer Giorgio and the populace; inasmuch as the mass of citizens had become entirely alienated from him by this last display of his insolence.

It seemed to them best therefore to avail of it before all those whose indignation had been aroused against Messer Giorgio Scali should have become reconciled to him; for they well knew that the favor of the multitude is easily lost and won by every little accident. They also deemed it necessary for their success in this matter to draw into their alliance Messer Benedetto Alberti, without whose concurrence the attempt seemed hazardous to them. Messer Benedetto was a very rich, humane, and austere man, and a great lover of the liberty of his country, to whom all tyrannous proceedings were most odious; it was easy, therefore, to satisfy him, and to obtain his consent to the destruction of Messer Giorgio. The insolence and tyrannical conduct of the Guelfs and of the noble citizens had made him their enemy and the friend of the people. But when he afterwards saw that the leaders of the people's party had become similar to those from whom he had separated himself a short time previous, and that the wrongs inflicted upon so many citizens had been committed wholly without his concurrence, he abandoned the party of the people for the same reasons that had caused him to take sides with them. Having therefore drawn Messer Benedetto and the chiefs of the guilds into their plans, and having provided themselves with arms, Messer Giorgio was arrested and Messer Tommaso fled. And on the following day Messer Giorgio Scali was beheaded, which struck such terror into his party that no one stirred, but all rather concurred in his destruction. When Messer Giorgio saw himself led to death before the very people who, but a short time before, had adored him, he complained of his unfortunate fate, and of the malignity of the citizens, who, having wrongfully injured him, had obliged him to favor and honor a populace who were devoid alike of good faith and gratitude. And recognizing amongst the armed men Messer Benedetto Alberti, he said to him: "And thou, Messer Benedetto, "thou consentest that this wrong should be done to me; which, "were I in thy place, I should never permit to be done to thee. "But I tell thee, this day is the end of my troubles and the "beginning of thine." Then he blamed himself for having confided too much in a people who were moved and corrupted by every voice, every act, and every suspicion. And with such lamentations he died, in the midst of his armed enemies, who rejoiced at his death. After him some of his nearest friends were put to death, and their bodies dragged through the streets by the populace.

21. The whole city was moved by the death of Giorgio Scali. His execution caused many persons to take up arms in support of the Signoria and the Captain; many also did so from ambition or from fear. And thus the city was full of different factions, each having their own aims, which they wished to follow out before laying down their arms. The ancient nobles, who were called grandees, could not bear being excluded from the public offices, and strove by every means to recover them; and for that reason wished to see the captains of the sections restored to their former authority. To the noble citizens and the major guilds it was offensive to share the government with the minor guilds and the common people; and the people feared to lose the colleges of their guilds. These differences caused frequent troubles in Florence during a year; at one time the grandees took up arms, at another the major or the minor guilds, and with these latter the common people; and several times all were armed at once in different parts of the city. Thus there occurred frequent fighting amongst them, and with the men at arms of the palace, although the Signoria did its utmost to remedy these disorders, at one time by yielding, at others by force of arms. So that at last after two parliaments and several "Balias," which were created for the purpose of reforming the government, and after much damage, many troubles and perils, a government was established, by which all who had been banished since the time when Messer Salvestro de' Medici was Gonfaloniere were restored to their country. All the offices and emoluments bestowed by the Balia of 1378 were revoked; the Guelfs were restored to their privileges; the two new guilds were deprived of their corporate powers and of their officers, and all their members were

placed in the old guilds. The office of Gonfaloniere of Justice was taken from the minor guilds, and their share of the public offices was reduced from one half to one third, and these were only those of the lower grade.

Thus the party of the noble citizens and that of the Guelfs recovered the government, which the party of the people lost after having controlled it from the year 1378 until 1381, when this new order of things was established.

22. This new government was not less injurious to the citizens, nor less oppressive in its beginning, than the government of the populace had been; for many noble citizens, who had been the noted supporters of the latter, were banished at the same time with the leaders of the populace. Amongst the latter was Michele di Lando, who was not saved from the fury of the party by all the services he had rendered, and to which he owed his authority at a time when an unbridled mob was destroying the city. His country showed him little gratitude for all his good deeds; an error often committed by princes and republics, and one which often causes those who are alarmed by such examples to injure their princes before they have experienced their ingratitude. These condemnations to exile and death, ever regrettable, greatly displeased Messer Benedetto Alberti, who censured them both privately and publicly. This caused him to be feared by the heads of the government, for they regarded him as one of the chiefest supporters of the populace, and believed that he had concurred in the death of Messer Giorgio Scali, not because he had disapproved of his conduct, but with the view to remaining alone in the control of the government. His language and conduct afterwards increased this suspicion, so that the whole party who now held the government kept their eyes upon him watching for an opportunity to oppress him.

Whilst matters were thus within Florence, nothing very grave disturbed their external relations, and if anything did trouble them it was more from apprehension than from any actual harm done. For it was at this time that Louis d'Anjou came into Italy for the purpose of re-establishing Queen Joanna on the throne of Naples and driving out Charles of Durazzo. This passage of Louis alarmed the Florentines greatly, for Charles asked their aid, in accordance with the custom of old allies; and Louis, like those who seek to form new alliances,

demanded that they should remain neutral. Whereupon the
Florentines, by way of making a show of satisfying Louis, and
yet at the same time aiding Charles, dismissed from their service Messer Giovanno Aguto, and had him transferred to that
of Pope Urban, who was a friend of Charles of Durazzo. This
trick was, however, quickly perceived by Louis, who considered
himself much injured thereby at the hands of the Florentines.
Whilst the war between Charles and Louis was being carried
on in Puglia, fresh troops came from France in support of
Louis, who upon reaching Tuscany were conducted by the
exiled Aretines to Arezzo, where they expelled those who governed that city in the name of Charles. At the moment when
they contemplated changing the government of Florence in
the same way in which they had accomplished that of Arezzo,
Louis died, which caused a change in the fortunes of Puglia
and of Tuscany, for Charles secured himself in the possession
of the kingdom of Naples, which he had come near losing;
and the Florentines, mistrusting their ability to defend their
own city, acquired Arezzo, which they purchased from the
troops who held it for Louis (1384). Charles thereupon, having made sure of Puglia, went to Hungary, the crown of
which came to him by inheritance, leaving his wife and two
children, Ladislas and Joanna, who were still small, in Puglia;
but soon after having acquired the crown of Hungary he
died.

23. The accession of Charles to the throne of Hungary
caused solemn rejoicings in Florence, such as no other city
had ever indulged in even to celebrate any victory of their
own. Public and private magnificence shone out alike on
that occasion, and many private citizens vied in their festive
displays with the public ones. But none equalled in pomp
and sumptuousness that of the Alberti; for the display made
by them and the jousts given by them were not like those of
private individuals, but were truly worthy of princes. This
ostentation greatly increased the general hatred and envy of
the Alberti, which, added to the suspicion with which the
government regarded Messer Benedetto, was the cause of his
ruin. For those at the head of the government did not feel
easy on his account, fearing lest he might at any moment,
with the support of the people, recover his influence and power
and drive them from the city. Whilst the chiefs of the gov-

ernment were filled with these apprehensions, it happened that, at the same time that Messer Benedetto was Gonfaloniere of the Companies (1387), his son-in-law Messer Filippo Magalotti was drawn as Gonfaloniere of Justice, which redoubled the fears of the chiefs of the state; they thought that Messer Benedetto was acquiring too much power, and the state incurring too much danger. And desiring to remedy this without creating any disturbance they induced Bese Magalotti, his associate and enemy, to inform the Signori that Messer Filippo lacked the age required for the exercise of that office and therefore ought not to hold it. The matter was examined into by the Signori, and some of them from hate, and some for the purpose of preventing a bad precedent, declared Messer Filippo incompetent to hold that dignity. And in his place Bardo Mancini was drawn, who was utterly opposed to the plebeian faction and personally hostile to Messer Benedetto. So soon as he entered upon this magistracy he created a Balia, who, in the reassumption and reform of the state, banished Messer Benedetto Alberti, and admonished the remainder of the family with the exception only of Messer Antonio. Before his departure Messer Benedetto called all his relatives together, and seeing them sad and weeping he addressed them as follows: " Fathers and seniors, you see how "fortune has ruined me and threatened you, at which I am "not surprised, nor should you be; for such is ever the fate of "those who, amongst the many wicked, wish to remain good, "and who desire to sustain that which the majority seek to "destroy. Love of country caused me to stand by Messer "Salvestro de' Medici and afterwards to keep aloof from Mes-"ser Giorgio Scali. The same feeling made me detest the "conduct of those who now hold the government; there being "no one to chastise them, they also wanted no one to censure "them. I am content by my exile to relieve them of that fear "which they have not only of me, but of every one that knows "and recognizes their wicked and tyrannical conduct; and "therefore do they threaten the others by my punishment. "I do not lament my own fate, for the honors which my coun-"try bestowed upon me, when she still enjoyed her liberty, "cannot be taken from me now that she is enslaved; and the "memory of my past life will always give me more pleasure "than the unhappiness caused by my exile can give me pain.

"But it grieves me much to see my country the prey of a few, and subject to their pride and avarice. For you, my dear relatives, I am sorry, for I doubt not that those ills which to-day terminate for me and commence for you will inflict greater injuries upon you than they have done upon me. I advise you therefore to fortify your courage against all misfortunes, and to bear yourselves in such manner that, if disasters befall you, (and you will have many,) every one will know that they have come upon you undeservedly and without any fault of your own."

After that Messer Benedetto Alberti, by way of preserving out of Florence the same good reputation which he had enjoyed within, made a pilgrimage to the sepulchre of Christ, but on his return from there he died at Rhodes. His remains were brought to Florence and buried there with the greatest honors by those who in his lifetime had persecuted him with every species of calumny and injury.

24. The family of the Alberti was not the only one that was persecuted during these dissensions. Many other citizens were also admonished and exiled. Amongst these were Piero Benini, Matteo Alderotti, Giovanni and Francesco del Bene, Giovanni Benci, and Andrea Adimari, and with these a great many of the smaller artisans. Amongst the admonished were the Covoni, the Rinucci, the Formiconi, the Corbizzi, the Mannelli, and the Alderotti. It was customary to establish the Balia for a given time; but those citizens who composed the present one resigned from motives of honesty, although their time had not yet expired. Believing that they had satisfied the requirements of the state, they desired now to lay down their office, according to custom. When this became known, a number of persons rushed, armed, to the palace, and demanded that, before resigning, they should exile and admonish others. This displeased the Signori greatly; but they entertained these men with fair promises until they had collected an armed force, and then they compelled them from fear to lay down their arms, which their fury had caused them to take up. Nevertheless, by way of satisfying in part this angry spirit, and to deprive these plebeian mechanics still more of authority, they provided that, whilst before the minor guilds had been entitled to one third of the public offices, they should henceforth have only a fourth. And so that there should always be amongst the Signori at least two in the closest confidence of

the government, they gave authority to the Gonfaloniere of Justice, and to four other citizens, to make a purse of chosen men, from which two should be drawn for every Signoria.

25. The government being thus regulated six years after its reorganization in 1381, things remained pretty quiet in Florence until the year 1393. It was at this time that Giovanni Galeazzo Visconti, called Conte di Virtu, made his uncle, Messer Bernabo, prisoner, and thereby became sovereign of all Lombardy. Galeazzo thought that he might by force make himself king of all Italy, as by fraud he had become Duke of Milan. In the year 1390 he carried on a most obstinate war against the Florentines, with such varying results that several times he was more in danger of defeat than the Florentines, who in the end would have lost if the Duke had not died. Nevertheless the defence was spirited and wonderful for a republic, and the end was much less unfortunate than might have been expected from so frightful a war. For, after having taken Bologna, Pisa, Perugia, and Sienna, and when he had already prepared the crown with which to have himself crowned king of all Italy, the Duke died. Thus death neither permitted him to enjoy his past victories, nor the Florentines to regret their present losses. During the progress of this war with the Duke of Milan, Messer Maso degli Albizzi was made Gonfaloniere of Justice, who, in consequence of the death of Piero, had become the enemy of the Alberti. And as the evil spirit of party still survived, Messer Maso thought that, although Messer Benedetto had died in exile, yet he would revenge himself upon the remaining members of that family before laying down his magistracy. He availed, therefore, of the occasion when some one was being examined in relation to certain dealings with the rebels, who named Alberto and Andrea degli Alberti, to have these promptly arrested (1393). At this act the whole city became greatly excited, so that the Signori provided themselves with arms, called the people to a parliament, and appointed a new Balia, by means of which they exiled a number of citizens, and had new purses made for the election of public officers. Amongst the exiled were pretty much all the Alberti; many artisans were admonished, and some were put to death. In consequence of all these wrongs, the guilds and the small people rose in arms; for it seemed to them as though they were being deprived of all honor and of life itself. A portion of them came into the Piazza, an-

other part went to the house of Messer Veri de' Medici, who, after the death of Messer Salvestro, had become head of that family. By way of quieting those who had come into the Piazza, the Signori put at their head as captains, with the banners of the Guelfs and of the people in their hands, Messer Rinaldo Gianfigliazzi and Messer Donato Acciaiuoli, who, being men of the people, were likely to be more acceptable to them than any others. Those who had gone to the house of Messer Veri begged him to take the government of the city into his hands, and to liberate them from the tyranny of those citizens who were destroyers of good men and of the public good.

All who have recorded the events of these times agree that, if Messer Veri's ambition had exceeded his goodness, he might without hindrance have made himself prince of the city. For the grave injuries that, rightly or wrongly, had been done to the guilds and their friends, had so exasperated their spirits that they lacked nothing to assuage their thirst for vengeance but a chief to lead them. Nor was there wanting some one to remind Messer Veri of what he had it in his power to do; for Antonio de' Medici himself, who had been for a long time his bitter enemy, endeavored to persuade him to assume the sovereignty of the republic. To which Messer Veri replied: "Thy threats when "thou wast my enemy never caused me any fear, nor shall thy "evil counsels now, since thou art my friend, mislead me to "evil." And then, turning to the multitude, he advised them to be of good cheer, for he was willing to be their defender provided they would allow themselves to be advised by him. And after having gone into their midst in the Piazza, he went up from there into the palace before the Signori, and addressed them as follows: "That he could in no way regret that his "course of life had made him beloved by the people of Flor- "ence; but that he was sorry indeed that they had formed such "a judgment of him as his past life did not warrant. For, in- "asmuch as he had never shown either a spirit of turbulence or "ambition, he did not know whence it came that the people "believed that he would sanction disturbances, like a turbulent "man, or that he would be willing to seize the government, like "an ambitious one. He therefore begged the Signoria not to "reckon the ignorance of the multitude as his crime; for so far "as he was concerned, he had submitted himself to their au- "thority so soon as he was able to do so. And that he felt

" sure that they would be content to use their good fortune
" modestly, and that they would have more satisfaction in the
" enjoyment of half a victory, with the safety of the city, than
" to ruin her by striving for a complete one." Messer Veri was
praised by the Signori, who urged him to induce the people to
lay down their arms, and that then they would do what they
had been counselled to do by him and by other citizens. After
these words Messer Veri returned to the Piazza, and, having
united his companions with those that were led by Messer Rinaldo and Messer Donato, he said to them " that he had found
" in the Signoria the best disposition towards them, and that
" he had discussed many matters with them; but, owing to the
" brief time and the absence of the magistrates, nothing definite
" had been concluded. Nevertheless he begged them to disarm
" and to obey the Signoria, assuring them that they would be
" moved more by humility than by pride, and more by prayers
" than by threats. And that they should neither lack their
" share in the public offices, nor in personal security, if they
" would be governed by him." Under these assurances from
Messer Veri, the people returned to their homes.

26. So soon as the people had disarmed, the Signori fortified
the Piazza, and then enrolled two thousand reliable citizens
whom the government could trust, dividing them equally into
companies with orders to hold themselves in readiness, at the
first signal, to come to the support of the government. And
all those who were not so enrolled were forbidden to carry
arms (1394). These preparations being made, the Signori condemned to exile and death a number of artisans from amongst
those who had shown themselves most audacious during the
riots. And for the purpose of giving to the office of the Gonfaloniere of Justice more majesty and consideration, they provided that no one should exercise that office who was not at
least forty-five years of age. They also made many other provisions for strengthening the government which were alike
unsupportable to those against whom they were aimed and
odious to the good citizens of their own party, who could not
regard a government good and secure that had to protect itself
with so much violence. All these exceeding rigors were offensive not only to those of the Alberti who remained in the city,
and to the Medici, to whom it seemed that the people had been
deceived, but also to many others who disapproved of so much

violence. The first who attempted to oppose these measures was Messer Donato di Jacopo Acciaiuoli; although he was one of the great of the city, and rather the superior than the equal of Messer Maso degli Albizzi, who from the events that occurred during his gonfalonierate had been almost like the head of the republic, yet could he not be satisfied in the midst of such general discontent. Nor would he, like so many others, seek his personal advantage in the general misfortunes; and therefore he thought of trying to obtain the recall of the banished, or at least restore the admonished to the privilege of holding office. For this purpose he disseminated his opinions amongst a number of citizens, demonstrating to them that it was the only means of quieting the people, and of putting an end to the discontent of the factions; he only waited to become himself one of the Signori, to have his plans carried into effect. But as in all human affairs delay brings weariness and haste danger, so he tried to escape the former by tempting the latter. Amongst the Signori were his relative Michele Acciaiuoli and his friend Niccolo Ricoveri; this seemed to afford Messer Donato an opportunity not to be lost, and he therefore requested them to propose a law in the councils that should provide for the restitution of the citizens. These two being persuaded by him spoke to their associates on the subject, who replied, however, that they were indisposed to try new things, the benefit of which was doubtful and the danger certain. Whereupon Messer Donato, having first tried in vain all other means, and being greatly excited by anger, gave them to understand that, since they were unwilling that the city should be reformed by the means in hand, it would have to be done by force of arms. These words so displeased them, that they communicated the matter to the chiefs of the government, who had Messer Donato summoned to appear before them; and being convicted by the testimony of those to whom he had committed his message, he was banished to Barletta (1396). Alamanno and Antonio de' Medici were also banished, together with the entire branch of that family who were descended from Messer Alamanno, and a number of the lower class of artisans who were influential with the common people. This occurred two years after the government had been reorganized by Messer Maso.

27. The city of Florence being in this condition, with many malcontents within and many banished without, it happened

that there were amongst the latter at Bologna, Picchio Cavicciulli, Tommaso de' Ricci, Antonio de' Medici, Benedetto degli Spini, Antonio Girolami, Cristofano di Carlone, and two others of low condition, but all brave young fellows and disposed to take every risk for the sake of returning to their country. These were secretly informed by Pigiello and Baroccio Cavicciulli, who were living as "admonished" in Florence, that if they would come into the city they would conceal them in their houses, whence they could afterwards issue and kill Messer Maso degli Albizzi and call the people to arms, who being discontented could easily be induced to rise, especially as they would be seconded by the Ricci, the Adimari, the Mannelli, and many other families. Encouraged by their hopes to accept this proposition, they came into the city on the 4th of August, 1397, and having secreted themselves in the appointed places, they sent to watch the movements of Messer Maso, intending to begin the riot with his death. Messer Maso left his house and stopped at an apothecary's shop near San Piero Maggiore. The man who was watching him ran to inform the conspirators, who, having armed themselves came to the place indicated, but found that Messer Maso had already left. Nothing daunted, however, by this failure of their first attempt, they went towards the Old Market, where they killed one of the adverse faction; and having raised a tumult and called the people to arms by shouts of "Liberty!" and "Death to the tyrants!" thence they turned towards the New Market, and at the end of the Calimara killed another man. They pursued their way with the same cries, but finding that no one took up arms, they went to the Loggia della Nighittosa; here they mounted a high place, surrounded by a great multitude who had run there more from curiosity than any intention of aiding them, and with a loud voice they exhorted the people "to take up arms "and to leave that servitude which they hated so much, affirm- "ing that their object was to redress the grievances of the mal- "content in the city, and not to avenge their own personal "wrongs. That they had heard that many of them prayed "God to give them the opportunity to be able to revenge them- "selves, which He would do whenever they had a chief to lead "them. But now that the opportunity was offered them, they "stood looking at each other like stupid men, waiting until the "promoters of their liberation were killed, and their own servi-

"tude aggravated. And that they were astonished that those "who were accustomed to take to arms for the slightest injury "remained unmoved when their wrongs were so numerous, and "were willing to submit to seeing so many of their fellow-"citizens exiled and admonished; whilst it was now in their "power to have the banished restored to their country and the "admonished reinstated in their rights to hold office." These words, although true, yet did not move the multitude, either because they were restrained by fear, or because the death of the two men had made the murderers hateful to them. When the instigators of the riot found that neither words nor deeds had power to stir the multitude, and saw too late the danger of attempting to make a people free who are in every way resolved to remain slaves, they despaired of the enterprise and retreated into the church of Santa Reparata, where they shut themselves up, not to save their lives, but to defer death. The Signori, disturbed by the first noise, armed and closed the palace; but when they learnt the facts and became aware who it was that had originated the disturbance, they became reassured, and commanded the Captain with a force of men-at-arms to go and arrest the rioters. Thus without much difficulty the doors of the temple were forced open and a portion of the conspirators were killed whilst defending themselves, and a portion were captured; and from their examination it appeared that outside of their number there were none others implicated except Baroccio and Pigiello Cavicciulli, who were condemned to death with the other conspirators.

28. (1400.) After this occurrence there happened another of greater importance. As we have related above, the city was carrying on a war at this time with the Duke of Milan, who, finding himself unable to overcome the Florentines by open force, resorted to indirect ways, and by means of the exiled Florentines, of which Lombardy was full, he formed a plot to which many in the city were parties. According to this it was agreed that on a given day those of the Florentine exiles who were skilled in arms should start from certain places in the immediate vicinity of Florence and enter the city by crossing the river Arno. These, together with their accomplices in the city, were then to rush to the houses of the heads of the government, and after having killed these they were to reorganize the government according to their own views. Amongst the

conspirators within the city was one of the Ricci, called Samminiato; and as often happens in conspiracies that few are insufficient to carry it into effect, whilst many cause its discovery, so in this instance, for whilst Samminiato sought associates he found an informer. He confided the matter to Salvestro Cavicciulli, whom the wrongs which his relatives and himself had experienced at the hands of the government ought to have made faithful to the cause of the conspirators. But heeding more his present fears than his distant hopes of revenge, he promptly revealed the whole plot to the Signori; these immediately had Samminiato arrested and compelled him to confess the whole conspiracy. But of all those who were parties to it in the city none were captured except Tommaso Davizi, who, coming from Bologna and being ignorant of what had taken place in Florence, was arrested immediately upon his arrival; all the others, being alarmed by the arrest of Samminiato, made their escape. Having punished Samminiato and Tommaso according to their crimes, the Signoria gave a Balia to a number of citizens, who, armed with this authority, should seek out the offenders and make the government secure. These declared as rebels six of the Alberti, two of the Medici, three of the Scali, two of the Strozzi, Bindo Altoviti, Bernardo Adimari, and many others of the people. They also admonished the entire families of the Alberti, Ricci, and Medici for ten years, exempting only a very few of them. Amongst those of the Alberti who were not admonished was Messer Antonio, because he was regarded as a quiet and peaceful man. But as the suspicions excited by this conspiracy were not entirely allayed, a monk was taken prisoner who had been seen during the time that the conspirators were communicating with each other to pass repeatedly between Bologna and Florence. He confessed that on several occasions he had brought letters for Messer Antonio, who was thereupon promptly arrested, and although he denied everything, yet he was convicted upon the monk's testimony, and banished to a distance of three hundred miles from the city. And so that the Alberti should no longer be a constant danger to the government, all of that family who were over fifteen years of age were likewise banished.

29. This event occurred in the year 1400, and two years after Duke Giovanni Galeazzo of Milan died; this put an end to the war, which had lasted twelve years. At this epoch the govern-

ment, having acquired more power and being now free from external and internal enemies, undertook an attempt upon Pisa, and conquered it gloriously, and retained it undisturbed from 1400 till 1423. Only in the year 1412 a new Balia was created for the express purpose of crushing and exiling the Alberti, which strengthened the government by new provisions and bore down the Alberti with new impositions. Within this period the Florentines also made war against Ladislas, king of Naples, which was terminated by the death of the king in 1414. In the course of this war Ladislas, finding himself unequal in strength to the Florentines, ceded to them the city of Cortona, of which he was lord. But shortly after that he recovered his forces and renewed the war, which became much more doubtful for the Florentines than it had been at first; and had it not been closed by the death of the king, the same as the previous war with the Duke of Milan, it would have exposed the liberties of Florence to great danger. This war with the king of Naples terminated no less happily for the Florentines than that with the Duke of Milan; for the king died after having made himself master of Rome, Sienna, La Marca, and all the Romagna; so that he lacked nothing but Florence to extend his power into Lombardy. And thus death was always a better friend to the Florentines than any other of their allies, and was more effective in saving them than their own valor.

After the death of the king of Naples Florence enjoyed entire tranquillity during eight years. At the end of that period she was agitated again by the war with Philip, Duke of Milan, and by the fresh breaking out of party violence, which was not allayed until the destruction of that government which had ruled from 1381 until 1434, and which had carried on so many wars with so much glory, and added to the dominions of the republic Arezzo, Pisa, Cortona, Livorno, and Montepulciano; and would have done even greater things if the old party feuds had not been rekindled, as will be shown more particularly in the following book.

FOURTH BOOK.

SUMMARY.

1. Defects in the government of republics: servitude and license. — 2. State of Florence, and resumption of the internal government of the city. — 3. Giovanni di Bicci de' Medici restores the authority of his family in Florence (1420). — Filippo Visconti, Duke of Milan, tries to make terms with the Florentines, and concludes peace with them. — 4. Owing to the suspicions which the Duke's bold enterprises in Italy excite in the minds of the Florentines, war breaks out (1424). — 5. Filippo seizes Furli. — 6. The Florentines are defeated near Furli by the Duke's forces. — 7. In consequence of this defeat the people murmur against those who have advised the war, but being quieted by Rinaldo degli Albizzi they provide for the prosecution of the war. — 8. The new tax for the expenses of the war is the cause of disturbances. — 9. Rinaldo degli Albizzi advises the restoration of the nobles to the government. — 10. His advice is disapproved by Giovanni de' Medici. — 11. He thereby gains in reputation with the masses, but is held in aversion by the party of Messer Rinaldo (1426). — 12. Gallantry of Biagio del Melano in defending the castle of Monte Petroso, and cowardice of Zanobi del Pino. — 13. The Florentines form a league with the Lord of Faenza and with the Venetians. — 14. Institution of the Catasto, under the advice chiefly of Giovanni de' Medici; which causes discontent amongst the rich. The parties that originate in consequence (1427). — 15. Peace with the Duke of Milan. — 16. Death of Giovanni de' Medici (1429). — 17. Revolt of the people of Volterra, which is however soon suppressed. — 18. Niccolo Fortebraccio, released from the conduct of the Florentine armies, assails the Lucchese. — 19. Deliberations on the war with Lucca. — 20. The Florentines appoint commissioners for the enterprise against Lucca, and agree with Fortebraccio to conduct the war in the pay of the republic, but that he must give up the places he has taken. — 21. Misgovernment of Seravezza by Astore Gianni. — 22. Arraignment of Rinaldo degli Albizzi. — 23. Filippo Brunelleschi proposes to inundate Lucca by damming up the Serchio, but does not succeed (1430). — 24. The troops of the Duke come to the aid of the Lucchese, and take some towns. — 25. Francesco Sforza causes the Lucchese to expel their Signori. The Florentines are defeated by the troops of the Duke. — 26. Cosimo de' Medici. His character and method for achieving greatness (1433). — 27. His growing power excites the suspicion of many citizens, and especially of Niccolo da Uzano and his associates. — 28. Rinaldo degli Albizzi causes Bernardo Guadagni to be elected Gonfaloniere, and makes him

seize Cosimo and confine him in the palace. — 29. The Albizzi attempt to restore the nobles in the government, and take up arms against the Signoria. — 30. Proceedings of the new Signoria in favor of Cosimo. — 31. Pope Eugenius IV. in Florence constitutes himself the mediator for quieting the tumults. — 32. Cosimo is reclaimed, and Rinaldo with the whole party of the Albizzi is confined (1434). Glorious return of Cosimo to Florence.

1. CITIES that govern themselves under the name of Republics, and especially such as are not well constituted, are exposed to frequent revolutions in their government, which make them pass, not, as is generally believed, from servitude to liberty, but from servitude to license. For it is merely the name of liberty that is extolled by the ministers of license, which are the popular faction, and by the ministers of servitude, which are the nobles, neither one nor the other of these being willing to submit either to laws or to men. On the other hand, it is true that when by good fortune some wise, good, and powerful citizen arises in the republic, (which, however, seldom happens,) who establishes laws that will quell the factious spirit of the nobles and of the people, and restrain it so that it can do no harm, — then I say that city may call herself truly free, and such a state may be considered firm and stable. For being founded upon good laws and institutions, it is not dependent upon the virtue of one man for its maintenance, as is the case with the others. Many of the republics of antiquity, whose governments endured a long time, were endowed with such laws. And similar laws and institutions will ever be needed in all those republics that have often changed, and continue to change, their governments from a state of tyranny to one of license, and from the latter to the former. For in such there is not, and cannot be, any stability, because of the violent enmities which each of them provokes; for the one does not please the good men, and the other displeases the wise ones; the one can easily work harm, and the other can with difficulty effect any good. In the one, the insolent have too much authority, and in the other, the foolish; and both one and the other require being sustained by the virtue and good fortune of one man, who may at any moment be removed by death, or his usefulness impaired by misfortune.

2. I say, therefore, that the organization of the government that was established in Florence after the death of Messer Giorgio Scali, in 1381, was maintained, first by the virtue of

Messer Maso degli Albizzi, and afterwards by that of Niccolo da Uzano. The city remained tranquil from the year 1414 until 1422; for King Ladislas was dead, and the state of Lombardy divided by parties, so that there was nothing from without or within to disturb her quiet. After Niccolo da Uzano, the citizens having most authority were Bartolommeo Valori, Nerone di Nigi, Messer Rinaldo degli Albizzi, Neri di Gino, and Lapo Niccolini. The factions that sprung from the feud between the Albizzi and Ricci, and which Messer Salvestro de' Medici rekindled with so much violence, had never been extinguished; and although the popular party ruled only three years, having been vanquished in 1381, yet, comprising as it did the greater part of the citizens, it could never be entirely suppressed. Still it is true that the frequent parliaments, and the continued persecutions against its leaders from 1381 to 1400, had well-nigh reduced it to nullity. The principal families that were persecuted as the chiefs of that faction were the Alberti, the Ricci, and the Medici, who many times had to suffer in their persons and in their wealth; and those of them who still remained in Florence were deprived of the honor of holding public offices. These frequent chastisements humbled that party so as almost entirely to destroy it. There remained nevertheless in the minds of many of them the remembrance of the wrongs endured, and the desire to avenge them; but not finding a favorable opportunity to vent that feeling, it remained concealed within their hearts. Those noble citizens, who governed the city thus peaceably, committed two errors, which proved the ruin of their government. The one was that, by continued possession of power, they became overbearing; the other, that mutual jealousies and long control of the government caused them to relax that vigilance which they should have exercised over those who were hostile and capable of injuring them.

3. Stimulating thus by their sinister conduct the hatred of the masses, and neglecting to watch the dangers because they did not fear them, or encouraging them by their jealousy of each other, they enabled the Medici to recover their influence and authority. The first of them that began to rise again was Giovanni di Bicci; who, having amassed great wealth, and being of a benign and humane disposition, was elevated to the supreme magistracy by those who held the government in the year 1420.

This caused the greatest satisfaction to the mass of the people, for they seemed to think that in him they had gained a defender; so that the most prudent men of the city became justly suspicious of him, seeing all the former ill-feeling to revive and gain strength. Niccolo da Uzano therefore made it a point to inform the other citizens of it, pointing out to them the danger of encouraging any one who had so much influence with the masses, and how easy it was to check disorders in the beginning; but that, having once allowed them to gain headway, it was difficult to remedy them; and that he well knew Giovanni to possess many qualities superior to those of Messer Salvestro. But Niccolo was not listened to by his compeers, who were jealous of his reputation, and were desirous of securing associates for themselves so as to put him down. Whilst this state of things prevailed in Florence, and dissensions began secretly to be fomented again, Filippo Visconti, second son of Galeazzo, who, by the death of his brother, had become sovereign of all Lombardy, believing himself capable of undertaking almost any enterprise, desired, above all things, to recover the mastery over Genoa, which at that time enjoyed independence under the government of its Doge, Messer Tommaso da Campo Fregoso. But he was doubtful whether success would be certain in this or any other enterprise, unless he first concluded a new treaty with the Florentines, and to have it made publicly known; for he thought that the credit he would gain thereby would suffice to enable him to accomplish his desires. He therefore sent ambassadors to Florence to obtain such a treaty. Many citizens advised that it should not be made, as, without any new treaty, they ought to continue the peace with Filippo, which had been maintained for so many years; for they knew the great advantage which such a treaty would afford to Filippo, and of how little benefit it would be to the city of Florence. Many others thought it best to make such a treaty, and by virtue of it to impose conditions upon Filippo, the transgression of which would make his evil intentions manifest to everybody; and that then, in case he broke the peace, they might with the greater justice make war against him. And thus, after the matter had been much debated, a treaty of peace was concluded (1421), in which Filippo pledged himself in no way to interfere with anything on the Florentine side of the rivers Magra and Panaro.

4. So soon as this treaty was made, Filippo seized Brescia (1422), and soon after he took Genoa, contrary to the expectations of those Florentines who had advised the making of the treaty; for they had believed that Brescia would be defended by the Venetians, and that Genoa would be able to protect herself. And inasmuch as in the terms which Filippo had made with the Doge of Genoa, he had left him Serezana, and other places situated on this side of the Magra, on condition that he should not part with them except to the Genoese, it was considered that Filippo had by this agreement violated the stipulations of his treaty with Florence. He had, moreover, concluded a treaty with the Legate of Bologna. These things caused great uneasiness to our citizens, who, apprehensive of further troubles, began to prepare means for their prevention. When this became known to Filippo, he sent ambassadors to Florence, either to justify himself, or to sound the feelings of the Florentines, or to lull them into security. He professed to be astonished at their suspicions, and offered to renounce all that he had done that could give rise to any such feelings. These ambassadors produced no other effect than to divide the city; for that part of the citizens who had most influence in the government thought it advisable to arm, and to prepare themselves to thwart the designs of the enemy; for if such preparations should cause Filippo to remain quiet, then a war would be avoided, and there would be every reason for a continuance of peace. Many others, either from jealousy of those who held the government or from fear of war, deemed it wrong so lightly to suspect an ally, whose conduct had given no cause for such mistrust, but felt convinced that the appointing of the Ten, and the hiring of troops, meant war; which, if undertaken against so powerful a prince as Filippo Visconti, would surely involve the city in ruin, without the least prospect of any good resulting from it. For they could not retain sovereignty over any territory they might acquire, because of the Romagna lying between; and it would be impossible for them to make themselves masters of the Romagna on account of the proximity of the Church. Nevertheless the influence of those who wanted the republic to prepare for war outweighed that of the advocates of peace. The Ten were appointed, troops were levied, and fresh taxes imposed, which, bearing much heavier upon the lower classes than upon the wealthy citizens, filled the city with complaints; and the con-

demnation of the ambition and avarice of the government were general; they were accused of wishing to make an unnecessary war only for the purpose of gratifying their passions and to oppress the people.

5. The republic had not yet come to an open rupture with the Duke, but everything was looked upon with suspicion; for Filippo had at the request of the Legate of Bologna (who feared Messer Antonio Bentivogli, who, being banished, happened to be at Castel Bolognese) sent troops into that city (1420), which being near the Florentine dominions kept the republic full of apprehensions. But that which alarmed everybody, and was the main cause for declaring war, was the attempt which Duke Filippo made upon Furli. Giorgio Ordelaffi, lord of Furli, upon his death had left his young son Tibaldo under the guardianship of Duke Filippo; and although the mother, being suspicious of this guardian, had sent her son to her father Lodovico Alidossi, who was lord of Imola, yet was she forced by the people of Furli to conform to the father's will, and place the boy in the hands of the Duke. Whereupon Filippo, by way of removing all suspicion and the better to conceal his intentions, ordered that the Marquis of Ferrara should send Guido Torelli in his place with troops to take possession of the government of Furli. It was thus that this place fell into the hands of Filippo. When this fact became known at Florence, together with the news of the arrival of troops at Bologna, it facilitated the determination to declare war. Still there was great opposition to it, and Giovanni de' Medici publicly counselled against it, pointing out that, however certain the Duke's evil intentions were, yet it would be better to wait until he should make an attack than at once to move against him; for in the latter case the war would be justified in the opinion of the other Italian sovereigns on the part of the Duke as well as on their own part; and that then they could not claim their assistance with the same confidence as they might do if they allowed the Duke to manifest his ambitious projects; and that, finally, people defend their own homes with more courage and determination than they attack those of others. To this it was replied, that one should not await the enemy at home, but that it was better to go to meet him, and that fortune favored the assailants more than the defendants; and that it was less injurious, even if more

costly in money, to carry the war into the enemy's country, than to have it in one's own. This opinion prevailed, and it was resolved that the Ten should take all means for recovering the city of Furli from the hands of the Duke.

6. Filippo, seeing the Florentines determined to take those places which he had resolved to defend, threw off the mask, and sent Agnolo della Pergola with a large force to Imola (1424), so that the lord of that city, being obliged to look to his own defence, could not think of the protection of his grandson Tibaldo. When therefore Agnolo reached Imola, the Florentine troops being still at Modigliana, and the weather being so intensely cold that the ditches of the city were frozen, he passed over them by stealth at night and entered the city, capturing Lodovico Alidossi, whom he sent as prisoner to Milan. Imola being lost and war openly declared, the Florentines sent their troops to Furli, and began the siege of that city by investing it on all sides; and to prevent the Duke's forces from uniting to relieve it, they employed the Count Alberigo, who scoured the country daily from Zagonara to the very gates of Imola. Agnolo della Pergola, seeing that he could not safely succor Furli, because of the strong position occupied by the Florentine troops, bethought himself of attempting the capture of Zagonara, judging that the Florentines would not allow that place to be taken; and that, if they wished to succor it, they would have to raise the siege of Furli and come to battle under great disadvantage. He soon forced the Count Alberigo to ask for terms of capitulation, which were conceded to them, on condition that they should surrender the place if not relieved by the Florentines within fifteen days. When this mishap became known in the Florentine camp and in the city, every one was anxious not to allow the enemy to obtain this victory, but unhappily they thereby afforded him the opportunity of gaining a much greater one. For having raised the camp of Furli to go to the rescue of Zagonara, they encountered the enemy and were completely routed, not so much by the valor of the Milanese as by the inclemency of the weather; for the Florentines, having marched for several hours through deep mud in a pouring rain, found the enemy fresh, and were easily defeated by him. Nevertheless, in so great a defeat, which become famous throughout all Italy, none were killed excepting Lodovico degli Obizzi, to-

gether with two of his men, who having fallen from their horses were suffocated in the mud.

7. This defeat threw all Florence into great consternation, but mostly so those prominent citizens who had advised the war; for they saw the enemy powerful, their own forces dispersed, without the support of allies, and their own people irritated, who assailed them in all the public places with insulting words, complaining of the heavy taxes imposed upon them, and of the war, for which there was no cause, saying: "Did they appoint the Ten to intimidate the enemy? Did "they relieve Furli and rescue it from the hands of the Duke? "We now see the result of their counsels, and what they are "aiming at! It was not to defend liberty, which is hateful "to them, but it was to increase their own power, which God "has justly diminished. Nor is this the only enterprise with "which they burdened the city, but there were several others; "for was not the war against King Ladislas similar to this "one? To whom would they now fly for help? To Pope "Martin, whom they had insulted, for the sake of Braccio? "To Queen Joanna, who had to throw herself into the arms "of the king of Aragon because they had abandoned her?" Besides these reproaches, they said all sorts of other insulting things, as an irritated people is apt to do. The Signori therefore deemed it well to call together a number of citizens who with good words should quiet the excited anger of the populace. Whereupon Messer Rinaldo degli Albizzi, the oldest remaining son of Messer Maso, who on the strength of his own merits and the memory of his father aspired to the highest offices in the city, spoke at length, showing that "it was "not wise to judge of things only by their results, for it often "happened that the best considered undertakings did not come "to a good end, whilst the most ill-advised were frequently "successful. And were we to approve evil counsels because "of the good which occasionally has attended them, we should "virtually be encouraging error, which might result disas-"trously for the republic; for certainly evil counsels do not "always produce happy results. And in the same way it "would be an error to blame a judicious enterprise because "it had had an unsuccessful issue; for such a course would "discourage the citizens from giving the city the benefit of "their counsels, and to say that which they thought." He

then pointed out the necessity that had existed for this war, and how it would have been waged in Tuscany, if they had not carried it into the Romagna. "But since it was the will "of God that their troops should have been beaten, their losses "would be still more serious if they abandoned themselves to "hopelessness; if, however, they showed a bold front to for-"tune, and made the best use of the means at their command, "they would not feel the loss, nor would Duke Filippo enjoy "the victory. Nor should they be alarmed by the cost of the "war and the prospect of future taxation; for the latter could "easily be modified, and the former would be much less in the "future than what it had been in the past; for less money suf-"ficed for defence than what was needed for attacking others. "And finally he counselled them to follow the example of "their fathers, who, undismayed by any reverses, had always "defended themselves courageously against whoever assailed "them."

8. The citizens, reanimated by the discourse of Messer Rinaldo, engaged the services of the Count Oddo, son of Braccio, and gave him as an adviser Niccolo Piccinino, a pupil of Braccio's, and the best reputed of all those who had fought under his banner; to these they added other Condottieri, and remounted a portion of their men who had lost their horses. They appointed twenty citizens to levy new taxes, who, seeing the prominent citizens much cast down by the late defeat, taxed them without consideration. (1426.) These imposts greatly offended many of the prominent citizens, who at first, from a sense of propriety, had not complained of the taxes for themselves, but objected to them on the general ground of their being unjust, and therefore urged their repeal. This proposition, however, was rejected when brought before the council. Therefore, by way of making the harshness of the tax felt the more, and to make it odious to the mass of the people, these citizens contrived that the tax-gatherers should enforce it with the utmost severity, giving them the authority to kill any one who resisted the officers of the law. This gave rise to many painful occurrences, by the wounding and killing of citizens. It became evident that this course of proceeding would soon provoke the old party violence, and many prudent men feared some immediate misfortune. The great, who had been accustomed to be treated with special regard, would not

submit to being thus spoliated, whilst the others wanted that all should be taxed alike. In this state of things a number of the principal citizens met, and concluded that it would be necessary for them to reconstitute the government; inasmuch as their indolence had encouraged the people to find fault with the acts of the government, and had emboldened the leaders of the masses. After several private conferences they resolved all to meet again at an appointed time; when upwards of seventy citizens assembled in the church of San Stefano, with the sanction of Messer Lorenzo Ridolfi and Francesco Gianfigliazzo, members of the Signoria. Giovanni de' Medici did not meet with them, either because he was not invited, being suspected, or because he did not wish to interfere by opposing their views.

9. Messer Rinaldo degli Albizzi addressed the assembly and began by " showing them the condition of the city, and how by
" their negligence Florence had fallen under the control of the
" populace, from whom it had been wrested by their fathers in
" 1381. He reminded them of the iniquity of that government
" which had ruled from 1378 to 1381, and how every one present
" had to deplore the death of a father or grandfather in conse-
" quence; that the same dangers now threatened the republic,
" and that the city was relapsing into the same disorders. For
" already the people had laid a tax after their own fashion, and
" that they would very soon appoint the magistrates according
" to their pleasure, if they were not restrained by superior force
" or by more vigorous institutions. And that if this came to
" pass then the populace would occupy their places, and would
" overturn the government which for forty years had ruled the
" city with so much glory. That Florence would then be gov-
" erned either by chance, according to the caprice of the multi-
" tude, when the one party would indulge in every license and
" the other would be exposed to every danger; or the city would
" become subject to the rule of some one man, who would in the
" end make himself sovereign of it. And therefore he affirmed
" that every one who loved his country and valued his honor
" ought to rouse himself and remember the virtue of Bardo
" Mancini, who by the ruin of the Alberti rescued the city from
" the dangers in which it then was. He showed them that the
" cause of the audacity of the multitude was to be found in the
" frequency of the elections, which they by their negligence had

"allowed to take place, and which had filled the palace with
"new and low people. He therefore concluded that there was
"but one way of remedying the evil, and that was to restore
"the government to the hands of the nobles; to deprive the
"minor guilds of all share in the public authority, and to re-
"duce their number from fourteen to seven; that thus the
"populace would have less influence in the councils, both by
"the diminution of their numbers as well as by the increased
"authority which it would give to the nobles, who, always pre-
"serving their old enmities, would be opposed to the others.
"He assured them that it was true wisdom to make use of men
"according to the times; for if their fathers availed of the
"people to put down the insolence of the nobles, so, now that
"the nobles had become humble and the people insolent, it was
"wise to check the arrogance of the latter by the help of the
"former. And to enable them to carry this out, they might em-
"ploy either craft or force, to either of which means they could
"easily resort, as some of their friends were members of the
"Council of Ten, and could easily bring troops into the city."

Messer Rinaldo was applauded and his counsels approved by all; amongst others Messer Niccolo da Uzano said: "All that
"Messer Rinaldo has spoken is true, and the remedies proposed
"by him are good and sure provided they can be carried out
"without producing an open rupture in the city; which could
"be done if they could draw Messer Giovanni de' Medici into
"their plans. For by his concurrence with them, the people,
"being deprived of their chief and their strength, could do no
"harm; but if he did not concur with them, nothing could
"be effected without arms, and he deemed any resort to arms
"perilous, either from failure of success or from not being able
"to enjoy the benefit of their victory. He modestly brought
"to their recollection his past record, how he wanted to remedy
"the difficulty at the time when it might have been done easily,
"but now the opportune moment had been allowed to pass
"when it might have been done without danger of greater evils;
"and therefore there was now no other remedy left them but
"to gain Giovanni de' Medici over to their side." Messer Rinaldo was therefore commissioned to call upon Giovanni, and try to draw him into their plans.

10. This gentleman executed his commission, and in the best terms at his command he urged Giovanni to unite with them

in their effort, and not to encourage the multitude in their audacity, which would lead to the ruin of the government and the city. To which Giovanni replied: "That he believed it the "duty of a good and wise citizen not to change the established "institutions of the city, as there was nothing so injurious as "such frequent changes, which always gave offence to many; "and where so many remained discontented, there was cause "for apprehending every day some unhappy occurrence. He "thought that their determination would have two most per-"nicious results: the one, to give the public offices to those "who, never having held them, would esteem the honor less, "and who would have less cause of complaint if they did not "have them; the other, to take the honors from those who, "being accustomed to have them, would never rest until they "were restored to them. And thus the injury done to the one "would be much greater than the benefit bestowed upon the "other, so that whoever might be the author of such a measure "would gain but few friends by it, and make himself many "enemies; and the latter would be more eager to injure him "than the former to defend him, men being naturally more "prone to revenge of injuries than to gratitude for benefits re-"ceived, regarding the latter as onerous, whilst the former was "alike sweet and profitable." Then, turning to address Messer Rinaldo personally, he said: "And you, if you would remem-"ber the things that have happened, and with how much craft "and deceit things are carried on in this city, you would be "less eager in your resolve; for those who counsel it, after "having with your aid deprived the people of their authority, "will in turn take it again from you, with their aid whom the "wrong done them will have converted into your enemies. "And it will happen to you as it did to Messer Benedetto Al-"berti, who, persuaded by those who did not love him to con-"sent to the destruction of Messer Giorgio Scali and Messer "Tommaso Strozzi, was a short time after sent himself into "exile by those who had thus persuaded him. He advised "him, therefore, to think more maturely of these matters, and "to imitate his father, who, for the sake of gaining the favor "of the masses, had lowered the price of salt, and had provided "that he who owed less than half a florin for taxes might pay "it or not as he pleased; and that on the day of the meeting "of the councils every one should be exempt from prosecution

"by his creditors. And finally he concluded that, so far as re-
"garded himself, he was in favor of leaving the city under its
"present organization."

11. When these negotiations became known, it increased the esteem in which Giovanni was held, and the detestation of the other citizens, from whom Giovanni kept himself aloof, so as to discourage any one's attempting to introduce innovations under cover of his favor; and in all his conversations he gave every one to understand that he did not wish to nurse factions, but rather to destroy them; and so far as regarded himself, he desired nothing but the union of the city. This caused many of the adherents of his party to be dissatisfied, for they could have wished that he should have shown himself more active in these matters. Amongst these was Alamanno de' Medici, who, being of a violent temper, did not cease to urge him to persecute his enemies and to favor his friends, condemning his coldness and want of energy, to which he attributed the intrigues of his enemies against him, which, he said, would some day ruin his family and friends. He also encouraged Cosimo, the son of Giovanni, to the same views. Nevertheless Giovanni, from some revelations or predictions made to him, did not swerve from his purpose; despite of which, however, the parties had already declared themselves, and the city was in open division. There happened at that time to be in the palace attached to the service of the Signoria two chancellors, Ser Martino and Ser Pagolo. The latter adhered to the party of Uzano, and the former to that of the Medici; and Messer Rinaldo, seeing that Giovanni would not agree with them, thought it advisable to deprive Ser Martino of his office, hoping thereby to have the palace afterwards more favorably disposed for his party. But he was anticipated in this move by his adversaries, for Martino was not only protected, but Ser Pagolo was deprived of office, to the great displeasure and damage of his party. This would immediately have produced evil consequences had it not been for the war which threatened the republic, which had become greatly alarmed by the defeat suffered at Zagonara. For whilst these things were transpiring in Florence, Agnolo della Pergola with the troops of the Duke had seized all the places which the Florentines possessed in the Romagna, excepting only Castrocaro and Modigliana; partly in consequence of the weakness of the places, and partly owing to the defection of those in charge

of them. In the taking of these places two circumstances occurred which show how true bravery is appreciated even by the enemy, and how cowardice and villany are despised.

12. Biagio del Melano was castellan of the castle of Monte Petroso, which was surrounded and closely pressed by the enemy; and seeing no means of saving the place, Biagio piled clothing and straw in that part which was not yet in flames, and, casting his two little sons upon the pile, he called out to the enemy: "Take for yourselves the goods which Fortune "has given me, and of which you can deprive me, but the "treasures of my heart, which constitute my honor and glory, "I shall neither yield nor can you take them from me!" The enemy rushed in to save the children, and brought him ropes and ladders so that he might save himself and them. But he did not accept for himself, preferring to die in the flames rather than be saved by the hands of his country's enemies. An instance truly worthy of the boasted examples of antiquity! but more admirable than those, because more rare. The enemy restored to the children of Biagio all the things they were able to save, and sent them with the greatest care to their relatives. Nor was the republic less kind to them, for they were supported during life at the public expense.

The reverse of this occurred at Galeata, where Zanobi dal Pino was Podesta, who surrendered the fortress to the enemy without making any defence, and moreover advised Agnolo to leave the mountains of the Romagna and come into the hills of Tuscany, where he could carry on the war more advantageously and with less danger. Agnolo was disgusted by the cowardice and baseness of Zanobi, and handed him over to his servants, who, after much taunting, gave him nothing to eat but paper painted with snakes, saying that by this means they wanted to change him from a Guelf into a Ghibelline; and thus he died in a few days from hunger.

13. In the midst of this Count Oddo, together with Niccolo Piccinino, had entered the Val di Lamona for the purpose of trying to force the lord of Faenza into an alliance with the Florentines; or at least to hinder Agnolo della Pergola from freely scouring the Romagna. But that valley being naturally strong, and its inhabitants accustomed to arms, Count Oddo was killed and Niccolo Piccinino taken prisoner and sent to Faenza. But fortune wanted the Florentines to obtain by

means of their losses what victory perhaps would not have given them; for Niccolo prevailed upon the lord of Faenza and his mother to become allies of the Florentines. By the treaty resulting from this Niccolo was set free; but he did not himself act up to the advice which he had given to others; for in negotiating with the city of Florence in relation to his employment, they disagreed, either because the terms seemed to him insufficient, or because he found better pay elsewhere. For he abruptly left Arezzo, where he was in quarters, and went into Lombardy, where he entered into the service of the Duke Filippo. The Florentines, alarmed at this and frightened by the enormous expenses, concluded that they were not able to carry on this war alone; and therefore sent ambassadors to the Venetians to pray them, whilst it was still easy for them to do so, to oppose the greatness of one man, who, if they allowed him to increase in power, would be as dangerous for them as he was for the Florentines. The Venetians had been advised to the same effect by Francesco Carmignuola, a man highly esteemed in those days for his ability as a general, and who had formerly been in the service of the Duke, but had subsequently revolted against him; but they were doubtful as to how far they could trust Carmignuola, thinking that his enmity towards the Duke might possibly be only feigned. Whilst he was thus suspected by the Venetians, the Duke had poison administered to him by one of the servants of Carmignuola; the poison, however, was not sufficiently powerful to kill him, though it reduced him to extremity. When the cause of his illness was discovered, the Venetians gave up their suspicions, and employed him in accordance with the advice of the Florentines, and concluded a league with them, by which both parties obligated themselves to carry on the war at joint expense; and that the conquests in Lombardy should belong to the Venetians, and those in the Romagna and Tuscany to the Florentines; and Carmignuola was appointed the commander-in-chief of the forces of the league. The war during the continuance of this league was confined to Lombardy, where it was valiantly conducted by Carmignuola, who in the course of a few months took a number of places from the Duke, together with the city of Brescia, the capture of which was regarded in those days as something marvellous.

14. This war lasted from 1422 to 1427, so that the citizens

of Florence were tired of the taxes imposed upon them and
agreed to revise them (1427). And by way of equalizing
them according to the wealth of the citizens, they provided
that the taxes should be laid upon property, and that whoever
had to the value of one hundred florins should be assessed one
half a florin. As it was therefore the law and not men that had
to adjust this tax, it was regarded very onerous by the powerful citizens, who strenuously opposed the new system before it
was finally adopted. Giovanni alone supported it openly, and
thus it was passed. And because in the assessing of this tax
the property of each one was valued in the aggregate, which
the Florentines call "accatastare" (to pile together), this tax
was called the "Catasto." This system in some measure put
a check upon the tyranny of the great, for they could no
longer oppress the lesser people, nor silence them with threats
in the councils, as they formerly could. The mass of the
people therefore gladly accepted this tax, but the great received it with the greatest oppugnancy. But as it happens
that men are never satisfied, and when they have obtained one
thing are not content with it, but desire something else, so the
people, not content with the present equality of the tax, which
commenced with the passage of the law, demanded that it
should be made retroactive, and that it should be ascertained
how much too little the nobles had paid according to the Catasto; and that they should be made to pay as much as
would bring them even with those who, to enable them to pay
the taxes which they ought not to have paid, had been obliged
to sell their property. This demand alarmed the nobles much
more than the Catasto itself; and they did not cease to condemn it as being most unjust, especially in being put also upon
movable property, which, they argued, is possessed one day
and lost the next; and besides, that there were many persons
who kept their money concealed, so that the Catasto could
not touch it; to which they added, that those who left their
business to govern the republic should be taxed less, as it
should suffice that they gave their personal services; and that
it was not just that the city should claim their property, as
well as their time and talents. The others, who were favorable to the Catasto, replied, that, if the personal property varied,
the assessments could be varied accordingly, and by doing so
frequently, that inconvenience would be remedied. And of

those who kept their money concealed it was not necessary to take any account, for their money brought them no return, and therefore it was not reasonable that they should pay; but if they wanted to have profit from their money, they would have to reveal it, in which case it would be taxed. And if it did not please them to serve the republic, they might leave it alone and need not trouble themselves about it; for it would be easy to find well-disposed citizens who would willingly give their money and their counsels to the city; inasmuch as the advantages and honors resulting from their being in the government were such that they ought to suffice them without wishing to be exempt from taxation. But that the evil was not where they said it was, and that the real cause of their regrets was being no longer able to carry on the war without injury to themselves, since they had to contribute to its expenses the same as the others. And if the present measure had been adopted sooner, they would never have made the war against King Ladislas, nor the one against the Duke Filippo, both of which had been made, not from necessity, but merely to enrich some of the citizens. These ill feelings were calmed by Giovanni de' Medici, who argued that it was not well to revert to the things of the past, but that they ought to provide for the future. And if the taxes in the past had been unjust, they should thank God that the means had been found to make them just for the future; and he wanted that these means should serve to unite, and not to divide the city, as would be the case if they attempted to collect the taxes for the past so as to make them equal to the present one; and that it was better to be content with half a victory, for those who wanted to gain too much often lost all. With these and other similar arguments he quieted these discontents, and caused the retrospective tax not to be resolved upon.

15. Meantime, whilst the war with the Duke thus went on, a peace was negotiated at Ferrara through the intervention of the Pope's Legate, the conditions of which, however, were from the first disregarded by Filippo, so that the league resumed arms anew; and having come to battle with the Duke's forces, these were routed at Maclovio (1428). After this defeat Filippo set new negotiations on foot for a treaty, which were acceded to by the Venetians and Florentines; by the latter, from jealousy of the Venetians, for it seemed to them that they had

spent enough to make others powerful; and by the former, because they had observed that Carmignuola after the defeat of the Duke had become less active, so that they thought that they could no longer trust him. Peace was therefore concluded in 1428; according to the terms of which the Florentines were to receive back the places lost in the Romagna, and the Venetians retained Brescia, besides which the Duke gave them Bergamo with its territory. Florence had spent in this war the sum of three and a half millions of ducats; and whilst the Venetians had gained in power and possessions, the Florentines increased their poverty and divisions. External peace being restored, the internal dissensions recommenced. The great citizens, unwilling to submit to the Catasto, and seeing no way of putting an end to it, thought of means for augmenting the number of opponents to that measure, so as to have more support in their efforts to have it annulled. For this purpose they instructed the official assessors to put the tax, in accordance with the law, also upon the property of the inhabitants of the subject districts, so as to ascertain whether any of that property belonged to the Florentines. All the inhabitants of the districts were therefore cited to present, within a given time, written schedules of their property. This caused the Volterrans to send a deputation to protest against it to the Signoria, which irritated the officials to that degree that they put eighteen of them in prison. This aroused the indignation of the Volterrans, but consideration for their imprisoned envoys caused them to refrain from any violence.

16. About this time Giovanni de' Medici fell sick, and, feeling his illness to be mortal, he called his two sons, Cosimo and Lorenzo, to him, and said to them: " I believe I have lived
" to the time appointed for me by God and nature at my birth.
" I die content, for I leave you rich and healthy, and of such
" quality that, if you will follow in my footsteps, you can live
" in Florence honored and beloved by every one. Nothing
" makes me die so content as the reflection that I have never
" injured any one, but that rather, according to my ability, I
" have benefited all. I advise you to do the same; and if
" you desire to live securely, take only such share of the gov-
" ernment as the laws and the citizens may choose to bestow
" upon you, which will never expose you to envy or danger.
" For it is that which a man takes, not that which is given

"to him, that renders him odious to others; and thus you will "always have much more than those who, wishing to take the "share of others, lose their own, and who, before losing it live "in constant anxiety. In this way have I, in the midst of so "many enemies and divisions, not only maintained, but in-"creased my influence in the city; and thus, if you follow my "example, will you maintain and increase yours. But if you "do otherwise, remember that your fate will not be different "from that of those who within our memory have ruined them-"selves and their families."

Soon after this he died, in 1429, greatly regretted by every one in Florence, as he deserved, because of his admirable qualities. Giovanni was most charitable, and not only gave alms to whoever asked them, but often succored the poor without being solicited. He loved all mankind; he praised the good, and had compassion upon the wicked. He never asked for honors, but had them all. He never went to the palace unless called there. He loved peace, and avoided war; he remembered men in their adversity, and aided them in prosperity. He was a stranger to public rapine, and only aimed to increase the wealth of the state. As a magistrate he was courteous; his eloquence was moderate, but his prudence very great. The expression of his countenance was sad, but his conversation was cheerful, and even facetious. He died rich in treasure, but richer in good fame and the general affection. The heritage he left both in wealth of fortune and of character was not only maintained, but increased, by his son Cosimo.

17. The Volterran envoys were tired of being in prison, and for the sake of obtaining their liberty they promised to consent to what had been demanded of them. Being thereupon liberated, they returned to Volterra at the moment when the new priors of the city were about to assume their magistracy. Amongst these one Giusto had been drawn, a plebeian who had much influence with the populace, and one of those who had been imprisoned by the Florentines. Being fired with hatred against them on account of his private and the public wrongs, and stimulated also by Giovanni di Contugi, a noble who sat in the magistracy with him, he resolved to stir up the people with the authority of the priors; and with the support of the masses, whose favor he enjoyed, to rescue the country from the hands of the Florentines, and to make him-

self master of it. By Giovanni's advice Giusto took up arms, scoured the country, captured the resident Florentine governor, and with the consent of the people made himself lord of Volterra. This occurrence greatly irritated the Florentines; but having concluded a peace with Duke Filippo, the terms of which had just been settled, they judged that they would still be able to recover Volterra. And by way of not losing any time, they at once appointed Messer Rinaldo degli Albizzi and Messer Palla Strozzi as commissaries to conduct this enterprise. Giusto, in the mean time, anticipating that he would be attacked by the Florentines, applied for assistance to the people of Lucca and Sienna. The latter declined on the ground of being in alliance with the Florentines; and Pagolo Guinigi, lord of Lucca, who was desirous of recovering the good will of the people of Florence, which he supposed he had lost during their war with the Duke Filippo when he had declared himself the friend of the latter, not only refused all aid to Giusto, but sent those who had come to ask it as prisoners to Florence. The commissaries meantime, desiring to fall upon the Volterrans unawares, assembled all their forces, and raised a large body of infantry from the lower Val d' Arno, and marched upon Volterra. But Giusto, undismayed by having been abandoned by his neighbors, and by the impending attack of the Florentines, and relying upon the strength of the place and the roughness of the country, prepared for defence.

There was in Volterra a certain Messer Arcolano, brother of that Giovanni di Contugi who had persuaded Giusto to seize the lordship, who had much influence with the nobility. He called together certain of his confidential friends, and showed them how by this event God had come to the aid of their city in its need; for if they would take up arms and deprive Giusto of the lordship, and restore the city to the Florentines, it would follow that they would remain the leading men of the country, and preserve their ancient privileges. Having agreed upon this, they went to the palace where the lord resided; a portion of them remained below, whilst Messer Arcolano with three others ascended into the hall, where they found Giusto with some citizens. They called him aside as though they wished to confer with him upon some important affair, and whilst conversing with him they led him into a chamber, where Arcolano and his companions attacked him with their swords. But they were not sufficiently quick in their movements to prevent Giusto from drawing his sword, so that before they killed him he wounded two of his assailants severely. Unable, however, to resist so many, he was slain, and his body thrown down to the lower floor of the palace. The party of Messer Arcolano, having taken up arms, gave the city up to the Florentine commissaries, who were near by with their troops, and who entered the city without further stipulations. This made the condition of the Volterrans much worse, for amongst other things the Florentines secured the greater part of the territory from the city, and reduced Volterra to a mere vicariate.

18. Volterra being thus, as it were, lost and regained at one blow, there appeared no reasons for any new wars, had it not been that ambition provoked another. Niccolo Fortebraccio, a son of a sister of Braccio da Perugia, had been for a considerable time in the service of the city of Florence during the war with Duke Filippo. Upon the declaration of peace he was discharged by the Florentines; but when the difficulty with Volterra occurred he was still in quarters at Fucecchio, where the commissaries charged with the enterprise against Volterra made use of him and his men. It was generally believed that whilst thus engaged Messer Rinaldo persuaded Niccolo under some pretext to attack Lucca, pointing out to him that, if he did so, it would cause the Florentines openly to declare war against Lucca, and that then he would be made commander of their forces. After Volterra was taken, and when Niccolo had returned to his quarters at Fucecchio, persuaded either by Messer Rinaldo or of his own accord, he seized, in November, 1429, with three hundred mounted men and three hundred infantry, the Lucchese castles of Ruoti and Compito, and then descended into the plain, where he took a large amount of booty. When this became known in Florence people of all sorts gathered in groups throughout Florence, the greater part of which wanted war to be declared against Lucca. Of the principal citizens who were in favor of this were the Medici and their adherents; also Messer Rinaldo, who was influenced either by the belief that it would be advantageous for the republic, or perhaps by the ambitious hope that he would be appointed to conduct the enterprise. Those who were opposed to it were Niccolo da Uzano and his party. It

would almost seem incredible that in the same city there should be such a diversity of opinion as to the undertaking of this war; for those very citizens and the same people who, after ten years of peace, had blamed the war undertaken against Duke Filippo in defence of their own liberty, now, after the heavy expenditures and affliction in which that war involved the city, eagerly demanded that a war should be undertaken against Lucca to rob her citizens of their liberty. And, on the other hand, those who had been in favor of the former war now strenuously opposed this one. Thus do opinions change with time, and thus are the multitude ever more ready to seize upon the goods of others than to defend their own. And thus are men more influenced by the hope of gain than by the fear of loss; for the latter, unless very near, excites no apprehension; and the former, being still remote, creates hopes. And thus the people of Florence were filled with hopes by the conquests already made and yet expected to be made by Fortebraccio, and by the letters written by their rectors from near Lucca. For the governors of Pescia and Vico had written that, if permission were given them to receive those castles that were willing to surrender to them, the whole Lucchese territory would very quickly be acquired. Added to this came the conduct of the envoy whom the lord of Lucca had sent to Florence to remonstrate against the attack made upon him by Fortebraccio, and to beg the Signoria not to make war upon a neighbor and a city that had ever been their friend. This envoy was called Messer Jacopo Viviani; he had been imprisoned by Pagolo Guinigi, lord of Lucca, for having conspired against him; and although found guilty, yet his life was spared and he was pardoned by Pagolo, who, in the belief that Messer Jacopo had also forgiven his injury, intrusted him with this mission. But when Messer Jacopo came to Florence, being more mindful of the danger he had escaped than of the benefit received, he secretly counselled the citizens in favor of the war against Lucca. This advice, added to their hopes, caused the Signoria to assemble the councils, at which four hundred and ninety-eight citizens came together, before whom the question was discussed by the principal men of Florence.

19. Amongst the first to speak in favor of the attempt against Lucca was, as we have said above, Messer Rinaldo. He pointed

out the advantages that would result from the acquisition, and demonstrated the opportunity to be favorable,—Lucca being left an easy prey to them by the Venetians and Duke Filippo. Nor could the Pope intervene, being occupied with the affairs of the kingdom of Naples. He furthermore showed the facility with which the city could be taken, being enslaved by one of her own citizens, and having lost her natural vigor and ancient zeal in defence of her liberties; so that the city would be given up to them, either by the people for the sake of ridding themselves of their tyrant, or by the tyrant from fear of the people. He recited the injuries done them by the lord of Lucca, his ill-will against the Florentine republic, and how dangerous he would prove if ever they should again be involved in war with either the Pope or the Duke; and concluded by saying that no enterprise ever engaged in by the Florentines had been more easy, more beneficial, or more just. Against this opinion Niccolo da Uzano spoke as follows: " That the city of Florence had never " attempted a more unjust nor more hazardous enterprise, and " from which greater injury would result. And, first, because " it was a Guelf city which it was proposed to attack, and one " that had ever been friendly to the Florentine people, and had " many times, at her own peril, received in her bosom the Guelfs " who were not permitted to remain in their own country; and " that never, within the memory of our times, had Lucca, when " free, offended Florence; and that, if she had done so when " enslaved, as formerly by Castruccio, and now by Pagolo, the " guilt could not be imputed to her, but to her tyrant. And if " they could make war against the tyrant without doing so " against the citizens, it would displease him less; but as that " could not be done, he could not consent that a city, hitherto " their friend, should be despoiled of her liberty and her prop-" erty. But as people nowadays took little account of what was " just or unjust, he would not now touch upon that point, but " would only look to the question of advantage to their own city. " He believed that only those things should be called advan-" tageous which could not readily be productive of injury; but " he did not know how any one could call an undertaking use-" ful in which the damage was certain and the benefit doubtful. " The certain damage was the cost, which would be unavoidable, " and which would be found so great that it should alarm a city " that for a long while had enjoyed the repose of peace, and

"much more so one that was wearied by a serious and pro-
"tracted war, as was the case with Florence. The benefit that
"could possibly result from it would be the conquest of Lucca,
"which he confessed would be a great one; but that it was
"proper to consider the uncertainty in which that was involved,
"which in his judgment was so great that he regarded the con-
"quest impossible. And that they must not believe that the
"Venetians and Duke Filippo would rest satisfied with such an
"acquisition on their part; for the former only made pretence
"of consent to avoid appearing ungrateful, having but a short
"time before added so largely to their dominions by means of
"Florentine money. And Duke Filippo would be glad to see
"them involve themselves in new wars and expenditures, so
"that, when wearied and exhausted in all respects, he might
"the more safely assail them anew; and that whilst they were
"engaged in this undertaking, and full of high hopes of victory,
"the Duke would not lack means of aiding the Lucchese cov-
"ertly, either with money or by disbanding some of his troops,
"and letting them go to their assistance as soldiers of fortune.
"He therefore advised them to abstain from the attempt, and
"to live on such terms with the tyrant of Lucca as would cause
"him to increase the number of his enemies as much as possi-
"ble within the city; for there would be no more convenient
"way of subjugating Lucca than to let her live under the rule
"of her tyrant, and to have her weakened and exhausted by
"him. For if the matter were managed prudently, things
"would soon come to that point in Lucca that, the tyrant not
"being able to hold her, the city, being incapable of governing
"herself, would of necessity fall into their hands. But that he
"saw the feelings that had been stirred, and that his words
"were not listened to; yet this he would predict to them, that
"they were about to make a war in which they would expend a
"great deal of money and expose themselves to many dangers;
"and, instead of taking Lucca, they would deliver her from her
"tyrant, and convert her from a friendly, feeble, and enslaved
"city into a free and hostile city, which in time would prove an
"obstacle to the greatness of their own republic."

20. After the speeches in favor of and against the enterprise, a secret vote was taken, according to custom; and of the whole number present only ninety-eight were against it. The war being therefore resolved upon, the Ten were appointed for its

conduct, and troops were levied, both mounted men and infantry. Messer Astorre Gianni and Messer Rinaldo degli Albizzi were appointed commissaries, and an arrangement was made with Niccolo Fortebraccio to receive from him the places he had taken, and for him to remain in the service of the Florentines during the continuance of the war. When the commissaries arrived with the army in the Lucchese territory, they divided their forces; and Astorre extended himself through the plain to Camajore and Pietrasanta, and Messer Rinaldo went towards the mountains, judging that, if the city were cut off from the country, it would then be easy to take it. These movements, however, proved unfortunate; not because they did not capture places enough, but because their conduct of the war had subjected them to various complaints and charges. And certainly the conduct of Messer Astorre Gianni was justly liable to the charges brought against him. There is near to Pietrasanta a rich and populous valley called Seravezza. When its inhabitants heard of the arrival of the commissaries, they went to meet them, and begged to be received by them as loyal servants of the Florentine people. Astorre made show of accepting the proffer, and then sent his troops to occupy the passes and strong places of the valley. Thereupon he caused all the men of the valley to come together in their principal churches, where he made them all prisoners, whilst his troops sacked and plundered the whole country in the most cruel and rapacious manner, respecting neither their sacred places nor their women, whether maidens or married. When these proceedings became known at Florence it caused the greatest indignation, not only of the magistrates, but of the whole city.

21. Some of the men of Seravezza, who had escaped from the hands of Astorre, rushed to Florence, and told the story of their woes to every one in the streets; and being encouraged by many who desired the punishment of the commissary, either because of his infamous conduct or because he was of the opposite faction, they went to the Ten, demanding to be heard. And being admitted, one of the men spoke as follows: " We are certain, " O magnificent Signori, that our words will find belief and " compassion with your lordships, when you shall know how our " country has been seized by your commissary, and how we have " been treated by him. Our valley was evermore Guelf, as your " ancient records will abundantly attest, and has often been a

"safe refuge for your citizens when persecuted by the Ghibel-
"lines. Our ancestors, as well as ourselves, have ever honored
"the name of your illustrious republic as the head and chief of
"the Guelf party. So long as the Lucchese were Guelf, we
"cheerfully served their power; but since they have fallen
"under the yoke of the tyrant who has abandoned his old
"friends and followed the Ghibelline party, we have obeyed by
"compulsion rather than of our own free will. And God
"knows how many times we have prayed him to give us an
"opportunity of manifesting our attachment to the old party.
"But how blind men are in their desires! That which we
"longed for as being for our welfare has proved our ruin! For
"so soon as we heard that your banners were marching towards
"us, we went to meet your commissary, not as an enemy, but
"as our ancient lord; and placed our fortunes and ourselves
"into his hand, and commended ourselves to his good faith,
"believing that, if he had not the soul of a Florentine, yet he
"had at least that of a man. Your lordships will pardon us,
"for we could not suffer worse than what we have suffered, and
"speak from the heart. Your commissary has nothing of the
"man but the appearance, and nothing of the Florentine but
"the name. He is a deadly pest, a wild and cruel beast, a
"horrid monster, such as no writer has ever before imagined;
"for after having called us together in our church, on pretence
"of wishing to confer with us, he destroyed and burnt the whole
"valley, plundered the inhabitants of their substance, sacked,
"despoiled, beat, and killed them, ravished the women, and
"violated the young maidens by dragging them from the arms
"of their mothers and giving them up to the lust of his sol-
"diers. Had we deserved all this ill treatment because of some
"injury done to the Florentine people or to him, or had he
"taken us with arms in hand defending ourselves, we should
"blame your commissary less, and rather accuse ourselves for
"having by such injuries or by our arrogance deserved it. But
"having given ourselves up to him freely and unarmed, he
"afterwards robbed and maltreated us, and subjected us to
"such insults and ignominy that we are compelled to complain
"of it to you. And although we might have filled Lombardy
"with our lamentations, and spread the story of our wrongs
"throughout Italy, to the eternal disgrace of your city, yet did
"we refrain from doing so, as we did not wish to stain so hon-

"orable and benevolent a republic with the dishonesty and cru-
"elty of one of her evil-minded citizens, whose ravenous soul,
"though boundless and bottomless, we would have endeavored
"to have satisfied with the larger part of our substance, so as
"thus to have saved the remnant, had we known his avarice
"and rapacity before. But as there is no longer time for that,
"we desired to have recourse to you, and by you to relieve the
"wretchedness of your subjects, so that other people may not
"be deterred by our unfortunate example from placing them-
"selves under your dominion. And if you are not moved by
"our infinite ills, may the fear of God's divine anger move you,
"who has seen his temples sacked and burnt, and our people
"betrayed in his very bosom!" Having spoken thus, they
threw themselves upon the ground, crying and praying that their
goods and their country might be restored to them; and that,
although the Signoria could not restore to them their honor,
yet they should at least order the wives to be returned to
their husbands, and the children to their parents. These atro-
cities having already come to the knowledge of the Florentines,
and having them now heard attested by the very men who had
borne them, the magistrates were moved, and ordered Astorre
to return without delay, who was thereupon condemned and
admonished. They had the property of the people of Seravezza
collected, and what was found of it was restored to them; and
for the rest they were compensated in time in various ways.

22. Messer Rinaldo degli Albizzi was reported by the other
party to be carrying on the war more for his own benefit than
for that of the Florentine people; and that since he had been
appointed commissary he had become lukewarm in his desire
to take Lucca, contenting himself with plundering the country
and filling his own estates with stolen cattle and his palace
with booty; and that, not satisfied with the plunder made for
his private benefit by his followers, he purchased the soldiers'
share, so that from a commissary he had become a mere trader.
When these reports came to the ears of Messer Rinaldo, it
excited his proud and honorable spirit more than what was
becoming to so grave a man; and so perturbed him, that, indignant against the magistrates and the citizens, and without
asking or awaiting leave of absence, he returned to Florence,
and presenting himself before the Ten, he said: "That he well
"knew the difficulty and danger of serving a divided city and

"an unbridled people; for the one magnified every report, and
"the other punished errors, but did not reward good actions,
"and accused doubtful ones. And however much a man might
"be victorious, yet no one would praise him; whilst every one
"is ready to condemn the slightest error, and overwhelm him
"with calumnies; for his own party will persecute him from
"jealousy, and the opposite party from hatred. Nevertheless I
"have never from fear of any idle complaint failed to do any
"act which I believed would prove a certain benefit to this city.
"True, the base dishonesty of the present calumnies has over-
"come my patience and excited my temper, and therefore do
"I pray the magistrates that they will in the future be more
"ready to defend their citizens, so that they may devote them-
"selves with the greater energy to labor for the good of the
"country. And as it is not the custom of Florence to bestow
"triumphal honors upon their successful commanders, it would
"at least be proper that they should defend them against mali-
"cious slanders; and that they ought to remember that they
"too were citizens of Florence, and that charges might at any
"moment be brought against them, and that then they would
"understand how deeply upright men were offended by base
"calumnies." The Ten endeavored as far as they could to
placate Messer Rinaldo; but confided the further command of
the expedition to Neri di Gino and Alamanno Salviati, who,
instead of scouring the Lucchese territory, moved their camp
nearer to the city. And as the season was still cold they established themselves at Campanola, where the commissaries
however seemed to think they were losing time; and when
they wanted to invest the place closer, the soldiers refused, on
account of the severity of the weather, although the Ten urged
the investment, and would take no excuse.

23. There lived at that time at Florence an eminent architect called Filippo di Ser Brunelleschi, who has filled our city
with his works, and whose merits were so great that after his
death a marble statue was erected to him in the principal
church of Florence, with an inscription at foot attesting his
great ability. Considering the position of the city of Lucca,
and the bed of the river Serchio, Brunelleschi demonstrated
how Lucca could be submerged; and so persuaded the Ten
that they ordered the experiment to be made; which unfortunately, however, resulted only in the discomfiture of our own

camp, and greater security to the enemy. For the Lucchese by means of a dam raised the ground on the side whence the Serchio came, and then at night broke the bank of the canal by which the Florentines were conducting the river; so that the water, meeting the raised ground on the side of Lucca, and the open bank of the canal, spread itself over the whole plain, so that, instead of being able to invest the city closer, the Florentine camp had to be removed.

24. This project having failed, the Ten who had been reappointed sent as commissary Messer Giovanni Guicciardini, who established his camp as promptly as possible near the city. When, therefore, the lord of Lucca found himself so closely pressed, by the advice of one Messer Antonio del Rosso, the resident representative of Sienna at Lucca, he sent two envoys, Messer Salvestro Trenta and Leonardo Buonvisi, to the Duke of Milan, to ask assistance of him. But finding him disinclined, they begged him secretly to send them troops, in return for which they pledged themselves on behalf of the people of Lucca to deliver Guinigi to him as prisoner, and then to give him possession of the city; informing him at the same time, that, if he did not accept this proposition at once, the tyrant of Lucca would surrender the city to the Florentines, which they had asked of him with many promises in return. The Duke, fearing that this would be done, put aside all other considerations, and directed Count Francesco Sforza, who was in his pay, publicly to ask leave of him to go to the kingdom of Naples; this leave being granted him, the Count Francesco marched direct upon Lucca with his troops. Although the Florentines understood this arrangement, yet being apprehensive of its results, they sent to his friend Count Boccacino Alamanni to interrupt this movement. When therefore the Count Francesco came to Lucca, the Florentines withdrew with their forces to Librafatta, whilst the Count promptly pitched his camp before Pescia. Pagolo da Diacceto was deputy governor of this place, and being counselled more by his fears than by any other and better motive, he fled to Pistoja; so that the place would have been lost, had it not been defended by Giovanni Malavolti, who was there in garrison. The Count Francesco therefore, unable to take Pescia at the first assault, went thence to the Borgo alla Buggiano and took that, and also burnt the neighboring castle of Stigliano. The Florentines,

seeing these disasters, resorted to a remedy that had saved them many times before: knowing that, with the mercenary nature of soldiers, corruption will succeed where force is insufficient, they offered a sum of money to the Count to induce him to depart and give them up the place. Francesco, finding that he could extract no more money from the Lucchese, promptly turned to extract it from those who had it to give; and agreed with the Florentines, not to give them up Lucca, which his honor would not permit him to do, but to abandon it upon receiving from them the sum of fifty thousand ducats. And having concluded a convention to this effect, so that the people of Lucca might excuse him with the Duke, he offered to assist them in expelling their tyrant.

25. Messer Antonio del Rosso, as we have said above, was the Siennese envoy at Lucca, and he, by authority of the Count Francesco, plotted with the citizens the ruin of Pagolo Guinigi. The chiefs of this conspiracy were Piero Cennami and Giovanni da Chivizano. Count Francesco was in quarters outside of the city on the Serchio, and with him was Lanzilao, the son of the Lord Pagolo. The conspirators, to the number of forty, went armed to find Pagolo, who, aroused by the noise, went towards them quite surprised, and demanded the reason of their coming. To which Piero Cennami replied, that they had for a long time been governed by him, and had been led to die by hunger and the sword, surrounded by enemies, and therefore they were resolved to govern themselves in future, and demanded of him the keys of the city and its treasure. To which Pagolo replied, that the treasure was exhausted and the keys of the city in their power; and he begged of them only this one thing, that, inasmuch as his government had been begun and continued without bloodshed, they might be satisfied that it should terminate in like manner. Pagolo Guinigi and his son were carried by Count Francesco to the Duke at Milan, where both died in prison soon after. The departure of the Count Francesco relieved Lucca of her tyrant and Florence of the fear of his troops; whereupon the former prepared for defence, and the latter resumed the offensive. The Florentines appointed the Conte d' Urbino as their captain, who invested Lucca closely, thus obliging the inhabitants again to have recourse to the Duke for assistance. He sent Niccolo Piccinino to their assistance under a similar pretext

to that on which he had previously sent the Count Francesco. When Niccolo was about to enter Lucca, our troops met him on the Serchio, and on his attempting to cross the river they came to battle with him and were routed, so that our commissary with only a few of our troops escaped to Pisa. This defeat cast a gloom over our whole city; and as the expedition against Lucca had been undertaken at the general desire of the people, they knew not whom to blame; and inasmuch as they could not censure those who had advised the war, they abused those who had been charged with its conduct, and revived the charges against Messer Rinaldo. But more than any one else they censured Messer Giovanni Guicciardini, it being charged against him that he might have terminated the war after the departure of the Count Francesco, but that he had been bribed with money, and had sent home a large sum; they even gave the name of the person who had paid it, and of him who received it. These rumors became so loud that the Captain of the people, influenced by these reports, and urged on by those of the opposite faction, summoned Messer Giovanni to appear before him. Messer Giovanni appeared, full of indignation, but his relatives exerted themselves so much in behalf of his honor that the Captain abandoned the prosecution. After their victory, the Lucchese not only recovered their own castles, but took all those in the territory of Pisa, excepting Bientina, Calcinaia, Livorno, and Librafatta (1433). And had it not been that a conspiracy, which had been set on foot in Pisa, was discovered, that city would also have been lost. The Florentines thereupon reorganized their forces, and gave the command to Micheletto, a pupil of the Count Francesco Sforza. The Duke on the other hand followed up the victory; and to enable him to carry on the war against the Florentines with greater power, he induced the Genoese, the Siennese, and the lord of Piombino to form a league for the defence of Lucca, and to secure the services of Niccolo Piccinino as their commander, which made the whole matter publicly known. Hereupon the Venetians and Florentines renewed their league, and the war began openly in Lombardy and Tuscany; several battles were fought in both territories, with varying fortune; so that both sides became weary of the contest, and peace was concluded in the month of May, 1433, according to the terms of which the Florentines, Lucchese, and Siennese, who during the war had seized each other's castles, surrendered them all, and each re-entered into possession of their own.

26. Whilst this war had been going on, the malign humors of the factions were kept all along in a state of fermentation. Cosimo de' Medici, after the death of his father, displayed more zeal in public affairs, and even more devotion and liberality towards his friends, than his father had done; so that those who had rejoiced at Giovanni's death became greatly depressed when they saw what Cosimo was. Cosimo was a man of rare prudence, of grave but agreeable presence, and most liberal and humane. He never attempted anything against the party opposed to him, or against the state, but endeavored to do good to all; and by his generosity he won the attachment of a great many citizens who became his partisans, so that his example increased the cares of those who held the government, whilst he judged that in this way he would be able to live in Florence as securely, and exercise as much power, as any one else; or if his adversaries from motives of ambition should attempt to resort to extraordinary measures against him, that he would be superior to them both in force of arms and by the support of his friends. The persons mainly instrumental in promoting the growth of his power were Averardo de' Medici and Puccio Pucci; the former by his audacity, and the latter by his prudence and sagacity, contributed largely to increase the popularity and influence of Cosimo. The counsels and judgment of Puccio were so much esteemed, and were so well known by everybody, that the party was named, not after Cosimo, but after Puccio.

It was by a city thus divided that the expedition against Lucca had been undertaken, by which the party feeling, instead of being allayed, became only the more inflamed. And although it had been the party of Cosimo that had been in favor of the expedition, yet in its conduct many of the opposite party had been employed, being some of the best reputed men in the republic. And as Averardo de' Medici and the others of his party could not prevent this, they strove by every device most industriously to calumniate them, and whenever any reverse was experienced, which happened repeatedly, it was ascribed, not to fortune or to the strength of the enemy, but to the lack of skill and prudence of the commissary. It was this that caused the offences of Astorre de Gianni to be exaggerated; it was this that caused the indignation of Messer Rinaldo degli Albizzi, making him throw up his commission without leave; and it was the same system of calumny that had caused the Captain of the people to summon Messer Giovanni Guicciardini. From this arose all the other troubles to which the magistrates and the commissaries were subjected; for real evils were exaggerated, and unreal ones were invented, and both true and false were alike believed by the people, who as a general thing hated the accused.

27. This whole system and extraordinary mode of proceeding were well understood by Niccolo da Uzano and the other chiefs of the party; and they had often discussed together the means for remedying them, but had not found any; for to allow these things to go on and increase seemed to them dangerous, and any attempt to put an end to them difficult. Niccolo da Uzano was the first to express himself openly dissatisfied with these extraordinary proceedings; and therefore, whilst there was war without and dissensions within the city, Niccolo Barbadori, desirous to induce Niccolo da Uzano to consent to the destruction of Cosimo, went to see him at his house, where he found him in his study wrapt in deep thought. He endeavored to persuade him with such arguments as best he could to concur with Messer Rinaldo in the expulsion of Cosimo, to which Niccolo da Uzano replied in the following words: —

"It would be better for thee and thy family, as well as for "our republic, that thou and the others who hold the same "opinions as you do had beards of silver-white rather than of "golden hue as thy name indicates, for then their counsels, "proceeding from hoary heads full of experience, would be wiser "and more beneficial to everybody. For it seems to me that "those who wish to drive Cosimo from Florence should, before "doing anything else, measure their own strength and that of "Cosimo. You have baptized this party of ours that of the "nobles, and the other that of the people; even if the name "corresponded with the truth, yet would success be doubtful, "and we should have reason to fear rather than to hope, ac"cording to the example of that ancient nobility which was "destroyed by the people. But we have much more to fear, "for our party is dismembered, and that of the adversary com"pact and entire. In the first place Neri di Gino and Nerone "di Nigi, two of our principal citizens, have never declared

"themselves in such a way that we could say they are more
"our friends than theirs. Many families and even houses are
"divided amongst themselves; for, owing to the jealousy of
"brothers or relatives, they are opposed to us and support the
"other party. I will cite only the most striking cases; others
"will readily suggest themselves to you. Of the two sons of
"Messer Maso degli Albizzi, Lucci has cast his fortunes with
"the Medici party from jealousy of his brother, Messer Rinaldo.
"In the house of the Guicciardini the two sons of Messer Luigi
"are divided, Piero being the enemy of Giovanni and support-
"ing the party of our adversaries. The same with Tommaso
"and Niccolo Soderini, who have openly declared against us
"from their hatred against their uncle Francesco; so that, if
"we consider well who are for them and who for us, I do not
"really know why our party more than theirs should be called
"that of the nobles. If it be because they have the people on
"their side, that places us only so much in a worse and them
"in a better position, in so far that, were it to come to arms or
"to voting, we should be unable to resist them. And if we
"still preserve our dignities, it arises from the ancient reputa-
"tion of our government, which maintained itself honorably
"during fifty years; but should it come to the test and our
"weakness be discovered, then we should also lose that dig-
"nity. And if thou wert to say to me that the justice of our
"cause should increase our influence and diminish theirs,
"I should reply, that that justice must be understood and
"believed in by others as it is by us, all of which, however,
"is just the very reverse; for the reasons that influence us
"are founded wholly upon the suspicion that Cosimo aims at
"making himself sovereign of the city. Now, although we
"have that suspicion, yet the others have it not, and what
"is worse, they accuse us of the very thing that we charge
"upon him.

"The acts of Cosimo which cause us to suspect him are that
"he aids everybody with his money, not only private persons,
"but even the state, and not only the Florentines, but even the
"Condottieri; that he supports the citizens in their reclama-
"tions upon the magistrates; and that through the good will
"of the masses, which he enjoys, he has advanced several of
"his friends to the highest honors. The reasons, therefore,
"which we would have to adduce for expelling Cosimo would

"be that he is benevolent, serviceable to his friends, liberal, and
"beloved by everybody. Tell me a little now, what law is there
"against charity, liberality, and love? And although these are
"the very ways which all men adopt who aim at sovereignty,
"yet they are not so regarded in the case of Cosimo; nor have
"we sufficient credit to make them so regarded. For our past
"conduct has caused all confidence to be withdrawn from us;
"and the city of Florence, which is naturally partisan and cor-
"rupt from having always been divided into parties, will not
"listen to such accusations. But suppose that you were to
"succeed in driving him out, — which might well be, having a
"Signoria well disposed to it, — how can you ever prevent his
"return, when so many of his friends remain here, who will
"labor most ardently for his return? You will find it impos-
"sible to guard against this danger, for his friends are so
"numerous and have the support and good will of the masses.
"And the more of his avowed friends you expel, the greater
"number of enemies will you make yourselves; so that in a
"little while he would be recalled in spite of you, and all you
"will have gained will be that you have driven him out a good
"man and that he returns a bad one; for his nature will be
"corrupted by those who will have recalled him, and whom he
"could not oppose being under such obligations to them. And
"should you wish to kill him, you will never succeed in doing
"it by legal means, for his money and your corruptible natures
"will always save him. But suppose him to be killed or ban-
"ished not to return, I do not see what our republic would gain
"by it; for if she were delivered from Cosimo she would be
"enslaved by Rinaldo. As for myself, I am one of those who
"desire that no one citizen shall exceed another in power and
"authority. But if either one of these two men must rule, then
"I know no reason for loving Messer Rinaldo more than Cosimo.
"And now I have nothing more to say to thee other than may
"God preserve our republic from having any one of her citizens
"become sovereign! but even if our sins should have deserved
"it, then may God preserve her from having to obey Messer
"Rinaldo! Do not then advise a course that would in every
"way prove injurious; and do not imagine that being supported
"by a few, you could successfully oppose the will of the many;
"for all these citizens, partly from ignorance and partly from
"malice, are ready to sell the republic; and fortune has so far

"favored them that they have found a purchaser. Govern thy-"self, therefore, according to my advice, and look to living "modestly, and so far as liberty is concerned, you will have "as much cause for suspecting our party as the opposite one. "And when trouble comes, you, having remained neutral, will "be acceptable to everybody, and thus will you benefit, and not "injure, your country!"

28. These words somewhat cooled the ardor of Barbadori, so that matters remained quiet so long as the war with Lucca lasted; but when peace came, and with it the death of Niccolo da Uzano, the city being without any war and without any control, the evil humors again increased unrestrained. Messer Rinaldo, who considered himself as remaining the sole chief of his party, did not cease to entreat and importune all those citizens whom he supposed might become Gonfalonieri, to arm themselves and free the city from that man, who, from necessity and by the malice of a few and the ignorance of the many, would assuredly reduce the city to servitude. This course pursued by Messer Rinaldo, and that taken by the adverse party, kept the entire city in a state of apprehension; and every time that a new magistracy was to be appointed, it was publicly discussed how many of each party should be chosen; and at the drawing of the Signoria the whole city was aroused. Every case that came before the magistrates, even the smallest, became a cause of contention; secrets were divulged, and the good and evil alike became objects of favor or disfavor; good men and wicked were assailed alike, and no magistrate performed his duty. Florence then being in this state of confusion, and Messer Rinaldo ever anxious to break down the power of Cosimo, and knowing that Bernardo Guadagni was likely to become Gonfaloniere, he paid his taxes for him, so that his indebtedness to the public treasury might not deprive him of the right to hold that office. Having come now to the drawing of the Signoria, fortune, ever favoring our dissensions, caused Bernardo to be drawn as Gonfaloniere for the months of September and October. Messer Rinaldo went promptly to call upon him, and told him that the party of the nobles, as well as the others who desired to live quietly, were rejoiced that he had attained that dignity; and that it now behooved him so to act that they should not have rejoiced in vain. He then showed him the dangers to which they would be exposed

by disunion; and that there was no other way to secure union but the destruction of Cosimo, — for he alone by his immoderate wealth kept them weak; and that he had already raised himself so high that, if not prevented, he would make himself sovereign of Florence. And therefore it behooved a good citizen to provide against this by calling the people to assemble in the Piazza, and to reorganize the government so as to restore his country to liberty. He recalled to him that Messer Salvestro de' Medici was enabled unjustly to check the greatness of the Guelfs, to whom by the blood of their ancestors, spilt in the service of the state, the government of right belonged; and that what Salvestro could unjustly do against so many, he ought to be able justly to do against only one man. He counselled him not to fear, for his friends were ready to aid and stand by him with arms in hand; and that he need not regard the populace, which adored Cosimo, who however would obtain no better support from them than what Messer Giorgio Scali had received from them; nor need he fear the wealth of Cosimo, which when he should once be in the hands of the Signoria would then belong to them. And he concluded by telling him that, if he followed these suggestions, he would make the republic secure and united, and himself glorious. To all this Bernardo replied briefly, "that he judged it necessary to do as "Rinaldo had told him; but as time was required to carry "these suggestions into effect, he should attend to preparing "himself to be ready with his forces, being persuaded that "his colleagues would join him." So soon as Bernardo had assumed the magistracy, and had disposed his colleagues favorably to the plan, and all points being agreed upon with Messer Rinaldo, he summoned Cosimo, who, despite of the advice of numerous friends, appeared, relying more upon his innocence than the mercy of the Signori. The moment Cosimo entered the palace he was arrested; and Messer Rinaldo issued forth from his house, together with many armed men and followed by the whole party, and went to the Piazza, where the Signoria caused the people to be assembled, and appointed a Balia of two hundred persons to reorganize the government of the city. So soon as they were able, this Balia discussed the questions of reform and of the life and death of Cosimo. Many wanted him sent into exile, others wanted his death, and some were silent either from compassion for him or from fear of the others; and this difference of opinion prevented anything definite from being resolved upon.

In the tower of the palace of the Signoria there is a chamber called the "Alberghettino," occupying the entire space of the tower; it was here that Cosimo was confined under the charge of Federigo Malavolti. Hearing from this place the assembling of the councils and the noise of arms in the Piazza, and the frequent ringing of the bells for calling the Balia together, Cosimo became apprehensive lest some attempt should be made upon his life. But what he feared still more was that his particular enemies might employ some extraordinary means for encompassing his death; and therefore he abstained from all food, so that within the space of four days he had eaten nothing but a small piece of bread. Federigo, having observed this, said to him: "You are afraid "of being poisoned, Cosimo, and will kill yourself by starva-"tion; it is little to my credit that you should believe me "capable of lending myself to such an act of villany. I do "not believe your life to be in danger, for you have many "friends within and without the palace; and yet, if you should "have to lose your life, be assured they would have to use "other means than to employ me as a minister in depriving "you of it; for I would not stain my hands with the blood of "any man, and least of all yours, who have never offended me. "Be therefore of good cheer, take your food and live for your "friends and your country; and so that you may do so with "the greater confidence I will myself share your meals with "you." These words comforted Cosimo very much, and with tears in his eyes he embraced and kissed Federigo, and thanked him most earnestly and affectionately for this kind and compassionate act, promising to be most grateful to him if ever fortune afforded him the opportunity. Cosimo being somewhat restored, and whilst the citizens were still discussing his case, it chanced that Federigo, for the purpose of giving Cosimo pleasure, brought home with him to dinner a familiar friend of the Gonfaloniere, called Il Farganaccio, a man of gay and facetious spirit. Having nearly finished dinner, Cosimo, thinking to profit by the visit of this man, whom he knew extremely well, beckoned to Federigo to leave the room, who, understanding the object, feigned to go out for something necessary to complete the repast;—and the two being thus left alone together, Cosimo, after some friendly words to Farganaccio, gave him a written order upon the director of the Hospital of Santa Maria Nuova for one thousand one hundred ducats; one hundred of which he was to take for himself, and the one thousand he was to carry to the Gonfaloniere and beg him to take an early occasion to come to see Cosimo. Farganaccio accepted the commission, and the money was paid; whereupon Bernardo Guadagni became more humane; and the consequence was that Cosimo was banished to Padua, contrary to the will of Messer Rinaldo, who wanted to have him put to death. Averardo and many others of the house of Medici were also banished, and with them Puccio and Giovanni Pucci. And by way of intimidating those who were dissatisfied with the exile of Cosimo, a Balia was given to the Eight of the Guard and the Captain of the people. After these matters were resolved upon, Cosimo was brought before the Signori, on the 3d of October, 1433, who then announced to him the limits of his banishment, and advised him strictly to conform to them unless he wished them to proceed more harshly against him and his property. Cosimo accepted the limits with cheerful countenance, assuring them that wherever the Signoria might send him, there he would cheerfully abide. He begged them however, that, inasmuch as they had spared his life, they would also afford him protection, for he was aware that there were many in the Piazza who desired his blood. And then he offered, wherever he might be, to place himself and all his substance at the service of the city, the people, and their lordships. The Gonfaloniere kindly comforted him, kept him in the palace until nightfall, and then took him home with him to his house and made him sup with him; after which he had him conducted under a strong guard to the place of his banishment. At every station Cosimo was received with honors, and he was publicly called upon by the Venetians, who did him honor as one high in office, and not as an exile.

29. Florence being thus widowed of so illustrious and beloved a citizen, was in a state of general consternation; the supporters as well as the adversaries of Cosimo were equally terror-stricken. So that Messer Rinaldo, foreseeing his future ruin, yet by way of not seeming wanting to himself and his party, called together a number of citizens, friendly to himself, and addressed them as follows: —

"That he saw their impending doom, because they had allowed themselves to be overcome by the prayers, tears, and money of their enemies; and that they themselves did not perceive that in a little while it would be their turn to pray and weep; but that then their prayers would not be heard, nor would their tears move any one to compassion for them. That of the money they had accepted they would have to make restitution of the principal, and pay usurious interest with torments of death and exile. That it would have been better to have left things as they were, rather than to have spared the life of Cosimo and to allow his friends to remain in Florence; for great men must either not be touched at all, or destroyed entirely. And that he saw no other remedy now but to strengthen themselves in the city, so that when their enemies recovered their power, as they assuredly would erelong, they might be able to drive them out by force, which they would not be able to do by civil proceedings. That he repeated now what he had long since counselled them as their sole remedy, namely, to secure to themselves again the support of the great nobles, restoring and conceding to them all the honors of the city, and to strengthen themselves by that party, the same as their adversaries had done with the party of the people. That their own party would gain strength in proportion as they displayed more activity, more ability, more courage, and more influence; affirming that, if they did not avail of this last resource, he could not see by what other means they could preserve the government in the midst of so many enemies; and in such case he only foresaw the speedy ruin of their party and of the city."

Mariotto Boldovinetti, one of the assembled, opposed these views, "pointing out the pride and insupportable nature of the nobles, and that it would not do for them to subject themselves to certain tyranny for the sake of avoiding the doubtful dangers apprehended from the people." Whereupon Messer Rinaldo, seeing that his counsels were not listened to, bewailed his own misfortunes and those of his party, imputing them more to Heaven who wanted it thus, than to human ignorance and blindness. Matters being left in this way without any necessary provision being made, a letter was found written by Agnolo Acciainoli to Cosimo de' Medici, making known to him the favorable disposition of the city towards him, and advising him to endeavor to stir up some war, and to secure for himself the friendship of Neri di Gino. For he judged that, as the city in such case would need money, they would find no one willing to supply it, and that then the recollection of his liberality would revive a most earnest desire for his return. And that, if at the same time Neri should declare against Messer Rinaldo, it would so weaken the party of the latter that it would be no longer able to defend itself. This letter having fallen into the hands of the magistrates, they had Messer Agnolo arrested, put to the torture, and then sent into exile. But even this example in no way abated the feeling in favor of Cosimo.

A twelvemonth had now nearly elapsed since the banishment of Cosimo; and the end of August, 1434, having come, Niccolo di Cocco was drawn as Gonfaloniere for the two following months, and with him eight Signori, all partisans of Cosimo, so that Messer Rinaldo and all his party became greatly alarmed at this election of the Signoria. And as it was the custom that three days are allowed to elapse before the new Signori assume the magistracy, Messer Rinaldo again convened the chiefs of his party, and pointed out to them the certain and new dangers, and that their only remedy lay in taking up arms and making Donato Velluti, who was then acting Gonfaloniere, call the people to assemble in the Piazza, to appoint a new Balia, deprive the newly elected Signori of the magistracy, and create new ones to be placed at the head of the government, burn the election purses, and by new elections to fortify themselves with friends. Many judged this plan safe and necessary; many others deemed it too violent, and likely to involve them in serious difficulties. Amongst those who objected to it was Messer Palla Strozzi, who was a quiet, courteous, and humane man, and better qualified for the pursuit of letters than for the restraining of a faction, and of contending with civil discords. He said, "That cunning or audacious measures always seemed "well in the beginning, but afterwards became difficult in the "execution, and in the end dangerous. And he believed that "the fear of external war (the troops of the Duke being upon "our frontiers in the Romagna) would cause the Signori to "think more of that than of their internal dissensions. Should "it become evident, however, that they were about to take a "different course, (which they could not do without its becom-"ing known,) then it would always be time enough to take up "arms, and act as the general good might require; which in "that case, being done from necessity, would cause less excite "ment to the people, and less difficulty to themselves." It was concluded, therefore, to let the new Signori come in, and that their conduct should be closely watched, and if they attempted to do anything adverse to the party, that then each should take up arms and meet in the Piazza of San Pulinari, a place near the palace, whence they might afterwards proceed wherever it seemed necessary.

30. Having resolved upon this course, the meeting separated, and the new Signoria entered upon the magistracy. The Gonfaloniere, by way of making a reputation for himself, and striking terror into those who designed to oppose him, condemned Donato Velluti, his predecessor, to prison for misappropriation of the public funds. After that, he sounded his colleagues as to the return of Cosimo, and finding them favorably disposed, he conferred with those whom he supposed to be the chiefs of the Medici party; and being encouraged by these, he cited Messer Rinaldo, Ridolfi Peruzzi, and Niccolo Barbadori as being the leaders of the opposite party. After this summons, Messer Rinaldo thought that it would not do to delay action any longer, and issued forth from his house with a great many armed followers, and was promptly joined by Ridolfo Peruzzi and Niccolo Barbadori. A great many other citizens joined the crowd, as also numerous soldiers who happened in Florence, being without any engagement; and all went, according to agreement, to the Piazza of San Pulinari. Messer Palla Strozzi, however, although he had collected a goodly number of men, did not come out; and Messer Giovanni Guicciardini did the same; whereupon Messer Rinaldo sent to request them to come out, and to reprove them for their tardiness. Messer Giovanni replied, that he would most effectually damage the other party if, by remaining at home, he prevented his brother Piero from going to succor the Signoria in the palace. After repeated messages, Messer Palla Strozzi came on horseback to San Pulinari, followed only by two unarmed attendants on foot. Messer Rinaldo met and reproved him severely for his remissness, and said, "that his "not coming with the others arose either from want of good "faith or lack of courage; and that a man who desired to en"joy the consideration that he did ought to avoid laying himself "open to such charges; that he greatly deceived himself if he

"believed that, by thus failing in his engagements to his own
"party, the enemy, in case of victory, would either spare his
"life or exempt him from exile. As regarded himself, in the
"event of disaster, he would at least have the satisfaction of
"not having withheld his counsels before the danger, nor his
"active support when danger had come. But as for him (Palla)
"and the others like him, their regrets would be increased mani-
"fold by the reflection that they had betrayed their country three
"times; once when they saved Cosimo, the second time when
"they rejected his advice, and the third time now by fail-
"ing to support him with arms." Messer Palla's answer to
these words was not sufficiently loud to be understood by the
bystanders; but murmuring something, he turned his horse's
head, and went back to his house.

The Signori, upon hearing that Messer Rinaldo and his party
had taken to arms, and seeing themselves abandoned, caused
the palace to be closed, and being without any one whom they
could consult, they were wholly at a loss what to do. Messer
Rinaldo on his part, however, by waiting for the forces that did
not come, delayed his arrival in the Piazza, and thus lost the
opportunity of victory; for he afforded to the Signori time to
recover their courage and to provide for their defence, and
allowed many citizens to join the Signori, and to advise them
as to the means for inducing Rinaldo to disarm. Thereupon
some of the less suspected of the party of the Signori went to
Messer Rinaldo, saying that the Signoria did not know the cause
of this movement, that they never had any intention of offending him, and, although the subject of Cosimo had been discussed amongst them, yet they had never thought of permitting
his return; and that if this was the cause of Messer Rinaldo's
suspicions, he might be reassured; that they were quite willing
to have him come to the palace, where they would be glad to
see him, and that all his demands should be conceded to him.
Messer Rinaldo, however, was not persuaded by these words to
change his purpose, but he replied, " that the only way to reas-
"sure him was for the Signori to return to private life, and that
"then the city would be reorganized for the benefit of all." But
it invariably happens that, when the authority is equally divided
and the opinions differ, nothing is resolved upon that results in
good; and so in this case. Ridolfo Peruzzi, persuaded by the
words of those citizens, said that, "for himself, he desired noth-

"ing else than that Cosimo should not be permitted to return, "and the Signoria's agreeing to this seemed to him victory "enough, which he had no wish to increase by flooding the city "with blood; and therefore he wished to obey the Signoria." And thereupon he went with all his followers to the palace, where he was gladly received. Thus the delay of Messer Rinaldo at San Pulinari, the want of courage of Messer Palla Strozzi, and the going off of Ridolfo Peruzzi, had the effect of depriving Messer Rinaldo of success in his attempt. The ardor of the citizens who had followed him abated after the first excitement was over; and his failure was made still more complete by the authority of the Pope.

31. Pope Eugenius, having been expelled from Rome by the people, happened to be in Florence at the time of these occurrences; and deeming it his duty to do what he could to tranquillize the city, he sent the Patriarch Giovanni Vitelleschi, who was an intimate friend of Messer Rinaldo, to request him to come to him, and to assure him that the Pope had sufficient influence with and confidence in the Signoria to obtain for him entire satisfaction and security, without the effusion of blood, or danger to any citizen. Messer Rinaldo, therefore, being persuaded by his friend, went with all his followers to Santa Maria Novella, where the Pope resided. Pope Eugenius explained to him the pledge which the Signoria had given him, and that he had the whole subject of difference in his hands, and that matters would be arranged according as he might deem best, whenever Messer Rinaldo should lay down his arms. Messer Rinaldo, having seen the coldness of Messer Palla Strozzi and the fickleness of Ridolfo Peruzzi, for want of a better course placed himself in the hands of the Pope, thinking that his authority would anyhow have to be respected. The Pope thereupon caused Niccolo Barbadori, and the others who were waiting outside, to be notified that they must go and disarm, whilst Messer Rinaldo remained with the Pope to arrange the particulars of an agreement with the Signoria; whereupon they all dispersed and disarmed.

32. The Signori, seeing that their adversaries had disarmed, continued the negotiations for an agreement through the intervention of the Pope; but at the same time they sent secretly into the mountains of Pistoja for infantry, which, as well as their other men-at-arms, they introduced by night into Florence,

taking possession of all the strong points in the city. And then they called the people together in the Piazza, and created a new Balia, which, immediately after having been convened, restored Cosimo to his country, as well as the others who had been exiled with him. And of the adverse party, they banished Messer Rinaldo degli Albizzi, Ridolfo Peruzzi, Niccolo Barbadori, and Messer Palla Strozzi, together with many other citizens, to such an extent that there were but few places in Italy to which some of them were not banished, and even many places outside of Italy were filled with these exiles.

Thus did Florence, by this and similar proceedings, deprive herself not only of many good and worthy citizens, but of much wealth and industry. The Pope, seeing such general destruction befall those who, at his request, had laid down their arms, was greatly dissatisfied, and condoled with Messer Rinaldo on the wrong done him under his pledge, and counselled him to have patience, and to hope for good from the mutability of fortune. To which Messer Rinaldo replied: " The little faith which those " have shown me who should have believed in me, and the too " great faith which I had in you, have ruined me and my party. " But I blame myself more than any one else for having believed " that you, who had been driven out of your own country, would " be able to keep me in mine. I have had sufficient experience " of the fickleness of Fortune, and, as I had but little confidence " in her during prosperity, I am not now made unhappy by ad- " versity; for I know that whenever it shall please her she will " show herself more kind to me. But even should it never please " her, I should value but little living in a city where the laws " are less potent than men; for that country only is desirable " where one can enjoy one's substance and friends in security, " and not that where you may easily be deprived of the former, " and where your friends, from fear for their own, abandon you " in your greatest need. It has ever been less painful for good " and wise men to hear of the misfortunes of their country than " to witness them; and it has ever been deemed more glorious " to be reputed an honorable rebel than an enslaved citizen." He then parted from the Pope, full of indignation, repeatedly recalling to himself his own counsels and the coldness of his friends, and went away into exile. Cosimo, on the other hand, having been notified of his restoration, returned to Florence; and it has seldom happened that a citizen, returning in triumph from a victory, was received in his own country by such a concourse of people, and with such demonstrations of good will as those with which Cosimo was received on his return from banishment. He was spontaneously greeted by every one as the Benefactor of the People and as the Father of his Country.

FIFTH BOOK.

SUMMARY.

1. Vicissitudes to which governments are subject in consequence of the frequent mutations natural to all human affairs. — 2. State of Italy. Armed bodies of the Braccesca and the Sforzesca (1434). They combine against the Pope, who is expelled by the Romans. Francesco Sforza makes terms with the Pope. — 3. War between the Duke of Milan and the Pope, who is joined by the Florentines and the Venetians. — 4. Cosimo having returned from exile, the party favorable to him, having increased in power and in boldness, tyrannize over the opposite faction. — 5. Joanna II., queen of Naples, dies, and Regnier of Anjou and Alfonso of Aragon contend for the crown; the latter, being defeated by the Genoese, is delivered by them into the hands of the Duke of Milan, who becomes his friend, and he is liberated by him (1435). — 6. Factions of the Fregosa and the Adorna in Genoa. — 7. The Genoese, through the efforts of Francesco Spinola, drive out the Duke of Milan's governor. — 8. They form a league against the Duke with the Florentines and the Venetians. The Duke of Milan is persuaded by Rinaldo degli Albizzi and other Florentine exiles to make war against Florence. — 9. He sends his captain, Niccolo Piccinino, to the disadvantage of Florence (1436). — 10. Sforza, the commander of the Florentines, defeats Piccinino under Barga; he moves thence against Lucca (1437), which is succored by the Duke of Milan. — 11. The Florentines march upon Lucca, which is abandoned by the Duke of Milan. — 12. The Duke returns to the disadvantage of the Florentines. — 13. Bad faith of the Venetians to the Florentines. — 14. Cosimo de' Medici at Venice. The Florentines make peace with the Lucchese (1438). — 15. Pope Eugenius IV. consecrates the Metropolitan Church, built after the designs of Arnolfo and Brunelleschi. — 16. Council of Florence, at which the union of the Greek and Latin Churches is effected (1439). — 17. Niccolo Piccinino, in the name of the Duke of Milan, invades many places belonging to the Church. — 18. He attacks the Venetians, who are succored by the Florentines with the Sforzesca troops. — 19. The war is continued with alternate success between Piccinino and Sforza. — 20. Neri Capponi is sent to Venice. — 21. Address of Capponi to the Venetian Senate. — 22. The Count Sforza comes into Lombardy. — 23. Piccinino defeats the Venetians on the Lake of Garda. — 24. He takes Verona. — 25. It is retaken by Sforza. — 26. The Duke of Milan turns against the Florentines; and the Venetians prevent Sforza from passing into Tuscany to aid the Florentines (1440). — 27. The Florentines make themselves masters of the Patriarch Vitelleschi, who, abusing the name of the

Pope, was betraying them. — 28. Niccolo Piccinino passes the Po. Tardiness of the help of the Venetians to the Florentines. — 29. Piccinino in the Romagna. — 30. Niccolo Piccinino makes himself master of Marradi, and scours the country around Florence. — 31. He also takes, after much resistance, the Castel San Niccolo, but does not succeed in taking Cortona. — 32. He is recalled to Lombardy by Duke Filippo. — 33. He is defeated by the Florentines at Anghiari. — 34. Death of Messer Rinaldo degli Albizzi. — 35. Neri Capponi goes to recover the Casentino. The Count Poppi surrenders. His speech before abandoning the state.

1. THE general course of changes that occur in states is from a condition of order to one of disorder, and from the latter they pass again to one of order. For as it is not the fate of mundane affairs to remain stationary, so when they have attained their highest state of perfection, beyond which they cannot go, they of necessity decline. And thus again, when they have descended to the lowest, and by their disorders have reached the very depth of debasement, they must of necessity rise again, inasmuch as they cannot go lower. And thus they always decline from good to bad, and from bad they rise again to good. For virtue brings peace, and peace leisure, and leisure begets disorder, and this in turn brings ruin; and in like manner from ruin springs order, from order virtue, and from that glory and good fortune. Whence it has been observed by wise men that literature follows arms, and that in cities and in provinces leaders of armies precede philosophers. For when brave and well-disciplined armies have achieved victory, and victory has produced peace, the vigor of warlike spirits cannot be enervated by a more honorable indulgence than that of letters; nor can idleness enter any well-regulated communities under a more alluring and dangerous guise. This was perfectly well understood by Cato when the philosophers Diogenes and Carneades were sent as ambassadors from Athens to the Senate of Rome; for when he saw the Roman youth begin to follow them with admiration, Cato, well knowing the evil that would result to the country from this excusable idleness, ordered that no philosopher should thenceforth be received in Rome. For it is thus that countries gradually come to their ruin; and when they have become wise by misfortune, they return, as I have said, to order, unless they remain oppressed by some extraordinary power. These causes made Italy by turns now happy and now wretched, first under the ancient Tuscans, and afterwards

under the Romans; and although no other state has since arisen from the ruins of Rome that could in any way redeem her former greatness, and which might well and gloriously have been achieved by any virtuous and able prince, yet in some of the new cities and states that have arisen out of the ruins of Rome there was sufficient virtue and bravery, so that, even if they did not dominate all the others, yet they succeeded by their union and good organization in liberating and defending Italy from the Barbarians.

Amongst these states, that of Florence, even if less in extent, yet was not less in power and influence than the others. Situated in the centre of Italy, rich and ever ready for attack, Florence not only successfully sustained all wars made upon her, but also gave victory to whomever she became allied. If then the courage and ability of these new states did not insure them any long-continued periods of peace, yet were they neither exposed to great dangers from the asperities of war. For that cannot be called peace when principalities assail each other; nor can that be called war where men do not kill each other, and the cities are not sacked, nor the principalities ruined. Their wars had so declined in vigor that they were begun without fear, conducted without danger, and terminated without damage; so that that virtue which in other countries is apt to become extinguished by long-continued periods of peace, was lost in the Italian provinces through cowardice, as will clearly appear from what we shall write of the period from 1434 to 1504, and wherein we shall show how, in the end, the way was opened again to the Barbarians, and how Italy sank to rest in slavery to them. And if the actions of our princes, both at home and abroad, do not inspire us with admiration for their virtue and greatness, like those of the ancients, yet will they perhaps be regarded with no less admiration for their other qualities, seeing how many noble peoples were restrained and controlled by such feeble and ill-constituted armies. And if in the account of the events of this corrupt age we may not have occasion to tell of bold deeds of soldiers, or of the ability of the commanders, or of the patriotism of the citizens, it will nevertheless show to what frauds and cunning devices the princes and soldiers and chiefs of republics resorted for the sake of maintaining an influence which they did not merit. This it will perhaps be not less useful to know than the events of antiquity; for if the latter kindle in generous hearts the desire to imitate them, the former will teach them to contemn and avoid similar baseness.

2. Italy had been brought by those who controlled her to the point, then, that when by the agreement of the states a peace was established it was quickly afterwards again disturbed by those who had arms in hand; so that there was neither glory won by war, nor quiet secured by peace. When, therefore, peace was concluded in 1433 between the Duke of Milan and the league, the hired soldiery, wishing to continue on a war footing, turned against the Church. There were at that time two bodies of mercenary troops in Italy, the Braccesca and the Sforzesca. Count Francesco, son of Sforza, was chief of the latter, and the commanders of the former were Niccolo Piccinino and Niccolo Fortebraccio. All the other Italian troops attached themselves, as it were, to these two principal companies. The Sforzesca troops were the most appreciated of the two, both on account of the valor and ability of the Count, as also because of the promise which the Duke of Milan had made him of the hand of his illegitimate daughter, the Lady Bianca; the prospect of which connection added greatly to the reputation of Count Francesco. After the peace of Lombardy, therefore, these two armed bodies assailed the Pope Eugenius. Niccolo Fortebraccio was influenced in this by the ancient enmity which Braccio had always entertained towards the Church; the Count Francesco was moved by ambition; thus Niccolo attacked Rome, whilst the Count made himself master of La Marca. In consequence of this the Romans, who did not want war, drove Pope Eugenius from Rome, who, having escaped with difficulty and danger, made his way to Florence. Considering the danger to which he was exposed, being abandoned by the princes who had with so much satisfaction just laid down their arms, which they were unwilling to resume again for the sake of the Pope, Eugenius made terms with the Count Francesco and conceded to him the lordship of La Marca, although Francesco had added insult to the injury of having seized it; for in indicating the place whence he sent his letters to his agents, he wrote, "From our hawk's nest of Fermo, in spite of "Peter and Paul." Nor was he content with having obtained possession of these places, but wanted to be made Gonfaloniere of the Church; all of which Pope Eugenius conceded to him,

being more afraid of a hazardous war than of an ignominious peace. The Count Francesco, having in this wise become the friend of the Pope, attacked Niccolo Fortebraccio, and for many months they fought within the territory of the Church with varying successes, which resulted however altogether more to the injury of the Pope and his subjects than to those who were carrying on the war. Finally, through the intervention of the Duke of Milan, an agreement was concluded by way of a truce, whereby both remained in possession of the places they had taken within the territory of the Church.

3. This war, extinguished at Rome, was rekindled in the Romagna by Battista da Canneto, who killed several citizens of the family of Grifoni in Bologna, and drove the Pope's governor, with others of his enemies, out of the city. And to enable him forcibly to hold that state, he applied for help to Duke Filippo, whilst the Pope by way of avenging the insult asked aid from the Venetians and Florentines. Both the one and the other obtained the desired assistance, so that in a very little while two considerable armies found themselves face to face in the Romagna.

Niccolo Piccinino commanded the forces of the Duke, and the Venetian and Florentine troops were under the command of Gattamelata and Niccolo da Tolentino. They came to battle near Imola, and the Venetians and Florentines were routed, and Niccolo da Tolentino was sent as prisoner to Milan, where he died within a few days, either by unfair means or from grief at his defeat. After this victory the Duke, either from having been weakened by the late wars, or because he believed that the league, having experienced this defeat, would disarm, did not follow up his success, and thus gave time to the Pope and his allies to gather their forces again. They appointed the Count Francesco their general, and attempted to drive Niccolo Fortebraccio from the states of the Church, and thus to terminate the war which had been begun only for the benefit of the pontiff. When the Romans saw the Pope take the field so bravely, they sought to make terms with him, and sent a messenger to him and received a commissioner from him in return. Amongst the other places which Niccolo Fortebraccio had taken, he held Tivoli, Montefiascone, Citta di Castello, and Ascesi. Unable to keep the field, he had taken refuge in the last-named place, where Count Francesco besieged him; and as the siege was becoming a protracted one in consequence of the vigorous defence of Niccolo, Duke Filippo thought it necessary either to prevent the league from obtaining the victory, or so to regulate his own movements that he might the better be able afterwards to defend his own estates. With the view therefore of making the Count raise the siege of Ascesi, he ordered Niccolo Piccinino to make a diversion into Tuscany through the Romagna; so that the league, deeming it more important to defend Tuscany than to possess Ascesi, might order the Count Francesco to dispute the passage of Niccolo, who was already with his army at Furli. Francesco, on the other hand, moved with his forces to Cesena, having left his brother Lione in charge of his states and of the war in La Marca. Whilst Piccinino sought to penetrate into Tuscany and Count Francesco strove to prevent his passage, Niccolo Fortebraccio attacked Lione, and after a glorious victory took him prisoner, and destroyed his army; and following up this success, he took possession with the same dash of many places in La Marca. This greatly afflicted the Count Francesco, who already imagined that all his states were lost; and leaving part of his army to confront Piccinino, he turned with the rest upon Fortebraccio, and fought and defeated him. Fortebraccio was wounded and taken prisoner in this rout, and soon after died of his wounds. This victory restored to the Pope all the places that had been taken from him by Niccolo Fortebraccio, and reduced the Duke of Milan to sue for peace, which was concluded through the intervention of Niccolo da Este, Marquis of Ferrara. By the conditions of this peace, also, the places occupied by the Duke in the Romagna were restored to the Church, and the troops of the Duke returned into Lombardy. And Battista da Canneto (like all usurpers who maintain themselves in any state by the force and valor of others), finding it impossible to hold his position in Bologna, took to flight; whereupon Messer Antonio Bentivogli, chief of the opposite party, returned.

4. All this took place during the time of Cosimo's exile. After his return those who had brought about his restoration, and had themselves been so much wronged by the adverse party, resolved anyhow to get control of the government. The Signoria that succeeded to the magistracy for November and December, not content with what had been done by their

predecessors for the party, prolonged and changed the place of banishment of many, and sent many other citizens into exile. And it was not so much the fact of belonging to the opposite party that proved dangerous to citizens, but their wealth, their relations, and their private friendships. If this wholesale proscription had been accompanied by bloodshed, it would have equalled those of Octavius or Sylla. In some instances it was tainted with blood, for Antonio di Bernardo Guadagni was beheaded, and likewise four other citizens, amongst whom were Zanobi de' Belfratelli and Cosimo Barbadori, who, having gone beyond the limits of their banishment, and happening to be at Venice, the Venetians, valuing the friendship of Cosimo more than their own honor, sent them to Florence as prisoners, where they were basely put to death. All this greatly increased the power of the party of Cosimo, and struck terror into the hearts of his opponents, especially when they saw that so powerful a republic as Venice sacrificed its independence to the Florentines, which it was believed that they had done, not so much to benefit Cosimo as for the purpose of stimulating party feeling in Florence to a still higher pitch, and by bloodshed to make the dissensions in our city still more dangerous. For the Venetians regarded the union of the Florentines as the only obstacle to their own aggrandizement.

The city being thus cleared of enemies or suspected enemies of the government, the party in power began to bestow benefits upon new people for the purpose of strengthening their party, and restored to their country the Alberti family and other exiles. All the great nobles with very few exceptions were reduced from their rank to that of plebeians, and they divided and sold the possessions of the exiled amongst themselves at very low prices. After this they strengthened themselves by new laws and ordinances, and had new elections made, withdrawing the names of their enemies from the purses and filling them with those of their friends. Admonished, however, by the ruin of their adversaries, they concluded that even these packed elections would not suffice to enable them to keep the control of the government in their hands; and therefore they resolved that the magistrates who exercised the power of life and death should always be chosen from amongst the chiefs of their party, and that the officers who had charge of the imborsations for the new elections, together with the old Signoria, should have the power of appointing the new Signoria. They gave to the Eight of the guard power over life and death, and provided that the banished should not be able to return at the expiration of their term without having first obtained the consent of thirty-four out of the thirty-seven Signori and their colleagues. They prohibited all correspondence with the banished; and every word or sign or practice that in any way displeased those who held the government was severely punished. And if any suspected individual still remained in Florence who had not been reached by these repressive measures, he was oppressed by new impositions which they ordered for the express purpose; so that in a little while, having expelled and impoverished the whole of the adverse party, they secured themselves firmly in the government. And by way of insuring to themselves foreign assistance, and at the same time depriving those of it who might design to attack them, they formed defensive alliances with the Pope, the Venetians, and with the Duke of Milan.

5. Whilst the affairs of Florence were in this condition, Joanna, queen of Naples, died, leaving by her will Regnier of Anjou heir to the kingdom. Alfonso, king of Aragon, happened to be at that time in Sicily, and, having friendly relations with many of the Neapolitan barons, he prepared to take possession of that kingdom. The Neapolitans and many of the barons favored Regnier; the Pope, on the other hand, wanted neither Regnier nor Alfonso to have the kingdom, but desired that it should be administered by a governor of his own. Meantime Alfonso came into the kingdom, and was received by the Duke of Sessa; he brought with him some princes whom he had taken into his pay, intending (as he already had Capua, which the Prince of Taranto held in his name) to compel the Neapolitans to acknowledge him as sovereign. Alfonso also sent his fleet to attack Gaeta, which was held by the Neapolitans. In consequence of this, the Neapolitans applied for assistance to the Duke Filippo, who persuaded the Genoese to take the enterprise in hand. These promptly armed a fleet for the purpose, not only of complying with the wishes of the Duke, their lord, but also to save their merchandise which they had in Naples and in Gaeta. Alfonso, on the other hand, hearing of this, increased his own fleet, and went in person with it to meet the Genoese; and having encountered them above the

island of Ponzio, the Aragonese fleet was defeated, and Alfonso together with many other princes made prisoner, and delivered by the Genoese into the hands of Filippo. This victory alarmed all the other princes of Italy, who feared the power of Filippo; for they judged the opportunity favorable for him to make himself master of the whole country. But, so diverse are the minds of men, Filippo took exactly the opposite course. Alfonso was a man of uncommon sagacity, and so soon as he had an opportunity of speaking with Filippo, he demonstrated to him " that it was a great error on his part to "support Regnier in opposition to himself. For," argued he, "if Regnier should become king of Naples, he would make "every effort to have Milan become the property of the king "of France, so as to have friendly support near at hand, and "not to be obliged in a moment of need to ask permission for "the passage of his allies; and that Regnier could not secure "this advantage for himself except by the ruin of Filippo in "causing Milan to become French. But that, on the contrary, "he, Alfonso, should he become king of Naples, would inter- "vene in favor of Filippo; for having no other enemy to fear "except the French, he would of necessity be obliged to love "and be friends with — if not obey — him, who had it in his "power to open the way to his enemies. And therefore, al- "though the title of king would be Alfonso's, yet the power "and authority would really be Filippo's. So that it really "concerned him more than himself to reflect upon the danger "of the one course and the advantage of the other, unless he "preferred to gratify his own feelings rather than to assure "the security of his state. For in the one case he would "really be prince, and free; and in the other, being between "two most powerful princes, he would either lose his state, or "he would live in perpetual apprehension, and obey them like "a slave." These arguments had such an effect upon the mind of the Duke, that, having changed his purpose, he set Alfonso at liberty, and sent him honorably back to Genoa, and thence to the kingdom of Naples. Alfonso landed at Gaeta, which city, so soon as Alfonso's liberation had become known, had been taken possession of by some of the princes who were his partisans.

6. The Genoese, seeing how the Duke without regard to them had liberated the king, and how he had gained all honor

at their risk and expense, and how the credit of the liberation accrued to Filippo, whilst the injury of the defeat and capture was theirs, became greatly exasperated against him. When the city of Genoa enjoyed her liberty, the chief of her government was elected by free suffrage; he was called the Doge, not because he was absolutely a prince, nor because he alone decided upon public measures, but merely proposed, as chief of the state, the measures which the magistrates and their counsellors should resolve upon. There are many noble families in this city, sufficiently powerful to make it difficult for the magistrates to enforce obedience from them; foremost amongst these are the families of the Fregosa and the Adorna. The frequent dissensions in the city, and consequent destruction of the civil institutions of the state, result from this. These families are constantly contending with each other for the government, not by legal means, but with arms in hand; whence it is that alternately one party is dominant and the other oppressed. And it ordinarily happens that that party which finds itself deprived of all share in the public offices and honors has recourse to foreign arms, and thus subjects the country, which they are not allowed to govern themselves, to the rule of a stranger. This is the reason why Genoa has so frequently been subject to the sovereigns of Lombardy, and was so at the time when Alfonso of Aragon was made prisoner.

Amongst the principal Genoese who were the cause of their country being subjected to Duke Filippo had been Francesco Spinola; who soon after having caused his country to be enslaved, as often happens in similar cases, became suspected by the Duke. Incensed by this he had chosen a sort of voluntary exile at Gaeta, where he happened to be at the time of the naval fight with Alfonso; and having rendered gallant services in this action, he thought that he had anew merited the confidence and favor of the Duke, and could therefore live with safety at Genoa. But he soon found that the Duke continued his suspicions of him, for he could not believe that any one who had betrayed his own country would be faithful to him. Spinola resolved therefore to tempt fortune anew, and with one blow to restore liberty to his country, and fame and security to himself. He felt that he had no other means of regaining the confidence of his fellow-citizens than by healing the wound which he had inflicted. Seeing, therefore, the universal indignation that had been excited against the Duke by his having set King Alfonso at liberty, Spinola deemed the occasion propitious for carrying his designs into effect; and communicated his views to some friends whom he knew to hold the same opinion with himself, and urged them to second him in his attempt.

7. On the day of the festival of San Giovanni Battista, the new governor, Arismino, who had been sent by Duke Filippo, was making his official entrance into Genoa. He had already entered the gates of the city accompanied by Opicino, the old governor, and many of the Genoese, when Spinola, thinking that it would not do to delay the execution of his design any longer, issued forth from his house, all armed, and accompanied by those whom he had drawn into his plans, and from the piazza in front of his house he raised the cry of "Liberty!" It was wonderful to see the eagerness with which the citizens rushed together at that cry; none of those who from interest or any other cause were attached to the Duke had time to arm, and were hardly able to think of the means of escape. The new governor, Arismino, and some Genoese who were with him, took refuge in the castle, which was guarded by some troops of the Duke. The old governor, Opicino, presuming that, if he should take refuge in the palace, where he had two thousand armed men under his command, he would be able to save himself or encourage his friends to defend themselves, turned into the road leading to the palace; but before reaching the piazza he was killed, and his body dragged through all Genoa and torn in pieces. And the Genoese, having placed the government in the hands of free magistrates, obtained possession in a few days of the castle and the other strongholds that were in the hands of the Duke's forces, and thus freed themselves entirely from the yoke of Filippo, Duke of Milan.

8. All these events in the beginning alarmed the princes of Italy, making them fear that Duke Filippo would become too powerful. But seeing now how his power in Genoa had come to an end, they were encouraged to hope that they would be able to keep his ambition in check; and notwithstanding the recent treaty, the Florentines and Venetians formed an alliance with the Genoese (1436). Whereupon Messer Rinaldo degli Albizzi and the other chiefs of the banished Florentines, seeing

the prospect of fresh perturbations, and the altered aspect of things, took hope of being able to induce Duke Filippo openly to declare war against Florence. Rinaldo therefore went to Milan, and spoke to the Duke as follows:—

"If we, formerly your enemies, come now confidently to "supplicate your aid to enable us to return to our country, "neither yourself nor any one else who observes the course "of human events and the mutability of fortune should be "surprised at it. Nor do we lack ample and manifest justifi- "cation of our past and our present actions, or of our present "conduct towards our country and our former conduct towards "you. No good man will ever find fault with any one who "seeks to defend his country, in whatever way he may deem "it proper to do so. Our aim never was to injure you, but to "protect our country from injury; and you can bear witness "yourself that after the greatest victories of our league, when "we knew you to be favorable to a real peace, we urged it even "more than yourself; so that we really believe that we have "never done a thing that could cause us to doubt our obtain- "ing any reasonable favor from you. Nor can our country "complain that we urge you now to take up those arms to "assail her, against which we have before defended her with "so much obstinacy; for only that country merits the affection "of all her citizens which in return loves all citizens equally, "and not that country which favors a very few at the expense "of the many. Nor should any one who raises arms against "his country be condemned under all circumstances; for cities, "although they are complex bodies, yet very much resemble "individual bodies. And as these are often afflicted with in- "firmities that can only be cured with fire and steel, so in the "former likewise similar troubles frequently occur, which "any good and devoted citizen would sin more by leaving un- "cured than by curing them, though it be with fire and steel. "What greater malady, I ask, can there be for a republic than "slavery? What remedy was it ever more necessary to em- "ploy than such as will relieve her of this evil? Those wars "alone are just that are necessary, and those arms are merci- "ful without which there is no hope. I know not what neces- "sity can be greater than ours, nor what mercy can exceed "that which saves our country from servitude. Assuredly "then our cause is just and merciful, which fact should not

"be lost sight of by you or ourselves. Nor is justice lacking
"on your side, for the Florentines have not been ashamed,
"after concluding a peace with so much solemnity, to form an
"alliance with the Genoese, who are rebels from your author-
"ity; so that if pity for our cause does not move you, a just
"indignation at the insult thus offered you should move you,—
"the more so as the undertaking is an easy one. Do not allow
"yourself to be deterred by the past exhibitions of the power
"of the Florentine people, and of their obstinacy in defence;
"these qualities might reasonably inspire you with apprehen-
"sions if the Florentines still possessed them in the same
"degree as formerly. But you will now find the very re-
"verse; for what power can a city have that has so lately
"driven out the best part of its wealth and industry? And
"how can you expect an obstinate defence from a people torn
"by such various and recent dissensions? The same dissen-
"sions prevent the wealth that still remains to them from
"being employed in the same way as formerly; for men will
"freely spend their fortunes when they see that it is for their
"own glory and for the honor and welfare of their country,
"because then they hope to recover in peace what the war has
"taken from them; but you cannot expect them to do the
"same when they find themselves equally oppressed in war
"and in peace, having in the one to bear the injuries of the
"enemy, and in the other the insolence of their rulers. For
"a people suffers more from the avarice of its magistrates
"than from the rapacity of an enemy; for of the latter you
"may sooner or later hope for an end, but of the former
"never. In your previous wars with Florence you had to
"contend against the entire republic, whilst now you would
"have to do so against only a very small portion. Then you
"came to take the government from a number of excellent
"citizens; now you would take it from the hands of only a
"few bad ones. Then you came to deprive the city of her
"liberty, but now you will go to restore it to her. It is not
"reasonable, therefore, to suppose that such different causes
"should produce the same effect; but rather should we look
"for certain success in this war, and how much that will add
"to the power of your own state you can readily judge. For
"Tuscany, having thus become your friend and ally, being
"bound to you by so many and such great obligations, will be

"worth more to you in your other undertakings than even
"Milan herself. And whilst at other times this acquisition
"would be regarded as the result of your ambition and vio-
"lence, it will now be looked upon as an act of justice and
"humanity. Do not, therefore, allow this favorable opportu-
"nity to be lost, and bear in mind that, if your former wars
"against Florence have brought you nothing but difficulty, ex-
"pense, and little credit, the present one will bring you with
"ease the greatest advantages and most honorable fame."

9. It did not need so many words to persuade the Duke to make war against the Florentines, for he was disposed to it by an hereditary hatred and a blind ambition; and was urged to it, moreover, by the new offence of the alliance with the Genoese. But his former expenditures, the dangers he had run, and the recollection of recent losses, as well as the extravagant hopes of the Florentine exiles, made him hesitate. So soon as Duke Filippo had heard of the rebellion of the Genoese, he had sent Niccolo Piccinino with all his forces, and such infantry as he could collect in the country, to make an effort to recover Genoa before the citizens should have time to become settled and establish a new government, relying much upon the citadel, which was still held for him. Although Piccinino drove the Genoese over the mountains and took from them the valley of Pozzenere, where they had fortified themselves, and compelled them to take refuge behind the walls of the city, yet he found so much difficulty in advancing further, owing to the obstinate defence made by the citizens, that he was obliged to withdraw. Whereupon the Duke, at the persuasion of the Florentine exiles, ordered Piccinino to attack the eastern shore, and to push the war vigorously into the Genoese territory on the frontier of Pisa, judging that this device would leave him free to decide from time to time upon the best course to follow. Niccolo thereupon attacked and took Serezana, and after having done considerable damage he marched upon Lucca; and for the purpose of allaying the suspicions of the Florentines he started the report that he was going down to the kingdom of Naples to assist the king of Aragon. Upon the occurrence of these events Pope Eugenius left Florence and went to Bologna, where he negotiated a new arrangement between the Duke and the league. He represented to the Duke that, if he did not consent to this

treaty, he should be obliged to transfer to the league the Count Francesco Sforza, who was formerly his ally, but was now in the military service of the Pope. Although the Pontiff exerted himself very much in this matter, yet it was all in vain; for the Duke would not make any terms until he should first have recovered Genoa, whilst the league wanted Genoa to remain entirely free; and thus each party, mistrusting peace, prepared for war.

10. When, therefore, Niccolo Piccinino came to Lucca, the Florentines became uneasy at his movements, and ordered Neri di Gino, with the cavalry, into the Pisan territory; and they obtained the Pope's consent that the Count Francesco should unite with him; and they established themselves, with their army, at Santa Gonda. Piccinino, who was at Lucca, demanded free passage for himself and his troops through the territory of the republic to go on to Naples; and upon its being refused, he threatened to take it by force. The two armies were nearly equal in numbers and in the ability of their respective commanders, and therefore neither of them wished to expose themselves to the hazards of fortune, being, moreover, restrained by the cold season (being in the month of December); and thus they remained many days without either making any movement to attack the other. Niccolo Piccinino, however, was the first to move, it having been represented to him that, if he were to make a night attack upon Vico Pisano, he would easily take it. Niccolo made the attempt, but failed to take Vico; whereupon he wasted the surrounding country, and plundered and burned the Borgo San Giovanni alla Vena. This attempt (in great measure useless, even if it had been successful) yet encouraged Niccolo to advance further; and having ascertained that Count Francesco and Neri di Gino had not moved, he attacked Santa Maria in Castello and Filetto, and took them both. With all this, the Florentine troops did not move, not because the Count Francesco was afraid, but because the magistrates of Florence had not yet definitely resolved upon war, out of reverence for the Pope, who was still treating for peace. Niccolo, mistaking the prudence and consideration of the Florentines for fear, felt encouraged to still more fresh attempts, and resolved to attack Barga with all his forces. This new attack caused the Florentines to put aside all considerations, and not only to succor Barga, but also to attack the territory of Lucca. Francesco

therefore, having gone to encounter Niccolo, engaged him in battle and defeated him; and having almost entirely dispersed his army, he raised the siege of Barga. The Venetians meantime, considering that Filippo Visconti had broken the peace, sent their general, Francesco da Gonzaga, to Ghiaradadda, where he ravaged the Duke's territory to that degree that Filippo found it necessary to recall Niccolo Piccinino from Tuscany. This recall of Piccinino, together with the victory which the Count Francesco had gained over him, encouraged the Florentines to make an attempt upon Lucca, with the hope of taking it. In this attempt they were neither restrained by fear, nor any other consideration, seeing that Duke Filippo, the only power they had to fear, was attacked by the Venetians, and that the Lucchese, having received the enemies of Florence within their territory, and permitted them from there to attack her, had thereby deprived themselves of all right to complain.

11. In April, however, Count Francesco set the army in motion; but before invading the enemy's territory the Florentines wished to recover their own, and recaptured Santa Maria in Castello, and the other places occupied by Piccinino. They then turned northward towards the Lucchese territory, and assailed Camajore; the inhabitants of which, though loyally attached to their lords, surrendered, for the fear of a present enemy had more power over them than their loyalty to a distant friend. With similar success, the Florentines took Massa and Serezana. Having accomplished this about the end of May, they moved towards Lucca, and destroyed all the grain and growing crops, burned the villages, cut down the vines and the trees, drove off the cattle, and left no injury undone that can be inflicted upon the bitterest enemy. The Lucchese, on the other hand, seeing themselves abandoned by the Duke, and despairing of being able to defend their country, abandoned it, and fortified the city with all the means in their power, confident of being able to defend it for some time, as they had plenty of soldiers within, and hoping that in the mean time something would occur to save them, as had been the case in the several previous attempts of the Florentines upon Lucca. The only thing they feared was the fickleness of the people, who, tired of the siege, might think more of their own dangers than of the liberty of others, and might thus force them to some disgraceful and injurious terms of capitulation. With the view, therefore, of stimulating them

to the most energetic defence, they called the people together in the Piazza, and one of the oldest and wisest citizens addressed them as follows:—

"You know well that what is done from necessity merits "neither praise nor censure. If, therefore, you accuse us of "having provoked this war with the Florentines by having re- "ceived the Duke's troops in our territory, and allowed them "thence to attack the Florentines, you will commit a very great "error. You know well the ancient enmity of the people of "Florence towards you, which has its origin not in injuries done "them by us, nor in any fear they have of you, but rather from "your weakness and their ambition; for the one gives them the "hope of being able to subjugate you, and the other urges them "on to do it. Nor must you believe that any service you could "render them would remove that desire from their minds, any "more than that any offence you might give them could still "more excite their desire to injure you. They think of nothing "but to rob you of your liberty, and you should think of nothing "but to defend it; and whatever may be done by either party "to further these objects may cause us regret, but should not "surprise us. Certainly we are much grieved that they should "attack us, that they seize our places, burn our houses, and lay "waste our country; but which of us is foolish enough to be "surprised at it? for if we could we would do the same to them, "or even worse. They pretend that they have begun this war "against us because we received Niccolo; but had we not done "so, they would have found some other pretext, and if thus the "evil had been deferred, it would probably have been the greater. "Thus, the coming of Niccolo should not be charged with it, but "rather your ill-fortune and the ambitious nature of the Floren- "tines. Moreover, we could not have refused to receive the "troops of the Duke of Milan; and having come as they did, it "was not in our power to prevent them from attacking the "Florentines. You know well that, without the support of "some powerful ally, we could not save our city, and there is "none that could have aided us more effectually and more in "good faith than Duke Filippo. It was he who restored you "your liberty; it is reasonable, therefore, that we should look "to him to aid us in maintaining it, and our enemies have no "more determined foe than he. If, then, we had irritated the "Duke for the sake of not offending the Florentines, we should

" have lost a good friend, and strengthened our enemy and made
" him more prompt in attacking us; so that it was better for us
" to have incurred this war, and preserve the friendship of Duke
" Filippo, than for the sake of peace to have exposed ourselves
" to his enmity. We have the right, therefore, to hope that he
" will help us out of the danger to which he has subjected us,
" provided that we are true to ourselves. You well know with
" what fury the Florentines have several times attacked us, and
" how gloriously we have defended ourselves against them. And
" many a time we had no other hope than in God and time, and
" the one and the other have saved us; and why should we not
" succeed now, if we defend ourselves courageously? Then all
" Italy abandoned us to fall a prey to the Florentines; but now
" we have Duke Filippo of Milan with us, and have besides good
" reason for believing that the Venetians would hesitate to offend
" us, as it is not to their interest that the power of Florence
" should increase. On former occasions when the Florentines
" attacked us, they were more free from embarrassments and had
" more hope of assistance, and were of themselves stronger;
" whilst we were in all respects weaker. For then we com-
" bated for a tyrant, but now we are defending ourselves.
" Then the glory of the defence accrued to others; now it is
" ours only. Then our assailants were united; but now they
" are divided amongst themselves, having filled all Italy with
" their banished citizens.

" But even if we had not all these encouragements, necessity
" alone commands us to the most determined resistance. Every
" enemy is reasonably to be feared, for they all aim at your de-
" struction and their own glory; but above all others should we
" fear the Florentines, for neither submission nor tribute nor the
" mastery over our city will satisfy them. They want our very
" persons and substance, so as to glut their cruelty and avarice
" with our blood and our possessions; and therefore are they to
" be feared in every way by each one of you. Be not troubled,
" therefore, at seeing your fields wasted, your villages burnt,
" and your lands seized by them; for if we save this city, we
" shall of necessity save all the rest. But if we lose Lucca,
" then it would be of little avail for us to save all the other
" things. If we maintain our liberty, the enemy will find it
" difficult to hold the rest, which we should strive in vain to
" save if our liberty were lost. To arms, then, fellow-citizens!

"and when you combat, think that the reward of your victory will be not only the safety of your country, but that of your homes and of your children."

These last words were received by the people with the utmost enthusiasm, and with one voice they pledged themselves to die rather than to yield or to entertain the thought of any arrangement that would in the least stain their liberty; and then they set to work to make all necessary preparations for the defence of the city.

12. The Florentine army meantime was not idle, and after doing infinite damage to the country they took Monte Carlo by capitulation, and then went into camp before Uzano; so that the people of Lucca, hemmed in on all sides and deprived of all hopes of succor, should surrender under the pressure of hunger. The castle of Uzano, however, was strong and well garrisoned, so that its capture was not as easy as the rest of the country. The Lucchese, as was most natural, finding themselves so closely pressed, had recourse to the Duke of Milan, employing prayers and remonstrances in their application, and pointing out their own merits and the offences of the Florentines, and how much it would encourage his other allies if he came to their rescue, and how much they would be alarmed if he abandoned them; and that, if they were destined to lose their liberty and their lives, he on his part would lose not only useful allies, but also his honor, and the confidence of all those who hereafter might have occasion to expose themselves to every danger from their devotion to him. They added tears to their entreaties, so that, if Filippo should not be influenced by his sense of obligation, he might perhaps be moved by compassion. So that the Duke, adding to his inveterate hatred of the Florentines the new obligations he owed to the Lucchese, and being above all desirous that the Florentines should not aggrandize their power by so important a conquest, resolved to send a large force into Tuscany, or to make so vigorous an attack upon the Venetians that the Florentines would be compelled to desist from their attempt upon Lucca for the sake of going to the assistance of the Venetians.

13. This being determined upon, the Florentines were quickly informed that Duke Filippo was preparing to send a force into Tuscany. This made the Florentines begin to give up all hopes of taking Lucca; and to keep the Duke occupied in Lombardy

they urged the Venetians to attack him with all their forces. But these were also alarmed because their commander, the Marquis of Mantua, had left them, and had entered the service of Duke Filippo. Finding themselves thus as it were disarmed, they replied to the Florentines, that, so far from being able to increase their efforts, they would hardly be able to continue the war unless the Florentines could send them the Count Francesco Sforza to command their army, and with the condition that he should obligate himself to pass the Po in person. Without this they would not adhere to their former treaty, according to which he was not obliged to pass the river. For they were not willing to carry on the war without a commander, and had no hope of any but the Count Francesco; but unless he bound himself to carry on the war wherever they might require it, he would be of no value to them. The Florentines considered it important that the war should be pushed with vigor in Lombardy; at the same time, they felt that their attack upon Lucca would prove in vain; and they knew perfectly well that the Venetians made this demand for Sforza, not so much because he was indispensable to them as for the purpose of preventing them from making so important a conquest as that of Lucca. The Count, on the other hand, was ready to go into Lombardy at the pleasure of the league, but was unwilling to change the terms of the original agreement with the Duke Filippo, as he did not wish to forego the hope of his alliance to the Duke's daughter which he had promised him.

The Florentines were thus agitated by two different feelings; the one the desire to possess Lucca, and the other the fear of war with the Duke of Milan. The latter, however, prevailed, as is generally the case with fear; and they consented that, after the capture of Uzano, the Count Sforza should go into Lombardy. There remained, however, one difficulty, which, not being within the control of the Florentines, caused them more anxiety and apprehension than the first: the Count was not willing to cross the Po, and the Venetians would not accept him unless he did. There being no other way of coming to an agreement except by one party freely yielding the point to the other, the Florentines persuaded the Count Francesco to obligate himself by a private letter to the Signoria to pass the river, demonstrating to him that such a private promise would not be considered an infraction of a public treaty; and that he could manage afterwards to avoid passing the river, which would have this advantageous consequence,—that the Venetians would be obliged to continue the war after it had once been begun, and that thus the evil which the Florentines feared so much would be averted. On the other hand, they argued with the Venetians, that this private letter would be binding upon the Count, and that therefore they ought to be content with it; and that it was well to afford him the means of preserving the appearance of respect due to his future father-in-law; and that it would be of no advantage to them to expose him without manifest necessity. And thus the passage of the Count Sforza into Lombardy was resolved upon; who, having taken Uzano and thrown up some intrenchments around Lucca for the purpose of keeping the inhabitants closely pressed, placed the conduct of the war in the hands of the commissaries. He then passed the mountains and went to Reggio, where the Venetians, suspicious of his advance and wishing above all to assure themselves of his real intentions, requested him to pass the Po, and there join their other forces. The Count absolutely refused this; so that high words passed between him and the Venetian envoy, Andrea Mauroceno, each accusing the other of presumption and bad faith. And after much mutual recrimination, the one claiming not to be obliged to perform that service and the other threatening to withhold the stipulated payments, the Count Sforza returned to Tuscany and the other to Venice. The Count was thereupon ordered by the Florentines to encamp on the Pisan territory, hoping to induce him to resume the war against Lucca, to which, however, they found him indisposed; for the Duke Filippo, having heard that the Count Francesco had refused to pass the Po out of regard for him, hoped still by his means to save the Lucchese; and begged him to endeavor to bring about an amicable arrangement between the Lucchese and the Florentines, and if possible to include him also in the arrangement, giving Sforza the hope that the promised marriage with his daughter might then take place at his own pleasure. This hoped for marriage had great weight with Count Francesco; for inasmuch as Duke Filippo had no sons, he hoped thereby eventually to become himself the sovereign of Milan. For this reason he embarrassed the movements of the Florentines, and declared that he would not move with the army unless the Venetians paid the amount due him and continued him in command of the army. The payments alone, however, did not satisfy him; for wishing to be assured of the safety of his own states, he deemed it desirable to have other support besides the Florentines, and therefore shrewdly threatened that, if he were abandoned by the Venetians, he would be obliged to look to his own interests, and make terms with the Duke of Milan.

14. These cavillings and evasions displeased the Florentines greatly, for they saw themselves disappointed in their attempt upon Lucca, and began moreover to have some doubts as to the safety of their own state if ever the Duke of Milan and the Count Francesco should become allied. By way of inducing, therefore, the Venetians to keep Sforza in command, Cosimo de' Medici went himself to Venice in the hope of being able to influence them by his reputation. He discussed the subject at length in their Senate, showing the condition of the Italian governments, the extent of the forces of the Duke of Milan, which armies were the most powerful and best reputed; and concluded that, if the Duke united with the Count Francesco, the Venetians might have to confine themselves again to the sea, whilst the Florentines would have to fight for their liberties. To this the Venetians replied: "That they knew their "own strength, as well as that of the other Italian states, and "believed themselves in every way competent to defend them-"selves; affirming at the same time that they were not in the "habit of paying soldiers who served others, and that the Flor-"entines had better pay the Count themselves, inasmuch as he "had been employed in their service. And that they deemed "it more necessary, if they wished to continue in the free en-"joyment of their institutions, to humble the pride of the "Count Sforza than to pay him; for there was no limit to "men's ambition; and if the Count were now paid, it would "not be long before he made other unfair and dangerous de-"mands. And therefore they deemed it well, once and for all, "to check his insolence, instead of allowing it to grow until it "became insupportable; and if the Florentines, either from "fear or any other reason, wished to preserve the Count's "friendship, they might pay him themselves."

And thus Cosimo had to return without any other conclusion. The Florentines, nevertheless, urged the Count not to separate himself from the league, to which he would willingly have adhered but for his desire to conclude his marriage with the daughter of Duke Filippo; this kept his mind in a state of doubt, so that the slightest incident, as indeed it happened, caused him to hesitate. Count Francesco had left his possessions in La Marca in charge of Furlano, one of his principal Condottieri, who was persuaded by the Duke of Milan to leave the service of the Count and to enter into his pay. In consequence of this, the Count, regardless of everything but his own safety, formed a compact with the Duke, one of the conditions of which was that the latter was not in any way to interfere in the affairs of the Romagna and of Tuscany. After making this arrangement with Duke Filippo, the Count earnestly persuaded the Florentines to make terms with the Lucchese; and pressed them in such manner, that, seeing they had no other alternative, they concluded a treaty with them in April, 1438, according to which the Lucchese preserved their independence, and the Florentines kept Monte Carlo and several other places. After that they filled all Italy with declarations of regret, saying that, since both God and man were opposed to their subjecting Lucca to their government, they had concluded to make peace with her. It seldom happens that any one regrets the loss of his own property so much as the Florentines regretted their failure to acquire that of others.

15. Although the Florentines were occupied at that time with such important enterprises, yet they did not omit to give attention to their neighbors, and to adorn and improve their own city. We have already related the death of Niccolo Fortebraccio, who had been married to a daughter of the Count Poppi, who at the time of the death of Niccolo held the Borgo of San Sepolcro and the fortress of that place, which he had commanded during the lifetime of his son-in-law in his name. After his death he claimed to hold them as the dowry of his daughter, and refused to yield them to the Pope, who demanded them as the property of the Church, and sent the Patriarch with his army to recover them. The Count Poppi, feeling himself unable to resist an attack, offered to turn these places over to the Florentines, who however declined to accept them. But when the Pope returned to Florence they interceded with him in behalf of the Count Poppi, but, failing to bring about an agreement, the Patriarch attacked Casentino, and took Prato Vecchio and Romena, which places he offered also to the Florentines. They declined to accept them, unless

the Pope should first consent to their restoring them to the Count Poppi. After long resisting, the Pope finally agreed to it, but wanted the Florentines to promise to induce the Count to surrender to him the Borgo of San Sepolcro. The Pope being satisfied with this negotiation, the Florentines asked him personally to consecrate the cathedral of the city, called the Santa Reparata, the construction of which had been begun a long time previous, but which was now so far completed that they could celebrate divine service in it. The Pope readily consented; and for the greater magnificence of the city and the cathedral, as well as for the greater honor of the Pope, the Florentines had a platform constructed all the way from the Santa Maria Novella, where the Pope resided, to the church that was to be consecrated. This platform was eight feet wide and four feet high, and was covered all over with the most costly drapery, and was to serve only for the passage of the Pope with his court, and the magistrates of the city, together with such citizens as had been deputed to escort the pontiff, whilst the other citizens and the people lined the streets, the windows, and the church to witness so grand a spectacle. After the customary ceremonies, the Pope, by way of giving a still greater proof of his affection for the city, bestowed the honor of knighthood upon Giuliano Davanzate, a citizen of the highest repute, and who was at that time the Gonfaloniere of Justice; and the Signoria, not wishing to appear less gracious than the Pope, gave to Giuliano the government of Pisa for one year.

16. There were at this time (1439) some grave differences between the Roman and the Greek Churches, so that they did not agree upon any one point in the divine service. And as there had been much discussion upon this subject at the last Council of Basle by the prelates of the Western Church, it was resolved that an effort should be made to induce the Emperor and the Greek prelates to attend the council, and to try if possible to reconcile them to the Latin Church. Although this proposition was derogatory to the majesty of the Greek empire, and distasteful to the pride of its prelates, yet, being at the time closely pressed by the Turks, and deeming themselves alone insufficient for their defence, they resolved to yield to the invitation for the purpose of being able with the greater certainty to ask for assistance. And thus the Emperor, with

the Patriarch and the other prelates and Greek barons, came to Venice in compliance with the resolution of the Council of Basle; but being alarmed by the plague which was then prevailing, they resolved that their differences should be settled at Florence. The Roman and Greek prelates having thereupon met for many days in succession in the cathedral of Florence, the Greeks yielded after repeated and protracted discussions, and the disputed points were agreed upon with the Roman Church and the pontiff.

17. Peace having now been restored between the people of Lucca and the Florentines, and an alliance formed between the Duke of Milan and Count Francesco Sforza, it was thought that the wars of Italy, and especially those that had so long plagued Lombardy and Tuscany, would now cease; although that which had originated in the kingdom of Naples between Regnier of Anjou and Alfonso of Aragon was not likely to be settled except by the ruin of either the one or the other. And although the Pope was dissatisfied at the loss of so much of his territory, and although the restless ambition of the Duke of Milan and of the Venetians was notorious, yet it was supposed that the Pope from necessity and the others from exhaustion would have to remain quiet. But matters went differently; for neither the Duke nor the Venetians were content in repose. Arms were therefore again resumed, and Lombardy and Tuscany were once more overrun by warring armies. The proud spirit of Duke Filippo could not brook that the Venetians should possess Bergamo and Brescia; and he was greatly annoyed at seeing them in arms and constantly running over and disturbing many parts of his territory. Thinking that he would be able not only to keep the Venetians in check, but also to recover his possessions whenever they should be abandoned by the Pope, the Florentines, and the Count Francesco, Filippo resolved to take the Romagna from the Pope; judging that, when once he held that country, the Pope would not be able to molest him, and that the Florentines, seeing the fire so near, would either not move from fear, or would not be able readily to attack him. The Duke was aware also of the indignation which the Florentines felt against the Venetians on account of their disappointment in regard to Lucca, and judged that on that account they would be less disposed to take up arms in their behalf. As to the Count Francesco, Filippo believed that the newly established alliance

between them, and the Count's hope of marrying his daughter, would keep him quiet; and to avoid responsibility, and to afford no one any cause to attempt any movement,—particularly as under his agreement with the Count Francesco he could not attack the Romagna,—he directed Niccolo Piccinino to undertake it himself, as though he had been prompted to it by his own ambition. At the time of the agreement between Duke Filippo and Count Francesco, Niccolo happened to be in the Romagna; and by an understanding with the Duke he pretended being indignant at this alliance between the Duke and his inveterate enemy, the Count, and went with his troops to Camarata, a place between Furli and Ravenna, where he fortified himself as though he intended to remain there a long while, or until he should determine upon some other course. The report of Piccinino's anger with the Duke having been very generally spread, Niccolo gave the Pope to understand how great his services to the Duke had been, and how great the Duke's ingratitude; who, from having the two principal captains in his pay, conceived that he thereby in a measure controlled all the armies of Italy, and intended to make himself the master of it. But if his Holiness desired it, he would bring it about that, of the two captains whom the Duke believed he controlled, one should become his enemy, and the other should prove useless to him. For if his Holiness would supply him with money and agree to keep him in his pay, he would attack those portions of the possessions of the Count which he had taken from the Church; so that Count Francesco, having to look to the protection of his own property, would not be able to serve the ambition of Duke Filippo. The Pope, believing these representations, which seemed reasonable to him, sent five thousand ducats to Piccinino, and made him besides many promises of estates for himself and his children. And although the Pope was cautioned by several persons against this fraud, yet he would not believe it, and would listen to no one who contradicted him.

The city of Ravenna was governed at that time, in the name of the Holy See, by Ostasio da Polenta; and Niccolo, thinking that there was no time to be lost in the execution of his designs,—his son, Francesco Piccinino, having sacked Spoleto in utter disregard of the Pope,—resolved to attack Ravenna, either because he thought it an easy undertaking, or because he had a secret understanding with Ostasio. And in a few days after, he made the attack, and took Ravenna by capitulation; after which he took Bologna, Imola, and Furli. And what was truly astonishing was, that, of twenty castles in the Romagna that were held by papal troops for the Church, there remained not one that did not fall into the hands of Piccinino, who, not content with outraging the Pope by sudden invasion, added insult to injury, and wrote him that he deserved to have these places taken from him, because he had not been ashamed to attempt to break up the friendship that existed between the Duke of Milan and himself, and because he had filled Italy with letters falsely representing that Niccolo had betrayed the Duke and gone over to the Venetians.

18. Niccolo, having thus made himself master of the Romagna, left it in charge of his son, Francesco Piccinino, whilst he himself with the greater part of his troops went into Lombardy, where, having united with the Duke's forces, he attacked the territory of Brescia, of which he made himself master in a few days, and then laid siege to the city itself. The Duke, who wanted the Venetians to be abandoned to him as a prey, disavowed the acts of Piccinino, and assured the Pope, the Florentines, and the Count, that, if the conduct of Niccolo was contrary to the treaties, it was equally so to his own wishes; and he gave them to understand by confidential messengers that he intended to make a signal demonstration against Niccolo for his disobedience whenever time and circumstances should permit it. The Count and the Florentines had no faith in these assurances, but believed, as in truth was the case, that these late military movements had been made merely to keep them quiet until the Duke should have subdued the Venetians, who, being filled with pride and believing themselves able alone to resist the Duke's forces, disdained to ask help of any one, and carried on the war single-handed through their general, Gattamelata. The Count Sforza was desirous of going to the assistance of King Regnier with the consent of the Florentines, if the events in the Romagna and Lombardy had not detained him. And the Florentines would cheerfully have consented, on account of the ancient friendship which their city had always cherished for the house of France; but that in such event the Duke would have given his support to King Alfonso, from the friendship contracted with him in the time of his need. Both however, being occupied with the wars

nearer home, abstained from more distant enterprises. In fact, the Florentines, seeing the Romagna invaded by the Duke's forces and the Venetians beaten, like men who saw their own ruin in that of others, begged the Count Francesco to come into Tuscany, where they would devise what means might be necessary to oppose the forces of the Duke Filippo, which were now greater than they had ever been before; affirming at the same time that, if the Duke's insolence were not restrained, every sovereign in Italy would soon suffer from it. Although the Count Francesco knew the apprehensions of the Florentines to be well founded, yet the desire to consummate his connection with the Duke by the promised marriage was supreme with him; and the Duke, well knowing this desire, gave him every encouragement, on condition that Sforza should not take up arms against him. And as the young lady was now of suitable age, things had several times been brought to that point that all the preparations for the marriage had been made, but the Duke upon one pretext or another had always set them aside. At the same time, by way of maintaining and increasing the Count's confidence, he added deeds to his words, and sent him thirty thousand florins, which he was to give him according to the marriage contract.

19. Meantime the war in Lombardy continued, and the Venetians lost daily more territory, and the fleets which they had placed upon the rivers were taken by the ducal forces. The whole country of Verona and Brescia was occupied, and the two cities were so closely pressed that according to general opinion they could hold out but a little while longer. The Marquis of Mantua, who had for many years been general of the forces of the republic, had quite unexpectedly left their service and gone over to the Duke of Milan; so that fear compelled them during the progress of the war to do that which their pride would not allow them to do in the beginning. For satisfied now that their only remedy was the friendship of the Florentines and of the Count Francesco Sforza, the Venetians began to solicit it, although with shame and full of doubts; for they feared to receive from the Florentines the same answer which they had given to them at the time of the attempt of the Florentines upon Lucca, and in their affair with the Count.

But they found the Florentines more ready to comply than

what they had hoped for, or than what they deserved for their former conduct. So much more were the Florentines influenced by their hatred of their ancient enemy, the Duke of Milan, than by resentment at the disregard by the Venetians of their old and habitual friendship. And having for some time previous anticipated the necessity to which the Venetians would be brought, they had pointed out to the Count Francesco "how their ruin would involve his own, and how "much he deceived himself in supposing that Duke Filippo "would value him more when fortunate than in misfortune; "and that the only reason why he had promised him his "daughter was the fear with which he had inspired him. "And inasmuch as promises made under the pressure of ne- "cessity are performed only under a similar pressure, so the "Duke would also have to be kept in that condition with "regard to the promise of his daughter's hand to Francesco, "which could only be done by maintaining the power of the "Venetians. He ought to bear in mind, therefore, that if the "Venetians were to lose their inland possessions he would "lose not only all the advantages which he had the right to "expect from their alliance, but also those which he could "hope for from the other Italian states, who were already "alarmed by the disasters of Venice. And if he reflected well "upon the condition of the different states of Italy, he would "see that some were without means, and that others were hos- "tile to him. Nor were the Florentines by themselves able "to sustain him (as he had several times said himself), and "therefore it was in every respect of the utmost importance "for him to do all he could to maintain the Venetians power- "ful by land."

These arguments, added to the hatred which the Count Francesco had conceived against Duke Filippo, by whom he believed himself to have been duped in the matter of the promised marriage, induced him to accede to a new agreement; but he would not yet obligate himself to pass the Po. This treaty was concluded in February, 1438; according to it the Venetians made themselves responsible for two thirds and the Florentines for one third of the expenses of the war; and both agreed jointly to bear the expense of defending the Count's possessions in La Marca. The league were not satisfied with their forces, and added to them the lord of Faenza, the sons of Messer Pandolfo Malatesta da Rimini, and Pietro Giampaolo Orsini. They also sought to seduce the Marquis of Mantua by great promises to unite with them, but could not tempt him to abandon the friendship and service of the Duke of Milan. The lord of Faenza also, after having agreed with the league for his services, finding that he could make better terms for himself, went over to the Duke. This defection deprived the league of the hope of being speedily able to dispose of the affairs of the Romagna.

20. Lombardy was at this time in a critical situation; Brescia was besieged by the forces of the Duke, and it was doubtful whether she might not any day be obliged to surrender from want of provisions. Verona, likewise, was so closely pressed, that a similar fate was apprehended for her; and it was considered that, if either of these cities were lost, all further preparations for war, as well as the amount of money expended thus far, would be in vain. So that the league saw no other remedy than to send the Count Sforza into Lombardy. This course, however, presented three difficulties: the first was to dispose the Count to pass the river Po, and to carry on the war wherever they might direct; the second was that the Florentines could not disguise from themselves that the sending the Count Sforza so far away would leave them at the mercy of the Duke, who might easily withdraw to some of his strongholds, keeping the Count at bay with a portion of his forces, and with the rest bring back the Florentine exiles into Tuscany, of which the government in power at the time were greatly afraid; and the third difficulty was as to the route which the Count Sforza should take so as to get safely to Padua, where the Venetian forces were stationed. Of these three difficulties the second, which especially concerned the Florentines, was the most serious. They however, knowing the necessities of the case, and wearied by the Venetians, who clamored with the utmost importunity for the Count Francesco, declaring that without him all would be lost, subordinated their own apprehensions to the necessities of others. There still remained then the question as to the route, the safety of which it was resolved should be provided for by the Venetians. Neri di Gino Capponi having been deputed to treat with the Count upon this point, and to induce him to pass the river, the Signoria of Florence deemed it proper that

Neri should also proceed to Venice in order to make this benefit the more acceptable to the Signoria of that city, and at the same time to arrange with them for the safety of the route and the passage of the river by the Count.

21. Neri thereupon departed from Cesena for Venice, where he was received by the Signoria with more honors than had ever been shown to any prince, for they believed that the safety of the state depended upon his coming, and upon the arrangements that were to be effected through his intervention. Neri, having been introduced to the Senate, addressed that body and the Doge in the following words: —

"Most illustrious Prince, the Signori of Florence have ever "been of the opinion that the power of the Duke of Milan con- "stituted the principal cause of danger to your republic and "their own; and that the safety of the two states depended "upon their respective greatness. Had your Signoria always "been of the same opinion we should have been in better con- "dition, and your state would have been secure from those "dangers by which it is threatened at this time. But as you "gave us neither your assistance nor your confidence at the "time when you should have done so, we could not hasten to "your relief in your troubles, and you could not ask it of us "so promptly, having known us but slightly in your adversity "and prosperity; for you did not know that it is our nature "to love those always whom we have loved once, and to hate "forever those whom we have hated once. You know your- "selves the love we have borne to your most illustrious Sig- "noria; for you have seen how on different occasions we have, "for your assistance, sent our troops and our treasure into "Lombardy. And the whole world knows the hatred we bear "and ever shall bear to Duke Filippo and the house of Vis- "conti; and certainly neither ancient love nor hatred can read- "ily be effaced by new benefits or injuries. We have been and "are still certain that we might have remained neutral in this "war, to the great satisfaction of Duke Filippo, and with little "risk to ourselves. For even if by your ruin he had made "himself master of Lombardy, there were enough resources "left to us in Italy to prevent our despairing of our safety; for "with the increase of the Duke's power and possessions, he "would have also increased the number of his enemies and "their jealousy of him, and this would have involved him in

"fresh wars and difficulties. We also know what heavy ex-
"penses and imminent dangers we should have escaped by
"avoiding this war, and how, in consequence of our taking part
"in it with you, it might be transferred from Lombardy into
"Tuscany. But all these considerations are counterbalanced
"by the ancient affection which we cherish for your state, and
"therefore we resolved to succor your government with the
"same alacrity that we should have employed in defence of our
"own if it had been assailed. My government, judging that
"before anything else Verona and Brescia should be relieved,
"which it supposed could not be done without the Count, sent
"me first to persuade him to pass over into Lombardy, and to
"carry on the war wherever directed; for you know that he
"was not obliged to pass the river Po. This I have done, em-
"ploying the same arguments with him that have influenced
"us; and he, invincible as he is in arms, and unwilling to
"be outdone in courtesy, determined to exceed even the liber-
"ality which he had seen us extend to you. Fully aware
"of the danger to which his departure would expose Tus-
"cany, but seeing that we had subordinated our dangers to
"your welfare, he resolved also to subordinate his considera-
"tions for us to the same object. I come, therefore, to offer
"to you the Count Francesco, with seven thousand cavalry
"and two thousand infantry, ready to go and meet the enemy
"anywhere, and I beg you most earnestly, and my Signoria
"likewise entreats you, that, inasmuch as the number of troops
"exceeds what by his agreement with us the Count is obliged
"to furnish, you will compensate him with your wonted lib-
"erality, so that he may have no cause to regret having
"placed himself at your service, nor we at having persuaded
"him to it."

Neri's address was listened to by the Senate as though he
had been an oracle; and they were so excited by it that they
did not wait for the Doge to reply, as is customary; but, rising
to their feet, the greater part of the Senators, with uplifted
hands, called out to thank the Florentines for this affectionate
and friendly service, and to thank Neri for having executed it
with so much zeal and promptness; promising at the same
time that it should never be cancelled from their hearts or those
of their descendants, and that their country should ever be a
common one to themselves and the Florentines.

22. When this excitement had subsided they discussed the route which the Count Francesco should take, so that bridges, pioneers, and all other necessary things, might be provided. Four routes presented themselves: one by Ravenna, along the sea, which, however, being in great part confined between the sea and morasses, was not approved; the next was by the direct road, but this was obstructed by a fortress called the Uccellino which was held by the troops of the Duke, and would have to be taken before it could be passed, which it was difficult to do in so short a time without delaying the succor so promptly needed. The third route was by the forests of the lake, but as the Po had risen over its banks, it made that route, not difficult, but impossible. There remained then the fourth, by the Campagna of Bologna, crossing by the bridges of Puledrano, Cento, and Pieue, and passing on to Ferrara between Finale and Bondeno; whence the army might be transferred by land and water into the Paduan territory, there to join the Venetian forces. This route, though very difficult and exposed to the attacks of the enemy, was chosen for want of a better; and so soon as it was made known to the Count, he started with the utmost promptness, and reached the Paduan territory on the 20th of June. The arrival of the Count Sforza in Lombardy filled all Venice with high hopes; and where at first the Venetians had despaired of their safety, they now began to indulge in hopes of new acquisitions. The first thing the Count did was to march to the relief of Verona; to prevent this, Niccolo Piccinino went with his army to Soave, a fortress between the territories of Vicenza and Verona, and which was protected by a ditch leading from the river Soave to the marshes of the Adige. Count Francesco, seeing the road through the plains impeded, judged that he might be able to pass around by the mountains and in that way reach Verona, thinking that Niccolo would not suspect his taking that route, which was steep and rugged; or if he did believe it, he would not be in time to prevent him. And having supplied himself with provisions for eight days, he passed the mountains with his forces and reached the plains below Soave. Although Niccolo had thrown up some intrenchments to embarrass Francesco on this road, yet he was not able to hold them. Niccolo thereupon, seeing that the enemy had passed where he had believed it impossible, and not wishing to come to an engagement with him at disadvantage,

retreated, across the Adige, and Francesco entered Verona without opposition.

23. The first difficulty having been so happily overcome, and Verona relieved of the siege, there remained the second, namely, to succor Brescia. This city lies, as it were, upon the lake of Garda; so that, although besieged by land, it could always be provisioned from the side of the lake. For this reason Duke Filippo had intrenched himself with his forces along the lake, and at the beginning of his successes had occupied all the places that could afford aid to Brescia by means of the lake. The Venetians also had galleys upon the lake, but not enough to contend against the forces of the Duke. Count Francesco therefore deemed it necessary to support the Venetian fleet with his land forces, hoping easily to take those places that prevented Brescia from obtaining supplies. Accordingly, he laid siege to Bardolino, a fortress situated on the lake, hoping that, when he should have taken that, the other places would surrender. Fortune, however, did not favor Francesco in this attempt, for a considerable portion of his forces fell sick, so that he abandoned that enterprise and went to Zenio, a Veronese fortress, which was healthy and well supplied with provisions. Piccinino, seeing that the Count had withdrawn, and unwilling to lose an opportunity, which he thought presented itself, for making himself master of the lake, left his camp at Vesagio, and with some chosen troops went upon the lake and attacked the Venetian fleet with such vigor and fury that he captured nearly the whole of it. In consequence of this victory nearly all the strong places on the lake surrendered to Niccolo. The Venetians, alarmed by this loss and fearing lest the Brescians should capitulate in consequence, sent letters and messengers to Count Francesco, urging him to go to the relief of that city. The Count, seeing that all chance of relieving Brescia by way of the lake was lost, and that it was unapproachable by the plains because of the ditches, intrenchments, and other obstacles interposed by Niccolo, to attempt to pass which in the face of a hostile army would be going to certain defeat, resolved that, inasmuch as the road by the mountains had enabled him to save Verona, it should equally serve him to succor Brescia. Having formed this design Count Francesco left Zenio, and went by the Val d' Acri to the lake of San Andrea, and came to Torboli and Peneda, above the lake of Garda.

Thence he went to Terma, which he besieged, as Brescia could not be reached without that castle being taken first. Piccinino, hearing of the Count's movements, led his army to Peschiera, and then went, together with the Marquis of Mantua and some of his choicest troops, to encounter Francesco. And having come to battle, Piccinino was defeated and his troops dispersed; some of them were taken prisoners, some made their way back to the main body of the army, and some took refuge on board of the fleet. Niccolo retreated to Terma, and, night having come on, he thought that if he waited in that place until daylight he would unavoidably fall into the hands of the enemy; and by way of escaping a certain danger he risked a doubtful one. Of all his forces Niccolo had but one servant with him, a German of remarkable strength, who had ever been most faithful to him. Niccolo persuaded him to put him into a sack, and to carry him on his shoulders to some safe place, as though he were carrying his master's armor. The troops of Count Francesco were encamped around Terma, but in consequence of the victory of the day, the whole camp was in disorder and without any guards, so that it was an easy matter for the German to save his master; for having taken him on his shoulders concealed in a sack, he passed through the camp without any hindrance, and so soon as he was safe he conducted Niccolo to his troops.

24. If this victory had been employed with as much wisdom as it was achieved with good fortune, Brescia would have been relieved, and the affairs of Venice would have been greatly benefited. But being badly availed of, the joy of the Venetians soon disappeared and Brescia remained in the same difficulties. For Niccolo, having returned to his troops, resolved to cancel the disgrace of his defeat by some new victory, and thus to deprive the Venetians of the chance of relieving Brescia. He knew the position of the citadel of Verona, and had learnt from prisoners taken during the war how insufficiently it was guarded, and the facility with which it might be taken. It seemed to him, therefore, that fortune had placed the means in his hands for recovering his honor, and of converting into grief the joy which the enemy had derived from the recent victory. The city of Verona is situated in Lombardy at the foot of the Alps that separate Italy from Germany; so that it is placed partly on the mountain slope and partly in the plain. The river Adige issues

from the valley of Trent, and on entering Italy, instead of spreading itself through the level country, turns sharply to the left along the mountains and runs through the city of Verona, not dividing it, however, into two equal parts, but leaving the part on the side of the plain much larger than that which lies on the slope of the mountain. Above this there are two forts, the one called San Pietro and the other San Felice, and which from their situation have the appearance of much greater strength than they really have; but being so high, they dominate the whole city. In the plain on the opposite side of the Adige, and within the city walls, are two other forts about one thousand paces distant from each other. One of these is called the old, and the other the new citadel; they are connected by a wall which forms as it were the chord of the arc which the regular city wall describes, and which goes from one citadel to the other. The whole space within these two walls is thickly inhabited, and is called the Borgo di San Zeno. It was these citadels and the Borgo which Niccolo Piccinino intended to seize, thinking that he would readily succeed, either because of the ordinary negligence of the garrison, or from their greater negligence in consequence of the recent victory; and knowing that in war no enterprise is so likely to succeed as that which the enemy thinks you incapable of accomplishing. Having thereupon made a selection of his best men, Niccolo went at night together with the Marquis of Mantua to Verona, and without being heard he escaladed and captured the new citadel. From there his troops descended into the place and burst open the gate of San Antonio, by which they let in all the cavalry. The garrison that held the old citadel for the Venetians, hearing the noise only after the guard of the new citadel had been killed, and concluding that it must be the enemy, began to shout and ring the bells to call the people to arms. The citizens being aroused were all in confusion; the most courageous of them seized their arms, and rushed to the Piazza dei Rettori. Meantime the troops of Niccolo had pillaged the Borgo di San Zeno, and as they were advancing further the citizens recognized that the ducal troops were within the city. And seeing no means of defending themselves, they advised the Venetian Rectors to take refuge in the fortress so as to save their persons and the place; representing to them that it was better for Venice that they should save their lives and so rich a city for a better fate, than, by attempting to avoid the present one, to expose themselves to the danger of death and their city to destruction. And thus the Rectors and all the other Venetians took refuge in the fortress of San Felice. After this some of the first citizens went to meet Niccolo and the Marquis of Mantua, and supplicated them to prefer a rich city, which they might possess with honor to themselves, to one that was devastated, and which would only bring shame upon them; especially as the fact of their having defended themselves entitled them neither to the thanks of their former masters nor to the vengeance of the present ones. They were comforted by Niccolo and the Marquis of Mantua, who restrained as far as they could the license of the soldiery and protected the city from being sacked. And being convinced that the Count Francesco would endeavor to recover possession of Verona, they made every effort to get the fortresses into their hands; and those which they could not take they isolated by means of ditches and barricades, so as to make it difficult for the enemy to enter them.

25. The Count Francesco was at Terma with his forces, and when he heard the news of the capture of Verona he at first discredited it; but when he became assured of its correctness, he wanted with immediate haste to make good the first neglect. All the captains of his army advised against this attempt upon Verona and Brescia and in favor of going to Vicenza, so as not to expose himself to being besieged by the enemy in his present position; but the Count would not listen to them, and persisted in tempting fortune by his effort to recover Verona. And turning in the midst of the discussion to the Venetian commissaries and to Bernardetto de' Medici, the Florentine commissary, he promised them the certain recovery of the city, provided that one of the forts held out until he came. Having thereupon organized his men, he moved with the utmost rapidity upon Verona. When Niccolo saw him coming, he believed him at first to be going to Vicenza, as he had been advised by his captains; but when he afterwards saw the troops turn to go to the fort of San Felice, he hastily attempted to organize its defence. But it was too late; for no barricades had been made, and Niccolo's soldiers were scattered in the eager pursuit of plunder and contributions, so that he could not collect them in time to prevent Count Francesco's men from entering the fort; whence they made a descent upon the city, and happily took it, to the dis-

credit of Niccolo, and great damage to his men, who together with the Marquis of Mantua fled first to the citadel, and then through the open country to Mantua, where they joined the other fragments of their forces that had escaped, and then went to unite with those who were engaged in the siege of Brescia. Thus was Verona won and lost by the ducal army within the short space of four days. Winter having now set in and the cold being very severe, the Count Francesco, after having first with great difficulty sent provisions into Brescia, went into quarters in Verona; and ordered some galleys to be built during the winter at Torboli, so as to be well prepared by spring for the relief of Brescia.

26. Duke Filippo, seeing the war stopped for the time, and himself deprived of all hope of taking Verona and Brescia, which he attributed entirely to the money and the counsels of the Florentines, who could neither be alienated from their alliance with the Venetians by the injuries they had received at their hands, nor gained over to him by the promises which he himself had made them, resolved to attack Tuscany, so as to make the Florentines taste the fruit of the seed which they had sown themselves. He was, moreover, urged to this resolution by the banished Florentines and by Niccolo Piccinino. The latter was influenced by his desire to acquire the estates of Braccio, and to drive the Count out of La Marca; and the former by their longing to return to their country, from which they had been exiled; and both urged the Duke with opportune reasons in conformity with their own desires. Niccolo pointed out to him how he might send him into Tuscany, and yet continue the siege of Brescia, as he was master of the lake and held all the strong places on land, which were amply supplied with everything, and had men and competent captains to resist the Count Francesco should he attempt any fresh enterprise, which, however, he would hardly do without first relieving Brescia, and that was impossible; and therefore he might carry the war into Tuscany, without giving up his operations in Lombardy. He also argued that the Florentines would be obliged, so soon as he entered Tuscany, to recall the Count Francesco, or be destroyed, and that, whatever course he might take, victory would be the certain result. The Florentine exiles affirmed that, if Niccolo with his army were to approach Florence, it would be impossible for the people not to take up arms against the nobles,

being weary of their insolence, and of the burdens that had been imposed upon them. They showed him that it was easy to approach Florence, and assured him that the way by Casentino would be open to him, owing to the friendship existing between Messer Rinaldo degli Albizzi and the Count Poppi. Thus the Duke Filippo, who was of his own accord inclined to go, was confirmed by these persuasions in his resolve to engage in this enterprise. The Venetians, on the other hand, notwithstanding the severity of the winter, urged the Count most earnestly to go to the relief of Brescia with all his forces. This the Count Francesco declined, as being impossible at that season, and advised them to wait until spring, and in the mean time to put their fleet in order, so as to be able to aid Brescia at the same time both by land and by water. This refusal greatly dissatisfied the Venetians, so that they became dilatory in supplying provisions, which caused a great many desertions from the army.

27. When the Florentines were informed of these movements, they became greatly alarmed at seeing the war coming upon them, whilst they had derived so little advantage from the operations in Lombardy. They were no less disquieted by the army of the Holy See; not that the Pope himself was hostile to them, but because they saw his troops show more obedience to the Patriarch, their mortal enemy, than to the Pope himself. Giovanni Vitelleschi of Corneto, at first apostolic notary, became afterwards Bishop of Recannati, and then Patriarch of Alessandria; and having finally been made Cardinal, he was called the Florentine Cardinal. He was courageous and astute, and therefore knew how to win the confidence and affection of the Pope, and to have himself appointed commander-in-chief of the armies of the Church; and thus he obtained the direction of all the wars in which the Pope became involved in Tuscany, the Romagna, in the kingdom of Naples, and in Rome. In this way he acquired such authority over the troops, and even over the pontiff himself, that the latter feared to give him any orders, and the troops would obey no one else. The Cardinal Vitelleschi happened to be in Rome with his forces when the report came that Niccolo Piccinino intended to invade Tuscany. This increased the alarm of the Florentines; for the Cardinal, ever since the banishment of Messer Rinaldo degli Albizzi, had been extremely hostile to their government, because the agree-

ments made by his intervention between the parties had not been observed, and had been used rather to the prejudice of Messer Rinaldo, in having caused him to lay down his arms, whereby he gave his enemies the opportunity of driving him from Florence. The chiefs of the government of Florence thought, therefore, that the time had come for recalling and indemnifying Messer Rinaldo, lest he should join Niccolo in the event of his coming into Tuscany. And they were the more apprehensive on this point because it seemed to them ominous that Niccolo should have left Lombardy, at a moment when his enterprise there was all but successful, to engage in another that was altogether doubtful; and which they could not believe he would have done unless he was acting upon some special intelligence, or was meditating some covert treachery. They informed the Pope of their apprehensions, who had already discovered his error in having endowed another with too much authority. But whilst the Florentines were in this state of suspense, fortune showed them the way in which they could secure themselves against the Patriarch. The government exercised at that time a strict surveillance over all correspondence, so as to discover whether any one was plotting against the state; and thus it happened that letters were intercepted at Montepulciano which the Patriarch had written to Niccolo Piccinino without the concurrence of the Pope. These were immediately communicated to the pontiff by the magistrates charged with the direction of the war; and although these letters were written in unusual characters, and their sense so involved as to make it difficult to extract from them any distinct meaning, yet that very obscurity and this dealing with the enemy so excited the suspicions of the Pope that he resolved to assure himself of the reality, and charged Antonio Rido of Padua with the task. Antonio was at the time in command of the garrison of the Castel San Angelo in Rome, and, immediately upon receiving this commission, prepared himself for its execution, and quickly had an opportunity for carrying it into effect. The Patriarch having resolved to go into Tuscany, and wishing to leave Rome the following day, notified the castellan to meet him upon the drawbridge of the castle in the morning when he should pass, as he desired to converse with him upon some matters. This seemed to Antonio the very opportunity wished for. He accordingly instructed some of his men what to do, and awaited the Patriarch upon the drawbridge at the appointed time; and when the Patriarch was fairly upon the bridge, he engaged him in conversation, and then gave the appointed signal to his men to hoist the draw of the bridge; and thus the Patriarch, from being a commander of armies, in one instant became the prisoner of the castellan. The Patriarch's followers at the first moment were disposed to make a disturbance, but became quiet when told that it had been done by order of the Pope himself. To the castellan's assurances and kind words that all would yet be well, the Patriarch replied, "Great men do not take prisoners to let them go again, "nor is it well to set those free who have been undeservedly "imprisoned." He died soon afterwards in his captivity. The Pope appointed in his stead Lodovico, the Patriarch of Aquileia, to the command of his troops; and although he had never before been willing to involve himself in the wars of the league with the Duke of Milan, yet now he agreed to take part in them, and pledged himself to furnish four thousand mounted men and two thousand infantry for the defence of Tuscany.

28. The Florentines, although relieved of this apprehension, were still afraid of Niccolo, and of the confusion of things in Lombardy, resulting from the difference in the views of the Venetians and the Count Francesco; and for the purpose of having a better understanding of these, they sent Neri di Gino Capponi and Messer Giuliano Davanzate to Venice, with instructions to arrange the conduct of the war for the following season. They charged Neri, after he should have ascertained the views of the Venetians, to go to the Count and learn his views, and to persuade him to such a course as the welfare of the league might seem to require. Before reaching Ferrara these ambassadors heard that Niccolo Piccinino had crossed the Po with six thousand horse, which made them hasten their journey; and having arrived at Venice, they found that the Signoria wanted that, above all, immediate succor should be given to Brescia, as that city could not hold out until spring, or until the new fleet should be ready, and, unless promptly relieved, would have to surrender to the enemy; and that this would insure the Duke's success everywhere, and expose them to the loss of all their inland possessions. Neri, therefore, went to Verona to hear what the Count might have to say to the contrary, who demonstrated to him, with ample reasons, that it would be useless at that time to move upon Brescia, and would also endanger their

future movements. For considering the season, and the position of Brescia, it could be of no possible benefit to her, and would only disorganize and fatigue their own forces; so that when afterwards the season came suitable for active operations, they would be obliged to return to Verona with their army, for the purpose of resupplying themselves with what had been consumed in the winter, as well as to provide for the coming summer, so that the very time best adapted to warlike operations would be consumed in going and returning. The Venetians had sent Messer Orsatto Justiniani and Messer Giovanni Pisani to Verona to treat with Sforza upon these matters; and after much discussion, it was agreed between them that the Venetians should pay him for the coming year the sum of eighty thousand ducats, and to his troops forty ducats per lance; and that the Count should be obliged, with his whole force, to attack the Duke, so as to compel him to recall Niccolo into Lombardy, from fear for his own safety. After concluding this arrangement, they returned to Venice, and, on account of the large sum of money to be paid the Venetians, were very dilatory in providing all the other things.

29. Niccolo Piccinino meantime followed his route, and had already reached the Romagna. He prevailed over the sons of Messer Pandolpho Malatesta to leave the Venetians and go over to the Duke, which displeased the Venetians greatly, and the Florentines even more, for they had counted upon being able to resist the advance of Niccolo by that route. But seeing the defection of the Malatesti they became alarmed, and feared particularly lest their general, Pietro Giampaolo Orsini, who was in the territory of the Malatesti, should be waylaid and plundered, and they should be left as it were disarmed. The Count was equally troubled by this intelligence, for he was afraid that Niccolo's going into Tuscany would cause him the loss of La Marca; and being desirous to go to the relief of his own home, he went to Venice, and upon being presented to the Doge he pointed out to him that "his going into Tuscany would prove "of greatest advantage to the league; inasmuch as the war "should be carried wherever the enemy's army and commander "might be, and not against his strong places and garrisons. "For the defeat of the enemy's army would end the war; but "if only his fortresses were taken and the army left entire, it "would only have the effect of making the war go on with in-

"creased activity. At the same time Count Francesco affirmed
"that Tuscany and La Marca would be lost unless the most
"vigorous resistance were made to Niccolo; and these once
"lost, there would be no help for Lombardy. But that so long
"as there was the least chance of saving them he did not in-
"tend to abandon his subjects and his allies; and that he had
"come into Lombardy as a sovereign, and did not mean to leave
"it as a mere condottiere." To all which the Doge replied:
"That it was manifest that, if Francesco left Lombardy and
"recrossed the Po with his army, the whole of their inland pos-
"sessions would be lost to the Venetians; and that in fact
"they were resolved not to incur any further expenditures in
"their defence, for it was not wise to defend anything that
"under any circumstances would be lost, and there was less dis-
"grace and harm in losing one's states only than in losing one's
"states and money at the same time. And if the loss of their
"inland possessions really resulted from Francesco's leaving
"Lombardy, it would then be seen how important the influence
"of the Venetians was for the preservation of Tuscany and the
"Romagna. And therefore they were entirely opposed to his
"views, for they believed that, if he were victorious in Lom-
"bardy, he would be equally so everywhere else. And that
"victory would be easy for him there, because the departure of
"Niccolo had weakened the Duke so that he could crush him
"before he had time to recall Niccolo or provide himself with
"other means of defence. And that if Francesco would care-
"fully consider the whole subject, he would see that the Duke
"had sent Piccinino into Tuscany for no other purpose than to
"withdraw the Count from his present enterprise, so as to trans-
"fer the war from his own door to some other place. So that
"if the Count were now to follow Niccolo, unless from some
"extreme necessity, the Duke would have the satisfaction of
"seeing his design successful. But that if the Count kept his
"troops in Lombardy, leaving Tuscany to take care of herself
"as best she could, the Duke would discover too late that by
"his unwise course he had lost Lombardy without having gained
"anything in Tuscany." After each had given his views, it was
concluded to wait a few days to see what result the agreement between Niccolo and the Malatesti might produce; and
whether the Florentines could depend upon Pierogiampaolo;
and whether the Pope would act in good faith with the league,

according to his promise. A few days after having come to this conclusion it was ascertained that the Malatesti had entered into the agreement with Niccolo more from fear than from any evil intention, and that Pierogiampaolo had moved with his troops towards Tuscany, and that the Pope was even more willing than before to aid the league. This information gave fresh courage to the Count Francesco, who consented to remain in Lombardy, and that Neri Capponi should return to Florence with one thousand horse of his own, and five hundred of those of the others. And if nevertheless matters in Tuscany should take such a turn as to make the Count's presence necessary there, that then he should depart regardless of all other considerations. Neri reached Florence with his troops in the month of April, and joined Giampaolo on the same day.

30. Niccolo Piccinino meanwhile, having settled the affairs of the Romagna, intended making a descent into Tuscany; and wishing to cross the mountains by the pass of San Benedetto and the valley of Montone, he found these places so well defended by the courage of Niccolo da Pisa that he deemed it useless to make any further attempts in that direction. The Florentines, illy prepared for so sudden an attack, both as regards men and officers, had sent a number of their citizens with some hastily organized infantry to guard these mountain passes. Amongst these was Messer Bartolommeo Orlandini, a cavalier, who was placed in charge of the castle of Marradi and the pass over the mountain there. Piccinino, having found it impossible to get over the San Benedetto pass because of the gallantry of its defenders, thought he might succeed in getting over the pass of Marradi through the cowardice of those charged with its defence. The castle of Marradi is situated at the foot of the mountains that separate Tuscany from the Romagna; although unprotected by walls on the side that looks to the Romagna and the head of the valley of Lamona, yet the river and the mountains, and the courageous character of the inhabitants, made it very strong; for the men are loyal and accustomed to bear arms; and the river has so eaten into the rock, as it were, and has such precipitous banks, that it is impossible to approach it by the valley, so long as a small bridge that crosses the stream is defended; and the mountain sides are so steep and rugged that it makes the place perfectly

secure. But the cowardice of Messer Bartolommeo made the men under his command also cowards, and changed the natural strength of the place into weakness. For no sooner did he hear of the approach of the enemy than he abandoned everything and fled with all his men, never stopping until he reached the Borgo San Lorenzo. Niccolo entered the abandoned place, amazed at its not being defended, and rejoiced at being in possession of it, descended to Mugello, where he took some castles, and then halted his troops at Puliciano, whence he scoured the whole country as far as the mountains of Fiesole, and had even the audacity to cross the Arno and to pillage the country within three miles of Florence, carrying off everything movable.

31. The Florentines, on the other hand, were not dismayed; and before anything else they saw to giving stability to the government, of which they had, however, no reason to doubt, owing to the good will of the people towards Cosimo, and the fact that they had confided the principal offices to a few of the most powerful citizens, who administered them with firmness and severity; and there had been no indications of any discontent or desire for change on the part of the people. They also knew, from the agreements made in Lombardy, the extent of the forces with which Neri would return, and moreover expected the troops of the Pope. This hope sustained them until the return of Neri, who, on finding the city in this state of disorder and apprehension, resolved to take the field at once for the purpose of checking Niccolo, and to put an end to his pillaging the country. With what cavalry he had, and some infantry raised entirely from the people, Neri issued from the city and took Remole from the enemy; and having established his camp there, he prevented Niccolo from making further depredations, and encouraged the Florentines to hope for speedy relief from the proximity of the enemy. Niccolo, finding that the tranquillity of the city had not been disturbed, although Florence was entirely bare of troops, concluded that it would be idle for him to waste his time there, and determined to attempt some other enterprise, so that the Florentines might be induced to send their troops after him, and thus afford him the opportunity of engaging them in battle; and if successful in that, he hoped to be equally prosperous in his other operations.

In Niccolo's army was the Count Francesco di Poppi, who had been an ally of the Florentines, but abandoned them when the enemy came to Mugello. The Florentines had in the beginning been doubtful of him, and for the purpose of insuring his fidelity by benefits they increased his emoluments and made him commissary over all the places in his neighborhood. Yet so powerful is the devotion to party with some men that neither benefits nor fear could make the Count Poppi forget his attachment to Messer Rinaldo degli Albizzi and to the others who had constituted the late government of Florence. So soon, therefore, as he heard of the approach of Niccolo, he went to join him, and urged him with the greatest solicitude to leave there and move to the Casentino, pointing out to him the strength of the country, and how he might from there in perfect security harass the enemy. Niccolo acted upon his advice, and having arrived in the territory of Casentino he seized Romena and Bibbiena, and then laid siege to Castel San Niccolo. This castle is situated at the foot of the mountains that separate the Casentino from the Val l' Arno; its elevated position and ample garrison made its capture very difficult, although Niccolo assailed it with catapults and other engines of war. The siege had lasted twenty days, during which the Florentines had gathered their troops, having already collected three thousand horse under several Condottieri, commanded by Pierogiampaolo as general, and Neri Capponi and Bernardo de' Medici as commissaries. The garrison of the Castel San Niccolo sent four messengers to these commissaries to entreat them to come to their rescue. Having examined the situation of the place, they found that no assistance could be rendered except by way of the mountains from the direction of the Val d' Arno. But as the crest of these mountains could be occupied sooner by the enemy, who had less distance to go, and as they would not be able to conceal their movements from the enemy, so that if they were to attempt it unsuccessfully it might cause the destruction of their troops, the commissaries could only commend the fidelity of the garrison, and advise them to surrender when defence was no longer possible. Niccolo thereupon took the castle, after a siege of thirty-two days; and this waste of time without any adequate result was in great part the cause of the failure of this expedition. For had Niccolo remained with his troops in the vicinity of Florence, it would have prevented the government from raising money from its citizens, and would have embarrassed them in collecting troops and making other provisions, from having the enemy so near them instead of at a distance. And in that case the Florentines would have been much more disposed to make terms with Niccolo, seeing that the war would be a protracted one. But the desire of the Count Poppi to revenge himself upon those castellans who had so long been his enemies, caused him to advise Niccolo to the course which he followed merely for the purpose of satisfying the Count Poppi.

Following up his success, Niccolo took also Rassina and Chiusi, where the Count Poppi advised him to halt, pointing out to him how he might there spread his forces between Chiusi and Caprese and the Piene, and thus make himself master of the Apennines, whence he might then descend at pleasure into the Casentino, the Val d' Arno, the Val di Chiana, and the Val di Tevere, and be prepared for every movement the enemy might make. But Niccolo, seeing the roughness of the country, said to him "that his horses could not eat stones," and went off to the Borgo San Sepolcro, where he met with a friendly reception; and from here he made overtures to the people of Citta di Castello, who however would not listen to him, being friends of the Florentines. Being desirous also to secure the good will of the people of Perugia, of which place he was a citizen, Niccolo went there with forty horse, and was kindly received. But in a few days he became suspect, and having in vain made great efforts to bring over the Legate and the Perugians, he accepted eight thousand ducats from them and returned to his army. He then attempted to seduce Cortona from the Florentines, but, the matter being discovered in time, his efforts proved fruitless. One of the most prominent citizens of Cortona was Bartolommeo di Senso, who, being about to go in the evening by order of the captain to guard one of the gates, was met by a countryman friend of his, who advised him not to go unless he wished to be killed. Bartolommeo, determined to probe this matter to the bottom, found out the arrangement that had been secretly made with Niccolo, and which Bartolommeo made promptly known to the captain; who, after securing the chiefs of the conspiracy, doubled the guards at the gates, and then awaited the coming of Niccolo, according to the agreement; so that when Niccolo came at the appointed hour of night, and found his plans discovered, he returned to his quarters.

32. Whilst these events were taking place in Tuscany with little advantage to the forces of Duke Filippo, affairs in Lombardy went on in an equally unpropitious manner for him. For so soon as the season permitted, the Count Francesco took the field with his army; and as the Venetians had re-established their fleet upon the lake, the Count wanted first of all to make himself master on the water and drive the Duke from the lake, judging that when this was done all the rest would be easy. He therefore attacked the Duke's fleet with that of the Venetians, and succeeded in scattering it, and then with his land forces he took the castles that were subject to the Duke. When the other ducal troops that invested Brescia by land heard of these losses they also withdrew, and thus Brescia, after having been besieged for three years, was finally relieved. After this victory the Count went in search of the enemy, who had retreated to Soncino, a castle situated on the river Oglio, dislodged him from his position, and forced him to retreat to Cremona, where the Duke made head and defended his states from that point. But being daily pressed closer and closer by the Count Francesco, and fearing to lose either the whole or a great part of his territory, the Duke discovered the error he had made in sending Piccinino into Tuscany. To retrieve this mistake he wrote to Niccolo telling him the straits in which he found himself, and how unfortunately his expedition had resulted, whereupon Niccolo left Tuscany as quickly as possible, and returned to Lombardy. The Florentines under their commissaries had meantime united their forces with those of the Pope, and took position at Anghiari, a castle situated at the foot of the mountains that divide the Val di Tevere from the Val di Chiana, and four miles distant from the Borgo San Sepolcro by a good road and a country well suited to the movements of cavalry and military operations. And as they had been informed of the victories of the Count Francesco, and of the recall of Niccolo Piccinino by the Duke, they considered that they had succeeded in this war without unsheathing their swords or burning powder, and wrote to the commissaries to avoid any engagement, as Niccolo would not be able to remain many days longer in Tus-

cany. These instructions came to the knowledge of Niccolo, who, aware of the necessity of leaving, and yet anxious to leave nothing untried, resolved to bring on an engagement, in the belief that he would find the enemy unprepared and far from expecting a battle. He was encouraged in this determination by Messer Rinaldo degli Albizzi and the Count Poppi, and the other Florentine exiles, who foresaw the certainty of their own destruction if Niccolo should leave; whilst in case of a battle they might yet succeed in their enterprise, or be honorably defeated. Having thus resolved, they moved the army from its position between Citta di Castello and the Borgo, and having arrived at the Borgo without the enemy being aware of it, they raised two thousand men from that country, who, trusting in the courage and skill of the general and in his promises, and eager for plunder, followed him.

33. Niccolo thence directed his march upon Anghiari, with his troops in battle array, and was already within less than two miles of it when Michelotto Attendolo observed a great cloud of dust, and, discovering it to be the enemy, gave the alarm. The confusion in the Florentine camp was extreme, for their army generally observed but little discipline when in camp, and now, believing the enemy far off, and more disposed to flight than to fight, they were more than ordinarily negligent; so that they were nearly all unarmed and away from their quarters, and scattered in every direction, wherever their inclination or the desire to escape the great heat of the day had led them. The commissaries and captain, however, acted with such promptness and energy that, before the arrival of the enemy, they got their men to horse and in position to resist the shock of the enemy's charge. Michelotto, who had been the first to discover the enemy, was also the first to encounter him, and rushed with his men upon the bridge over the stream that crosses the road not far from Anghiari. Before the appearance of the enemy, Pierogiampaolo Orsini had caused the ditches on each side of the road between the bridge and Anghiari to be filled up. Michelotto being now posted at the head of the bridge, Simoncino, the Condottiere of the Church, together with the Legate, took position on his right, and on his left the Florentine commissaries with their captain, Pierogiampaolo Orsini, the infantry being stationed all along on the upper side of the river. There was, therefore, no way left open for the enemy to make an attack

except straight over the bridge, which consequently was the only point which the Florentines had to defend. And they had ordered their infantry, in case the enemy should attempt to leave the road for the purpose of attacking them in the flank, to assail him with their crossbows, so as to prevent his wounding their horses in the flank when they should pass the bridge. Michelotto bravely sustained the charge of the first of the enemy, and would have repulsed them but that Astorre and Francesco Piccinino came up with a body of picked men, and threw themselves with such fury upon Michelotto that they took the bridge from him, and drove him back to the heights that rise at the Borgo of Anghiari. They were, however, afterwards repulsed by those who attacked them in the flank. This struggle lasted two hours, the bridge being alternately held now by Niccolo and now by the Florentine troops. And although the contest upon the bridge was equal, yet on either side Niccolo fought to great disadvantage; for when his troops got across the bridge, they found the enemy numerous, and able to manœuvre upon the level ground where the ditches had been filled up, so that those who were exhausted could at once be replaced by fresh men. But when the Florentines took the bridge, so that their men could pass over, Niccolo was not able, in like manner, to reinforce his men, being hemmed in by the ditches and banks on either side of the road. And thus it happened that, although Niccolo's men took the bridge several times, yet were they driven back each time by the fresh troops of the enemy. But when the Florentines took the bridge, and their men passed over into the road, Niccolo could not, on account of the fury of the onset and the inconvenience of the ground, reinforce his men; so that the front ranks got mixed up with the rear, thus throwing one another into confusion, and obliging the whole to turn back, whereupon they all, regardless of one another, fled to the Borgo. Then the Florentines looked after the booty, which was very large, consisting of prisoners, accoutrements, and horses; so that only about one thousand horse made their escape with Niccolo. The men of the Borgo, who had followed Niccolo for the sake of plunder, became themselves booty, for they were all taken, and were obliged to be ransomed. The banners and wagons also were taken. This victory proved much more advantageous for Tuscany than injurious to Duke Filippo; for if the Florentines had lost the battle, Tuscany would have been his; but the Duke losing it cost him only the horses and accoutrements of his army, which could be replaced without any serious outlay of money. Nor was there ever a time when a war waged in the territory of others was less dangerous for the invader than the present; and in so complete a rout and so long a combat, which lasted nearly twenty-four hours, there was only one man killed, and he was not wounded nor struck down by a valiant blow, but fell from his horse and was trampled to death. Men fought in those days with so much security, being mounted and protected by armor, that they were safe against death; and although they often surrendered, yet that was no reason why they should die. Whilst fighting, they were protected by their armor, and when they could no longer fight, they surrendered.

34. This battle, from the circumstances that attended and followed it, furnishes a striking illustration of the wretched military discipline that prevailed during those wars; for after the enemy was beaten, and Niccolo driven into the Borgo, the Florentine commissaries wished to follow and besiege him there, so as to make the victory complete. But neither the Condottieri nor the soldiers were willing to obey, alleging that they wanted first to secure their plunder and attend to the wounded. And what is most notable is, that the following day at noon, without leave, and regardless of commissaries and captains, the soldiers went off to Arezzo, and having deposited their plunder there, they returned to Anghiari; a proceeding so contrary to all good order and discipline that any mere remnant of a well-disciplined army could easily and deservedly have deprived them of that victory which they had achieved without merit. Besides this, the commissaries wanted to keep the men-at-arms that had been taken prisoners, so as to prevent the enemy from reorganizing his forces; but they were all set at liberty, contrary to the express wish of the commissaries. It is wonderful that so ill-disciplined an army should have had valor enough to gain a victory, and that there should have been such cowardice in the enemy as to allow himself to be beaten by such an undisciplined force.

During the going to and returning of the Florentine soldiers from Arezzo, Niccolo had time to get away with his men from the Borgo, and to move towards the Romagna. The Florentine exiles also fled with him, and, seeing all hope of returning to

Florence lost, they scattered in various directions, within and beyond Italy, according to the convenience of each. Of these, Messer Rinaldo degli Albizzi chose his abode at Ancona; and, by way of gaining the heavenly fatherland after losing his terrestrial one, he made a pilgrimage to the sepulchre of Christ. On his return from there, and whilst celebrating the nuptials of his daughter, he died suddenly at table, fortunate in this, that his death occurred at the least unhappy moment of his exile. Equally honored in good and in ill fortune, Messer Rinaldo would have even received a higher consideration had it been his fate to live in a city not torn by factions; for many of his qualities, which proved injurious to him in a city divided by the fury of parties, would have been a cause of high advancement for him in a tranquil and undivided republic.

After the return of the men from Arezzo, and the departure of Niccolo, the commissaries presented themselves before the Borgo, the inhabitants of which were willing to yield themselves to the Florentines, but these declined the offer; and whilst these negotiations were going on, the Pope's Legate became suspicious of the Florentine commissaries, lest they should wish to take this place from the Church. This led to high words between them; so that difficulties would have arisen between the Florentines and the ecclesiastics if the misunderstanding had continued much longer; but as it was finally settled according to the Legate's wishes, matters were amicably arranged.

35. Whilst these things were taking place at the Borgo San Sepolcro, word came that Niccolo Piccinino had gone towards Rome, whilst other intelligence represented that he had gone towards La Marca; whence the Legate and the Count Francesco's troops deemed it best to go towards Perugia, so as to be in position to afford assistance either to Rome or La Marca, to whichever of the two Niccolo might have gone. With them went Bernardo de' Medici, whilst Neri Capponi went off with the Florentine troops to recover the Casentino. This having been resolved upon, Neri went to Rassina, which he took, as also Bibbiena, Prato Vecchio, and Romena; and afterwards he besieged the castle of Poppi, and invested it on two sides, the one towards the plains of Certomondo, the other by the hill that stretches towards Fronzola. The Count Poppi, imagining himself abandoned by God and men, had shut himself up in this castle, not because he hoped for any help, but for the sake if possible of

making better terms of surrender. When therefore closely pressed by Neri, he asked for terms, and was granted as favorable conditions as he could have hoped for under the circumstances; namely, safety for himself and his sons, and all they could carry away with them, but yielding the place and its government to the Florentines. And whilst capitulating he descended on to the bridge over the Arno, which river flows by the foot of the place, and said to Neri, full of sorrow and affliction: "Had I justly measured my fortune and your power, I "should now have to rejoice with you as a friend at your vic- "tory, instead of being now obliged as an enemy to supplicate "that my ruin may be less complete. But present fate, which "brings to you glory and happiness, brings to me only sorrow "and misery. I had horses, arms, subjects, state, and riches; "what wonder, then, if I give them up reluctantly? But as you "are able and determined to command all Tuscany, we others "of necessity have to obey. Had I not committed an error "misfortune would not have befallen me, nor would you have "had the opportunity of displaying your liberality; if then you "preserve me from entire ruin, you will give to the world an "eternal example of clemency. Let your benevolence, therefore, "exceed my fault, and leave at least this one house to the de- "scendant of those from whom your ancestors have received in- "numerable benefits." To which Neri replied, "that relying too "much upon those who were able to do but little had in great "measure been the cause of his erring against the republic of "Florence; and taking into view the present condition of the "times made it necessary that he should surrender all his pos- "sessions, and cede those places to Florence as an enemy which "he had been unwilling to hold as a friend. For by his con- "duct he had set such an example as could not be tolerated, "and which under all circumstances would have proved injuri- "ous to the republic, and that it was not himself, but his pos- "sessions, that made him feared by the Florentines. But if he "could obtain a principality and reside in Germany, it would be "entirely satisfactory to the city of Florence, and out of regard "for those ancestors to which he had alluded, they would "favor his doing so." To which the Count replied, in great anger, that "he would like to see the Florentines at a much "greater distance." And thus breaking off all further friendly discussion, the Count Poppi, seeing no help for it, ceded his castle, lands, and jurisdiction to the Florentines, and departed with his wife and sons, and with all his chattels, lamenting and complaining that he had lost a state which his ancestors had possessed for four hundred years.

The news of these victories was received by the chiefs of the government as well as by the people of Florence with the greatest demonstrations of joy, and as Bernardetto de' Medici found the report of Niccolo Piccinino's having gone either to Rome or La Marca to be incorrect, he returned with his troops to join Neri; and having afterwards gone together to Florence, all the highest honors were decreed to them that it was the custom of the city to bestow upon her most distinguished citizens; and they were received by the Signoria and the captains of the sections, and afterwards by the whole city, in a triumphal manner.

SIXTH BOOK.

SUMMARY.

1. Considerations upon the end of the war, and the utility of victories. — 2. The Duke of Milan treats with Count Francesco Sforza, captain of the Venetians; in consequence of which negotiations, ill-humors and suspicions arise in the minds of the Count and the Venetians. — 3. Ravenna places herself under the power of Venice (1440). The Pope sells Borgo San Sepolcro to the Florentines. Niccolo Piccinino has the Venetian territory well scoured during the winter. — 4. The coming of spring and the resumption of arms oblige Sforza to raise the siege of Martinengo. His victories have made him so insolent that the Duke of Milan, by way of revenging himself upon him, makes peace with his allies (1441). Francesco Sforza, according to agreement, marries the daughter of the Duke, and receives Cremona as her dower. — 5. Alfonso of Aragon stirs up afresh the war for the possession of Naples, Benevento, and of other cities and places in the kingdom. The Duke of Milan and the Pope form a league with him against Sforza, and give the conduct of the war into the hands of Niccolo Piccinino (1442). Regnier, king of Naples, is driven out by Alfonso, and is honorably relieved by the Florentines, who make common cause with him and Sforza. — 6. Fresh discords in Florence. Jealousy against Neri di Gino Capponi (1443). — 7. Baldaccio d' Anghiari is killed by the treachery of Bartolommeo Orlandini. Reform of the government in favor of the Medici party (1444). — 8. Death of Niccolo Piccinino, and end of the war. — 9. Annibale Bentivogli is killed in Bologna by Battista Canneschi, and the latter is afterwards slain by the people, whence grave disturbances arise in the city (1445). — 10. Santi, the supposed son of Ercole Bentivogli, is called to Bologna to assume the government of the city. — 11. General war in Italy, with loss to the Duke of Milan. — 12. The Duke comes to terms with Sforza. — 13. Death of Duke Filippo Visconti. The Milanese make Sforza their captain (1447). — 14. Negotiations of the Pope for the pacification of Italy, which are opposed by the Venetians. — 15. Alfonso of Aragon assails the Florentines. — 16. He is constrained to sue for peace and to depart (1448). — 17. Count Sforza makes war against the Venetians, and is successful. — 18. Continuation of the war. — 19. The Count compels the Venetians to sue for peace. — 20. The terms of the peace not being satisfactory to the Milanese, they make terms with the Venetians against Count Sforza. — 21. They are closely besieged by him. — 22. The Count feigns to withdraw from the siege of Milan. — 23. Diversity of opinions in Florence as regards their conduct

towards Sforza. — 24. The Milanese, being anew besieged, and reduced to extremity, rise against their magistrates and give themselves to the Count Sforza (1450). — 25. League between the new Duke of Milan and the Florentines on the one part, and the king of Naples and the Venetians on the other part. — 26. Consequences of this league. — 27. Emperor Frederick III. at Florence (1451). War in Lombardy, between the Duke of Milan and the Venetians. — 28. Fernando, son of Alfonso, king of Naples, enters Tuscany against the Florentines (1452). — 29. Conspiracy of Messer Stefano Porcari, in Rome, against the Pontifical government: it is discovered and he is punished. — 30. Gherardo Gambacorti, lord of the Val di Bagno, negotiates with the king of Naples to give him the government, but his designs are frustrated by the courage and firmness of Antonio Gualandi (1453). — 31. Regnier of Anjou comes into Italy at the call of the Florentines, but soon afterwards returns to France (1458). — 32. Through the Pope's influence, peace is concluded between the princes engaged in war (1454). — 33. Jacopo Piccinino attacks the Sienuese. The Turks are routed at Belgrade (1456). — 34. Frightful storm in Italy. — 35. Genoa gives herself to the king of France (1458). — 36. Death of Alfonso of Aragon, king of Naples. He is succeeded by his son Ferdinand. Pope Calixtus III. dies, whilst meditating the gift of the kingdom of Naples to his nephew, Piero Lodovico Borgia; and Æneas Sylvius Piccolomini, of Sienna, is elected his successor under the name of Pius II. — 37. Discord in Genoa between John of Anjou and the Fregosi, to the disadvantage of the latter (1459). John of Anjou assails the kingdom of Naples, and defeats King Ferdinand. — 38. The latter re-establishes himself with the help of the Pope and the Duke of Milan (1460.) Genoa shakes off the yoke of the French. John of Anjou, abandoned by Jacopo Piccinino, is defeated in the kingdom of Naples, whence he retreats after defeat to the island of Ischia, and returns thence to France (1462).

1. It has ever been the aim of those who make war to enrich themselves and to impoverish the enemy; and it is reasonable that it should be so, for victories and conquests are sought for no other object than to gain an increase of power and to weaken the enemy. Whence it follows that those who are impoverished by their own victories, or enfeebled by their conquests, have either gone beyond or fallen short of the object for which the war was made. That prince or republic is enriched by war which crushes the enemy and remains master of the booty and ransoms; and those are impoverished who, although victorious, yet are unable to destroy their adversaries, and have to leave the plunder and the ransoms to their soldiers. Such are unfortunate in defeat, and still more unfortunate in victory; for, losing, they have to submit to the injuries inflicted upon them by the enemy; and gaining, they have to bear those of their friends, which are less excusable and

harder to be borne, seeing that it obliges them to afflict the subjects with fresh taxes and impositions. If then such government has any feelings of humanity, it cannot altogether rejoice at a victory by which all its citizens are afflicted.

The ancient and well-constituted republics were wont victory to fill their treasuries with gold and silver, to distribute donations to the people, to remit taxes and tribute to the subjects, and to celebrate the victories with games and solemn festivities. But those of the period of which we write first exhausted the public treasury, and afterwards impoverished their people, without securing themselves against renewed aggressions of the enemy; all of which results from the disorderly and wretched manner in which their wars were conducted. For by merely despoiling the vanquished enemies without keeping them prisoners or killing them, they caused these to defer a renewal of their attacks only until they could induce their employers to resupply them with arms and horses. Besides this, the booty and ransoms being left to the soldier, the victorious prince or republic could not avail of them for the further expenses of the war, which had to be wrung out of the bowels of their people; and the only result of these victories for the people was that it made their rulers more eager and reckless in their new impositions. And to such a point had these soldiers carried the practice of war, that both victor and vanquished alike needed fresh supplies of money whenever they wanted to command their services; for the one had to re-equip them, and the other had to give them fresh bounties to induce them to serve; for as the soldiers of the former could not serve without being remounted, so the others would not fight without fresh rewards. Thus the conqueror derived but little advantage from his victory, and the conquered did not feel his defeat so much; for the vanquished had time to reorganize his forces, and the victor was not in condition to follow up his successes.

2. This irregular and perverse military system enabled Niccolò Piccinino to remount his men before his defeat became known in Italy, and to carry on the war more effectually than he had done before. It was this system that enabled him, after the rout at Terma (1440), to take Verona; it was this that permitted him, after having lost his army at Verona, to come with a strong force into Tuscany; and it was this that enabled him, after having

been beaten at Anghiari and before reaching the Romagna, to reappear in the field stronger than he had been before, so as to inspire the Duke of Milan with the hope of being able to defend Lombardy; which, in consequence of his absence, was almost looked upon as lost by the Duke. For, whilst Niccolo spread consternation throughout Tuscany, Duke Filippo was reduced to that point that he feared the loss of his entire possessions before Niccolo, whom he had recalled, could come to his rescue and check the impetuous progress of the Count Sforza. For the purpose, therefore, of obtaining by a temporizing policy what he could not achieve by force, the Duke resorted to such means as had many times stood him in good stead in similar difficulties. He sent Niccolo da Este, Prince of Ferrara, to Peschiera, where Count Francesco then was, to persuade him to make peace on his own account, and to point out to him that the war was not to his advantage, because, if the Duke should be so weakened as no longer to be able to maintain his influence, the Count himself would be the first to suffer from it; for he would lose consideration both with the Venetians and the Florentines. And in proof of his good faith in desiring peace, the Duke offered to Count Francesco the conclusion of the marriage, and declared himself willing to send his daughter to Ferrara, and pledged himself to place her in Francesco's hands upon the conclusion of peace. To all this Count Francesco replied, that, if the Duke really desired peace, he could easily have it, as it was equally wished for by the Venetians and the Florentines; but in truth he could hardly believe him, knowing that he never made peace except from necessity, which no sooner passed than his passion for war would again control him. Nor could he place any reliance upon his offer respecting the marriage, having been already so many times deceived by him. Nevertheless, upon the conclusion of peace, he would act in the matter of the marriage as his friends might advise him.

3. The Venetians, who were always suspicious of their generals, even in matters that offered no occasion for it, very naturally looked upon these negotiations with the greatest suspicion, to remove which Count Sforza resumed the war most actively. Nevertheless, ambition and the suspicions of the Venetians had in so far cooled his ardor that he attempted but little during the remainder of the season; so that, Niccolo Piccinino having returned into Lombardy, and winter having

set in, both armies went into quarters,— the Count in Verona, the Duke in Cremona, the Florentine troops in Tuscany, and those of the Pope in the Romagna. After the victory at Anghiari, these latter had attacked Furli and Bologna, for the purpose of wresting them from the hands of Francesco Piccinino, who governed them in the name of his father. But they did not succeed in this attempt, owing to the gallant defence made by Francesco. Nevertheless, the approach of the papal forces so alarmed the people of Ravenna with the thought of being again brought under the dominion of the Church, that, with the consent of their lord, Ostasio di Polenta, they placed themselves under the protection of the Venetians, who in reward for the place and territory they had received sent Ostasio, with his son, to die in Candia; so that he might not at any future time attempt to recover by force what from lack of prudence he had surrendered to them. As the Pope, notwithstanding the victory at Anghiari, lacked money for these various enterprises, he sold the castle of the Borgo San Sepolcro to the Florentines for the sum of twenty-five thousand ducats. Matters being in this condition, and each believing himself secure from attack, owing to the winter season, peace was no longer thought of, and least of all by the Duke of Milan, who had been reassured by the presence of Piccinino and the winter, and had therefore broken off negotiations with the Count Francesco; and with the greatest diligence he remounted Niccolo's forces and made every requisite provision for future military operations. When this became known to the Count Sforza, he went to Venice to confer with the Senate as to the operations during the next season. Niccolo, on the other hand, having now fully reorganized his forces, and seeing those of the enemy disordered, did not wait for the coming of spring, but passed the Adda at the coldest season (1441), and entered the Brescian territory, occupying the whole country excepting Adula and Acri, where he captured two thousand of Sforza's horse, who did not expect such an attack. But what most displeased the Count and alarmed the Venetians was the defection of Ciarpellone, one of the Count's principal captains. So soon as advised of this the Count Francesco left Venice, and having arrived at Brescia he found that Niccolo, after having done this mischief, had returned to quarters; and finding active operations thus ended, he did

deem it advisable to renew them. But as the season and the
enemy afforded him the opportunity of reorganizing his forces,
he resolved to avail of it, so as to be in condition, at the opening of spring, to revenge himself for the injuries received. He
therefore caused the Venetians to recall the troops that served
under the Florentines in Tuscany, and to give the command to
Michelotto Attendolo, instead of Gattamelata, who had died.

4. At the opening of spring Niccolo Piccinino was the first
to take the field, and laid siege to Cignano, a castle some
twelve miles distant from Brescia. The Count Francesco went
to its relief, and the war was carried on in the usual fashion
by these two generals. Sforza, fearing for the city of Bergamo, laid siege to Martinengo, a castle so situated that assistance could thence easily be rendered to Bergamo, which was
closely pressed by Niccolo, who having foreseen that the enemy
could interfere with him only from Martinengo, had supplied
that castle with all the means of defence, so that the Count
was obliged to employ all his forces for its capture. Niccolo
thereupon took a position with his army that enabled him to
cut off the Count's supplies, and protected himself by intrenchments so that the Count could not attack him without manifest
danger. And thus in the end it came to pass that the besiegers
were in greater danger than those who were besieged in Martinengo; for the Count was no longer able to continue the siege
for want of supplies, nor to raise it without imminent danger;
and it became evident that the Duke would have a manifest
victory, and the Venetians and the Count a decided defeat.
But Fortune, who never lacks means to aid her favorites and
injure their enemies, caused Niccolo, in consequence of his
anticipated victory, to become so filled with ambition and insolence that, regardless of all respect due to the Duke of
Milan or to himself, he sent word to the Duke, that, having
fought under his banner for a long time without ever acquiring as much land as would serve him for burial, he wanted
now to understand from him what reward he was to have for
all his labors; that it was now in his power to deliver the
Duke's enemies into his hands, and make him undisputed
master of Lombardy; but that he considered that a certain
victory should also have a certain reward, and therefore he
wanted the Duke to grant him the city of Piacenza, so that
when tired by his long military service he might have some

place where to repose himself. Nor was he ashamed, as a last resort, to threaten the Duke with abandoning the enterprise unless his demands were acceded to. This insolent and insulting message so offended Duke Filippo, that, rather than yield to Piccinino's demands, he resolved to give up the whole enterprise. And thus the Duke, whom neither the many dangers nor the threats of enemies could induce to give way, was prompted to do so now by the insolence of his friend; and accordingly he resolved to make terms with the Count Francesco Sforza, and sent Antonio Guidobuono of Tortona to offer him his daughter and conditions of peace, which were eagerly accepted. And after a secret treaty of peace had been concluded between them, the Duke sent to order Niccolo to make a truce for one year with the Count Francesco, explaining to him that he was weary of the expenses of the war and would not forego a certain peace for a doubtful victory. Piccinino was astonished at this determination, and unable to comprehend the reasons that induced the Duke to forego so glorious a victory; for he could not believe that the Duke, for the sake of not rewarding his friend, should be willing to save his enemy. He therefore objected to the Duke's instructions in the manner that seemed to him best, so that the Duke was constrained, by way of making him submit, to threaten that unless he obeyed he would hand him over as a prey to his soldiers and his enemies. Whereupon Niccolo conformed to his orders, but much with the same sort of feeling as one who is compelled to abandon his friends and his country, lamenting his unhappy fate because at one moment Fortune and at another the Duke deprived him of victory over his enemies.

The truce having been concluded, the nuptials of the Lady Bianca Visconti with the Count Francesco Sforza were celebrated, and as a dower her father the Duke gave her the city of Cremona. This done, peace was formally concluded in November, 1441, and was signed on the part of the Venetians by Francesco Barbarico and Pagolo Trono, and on the part of the Florentines by Agnolo Acciaiuoli; whereby the Venetians gained Peschiera, Asola, and Leonato, a castle belonging to the Marquis of Mantua.

5. Whilst the war in Lombardy had ceased, the disturbances in the kingdom of Naples continued; and as these could not be composed, they led to a resumption of arms in Lombardy. For

whilst the war had been going on there King Regnier had been deprived by Alfonso of Aragon of his entire kingdom except the city of Naples. Alfonso, confident of victory, resolved, whilst besieging Naples, also to take from Count Francesco Sforza the town of Benevento, and other possessions which he had in the neighborhood, thinking that he could do so without risk, as the Count was occupied by the war in Lombardy. But when the news of the peace in Lombardy reached Alfonso he became afraid lest the Count Sforza should now intervene in favor of Regnier; which, in truth, the latter was hoping for, having already sent to solicit the Count to come to succor a friend and to revenge himself upon an enemy. On the other hand, Alfonso entreated Duke Filippo, by the friendship which he bore him, to harass the Count Francesco, so that, being occupied by more important matters, he would be compelled to give up all attempts at interfering with him. Filippo acceded to this request, not thinking that it would be an infraction of the peace that had been concluded but a short time before to his great disadvantage. And therefore he gave Pope Eugene to understand that now was the time to recover the places belonging to the Church, and of which Count Francesco held possession; and for this purpose he offered him the services of Niccolo Piccinino, who, since the conclusion of the peace, was with his men in the Romagna, and whom he offered to pay during such service. Pope Eugene eagerly accepted this suggestion, both from the hate he bore the Count Francesco and from the desire to get back his own. And although on a former occasion he had been deluded with the same hope by Niccolo Piccinino, yet now he thought, as the Duke himself had intervened, he need apprehend no disappointment; and having united his forces with those of Niccolo, he attacked La Marca. Count Sforza, surprised at so unexpected an attack, made head with his forces and went to encounter the enemy. In the midst of this King Alfonso took Naples (1442), so that the whole of the kingdom, Castelnuovo alone excepted, fell under his dominion. King Regnier, therefore, left a strong garrison in Castelnuovo and departed, and was received with great honors upon his arrival at Florence, where he remained a few days, and then, seeing that he could no longer carry on the war, he went off to Marseilles.

Meantime Alfonso had taken Castelnuovo; and Sforza, finding himself unable to cope with the Pope and Piccinino in La Marca, applied to the Venetians and Florentines for assistance in men and money, pointing out to them that, if they did not now make an effort to check the Pope and King Alfonso whilst he himself was still living, they would very soon after his death have to look to their own safety, for then Alfonso would unite with Duke Filippo, and then they would divide Italy between them. The Florentines and Venetians were for a time undecided, partly because they did not deem it well to meddle with the Pope and the king, and partly because they were occupied with the affairs of Bologna. Annibale Bentivogli had driven Francesco Piccinino from that city; and so as to be able to defend himself against Duke Filippo, who favored Francesco, he had asked for help from the Venetians and Florentines, which they agreed to furnish him; so that, being engaged in this affair, they could not decide to give the asked for aid to the Count Sforza. But as it happened that Annibale had defeated Francesco Piccinino, which it was supposed had settled the troubles of Bologna, the Florentines determined to support the Count Sforza. But, by way of securing themselves against Duke Filippo, they first renewed the league with him. Duke Filippo had been willing that war should be made against the Count Sforza so long as King Regnier was in the field with an army; but seeing him ruined and deprived of the whole of his kingdom, he did not like to have the Count also despoiled of all his possessions, and therefore he not only consented that aid should be given him, but he wrote to King Alfonso that he would be pleased to see him return to his kingdom and no longer make war against the Count Sforza. Alfonso very reluctantly, yet mindful of his obligations to the Duke, resolved to comply with his request, and retreated with his forces beyond the Tronto.

6. Whilst these events were transpiring in the Romagna, things were not quiet amongst the Florentines themselves. One of the most prominent men in the government of Florence was Neri di Gino Capponi, whose influence Cosimo de' Medici feared more than that of any other man. For besides the great estimation in which he was held by the citizens, he had also great influence with the soldiery, which he had gained by his bravery and merit when at different times chief of the Florentine armies. Besides this, the memory of the victories gained by

him and his father, Gino, who had taken Pisa, whilst he had defeated Niccolo Piccinino at Anghiari, made him much beloved by many, and feared by those who did not wish to share the government with any one else. Amongst the many generals of the Florentine army at that time was Baldaccio d'Anghiari, a most distinguished soldier; for there was no one in all Italy in those days who excelled him in personal strength or courage; and such was his reputation with the infantry, which he had always commanded, that every man was ready to follow him blindly in any enterprise. Baldaccio was devoted in friendship to Neri, who loved him in return for his bravery, of which he had on every occasion given the most signal proofs. This mutual friendship excited the mistrust of other citizens, who, deeming it dangerous to dismiss Baldaccio, and equally perilous to keep him, resolved to destroy him; and fortune favored their intent. Messer Bartolommeo Orlandini was Gonfaloniere of Justice at that time. As we have related above, he had been sent to guard the castle of Marradi at the time when Piccinino invaded Tuscany, and had fled ignominiously on his approach, abandoning that pass, which by nature was almost impregnable. Such cowardice had disgusted Baldaccio, who publicly denounced, by insulting words and letters, this want of courage of Messer Bartolommeo, which caused the latter so much shame and anger that he eagerly desired to revenge himself upon Baldaccio, thinking to efface the infamy of his conduct by the death of his accuser.

7. As this resentment of Messer Bartolommeo was well known to the other citizens, they had no difficulty in persuading him to destroy Baldaccio, and thus at one blow revenge himself for the injuries received and rid the state of a man whom it was equally dangerous to retain or dismiss from their service. Orlandini therefore, having resolved to kill Baldaccio, concealed a number of armed men in his chamber, and when Baldaccio came to the Piazza, where he went daily to negotiate with the magistrates about the pay of his troops, the Gonfaloniere sent for him, and he obeyed the call without the least suspicion. Orlandini went to meet him, and walked up and down with him several times in the hall of the Signoria, discussing the subject of the pay of his troops; and when the right moment seemed to him to have come, being near the chamber where the armed men lay concealed, he gave a signal, upon which they rushed forth, and,

Baldaccio being unarmed, they quickly despatched him and threw his dead body out of the window that looks towards the custom-house, whence it was dragged into the Piazza and the head cut off, which was exhibited during the whole day to the people (1443). Baldaccio left an only son, which his wife, Annalena, had borne him a few years previous, but he did not long survive his father. Annalena, thus deprived of her husband and son, and unwilling to unite herself again to another man, converted her house into a convent, within which she secluded herself, together with a number of other noble ladies who had joined her, and where she led a most holy life until her death. The convent which she founded, and which was named after her, will preserve her memory forever. This assassination of Baldaccio abated in a measure the power of Neri, depriving him of influence and friends, which, however, did not satisfy the citizens who held the government. For ten years having passed since their accession to power, and the authority of the Balia having expired, many of the people were encouraged to speak and act in a manner not acceptable to them; so that the chiefs of the state judged it necessary for the preservation of their power to adopt measures for renewing their authority by strengthening their friends and defeating their enemies. They therefore caused the councils to create a new Balia in 1444, which reformed the offices, gave authority to a few to form the Signoria, renewed the chancery of reform, taking it from Ser Filippo Peruzzi and placing at the head of it one who should administer it in accordance with the wishes of the nobles. They prolonged the term of banishment of the exiles, imprisoned Giovanni di Simone Vespucci, deprived the magistrates of the opposite party who were charged with the making up of the lists from which the Signoria was drawn of all the honors of public employment, and likewise the sons of Piero Baroncelli, all the Serragli, Bartolommeo Fortini, Messer Francesco Castellani, and many others. And by these means they restored their own authority and influence, and humbled the pride of their enemies, and of all whom they suspected of being unfriendly to themselves.

8. Having thus remodelled and confirmed their government within Florence, they turned their attention again to matters without. Niccolo Piccinino, as we have related above, had been abandoned by King Alfonso; whilst on the other hand

the Count Francesco Sforza had recovered his strength through the assistance afforded him by the Florentines; so that he attacked Niccolo near Fermo, and routed him; so that having lost nearly all his men, Piccinino took refuge with the remaining few in Montecchio, where he fortified and defended himself so vigorously that he was able in a short while to gather his scattered forces again, and in such numbers that he could easily have defended himself against the Count Sforza, especially as winter was at hand, which obliged both generals to send their troops into quarters. Piccinino devoted himself all winter to reinforcing his army, in which he was aided by the Pope and King Alfonso; so that when spring came, and the two armies took the field, Niccolo proved so much the superior in force that Sforza was reduced to the greatest straits, and would have been beaten if Niccolo's plans had not been thwarted by the Duke. Filippo had sent to request Niccolo to come to him immediately, as he wished to confer with him personally about some highly important matters; whereupon Niccolo, eager to hear what it was, gave up a certain victory for an uncertain advantage, and, leaving his son Francesco in command, went himself to meet the Duke at Milan. When the Count Sforza heard this he promptly resolved not to lose the opportunity of attacking Niccolo's forces during his absence; and having engaged them near Castel di Monte Loro, he routed them and took Francesco Piccinino prisoner. When Niccolo arrived at Milan he found that he had been deceived by the Duke, and on hearing of the rout of his troops and the capture of his son he died of grief, in the year 1445, at the age of sixty-four, having been more able than fortunate as a commander. He left two sons, Francesco and Jacopo Piccinino, who were not less able than their father, but even more unfortunate. Thus ended, as it were, the army of the Braccios, whilst that of Sforza, being always favored by fortune, became more and more renowned.

The Pope, seeing the army of Piccinino defeated and himself dead, and not having much confidence in the help from the king of Aragon, sought to make peace with the Count Sforza, which was concluded through the mediation of the Florentines. By this treaty there were restored to the Pope the following places in La Marca, namely, Osimo, Fabriano, and Ricanati, whilst all the rest remained under the dominion of the Count Sforza.

9. After the peace of La Marca all Italy would have been tranquil, had it not been disturbed by the Bolognese. The two most powerful families of Bologna were the Canneschi and the Bentivogli; Annibale was the chief of the latter, and Battista of the former. By way of establishing a greater degree of mutual confidence they had contracted a family alliance between them. But it is much easier for men having the same ambitious aims to contract a relationship than a real friendship. After the expulsion of Niccolo Piccinino, Bologna formed a league with the Venetians and the Florentines through the agency of Annibale Bentivogli; but Battista Canneschi, knowing how desirous the Duke of Milan was to have the city of Bologna favorably disposed towards him, secretly intrigued with him for the murder of Annibale, and then to bring the city under the dominion of Duke Filippo. And having agreed as to the mode of proceeding, Battista attacked Annibale with a body of his armed followers on the 24th of June, 1445, and killed him, and then rushed through the town proclaiming the Duke's name. The Venetian and Florentine commissaries, who were in Bologna at the time, retreated to their houses so soon as they heard the noise. But seeing afterwards that the people did not support the murderers, but rather lamented the death of Annibale, and had gathered armed and in great numbers in the Piazza, they took courage and joined them; and having made a stand they attacked the Canneschi, and in a few hours defeated them, killing a portion and driving the rest from the city. Battista not having been in time to make his escape, nor his enemies in time to kill him, concealed himself in a barn behind the house, used for the storage of grain. His enemies, having sought him in vain all day, yet knowing that he had not left the city, so terrified his servants with threats, that one of the boys from fear showed them his master's place of concealment. Having been dragged from there still covered with his armor, Battista was killed, and his body dragged through the city, and then burnt. Thus the Duke of Milan's authority had been enough to cause Battista to engage in this attempt, but his power could not intervene in time to save him.

10. The death of Battista and the flight of the Canneschi having put an end to these troubles, the Bolognese however still remained in great confusion, for there was none of the

family of the Bentivogli fit to take the government, Annibale having left an only son called Giovanni, who was only six years old. It was feared, therefore, that divisions would arise amongst the friends of the Bentivogli, which would cause the return of the Canneschi, and with them the ruin of their country and party. Whilst in this state of uncertainty, Francesco, the former Count Poppi, who happened to be in Bologna, gave the principal men of the city to understand that, if they desired to be governed by one of the blood of the Bentivogli, he could tell them where to find one. And he related to them that about twenty years ago, Ercole Bentivogli, cousin of Annibale, being at Poppi, had to his knowledge an intimacy with a young girl of that castle, the result of which was the birth of a boy named Santi, whom Ercole had several times acknowledged as his child. Nor could it be denied, for whoever knew Ercole and the youth was struck by the remarkable resemblance between them. The citizens put faith in these representations, and promptly sent some of their number to see the youth, and they managed through Cosimo and Neri to have him given up to them. The putative father of Santi was dead, so that he lived under the guardianship of an uncle, called Antonio de Cascese, who was rich and without any son of his own, and at the same time a great friend of Neri's. When the matter was made known to him, Neri advised him that it would not do either to decline or to accept the offer hastily; and suggested that Santi should speak with the Bolognese envoys in the presence of Cosimo. This was agreed upon, and Santi was not only honored, but almost worshipped by them, such was the power of party feeling in those days. Nothing definite, however, was concluded, except that Cosimo took Santi apart, and said to him: "No one can advise you "in this matter so well as yourself, and you must take what-"ever course your own feelings incline you to. For if you are "the son of Ercole Bentivogli you will naturally choose to "engage in such enterprises as shall be worthy of your father "and his lineage; but if you are the son of Agnolo da Cascese "you will remain in Florence and pass your life humbly in "some branch of the wool business." These words moved the youth, who, although he had at first declined the proposition, yet now expressed himself ready to do whatever Cosimo and Neri might decide upon. These promptly arranged matters with the Bolognese envoys, and the young man was honorably provided with clothing, horses, and servants, and was soon after conducted to Bologna by a numerous escort; and the guardianship of the young son of Annibale and the government of the city were placed in his hands. He conducted himself with so much prudence that, although his ancestors had all been killed by their enemies, yet he passed his life in peace and tranquillity, and died greatly honored.

11. After the death of Niccolo Piccinino and the peace of La Marca, Duke Filippo, being in search of a captain to command his troops, secretly negotiated with Ciarpellone, one of the best captains of the Count Francesco Sforza. An engagement having been agreed upon, Ciarpellone asked the Count Sforza for leave to go to Milan, for the purpose of taking possession of some castles that had been given to him in the late wars by the Duke of Milan. The Count, mistrusting the real motive of this journey, and with the view of thwarting the designs of the Duke, first had Ciarpellone imprisoned, and soon after put to death, alleging that he had discovered his plotting treason against him. Duke Filippo was much displeased and angered by this, whilst the Venetians and Florentines were gratified by it, for they feared nothing more than a union between Duke Filippo and the Count Sforza; but the Duke's resentment gave occasion for fresh wars in La Marca. Gismondo Malatesti, lord of Rimini, and son-in-law to the Count Francesco Sforza, hoped on this account to obtain the lordship of Pesaro; but upon the taking of this town by the Count Sforza, he bestowed it upon his brother, Alessandro, which greatly irritated Gismondo. This feeling was increased still more when he saw his enemy, Federigo di Montefeltro, invested by the Count Sforza with the lordship of Urbino. All this caused Gismondo to throw himself into the ranks of the party of the Duke Filippo, and to solicit the Pope and the king of Naples to make war upon the Count Sforza. The latter, for the purpose of making Gismondo himself taste the first fruits of the war which he wished for, resolved to forestall him, and therefore suddenly attacked him. In consequence of this the Romagna and La Marca were quickly involved in confusion; for Duke Filippo, the king of Naples, and the Pope sent powerful aid to Gismondo, whilst the Florentines and Venetians provided the Count Sforza with money, if not with men. Filippo, not content with

making war upon Sforza in the Romagna only, attempted also to take Cremona and Pontremoli from him; but Pontremoli was defended by the Florentines, and Cremona by the Venetians. Thus the war was also renewed in Lombardy, where, after general engagements in the Cremonese territory, Francesco Piccinino, general of the Duke of Milan's forces, was defeated by Michelotto and the Venetian troops, at Casale, in 1446. This victory made the Venetians conceive the hope of being able to drive Duke Filippo from his states; they sent a commissary to Cremona, and attacked the Ghiaradadda, and took the whole of it excepting Crema. Afterwards they crossed the Adda, and scoured the country up to the very gates of Milan; in consequence of which the Duke had recourse to King Alfonso, begging him for assistance, and pointing out to him the danger to which the kingdom of Naples would be exposed if the Venetians should become masters of Lombardy. Alfonso promised to send him troops, which, however, could not pass into Lombardy except with great difficulty, unless with Count Sforza's consent.

12. Duke Filippo thereupon entreated Sforza not to abandon his father-in-law, who was now old and blind; but the Count was offended with him for having provoked this war against him. On the other hand, he did not like the aggrandizement of the Venetians, and besides began to lack funds, which the league provided but sparingly; for the Florentines had no longer that fear of Filippo which had made them value the Count Sforza so highly, and the Venetians desired his ruin, believing him to be the only man that could take Lombardy from them. Nevertheless, whilst Duke Filippo sought to draw the Count into his pay, and offered him the command of all his troops provided he would leave the Venetians and restore La Marca to the Pope, the Venetians also sent messengers to him promising him the sovereignty of Milan if they should take it, and the command in perpetuity of their forces, provided he carried the war into La Marca and prevented Alfonso from sending assistance into Lombardy. The promises of the Venetians were large and tempting, and they had rendered important services to the Count in having gone to war to save him Cremona; and, on the other hand, the injuries received at the hands of the Duke were still fresh in his mind, whilst his promises were insignificant and not to be relied upon. With

all this, the Count Sforza was in doubt as to which side he should take; for on the one hand he was influenced by his obligations to the league, his pledged faith, the recent benefits received, and the promises for the future. On the other hand were the entreaties of his father-in-law, and, above all, his suspicions that there was some secret poison concealed under the great promises of the Venetians; and judging that, even in case of victory, he would still be at their discretion, both as regarded the government of Milan and the other promises,— a position to which no prudent man should expose himself except in case of necessity. These difficulties in coming to a determination were removed by the ambition of the Venetians, who, from some secret intelligence they had obtained, were hopeful of taking Cremona, and had, under some other pretext, sent their troops into the neighborhood of that city. But the affair was discovered by those who guarded Cremona for the Count Sforza, who now, regardless of all other considerations, joined the Duke of Milan (1447).

13. Meantime Pope Eugenius had died, and Nicholas V. had been chosen his successor; and Sforza was already with his whole army at Cotignola, for the purpose of passing into Lombardy, when news came to him of the death of the Duke Filippo Visconti, on the last day of August, 1447. This intelligence filled the Count Sforza with consternation, for his troops did not seem to him in condition to proceed on account of their pay being in arrears; he feared the Venetians, who were armed, and were now his enemies, as he had so lately left them and gone over to the Duke; he was apprehensive of King Alfonso, who was his inveterate enemy, and he had nothing to hope from the Pope or the Florentines, the latter being allies of the Venetians, and the former hostile to him on account of his having seized the lands of the Church. With all this he resolved to face fortune, and to govern himself according to circumstances; for often valuable suggestions develop themselves in action that would otherwise not be thought of. He took much hope from the belief that, if the Milanese wished to defend themselves against the ambition of the Venetians, they could not look to any one but himself for armed assistance. He was therefore of good courage, and entered the Bolognese territory; and, passing by Modena and Reggio, he halted above the Lenza, and sent to Milan to offer his services. After the

death of Duke Filippo a portion of the Milanese desired to live as a republic, and a portion under a prince; and of those who wanted a prince, some wanted the Count Sforza and others the King Alfonso. Therefore, those who wanted a republic, being more united, prevailed, and organized a government in their fashion, which, however, was not obeyed by many of the other cities of the duchy, who wanted to enjoy their independence the same as Milan; and such as did not aspire to independence were yet unwilling to submit to the rule of Milan. Lodi and Piacenza gave themselves to the Venetians, and Pavia and Parma declared themselves independent. When Count Sforza heard of these complications he went to Cremona, where it was agreed between the Milanese ambassadors and himself that he should be the general of the Milanese on the same terms and conditions as had been agreed upon between him and Duke Filippo before his death; and further, that Sforza should have Brescia, and in case of the capture of Verona he was to have that city in place of Brescia, which he was then to give up.

14. After the assumption of the pontificate, and before the death of the Duke, Pope Niccolo sought to restore peace amongst the Italian princes; and for this purpose he endeavored, together with the ambassadors whom the Florentines had sent to congratulate him on his accession, to have a Diet convened at Ferrara, for the negotiation of either a long truce or a lasting peace. Accordingly there assembled in that city the Legate of the Pope, the Venetian, the Milanese, and the Florentine ambassadors; those of King Alfonso did not attend. He himself was at Tivoli, with a large force of horse and foot, and was disposed to support the Duke; and it was generally believed that, after having drawn the Count Sforza over to their side, they intended openly to attack the Venetians and the Florentines; prolonging the negotiations for peace so as to afford time to Sforza's troops to pass into Lombardy. King Alfonso had declared that, although his representatives were not present, yet he would ratify whatever Duke Filippo might conclude. The negotiations lasted some days, and after much debating it was resolved to have either a truce for five years or a definite peace, whichever might be approved of by the Duke Filippo. But when the ducal envoys returned to Milan to obtain his decision, they found the Duke dead. The Milanese wished, nevertheless, to carry out the agreement; but the Venetians

were not willing, as they cherished the hope of becoming masters of Milan, particularly as they found that immediately after the Duke's death Lodi and Piacenza had voluntarily placed themselves under their dominion. They expected, either by treaties or by force, to strip Milan of all her possessions, and then to press her so hard that she would surrender to them before any one could come to her assistance; and they were the more confident of succeeding in this from the fact that the Florentines had involved themselves in war with King Alfonso.

15. King Alfonso, who was at Tivoli at that time, was determined to carry out the project of attacking Tuscany which he had concerted with Duke Filippo, and thought that the war which had been rekindled in Lombardy would afford him a favorable opportunity. But before commencing open hostilities, he was anxious to secure himself a foothold upon the Florentine territory, and therefore opened negotiations with the castle of Cennina in the Val d'Arno, and took possession of it. The Florentines, surprised by this unexpected attack, and seeing the king engaged in open hostilities against them, levied troops, created a Council of Ten on the war, and made all the other customary preparations. Meantime Alfonso had advanced with his army into the Siennese territory, and made every possible effort to draw that city over to his side; but the Siennese remained true to their friendship for the Florentines, and refused to admit the king into their city, or any of their other places. They, however, supplied the king well with provisions, for which they excused themselves on account of their own weakness and the strength of the enemy. Alfonso had at first contemplated entering the Florentine territory by way of the Val d'Arno; but this seemed to him now undesirable, either because of his having lost Cennina again, or because he saw that the Florentines had already to some extent provided themselves with troops. And therefore he turned towards Volterra, and captured a number of castles in that territory. Thence he entered the Pisan territory, and with the aid of the Counts Arrigo and Fazio della Gherardesca he took some castles there. After that he attacked Campiglia, but did not succeed in taking it, as it was defended by the Florentines and the severity of the winter. Alfonso thereupon left garrisons in the places he had taken, both to defend them and to scour the country, and

retired himself with the remainder of his army into quarters in the Siennese territory. The Florentines meantime, favored by the season, made great exertions to provide themselves with more troops; their generals were Federigo, lord of Urbino, and Gismondi Malatesti di Rimini; and although these generals differed upon some points, yet the good sense and prudence of the commissaries Neri di Gino and Bernardetto de' Medici harmonized their differences sufficiently to enable them to take the field, although still midwinter, and to recover the places that had been lost in the Pisan and in the Volterran territories. And King Alfonso's troops, which until then had scoured the low country, were so effectually checked that they could with difficulty maintain themselves in the places which they had been left to guard. With the first opening of spring, the commissaries took position with their whole force at Spedaletto, to the number of five thousand horse and two thousand foot; whilst King Alfonso with his forces, numbering fifteen thousand, established himself within three miles of Campiglia. It was supposed that he would lay siege to this place, but instead of that he threw himself suddenly upon Piombino, hoping to take it easily, as it was insufficiently supplied, and because he thought that its possession would prove most advantageous to him, and most damaging to the Florentines. For from there he could harass and exhaust the Florentines by a long war, whilst he was able to procure supplies of every kind for himself by sea, and at the same time keep the whole Pisan country disturbed. The Florentines, therefore, were greatly disquieted by this attack upon Piombino, and, having consulted as to the best course to pursue, they resolved to remain with their army encamped in the woods of Campiglia, hoping in that way to force the king to depart, or to run the risk of a disgraceful defeat. And for this reason they armed four small galleys which they had at Livorno, and by means of which they transported three hundred men to Piombino, establishing themselves at Caldane, where they could with difficulty be attacked; for it was deemed dangerous to remain encamped in the thickets of the plains.

16. The Florentine army depended for its provisions upon the surrounding country, which, being but sparsely inhabited, made the supply very difficult. The soldiers consequently suffered from want, and what they mainly lacked was wine, as the coun-

try did not produce any; and as it could not be obtained from a distance, it became impossible to supply the men. King Alfonso, on the other hand, although closely pressed by the Florentines, had abundance of everything, as he was able to obtain his supplies by sea. The Florentines, therefore, wished to try whether they could not also supply their troops by water, and for that purpose they loaded their galleys with provisions; but being met on the way by seven of the king's galleys, these captured two and put the others to flight. This loss deprived the Florentine troops of all hopes of obtaining the needed provisions, so that two hundred or more foragers deserted to the king, mainly on account of the want of wine. The other troops complained that they could not remain in that extremely hot country without wine, as the water was not drinkable. The commissaries therefore resolved to abandon that position, and to endeavor to recover some of the castles that yet remained in the hands of the king. Alfonso, on the other hand, though not suffering from want of provisions, and superior in numbers, yet saw that he could not succeed, owing to the fact that a large part of his men were ill from the fevers that prevail in that swampy country during the warm season, so that many of them died, and nearly all were more or less affected. Negotiations for peace were therefore set on foot. The king demanded fifty thousand florins and the unconditional surrender of Piombino. This proposition was submitted to the government at Florence, and many who were anxious for peace were willing it should be accepted, affirming that they could not see how they were to succeed in so costly a war. But Neri Capponi, who had gone to Florence, dissuaded them with such arguments that all agreed that the proposed terms could not be accepted. And it was unanimously agreed to take the lord of Piombino under the protection of the republic, promising to sustain him in war and in peace, on condition that he should not surrender, but continue to defend himself, as he had done until then. When King Alfonso heard of this determination, seeing that he could not hope to take the place with an army so enfeebled by disease, he raised the siege, after having suffered all the disasters of a defeat, having lost over two thousand men; and with the remainder of his army he withdrew to the Siennese territory, and thence to his kingdom, furious against the Florentines, whom he threatened with a renewal of the war during the next season.

17. Whilst these events were taking place in Tuscany, Count Francesco Sforza, having become general of the Milanese forces, sought, before everything else, to win the friendship of Francesco Piccinino, who was also in the pay of the Milanese, so as to secure his support in his undertakings, or at least to make him less disposed to thwart them. He then took the field with his army; and the people of Pavia, believing themselves unable to resist him, and unwilling, on the other hand, to yield obedience to the Milanese, offered to give themselves to him on condition that he should not subject them to the government of Milan. Sforza greatly desired possession of this city, which he thought would serve him admirably as a means for covering his ulterior designs. And it was neither fear nor shame at breaking his faith that restrained him, for great men deem it a shame to lose, but not to gain, by fraud and perfidy; but he apprehended that his accepting Pavia would so irritate the Milanese as to cause them to transfer their allegiance to the Venetians. And, on the other hand, he feared that, if he did not take it, it would advance the interests of the Duke of Savoy, to whom many citizens wished to give the city. In either case, it seemed to him that he would lose the sovereignty of Lombardy. After much reflection, however, he concluded that there was less danger in accepting Pavia, than in allowing it to be taken by some one else; and therefore he resolved to accept the offer of the people of Pavia, trusting to be able afterwards to satisfy the Milanese by explaining to them how dangerous it would have been to their cause had he declined Pavia. For in that case the citizens would have given themselves to the Venetians or to the Duke of Savoy, and that in either case it would have been lost to them; and that they ought to be better satisfied to have him for a neighbor and friend than such a power as either of the others, which would be hostile to them. The Milanese were much perplexed by this matter, which seemed to them to disclose Sforza's ambition, and the end at which he aimed. But they deemed it best not to make their suspicions known, as they did not know where else to turn, if they alienated the Count from them, except to the Venetians, whose pride, and the onerous conditions they were likely to impose, they feared greatly. They resolved, therefore, not to break with the Count Sforza, but for the present to avail of his aid in meeting the impending difficulties, hoping that, when they should be relieved

of these, they would be able to rid themselves of the Count also. In fact, they were assailed not only by the Venetians, but also by the Genoese and by the Duke of Savoy, acting on behalf of Charles of Orleans, a son of Duke Filippo's sister. Sforza, however, easily repulsed these latter enemies, so that the Milanese had only to fear the Venetians, who had raised a powerful army, and were trying to make themselves masters of all Lombardy, holding already Lodi and Piacenza. The Count Sforza besieged the latter city, and took and sacked it, after an obstinate defence. After this, winter having set in, he led his troops into quarters, and went himself to Cremona, where he passed the winter in repose with his wife.

18. With the first return of spring, both the Venetian and the Milanese armies took the field. The Milanese were desirous of taking Lodi, and then to make peace with the Venetians; for the expenses of the war became daily more onerous, and they seriously suspected their general, so that they became exceedingly anxious for peace, to enable them to enjoy some repose, and to make themselves secure against the Count Sforza. They resolved, therefore, to have their army attempt the capture of Caravaggio, hoping that when that castle should have been taken Lodi would surrender. Sforza obeyed the wishes of the Milanese, although his own intention had been to cross the Adda, and to attack the Brescian territory. Having, therefore, encamped before Caravaggio, he fortified himself with ditches and intrenchments, so that, if the Venetians should attempt to compel him to raise the siege, they would have to attack him at great disadvantage. The Venetians, on the other hand, advanced with their army, under command of Michelotto, to within two bowshot lengths of Sforza's camp, where they remained several days, and had a number of skirmishes with the Count's troops. Despite of this, Sforza continued to press the besieged very hard, and reduced them to that point that there was nothing left for them but to surrender. This caused the Venetians the greatest uneasiness, for they regarded the loss of Caravaggio as ruinous to their whole enterprise; and was the occasion of a violent dispute between their generals as to the best means of succoring it. They saw no other way than to seek the enemy behind his intrenchments, which was in the highest degree disadvantageous for them; but they looked upon the preservation of that castle as of such importance that the Venetian Senate,

naturally timid and averse to every doubtful and hazardous course, were yet willing to risk all for the sake of saving Caravaggio, rather than by its loss to incur the failure of their whole enterprise. They resolved, therefore, to attack the Count anyhow; and having started one morning at a very early hour, they assailed him on the side where he was least protected; and at the first rush, as is often the case with sudden and unexpected assaults, the whole Sforzescan army was thrown into confusion. But the Count quickly restored order, so that the Venetians, after desperate efforts to pass the intrenchments, were not only repulsed, but put to flight, and so completely routed that of the whole army, which consisted of over twelve thousand horse, not one thousand were saved, and all the baggage and camp equipage was captured. Never did the Venetians experience a more complete and terrible defeat.

Amongst the booty and the prisoners taken was one of the Venetian commissaries, who before the fight, and in fact during the whole progress of the war, had spoken in the most abusive terms of the Count Sforza, calling him a coward and a bastard. But now, finding himself his prisoner after the defeat, and mindful of his previous conduct, he was very melancholy and depressed, for he feared that he would be dealt with according to his deserts. Having been brought before the Count all cowed and frightened, according to the nature of proud and pusillanimous men, who are insolent in prosperity and in adversity abject and humble, he threw himself upon his knees before Sforza, beseeching him with tears to forgive him the insults and injuries he had done him. The Count raised him up, took him by the arm, and bade him be of good cheer and hope for the best; and then he told him "that he wondered how a man of his prudence "and gravity, or at least who wished to be considered as such, "could fall into so great an error as to speak so abusively of "one who did not deserve it. And as for the reproaches which "he had cast upon him personally, he did not know how his "father Sforza had conducted himself towards the lady Lucia, "his mother, as he had not been present, and could not there- "fore be in any way held responsible for their proceedings; so "that he did not think that he merited either praise or blame "for whatever they might have done. But that he knew well "that, in all matters which it had devolved upon him to do, he "had conducted himself so that nobody could censure him; of

" which he himself and his Senate could give the latest and best
" testimony. And then counselled him in future to be more
" prudent in speaking of others, and more cautious in his enter-
" prises."

19. After this victory, the Count marched with his victorious army into the Brescian territory and took possession of the whole of it, and then pitched his camp within two miles of Brescia. The Venetians, on the other hand, having experienced defeat, and apprehending, as indeed it happened, that Brescia would be the first to be attacked, supplied it as quickly and as well as they could with a garrison and munitions; and then they set to work, with all diligence, to gather the fragments of their army and to collect more troops, and called upon the Florentines for assistance, according to the conditions of the treaty. The Florentines, being now relieved of the war with the King Alfonso, sent them fifteen thousand infantry and two thousand horse,— which accession of force gave the Venetians time to think of making terms. It was almost always the fate of the republic of Venice, at that time, to fail in war and to be successful in negotiations; so that what they lost in war was restored to them by peace many fold. The Venetians were not ignorant of the mistrust which the Milanese had of Count Sforza, and that the Count aimed, not at being their general, but their sovereign. And as they could at will make peace with either party, the one desiring it from ambitious motives and the other from fear, they elected to make it with the Count Sforza, and offered him their assistance in effecting the desired acquisition; persuading themselves that the Milanese, on finding themselves duped by Sforza, would from resentment subject themselves rather to any other authority than his, and that, being brought to the condition that they could neither defend themselves nor place any confidence in their general, the Count, they would be obliged, not knowing where else to go, to throw themselves into the arms of Venice. Having resolved upon this course they sounded the Count's disposition, and found him greatly inclined to peace, being determined that the victory of Caravaggio should prove to his own advantage, and not to that of the Milanese. A treaty was therefore concluded between them, according to which the Venetians obligated themselves to pay the Count the sum of thirteen thousand florins per month, until he should have effected the acquisition

of Milan, and moreover to furnish him during the war four thousand horse and two thousand infantry. Sforza, on the other hand, bound himself to restore to the Venetians the places, prisoners, and whatever else he might have taken from them during that war, and to remain satisfied with only those places which Duke Filippo held at the time of his death.

20. When the news of this treaty became known to the Milanese, they were more afflicted by it than they had before been rejoiced at the victory of Caravaggio. The rulers of the city lamented, the people complained, the women and children cried, and all united in calling the Count disloyal and a traitor. And although they did not believe that they could with prayers and promises induce him to abandon his unjust intentions, yet they sent ambassadors to him to see with what face and words he would attempt to carry out his villany; and having appeared before Sforza, one of them addressed him as follows:—

"It is usual for those who desire to obtain anything by con-
"cession to employ prayers, gifts, or menaces, so that by the
"influence of pity, the hope of gain, or by fear, they may obtain
"a compliance with their request. But as these means are of
"no avail with cruel and avaricious men, and such as are filled
"with the pride of their power, it is vain to attempt to soften
"them with prayers, or to win them by gifts, or alarm them
"with menaces. Knowing therefore now, although too late,
"your cruelty, ambition, and pride, we come not for the pur-
"pose of entreating you for anything, nor in the belief that we
"should obtain it even were we to ask for it; but to recall to
"your memory the benefits you have received at the hands
"of the people of Milan, and to show you with what ingrati-
"tude you have rewarded them; so that, amidst the great afflic-
"tions we are experiencing, we may at least have the small
"gratification of upbraiding you as being the cause of them.
"For you must not forget what your condition was after the
"death of Duke Filippo. Then you were at enmity with the
"Pope and the king of Naples; you had betrayed the Floren-
"tines and Venetians, who became your enemies from their
"recent and just resentment, and from having no longer any
"need of your services. You found yourself exhausted by the
"war with the Church, having but few troops, and without
"allies or money, and hopeless of being able to maintain your
"states and ancient reputation; all of which would easily have

"caused your overthrow had it not been for our confiding sim-
"plicity. For we received you in our homes because of the
"reverence we had for the happy memory of our Duke, with
"whom you had formed a relationship and recent friendship,
"believing that that friendship would be transferred to his
"heirs, and that if to the benefits you have received from him
"you were to add those which we have bestowed upon you, that
"friendship would not only be firm but unalterable; and there-
"fore we added Verona or Brescia to the original stipulations
"of the convention. What more could we give or promise
"you? And what more, I say, could you at that time have
"had or have desired from us, or from any one else? The
"benefits which you have received at our hands were as un-
"expected by you as the evil which you have returned us
"therefor was unlooked for by us. Nor did you delay until
"now to manifest your iniquitous intentions towards us, for no
"sooner had you become the general of our armies than you
"accepted Pavia, contrary to all justice, which act ought to
"have revealed to us what your friendship would come to in
"the end. We bore this injury, thinking that this acquisition
"would satisfy your ravening ambition. But alas! those who
"aim at the whole will never be satisfied with only a part.

"You had promised us that whatever acquisitions you might
"make after that should inure to our benefit, for you knew
"well at the time that you could at one blow take from us
"what at different times you had conceded us. Such was your
"conduct after the victory at Caravaggio, which, having been
"achieved with our blood and treasure, was followed by our
"ruin. Alas! unhappy are those cities that have to defend
"their liberties against the ambition of a ruthless usurper! but
"twice unhappy are those that are obliged to rely for their
"defence upon mercenary and faithless arms like thine! May
"our example at least be of some value to posterity; although
"we ourselves were not benefited by that of Thebes and Philip
"of Macedon, who, after overcoming her enemies, became her
"captain, and finally her enemy and master. We cannot, how-
"ever, be accused of any other fault than that of having con-
"fided too much in one whom we should have trusted but
"little; for your past life and your ambition, which no state or
"station could ever satisfy, ought to have served us as a warn-
"ing. Nor ought we to have placed our hopes upon one who,

"having betrayed the lord of Lucca, wrung tribute from the
"Florentines and Venetians, treated our Duke with disrespect,
"and reviled the king of Naples, and, above all, one who so
"many times outraged God and the Church. Nor ought we
"ever to have supposed that the Milanese would have more
"power over the mind of Francesco Sforza than so many other
"potentates; or that he would have observed towards us that
"faith which to others he had so often violated. The want of
"prudence with which we are chargeable is, however, no ex-
"cuse for your perfidy; nor will it purge you of that infamy
"with which our just complaints will brand you before the
"whole world. Nor will it assuage the just stings of thy con-
"science when the arms which we prepared for the purpose
"of attacking and alarming others shall be employed by you
"against us; for you will feel yourself that you have merited
"the punishment that is reserved for parricides. And though
"your own ambition may blind you, yet the whole world, wit-
"ness to your iniquity, will make you open your eyes. Yes,
"God himself will open them for you, if it be true that perju-
"ries, violated faith, and treason be hateful to him, unless he
"should continue forever as, for some occult reason, he seems
"to have been until now, the seeming friend of the evil-doers
"amongst men. Do not therefore anticipate a certain victory,
"which God in his just anger will prevent; for we are resolved
"to yield our liberty only with our lives; and even should we
"not be able to defend it, we would prefer to surrender it to any
"other prince rather than to you. And if from the excess of
"our sins we should, contrary to our will, fall into your hands,
"rest assured that a reign begun by you in fraud and iniquity
"will end with you or your children in infamy and ruin."

21. Count Sforza, although stung by every word the Milanese had said, yet manifested neither by words nor gestures any extraordinary displeasure. He replied that "he was content to
"ascribe to their angry feelings all their grave charges and the
"imprudence of their words, to which he would reply more par-
"ticularly if he were before any one who could be a judge of their
"differences; for then it would appear that he had not injured
"the Milanese, but had merely taken precautions that they
"should not injure him. For they well knew their own conduct
"after the victory of Caravaggio, when, instead of rewarding
"him with Brescia or Verona, they sought to make peace with

"the Venetians, so that he would have had nothing but the
"burden of the quarrel, whilst they would have had the fruits
"of victory and the satisfaction of peace. They could not there-
"fore complain of his having concluded that peace which they
"themselves had been the first to try to make. And if he had
"delayed somewhat in taking this course, it was for him now to
"reproach them with that ingratitude with which they had up-
"braided him. And the truth or falsity of this would be made
"manifest at the end of the war by that God whom they invoked
"to avenge their wrongs, and who would also see who was most
"devoted to him, and which of the two had fought with most
"justice on their side."

The ambassadors having left, the Count prepared to attack the Milanese, and they in turn to defend themselves; and for this purpose they appointed to the command of their forces Francesco and Jacopo Piccinino (whom the ancient hatred between the Braccesca and Sforzesca had kept faithful to the Milanese) to defend their liberties until they should have succeeded at least in detaching the Venetians from the Count Sforza, persuaded that these would not remain his faithful allies long. Sforza, on the other hand, being fully cognizant of all this, judged that it would be wise to bind the Venetians to him by interest, where the treaty obligations were insufficient to do so. And therefore in assigning to each their respective share of the enterprise he agreed that the Venetians should assail Crema, whilst he with his own troops would attack the other parts of the state. This arrangement caused the Venetians to adhere to their alliance with the Count Sforza sufficiently long to enable him to take possession of the whole Milanese territory; and to press them so close in the city that they could not obtain any supplies. So that, despairing of any other help, they sent messengers to the Venetians to beg them to have compassion upon their condition, and in accordance with the custom of republics to support them in the defence of their liberties, and not a tyrant whom, after he should have succeeded in making himself master of their city, they would be unable to resist in their turn. Nor was it likely, they added, that Sforza would remain satisfied with the conditions of the treaty, but would want to have the ancient limits of the state recognized. The Venetians had not yet made themselves masters of Crema, and, desiring to do so before changing sides, they replied publicly to the Milanese envoys, that according to their treaty with the Count they could not come to their assistance, but privately they encouraged them to give the Signori of Milan every hope of help from them.

22. Sforza was already so close upon Milan with his troops that they were fighting in the suburbs; whilst the Venetians, having now taken Crema, thought the time had come for their alliance with the Milanese, with whom they concluded a treaty, one of the first conditions of which was that they were to aid them in the defence of their liberty. This treaty made, they ordered such of their troops as were with the Count to leave his camp and retire into the Venetian territory. They also signified to the Count that they had made peace with the Milanese, and gave him twenty days' time to accept it also. Sforza was not surprised at this action of the Venetians, which he had expected for some time and looked for any day. Nevertheless, when it actually took place he could not but regret it, experiencing the same annoyance which the Milanese felt when he deserted them. He asked for two days' time to give his answer to the Venetian ambassadors, resolving, however, to deceive them, and not to desist from his enterprise. And therefore he declared publicly that he was willing to accept the peace, and sent ambassadors of his own to Venice with ample powers to ratify it; but privately he instructed them under no circumstances to do so, but to delay its conclusion by various objections and cavillings. And by way of making the Venetians believe the more that he was in earnest, he made a truce with the Milanese for one month, and withdrew from the city, distributing his troops in quarters in the surrounding places which he had taken. This course was the cause of his success and of the ruin of the Milanese; for the Venetians, confident of peace, became dilatory in making the necessary provisions for the war, and the Milanese, seeing the truce concluded and the enemy withdrawn, and having secured the alliance of the Venetians, fully believed that Sforza had given up the enterprise. This belief proved ruinous to them in two ways; one, because they neglected to make the necessary dispositions for their defence; and the other, because, it being seedtime, they planted the whole country not occupied by the enemy with grain, thus enabling Sforza the more easily to sustain himself and starve them. All these things, which proved so injurious to

the Milanese, were highly advantageous to the Count, besides affording him time for the repose of his army, and to provide reinforcements.

23. In this war in Lombardy the Florentines had not declared themselves in favor of either of the belligerents, nor had they given any support to the Count Sforza, either when he defended the Milanese or afterwards; for not standing in need of it, the Count had not asked for it. The only thing the Florentines had done was after the defeat at Caravaggio to send assistance to the Venetians in virtue of the obligations of the league. But Sforza being now reduced to his own forces, and not knowing where to look for help, was obliged by necessity to ask for help from the Florentines in the most pressing manner. He addressed himself publicly to the government and privately to his friends, and especially to Cosimo de' Medici, with whom he had always kept up an uninterrupted friendship, and who had in all his enterprises counselled him faithfully and aided him liberally. Nor did Cosimo forsake him now in his great strait, but aided him largely in his private capacity and urged him to persevere in his present enterprise. He endeavored also to make the city aid Sforza, in which, however, there was a difficulty. Neri di Gino Capponi was at this period very influential in Florence (1449), and he thought it would not be advantageous for Florence that Sforza should succeed in making himself master of Milan; believing it to be more for the benefit of all Italy that the Count should ratify the peace rather than continue the war. In the first instance he feared that the indignation of the Milanese against Sforza would induce them to give themselves entirely to the Venetians, which would be most dangerous to all; and next it seemed to him that, if the Count should succeed in taking Milan, the union of such large forces and such extensive possessions under one man would be most formidable, and that, if Sforza had been insupportable as Count, as Duke he would be wholly unbearable. He argued, therefore, that it would be better for the republic of Florence, and for all Italy, that Sforza should not increase his military power, and that Lombardy should be divided into two republics, which should never be allowed to combine for any attack upon others, whilst each by itself would be too feeble to attempt it. And to effect this Neri saw no better means than not to furnish aid to the Count, but

strictly to maintain the old league with the Venetians. The friends of Cosimo did not accept this argument; for they feared that Neri had reasoned thus, not because he deemed it for the good of the republic, but because he did not wish Sforza, who was the friend of Cosimo, to become Duke of Milan, which in the opinion of Neri would strengthen the influence of Cosimo. On the other hand, Cosimo pointed out that aiding the Count would prove most beneficial to the republic, as well as to the whole of Italy; for it was not reasonable to suppose that the Milanese would be able to maintain their independence, because the character of the citizens generally, their mode of life, and the ancient factions in that city, were in all respects most unfavorable to a republican form of government; so that it was necessary either that Sforza should become Duke of Milan, or that the Milanese should throw themselves into the arms of the Venetians. And in that state of the case, Cosimo thought that none would be so foolish as to doubt which would be the best for Florence, either to have a powerful friend for neighbor, or a still more powerful enemy. Nor could he believe that there was any reason to apprehend that the Milanese, from their enmity to the Count, would yield themselves to the Venetians; for the Count had a party in Milan, whilst the Venetians had not; so that whenever the Milanese should no longer be able to defend their liberty, they would always be more apt to subject themselves to the Count Sforza than to the Venetians. This diversity of opinion kept Florence for some time in suspense; and finally it was resolved to send ambassadors to the Count Sforza to arrange a treaty with him, with instructions to conclude it promptly in case they found him strong and confident of victory; otherwise, to delay its conclusion on some pretext or other.

24. (1450.) The ambassadors had hardly reached Reggio, when they learned that Sforza had taken Milan; for upon the expiration of the truce the Count closed in upon the city with his forces, in the hope of making himself master of it in spite of the Venetians, inasmuch as they could render it no assistance except from the side of the Adda, which route he could easily block. And as it was winter time he was not afraid that the Venetians would press him very close; so that he hoped before the close of the winter to have secured the victory, especially as Francesco Piccinino had died, and his brother Jacopo remained the only general of the Milanese.

The Venetians meantime sent an ambassador to Milan to exhort the inhabitants to a vigorous defence, and to promise them large and speedy succor. Some slight skirmishing occurred during the winter between the Venetians and the Count; but when the season became milder, the Venetian forces, under command of Pandolfo Malatesti established themselves above the Adda, where they resolved to attack the Count, and try the fortune of battle in aid of the Milanese. Pandolfo himself, however, advised against the attempt, well knowing the Count's valor and that of his army, and believing that it would be more safe to conquer him without fighting, because the Count would be compelled to retire from want of provisions and forage. He therefore counselled the holding of that position, as they would thereby encourage the Milanese to hope for speedy succor, and prevent their surrendering to the Count. This plan was approved by the Venetians, partly because they considered it a safe one, and partly also because they had the hope that, by keeping the Milanese in this necessitous condition, these would be forced to place themselves under their government; for they had persuaded themselves that the Milanese would never give themselves to the Count because of the injuries they had received at his hands.

The Milanese were meantime reduced to the extremest misery; and as that city habitually abounds in poor, many of these died in the streets from starvation; so that the whole city was filled with lamentations and disturbances which greatly alarmed the magistrates, who, in consequence, took every precaution to prevent the people from assembling together. The multitude is always slow in being moved to evil, but, once so disposed, the slightest accident will start them to violence. Two men of low condition were conversing near the Porta Nuova about the calamities of the city and their own misery, and as to what means there were for their safety; a few others began to join them, so that it very soon became a numerous group. This gave rise to a report in Milan that the people at the Porta Nuova were in arms against the magistrates. Upon this all the lower classes, who were only awaiting an opportunity, seized their arms, and chose for their captain Gasparo da Vicomercato, and marched to where the magistrates were assembled. And this was done with such a rush that all who were not able to fly were killed; amongst these was Leonardo Veneto, the Venetian ambassador, whom the people looked upon as the cause of the famine and as rejoicing at their wretchedness, and therefore they killed him. Having thus in a manner become masters of the city, they consulted amongst themselves as to what should be done to relieve them from all their troubles and give them peace; and all agreed that, inasmuch as they were not able to preserve their liberty, it was best to take refuge under some prince who was competent to defend them. Some were for calling in the King Alfonso, some wanted the Duke of Savoy, and some the king of France, but no one mentioned the name of Sforza, so strong was still the feeling against him. But as the people could not agree upon any other, Gasparo Vicomercato was the first to suggest the name of Count Francesco Sforza, showing them plainly that, "if they wanted to get rid of the war, there was "no other way but to call him; for the people of Milan had "need of a certain and immediate peace, and not of the distant "hope of future succor." He excused the attempt of the Count, and blamed the Venetians and all the other princes of Italy, who, some from ambition and some from avarice, were not willing that they should enjoy independence and liberty. "And "as after all they would have to give up their liberty, it was "best to surrender it to some one who had the ability and skill "to defend them; so that at least they might have peace as "the result of their servitude, and not increased sufferings "and perilous wars." Gasparo was listened to with wonder- "ful attention, and after he had finished speaking all cried out that Count Sforza should be called in, and they deputed Gasparo for that purpose. He went by command of the people to seek the Count, and made known to him the joyful and happy news, which Sforza accepted most gladly. He entered Milan as Prince on the 26th of February, 1450, and was received with the greatest and most wonderful rejoicings by the very men who but a short time before had loaded him with imprecations.

25. When the news of this revolution became known to the government of Florence, they instructed their ambassadors, who were on the way to the Count Sforza, instead of negotiating a treaty with him, to congratulate him as Duke of Milan upon his success. These ambassadors were received with greatest distinction by the Duke and bountifully honored; for he well

knew that he could not in all Italy have more faithful or braver allies against the power of the Venetians than the Florentines. For being relieved now of the fear of the house of Visconti, they felt that they would have to contend against the combined forces of the Aragonese and the Venetians; for the Aragonese kings of Naples were their enemies on account of the friendship which the Florentine people had always borne to the house of France; and as to the Venetians, they were aware that their ancient fear of the Visconti had been transferred to themselves, and knowing with how much zeal the former had persecuted the Visconti, they feared similar persecutions now themselves, and therefore naturally sought their ruin. Such were the considerations that induced the new Duke so readily to form a friendship with the Florentines; whilst the Venetians and King Alfonso united against their common enemies, obligating themselves mutually to put their armies into the field simultaneously. King Alfonso was to attack the Florentines, and the Venetians the Duke Francesco of Milan, who, being but recently established in that state, was believed by them unable to sustain himself either by his own forces or by the aid of others. But as the league between the Florentines and the Venetians had not yet expired, and the King Alfonso, after the war of Piombino, had made peace with the latter, it did not seem well to them to break the peace unless they could first with some color of right justify the war (1451). And therefore they both sent ambassadors to Florence to explain that the league had not been made for the purpose of attacking any one, but only for the defence of their respective states. Afterwards the Venetian ambassador complained " that the Florentines had allowed "Alessandro, the Duke's brother, to pass with troops through "Lunigiana into Lombardy; and moreover that they had been "the authors and advisers of the treaty made between the Duke "and the Marquis of Mantua; all of which acts, he affirmed, "were adverse to their state and to the terms of the alliance "existing between them; and therefore he reminded them "amicably that he who offends wrongfully gives cause to the "other party to be rightfully offended, and that he who breaks "the peace must expect war." The Signoria commissioned Cosimo to reply, who in a lengthy and judicious speech went over all the benefits conferred by his city upon the Venetian republic; he pointed out what extensive possessions they had gained by means of the money, troops, and counsel of the Florentines, and reminded them "that, since the friendship "had originated with the Florentines, so they would never be "the cause of enmity. And having ever been lovers of peace, "they were well pleased with the treaty made between them, "in so far as its object was peace, and not war. In truth, he "wondered much at the complaints made, and that so great "a republic should make so much account of such a slight "and trivial cause. But even if it were a matter worthy of con- "sideration, they wanted every one to understand that they "intended their country to be free and open to everybody; and "that the Duke's character was such, that, to enable him to "form an alliance with Mantua, he had no need of either their "counsels or support. And therefore he thought that these "complaints must have been caused by some other offence "than what appeared on the surface. Be that, however, as it "might, it would readily be seen by every one, that in propor- "tion as the friendship of the Florentines was advantageous, "so their enmity would prove dangerous."

26. For the present the matter passed lightly over, and the ambassadors retired seemingly satisfied; but the alliance of the Venetians with the king of Naples, and their proceedings, caused the Duke and the Florentines to fear a renewal of the war, rather than to hope for a lasting peace. The Florentines, therefore, formed an alliance with the Duke, and soon after the hostile disposition of the Venetians began to manifest itself, for they allied themselves with the Siennese, and expelled all the Florentines and their dependents from their city and terri- tory. King Alfonso very soon after did the same thing, wholly regardless of the peace concluded the preceding year, and with- out any just grounds or even color of pretext for such action. The Venetians also sought to obtain possession of Bologna, and, having armed the banished, they introduced them into the city one night through one of the sewers. Their entrance was not perceived until they themselves raised the cry. Santi Benti- vogli, being aroused by it, was told that the entire city was in the hands of the rebels; and although he was urged by many to save himself by flight, as he could not possibly save the city by remaining, yet he resolved to face fortune; and having armed, he encouraged his followers, and, making head with

a few friends, he attacked a portion of the rebels and routed them, killing many and driving the rest from the city. By this conduct Santi was said by every one to have given the best proof of being of the true blood of the Bentivogli. These events and demonstrations convinced the Florentines that other wars were near at hand. They therefore made their usual preparations for defence, appointed a Council of Ten, engaged new Condottieri, and sent envoys to Rome, Naples, Venice, Milan, and Sienna, to ask help of their friends, detect the suspicious, win over the doubtful, and to discover the designs of the enemy. From the Pope they received nothing but vague words, protestations of good will, and counsels of peace; from the king of Naples, vain excuses for having expelled the Florentines, and offering a safe conduct to whoever might ask for it; and although he sought in every way to conceal the fact that he had advised the renewal of the war, yet the ambassadors became convinced of his unfriendly disposition, and discovered many of his hostile preparations against their republic. The league with the Duke of Milan was strengthened by fresh mutual obligations, and through the Duke's mediation an alliance was concluded with the Genoese, and all the old differences as to reprisals and other complaints were adjusted, although the Venetians sought in every possible way to disturb the settlement of these disputes, and even appealed to the Sultan of Turkey to expel the Florentines from his dominions. Such was the bitterness of feeling with which they resumed this war; and so powerful was this thirst for dominion with them, that, regardless of every consideration, they sought to destroy a people to whom they were indebted for so much of their greatness. The Sultan, however, gave no heed to their request. The Venetian Senate forbade the Florentine ambassadors from entering the territory of that republic, alleging that, being bound by alliance to the king of Naples, they could not listen to them without his participation. The Siennese received the ambassadors with kindly words, fearing lest they should be assailed and defeated before their allies could come to their defence. They preferred, therefore, to lull into inaction an enemy whom they would be unable to resist. The Venetians and the king of Naples, according to what was then conjectured, wanted to send ambassadors to Florence to justify the war; but the Venetian ambassador was not permitted to enter the Florentine dominions, and the king's ambassador being unwilling to undertake the office by himself, that mission was left unaccomplished. And thus the Venetians learned that the Florentines showed them even less respect than they had shown the Florentines a few months before.

27. In the midst of the general uneasiness caused by these movements the Emperor Frederick III. came to Italy to be crowned. He entered Florence on the 30th of January, 1451, and was received with the utmost demonstrations of honor by the Signoria, and remained until the 6th of February, when he departed for Rome for his coronation. This having been duly solemnized, as also his nuptials with the Empress, who had come there by sea, he returned to Germany, passing again through Florence, where they paid him the same honors as at his coming. After his return he bestowed the cities of Modena and Reggio upon the Marquis of Ferrara, as a reward for services rendered. The Florentines meantime did not cease their preparations for the impending war; and by way of increasing their reputation and intimidating the enemy, they, in conjunction with the Duke of Milan, formed a league with the king of France for the mutual defence of their states, which treaty was published throughout Italy with great pomp and manifestations of gladness. With the opening of May, 1452, the Venetians concluded no longer to defer open hostilities against the Duke, and attacked him with six thousand infantry and sixteen thousand horse, in the direction of Lodi; and at the same time the Marquis of Monferrato, prompted either by his own ambition or by the Venetians, assailed him near Alessandria. The Duke, on the other hand, having collected eighteen thousand horse and three thousand infantry, and having garrisoned Lodi and Alessandria, as well as the other places where the enemy might annoy him, attacked the Brescian territory, where he damaged the Venetians seriously, ravaging the country in every direction and sacking the feeble towns. The Marquis of Monferrato having been defeated by the troops of the Duke, the latter was enabled to move with greater force against the Venetians, and to invade their territory.

28. Whilst the war was going on in Lombardy with varying and inconsiderable incidents little worthy of note, it had also broken out in Tuscany between the Florentines and King Alfonso, in which, however, there occurred no greater display

of gallantry nor any greater danger than in the operations in Lombardy. Ferdinand, an illegitimate son of King Alfonso, had come into Tuscany with twelve thousand men, under the command of Federigo, lord of Urbino. His first attempt was upon Foiano in the Val di Chiana, for, being friends with the Siennese, they had entered the Florentine territory from that side. The castle was small, with feeble walls; and although having but few inhabitants, yet they were reputed, according to the times, as brave and faithful. The Signoria of Florence had sent, moreover, two hundred soldiers to garrison it. This castle, so provided, was besieged by Ferdinand; and whether it was the bravery of the men within, or the lack of it on the part of the Neapolitans, it took Ferdinand thirty-six days before he became master of it. This length of time afforded the republic the opportunity to provide for the defence of the other and more important places, by garrisoning them and making them in every way more capable of defence than before. After the taking of the castle of Foiano, the enemy went to Chianti, where they were unable to take two little villas owned by private individuals. Leaving these, therefore, they laid siege to Castellina, a castle near Chianti, ten miles from Sienna, feeble as regards artificial means of defence, and still more feeble as regards position. But the weakness of the assailants could not overcome the twofold weakness of the castle, for after forty-four days of siege they were obliged shamefully to give it up. Such was the terror of those armies, and so dangerous were those wars, that places which nowadays are abandoned as incapable of defence were in those days defended, being looked upon as impregnable. Whilst Ferdinand remained encamped near Chianti, he made many predatory incursions into the Florentine territory, coming within six miles of the city of Florence, to the great terror and damage of the Florentine subjects. The Florentine army, to the number of eight thousand, under Astorre da Faenza and Gismondo Malatesti, had been led towards the castle of Colli, so as to keep them at a distance from the enemy, for the purpose of avoiding an engagement. For they thought that, so long as they had not been defeated in a general battle, the war would result favorably to them. They had no uneasiness about the small castles they had lost, and which would be recovered at the re-establishment of peace; and they felt safe as to the larger cities, knowing that the enemy could not attack them. King Alfonso had also a fleet of about twenty sail, galleys and small craft, lying in the Pisan waters, and, whilst Ferdinand was carrying on the war by land, he attacked with this fleet the castle of Rocca di Vada, which the negligence of the castellan enabled him to take; and from there they began to harass the surrounding country. The Florentines, however, soon put a stop to this, by sending a few soldiers to Campiglia, who kept the enemy strictly confined to the seacoast.

29. The Pope took no part in these wars, other than to endeavor to restore harmony amongst the parties, although whilst avoiding foreign wars he experienced more dangerous troubles at home. There lived at that time in Rome a citizen called Messer Stefano Porcari, equally illustrious by his birth and his learning, but still more so by the excellence of his character. According to the nature of men who are eager for glory, he desired to do, or to attempt to do, something worthy of being remembered; and thus he concluded that he could do nothing better than to attempt to rescue his country from the hands of the prelates, and to restore the ancient laws and institutions, hoping, in the event of success, to be called a new founder and second father of the city of Rome. He was encouraged to hope for success in this attempt by the general corruption of the prelates, and the discontent of the barons and the Roman people; but what inflamed him still more was this passage from the ode of Petrarch which begins, "Spirto gentil che quelle membra reggi," viz. :—

"Sopra il Monte Tarpeio, Canzon, vedrai
"Un cavalier ch' Italia tutta onora,
"Pensoso più d' altrui, che di se stesso." *

Messer Stefano knew that poets are filled with a divine and prophetic inspiration, and therefore thought that what Petrarch had prophesied was sure to happen, and that to him was reserved the distinction of carrying that glorious enterprise into execution; believing himself in eloquence, learning, influence, and the number of friends, superior to any other Roman. Deeply imbued with this idea, he could not control himself with sufficient caution not to betray his design by his speech, conduct, and mode of life. So that he became suspect

---

* "On the Tarpeian Mount, O Muse, thou 'lt see a knight honored by all Italy, and more devoted to the interests of others than his own."

to the Pope, who, for the purpose of depriving him of all opportunity of doing harm, banished Porcari to Bologna, and ordered the governor of that city to make Porcari report himself daily. Messer Stefano, however, was not discouraged from his purpose by this first check, but rather pursued his object with increased zeal; and by more cautious proceedings he kept up secret relations with his friends in Rome, and went to and fro between Bologna and Rome with such celerity as to be back always in time to present himself to the governor at the appointed periods. Having drawn a sufficient number of persons into his project, he resolved no longer to delay its execution, and directed his friends in Rome, on a given day, to prepare a splendid supper, where all the conspirators should meet, with the understanding that each was to bring with him his most trusty friends, and he promised to be there himself before supper should be served. Everything was done according to his directions, and Porcari himself had already arrived in the house where the feast was to take place. So soon as supper was served, Porcari appeared all arrayed in garments of cloth of gold, and with collars, orders, and other decorations, which gave him a majestic and commanding aspect; and having embraced each one of the company, he counselled them in a lengthy speech to take courage, and to dispose their minds to the glorious enterprise in hand. He then arranged the mode of proceeding, and ordered that one part of them should, on the following morning, seize the pontifical palace, and that the others should call the people of Rome to arms. But during the night the matter was communicated to the Pope; according to some, by treachery on the part of some of the conspirators; according to others, because the Pope knew of Porcari's presence in Rome. Be this as it may, during the night of the supper the Pope had Porcari and the greater part of his associates seized, and, according to their crime, put to death. Such was the end of this attempt; and although some may praise Porcari's intentions, yet every one will blame his judgment; for all such enterprises, even if they possess some shadow of glory in their conception, yet their execution almost invariably ends in ruin.

30. The war in Tuscany had lasted nearly a year, and the period had arrived, in 1453, for the armies to take the field, when the Florentines saw Alessandro Sforza, brother of the Duke Francesco, come to their aid with two thousand horse.

The Florentine army having been thus reinforced, whilst that of the king was diminished, the Florentines deemed the occasion favorable for recovering the places that had been taken from them by the enemy, in which they succeeded with very little trouble. They then besieged Foiano, which was sacked in consequence of the negligence of the commissaries; so that the inhabitants became dispersed, and it was with difficulty afterwards that they were induced to return by promises of rewards and immunities from impositions. They also recovered Rocca di Vada; for the enemy, seeing that they could not hold it, burnt and abandoned it. Whilst these things were being accomplished by the Florentines, the Aragonese army, having no desire to approach that of the enemy, moved to the vicinity of Sienna, whence they made numerous incursions into the Florentine territory, committing robberies and disturbances, and spreading general alarm. Nor did King Alfonso cease his efforts to injure the enemy in other ways, to divide their forces, and to dishearten them by various annoyances and attacks.

Gherardo Gambacorti was lord of the Val di Bagno; his ancestors as well as himself had, either from friendship or from obligation, always been in the pay or under the protection of the Florentines. King Alfonso opened secret negotiations with him for the surrender of that district, in return for which he offered him another principality in the kingdom of Naples. When these negotiations became known at Florence the Signoria sent an envoy to Gherardo for the purpose of ascertaining his intentions, and to remind him of the obligations which he and his ancestors owed the Florentines, and to exhort him to continue loyal to that republic. Gherardo pretended to be astonished, and affirmed with solemn oaths that such villanous thoughts had never entered his mind, and that he would go in person to Florence to prove his good faith; but being indisposed and unable to go, he would send his son, whom he handed over to the ambassador to take with him to Florence as a hostage. These assurances and demonstrations made the Florentines believe in the sincerity of Gherardo, and that he had been basely slandered by his accusers, and therefore they felt reassured upon that point. Meantime Gherardo carried on the negotiations with the king with increased earnestness, and when they were concluded, the king sent Fra Puccio, a Knight of Jerusalem, with a considerable force, into the Val di Bagno to take possession of Gherardo's castles and towns. But the people of the Val di Bagno, being devoted to the Florentines, most unwillingly promised obedience to the royal commissaries. Fra Puccio had nearly taken possession of the entire district, and all he lacked was to make himself master of the castle of Corzano. Whilst Gherardo was about to make the formal transfer of this castle, there was amongst his followers who surrounded him one Antonio Gualandi, a Pisan, young and bold, who did not like this treason of Gherardo's. Considering the position of the castle, and judging from the expression of the countenances and gestures of the garrison that they were ill content with the proceeding, and seeing Gherardo standing at the gate for the purpose of admitting the Aragonese troops, Antonio went behind him and suddenly with both hands pushed Gherardo outside of the castle gate, which he ordered the guard to close upon such a villain, and to save the castle for the Florentine republic. When this became known in Bagno and the neighboring places, all the people took up arms against the Aragonese, and having raised the Florentine banner they successfully drove them out. When this intelligence reached Florence they imprisoned the son of Gherardo, who had been given to them as a hostage, and sent troops to Bagno to defend the country for the republic, and to reduce that province, which until then had been governed by its own prince, to a mere vicariate. Gherardo, traitor alike to his government and to his own son, escaped with much difficulty, leaving his wife and family and all his possessions in the power of the enemy. This occurrence was highly appreciated at Florence, for if King Alfonso had succeeded in making himself master of that part of the country, he could with little risk have made incursions into the Val di Tevere and the Casentino, whence he could have annoyed and harassed the republic to that degree that the Florentines, with all their forces, would have been unable to resist the Aragonese army, which was at Sienna.

31. Besides the preparations made in Italy for repelling the forces of the hostile league, the Florentines had sent Messer Agnolo Acciaiuoli as their ambassador to the king of France, to induce him to empower King Regnier of Anjou to come into Italy to aid his friends; and that then, once being in Italy, he might again attempt the conquest of the kingdom of Naples; and to this effect they promised him assistance of men and

money. Thus, whilst the war was being carried on in Tuscany and Lombardy in the manner we have narrated, the ambassador concluded an arrangement with King Regnier to come into Italy during June with three thousand four hundred horse; and upon his arrival at Alessandria the allies were to pay him thirty thousand florins, and during the continuance of the war ten thousand florins per month. But when King Regnier in accordance with this arrangement wanted to pass into Italy, he was prevented by the Duke of Savoy and the Marquis of Monferrato; who, being friends of the Venetians, refused him passage through their possessions. King Regnier was thereupon advised by the Florentine ambassador to return to Provence, and to come thence by sea into Italy with some of his forces, and thereby to increase the preponderance of his friends. And that, on the other hand, he should induce the king of France to prevail upon the Duke of Savoy to allow the remainder of his troops to pass through his territory. This advice was accepted and acted upon successfully; for Regnier came by sea into Italy, and his troops were permitted, out of regard for the king of France, to pass through Savoy. King Regnier was most honorably received by Duke Francesco; and after uniting the French and Italian forces, they attacked the Venetians with such vehemence, that they recovered in a little while all the places which the Venetians had taken in the Cremonese territory. Not satisfied with this, they also occupied the whole of the Brescian territory; so that the Venetian army, feeling no longer secure in the open field, retreated close under the walls of Brescia. But upon the setting in of winter the Duke deemed it prudent to move his troops into quarters, and established King Regnier and his troops in Piacenza. Thus the winter of 1453 was passed without any movement being attempted; but when the warm season returned, and the Duke thought the time fit to take the field and to attempt to take their inland possessions from the Venetians, King Regnier notified the Duke that he was obliged to return to France. This unexpected determination surprised the Duke most unpleasantly; he went at once to dissuade King Regnier from leaving, but neither entreaties nor promises could move him from his resolve, and all he obtained from King Regnier was an agreement to leave a portion of his forces, and to send his son John to serve the league in his stead. The Florentines did not regret King Regnier's departure, for having recovered their own places and castles they no longer feared the king of Naples, and on the other hand they did not wish that the Duke should recover anything more than his places in Lombardy. Regnier therefore departed, and according to promise he sent his son into Italy, who without stopping in Lombardy came direct to Florence, where he was received with the greatest honors.

32. King Regnier's departure caused Sforza readily to entertain the idea of peace; and the Venetians, King Alfonso, and the Florentines, being all tired of war, were equally desirous of peace. The Pope likewise had manifested and still expressed the greatest anxiety for it; for it was in that very year that Sultan Mahomet had taken Constantinople, and had made himself master of all Greece. This conquest alarmed all Christendom, and more than all the rest the Venetians and the Pope, who both seemed already to hear the tramp of the infidel hosts on the soil of Italy. The Pope, therefore, invited all the Italian states to send ambassadors to him with plenary powers to establish a universal peace. They all complied with this request; but when the ambassadors met and came to discuss the merits of the question, they found great difficulty in the negotiations. The king of Naples wanted the Florentines to reimburse him the expenses of the war, whilst the Florentines made the same pretensions. The Venetians demanded Cremona from the Duke of Milan, whilst the Duke wanted Bergamo from them, as also Brescia and Crema; so that it really seemed impossible to solve these difficulties. And yet that which seemed so difficult to accomplish at Rome by so many ambassadors was easily effected by two negotiators at Milan and Venice; for whilst the negotiations were being protracted at Rome, the Duke of Milan and the Venetians concluded the terms of an agreement on the 9th of April, 1454, according to which each resumed the places which they had before the war, and it was conceded to the Duke that he might retake the places which the Dukes of Monferrato and of Savoy had taken from him; and the other Italian princes were allowed one month's time to ratify this treaty. The Pope and the Florentines, and with them the Siennese and the other smaller powers, ratified it within the given time; and, moreover, a peace for twenty-five years was concluded between the

Florentines, the Duke of Milan, and the Venetians. Of all the Italian princes, King Alfonso alone was dissatisfied with this peace, for it seemed to him that in the making of it but little regard was had to his dignity, he having been treated in the matter not as a principal, but as a mere secondary party; and therefore he remained a long while undecided without letting his intentions be known. But as the Pope and the other princes sent many solemn embassies to him, he allowed himself finally to be persuaded, mainly by the Pope, and joined the league with his son for thirty years. Thereupon King Alfonso and the Duke of Milan concluded a double alliance by giving their daughters reciprocally in marriage to each other's sons. By way of preserving, however, the seeds of war in Italy, King Alfonso did not consent to make peace unless his allies first conceded to him full liberty to make war, without injury to them, against the Genoese, Gismondo Malatesti, and Astorre, lord of Faenza. After concluding this treaty, his son Ferdinand, who was at Sienna, returned to the kingdom of Naples, having lost a large portion of his forces by his expedition into Tuscany, and without having made any acquisition of territory.

33. A general peace having thus been established, the only fear was that it would be disturbed by King Alfonso from his enmity against the Genoese. But it happened otherwise; for the peace was not broken openly by Alfonso, but indirectly, as is generally the case, by the ambition of the mercenary soldiers. The Venetians, as was customary upon the establishment of peace, dismissed from their pay their Condottiere, Jacopo Piccinino, with whom some other Condottieri, equally without engagement, united, and passed into the Romagna, and thence into the Siennese territory. There Jacopo halted and commenced hostilities against the Siennese, by taking some of their castles. It was in the beginning of these movements, and in the early part of the year 1455, that Pope Nicholas died, and Calixtus III. was chosen his successor. This Pope, for the purpose of repressing this fresh war in his immediate vicinity, quickly collected what troops he could, and sent them under his general, Giovanni Ventimiglia, against Jacopo, together with the troops of the Florentines and those of the Duke of Milan, who had already united for the purpose of suppressing these disturbances. They came to an engagement near Bolsena, and although Ventimiglia was taken prisoner,

yet Jacopo was defeated and obliged to retreat to Pescaia; and had he not been assisted with money by King Alfonso, he would have been entirely destroyed. This gave rise to the general belief that this attempt of Jacopo's had been instigated by King Alfonso; so that, deeming himself discovered, Alfonso, for the purpose of conciliating his associates in the general peace, whom he had in a measure alienated by this feeble attempt at war, caused Jacopo to restore to the Siennese the places which he had taken from them, and they paid him twenty thousand florins; and after this arrangement, Alfonso received Jacopo Piccinino, together with his troops, into the kingdom. Notwithstanding that the Pope was thus engaged in repressing Jacopo Piccinino, he did not cease to do all he could to organize the means for averting the danger from Christendom of being oppressed by the Turks. And for this purpose he sent messengers and preachers throughout all Christian lands, to exhort the princes and the people to arm in defence of their faith, and to aid with their money and their persons the enterprise against the common enemy. Thus large collections of money were made in Florence; and many people assumed the emblem of the red cross, in evidence of their intention personally to take part in this war against the infidels. There were also solemn processions, and no lack of other demonstrations, both public and private, to aid the enterprise with their counsel and with money and men. But this zeal for the crusade was somewhat checked by the intelligence that the Sultan, in his attempt to take Belgrade, a fortress on the river Danube, in Hungary, had been defeated and wounded by the Hungarians. Thus the alarm which the taking of Constantinople had caused to the Pontiff and all Christians having subsided, they proceeded more coolly in the preparations for the war; and even in Hungary itself their zeal was chilled by the death of their Vaivode, John Corvinus, who had gained the victory at Belgrade.

34. But to return to the affairs of Italy. In the course of the year 1456, when the disturbances caused by Jacopo Piccinino were quelled, and men had in consequence laid down their arms, it seemed as though the Almighty himself took them up in turn; for there occurred a most frightful tempest in Tuscany, causing the most marvellous and unheard of effects. At one o'clock in the morning on the 24th of August there arose a whirlwind

from the sea above Ancona, passing across Italy, and re-entering the sea below Pisa, driving before it a huge mass of dense clouds, which occupied a space of nearly two miles in width, and, impelled by a superior force, natural or supernatural, was broken up into many parts that seemed to be contending amongst themselves. And these broken clouds, now mounting towards heaven, now descending to the earth, rushed against each other violently, now moving in circles with incredible velocity, stirring up before them a tempest of inconceivable violence, and throwing out frequent vivid flashes of lightning of the utmost intensity. From these seemingly broken and confused clouds, and these furious winds and frequent flashes, there arose a noise exceeding anything that had ever been heard from either thunder or earthquake, and which excited such alarm that every one thought the end of the world had come, and that the earth and the water and the heavens and the whole world were about to return to their original chaos. This frightful tornado caused unheard of and wonderful effects wherever it passed, but more notably than elsewhere around the castle of San Casciano. This castle is situated within eight miles of Florence, on the hill that separates the valleys of Pisa and Grieve. The most violent portion of this furious tempest passed between the Borgo and the castle of San Andrea, situated on the same hill, not, however, reaching San Andrea, and just grazing San Casciano; so that only a few of the battlements of the castle and some chimneys of houses were thrown down. But within the space comprised between these two places many houses were levelled with the ground. The roofs of the churches of San Martino a Bagnuolo and Santa Maria della Pace were carried off entire to a distance of more than a mile. A teamster and his mules were found dead in a valley near the road. All the largest oaks and the strongest trees that did not yield to the fury of the hurricane were not only stripped of their branches, but torn up by the roots and carried to a great distance. When the tempest had passed and daylight came, the people remained stupefied; for they saw their fields desolated and wasted, they heard the lamentations of those who had their homes and possessions destroyed and had left their relatives and their cattle buried under the ruins; and all who saw and heard this were filled with pity and extreme terror. No doubt the Almighty wanted rather to threaten than to chastise Tuscany; for if so furious a tempest had passed over a city with many houses and inhabitants, as it had passed amongst the oaks and the other trees and the few scattered dwellings, beyond all doubt the ruin and chastisement would have been far greater than the mind can conceive. But the Almighty wanted rather that these few instances should suffice to remind men of his power.

35. But to resume where I left off, King Alfonso, as I have said above, was not satisfied with this peace; and, seeing that the war which Niccolo Piccinino, at his instigation, had begun against the Siennese without any reasonable cause had not had the success he had hoped for, Alfonso resolved to see what advantage he could gain from a war which he was authorized to begin according to the articles of the treaty. And therefore he attacked the Genoese by sea and by land, in the year 1456, resolved to restore the government of Genoa to the Adorni, and take it from the Fregosi, who held it at the time; and, on the other hand, he made Jacopo Piccinino pass the Tronto against Gismondo Malatesti. Gismondo had thoroughly garrisoned all his castles, and therefore cared little for Jacopo's attack; so that in this direction the king's attempt proved entirely futile. But that upon Genoa involved Alfonso and his realm in more wars than he had foreseen or could have wished. Pietro Fregoso, at that time Doge of Genoa, fearing not to be able to resist the attacks of Alfonso, resolved at least to yield what he could not hold himself to some one else, who could defend it from his enemies, and who at some future time might make him a just compensation for so important a gift. He therefore sent an ambassador to Charles VII., king of France, and offered him the sovereignty of Genoa. Charles accepted the offer, and sent John of Anjou, the son of King Regnier, to take possession of that place (1458), John having a short time before left Florence and returned to France. King Charles believed that John, who had adopted some Italian customs, was better qualified to govern Genoa than any one else. He thought also that John might proceed from there with an attempt to recover the kingdom of Naples, of which his father, Regnier, had been dispossessed by Alfonso. John therefore departed for Genoa, where he was received as a sovereign, and all the forces of the city and the state placed at his disposal.

36. This occurrence disquieted Alfonso, for he felt that he

had drawn upon himself too powerful an enemy. But so far from being intimidated by it, he pursued his enterprise against Genoa with unhesitating courage, and had already sent the fleet under Villamarina to Portofino, when he was suddenly taken ill and died. This death relieved John and the Genoese from the war that threatened them, and filled Ferdinand, who succeeded his father, Alfonso, on the throne of Naples, with apprehensions at having so considerable an enemy in Italy as John of Anjou; besides, he mistrusted the fidelity of many of his barons, lest love of change should cause them to desert him and go over to the French. He also feared the Pope, whose ambition he knew, and who, taking advantage of his having but so recently succeeded to the crown, might attempt to wrest it from him. Ferdinand's only hope was in the Duke of Milan, who felt no less solicitous about the kingdom than Ferdinand himself; for he feared that the French, once masters of Naples, would attempt also to get possession of Milan, which he knew they might demand as legitimately belonging to them. The Duke Francesco, therefore, immediately upon the death of Alfonso, sent letters and troops to Ferdinand; the latter to aid him and to add to his consideration, and the former to counsel him to be of good cheer, promising that he would under no circumstances abandon him. The Pope, after the death of Alfonso, resolved to bestow the crown of Naples upon his nephew, Pietro Lodovico Borgia; and, by way of covering this attempt with the appearance of honesty, and to secure the concurrence of the other princes of Italy, he pretended publicly that he wanted to make the kingdom a province of the Holy See. He therefore urged the Duke of Milan not to afford any support to Ferdinand, offering Sforza to leave him the places which he already possessed in the kingdom. But in the midst of these schemes and labors Calixtus died, and was succeeded in the pontificate by Pius II., of the family of the Piccolomini of Sienna, and who bore the name of Æneas Sylvius. This Pope, wholly occupied with the advancement of Christianity and the honor of the Church, and disregarding all private considerations, yielded to the instances of the Duke of Milan, and crowned Ferdinand king of Naples. Pius II. judged that he would sooner be able to restore peace in Italy by sustaining him who was in possession of the kingdom, than by favoring the attempt of the French to obtain it, or, like Calixtus, attempting to take it for himself.

Nevertheless Ferdinand, in return for this benefit, created Antonio, a nephew of the Pope's, Prince of Malfi, and gave him one of his illegitimate daughters for his wife; and, moreover, restored Benevento and Terracina to the Church.

37. Thus it seemed that peace was restored to Italy, whilst the pontiff was occupying himself to move all Christendom against the Turks, in accordance with the beginning previously made by Calixtus; when dissensions arose between the Fregosi and John of Anjou, lord of Genoa, which rekindled greater and more important wars than those of the past. Pietrino Fregoso had retired to one of his castles on the coast of Genoa, when it occurred to him that he had not been sufficiently remunerated by John of Anjou according to the merits of himself and his family, who had been mainly instrumental in making John sovereign of that city; and this led to an open rupture between them. Ferdinand rejoiced at this, for he saw in it his only remedy and means of salvation; and therefore he supplied Pietrino liberally with men and money, hoping by his means to see John driven from Genoa. When this became known to John he sent to France for reinforcements, with which he marched against Pietrino, who was however very strong in consequence of the extensive aid that had been sent him by Ferdinand. John of Anjou confined himself therefore merely to the guarding of the city of Genoa; Pietrino succeeded one night in entering the city and making himself master of some positions in it, but when daylight came he was attacked by the troops of John of Anjou and killed, and all his men were either slain or made prisoners. This victory encouraged John to attempt an invasion of the kingdom of Naples; and in October, 1459, he sailed with a powerful fleet from Genoa for that purpose, and landed at Baia, whence he marched to Sessa, where he was favorably received by the Duke of that name. John was joined by the Prince of Taranto, the Aquilani, and many other princes and towns, so that the loss of the whole kingdom seemed almost inevitable. Seeing this, Ferdinand had recourse for assistance to the Pope and the Duke of Milan, and by way of diminishing the number of his enemies he made terms with Gismondo Malatesti (1460). This, however, irritated Jacopo Piccinino, who was the natural enemy of Gismondo, to that degree that he left the service of Ferdinand and went over to John of Anjou. Ferdinand also sent money to Federigo,

lord of Urbino, who as quickly as possible gathered what, according to the times, was considered a respectable army, with which he met the enemy above the river Sarni; and having brought on an engagement, King Ferdinand was routed, and many of his principal officers were taken prisoners. After this disaster the city of Naples alone, with a few princes and places, remained faithful to Ferdinand. Jacopo Piccinino urged that on the strength of this victory John should march upon Naples and make himself master of the capital of the kingdom; but John refused this advice, saying that he wanted first to deprive Ferdinand of all his territory and then to assail Naples, thinking that, after having taken all the smaller places, the conquest of the capital would be more easy. This determination, however, caused John to lose all the fruits of his victories; for he did not know how much more readily the members follow the head than the head the members.

38. After his defeat Ferdinand had taken refuge in Naples, where he was joined by the fugitives from the provinces; he raised some money by the least oppressive means, and formed the nucleus of a little army. He sent again for assistance to the Pope and the Duke of Milan, which was rendered by both with the greatest alacrity, and more abundantly than before, for they were in great apprehension lest Ferdinand should lose the kingdom. After Ferdinand had gained some strength he issued from Naples, and, once having begun to re-establish his reputation, he recovered a number of the places he had lost. But whilst this war was progressing in the kingdom an occurrence took place which deprived John of Anjou of his preponderance, and of all chance of success in his attempt. The Genoese were tired of the proud and grasping government of the French, so that they rose in arms against the royal governor, obliging him to take refuge in the Castelletto. In this movement the Fregosi and the Adorni acted together, and were aided by the Duke of Milan with men and money, for the purpose both of recovering and preserving the state. King Regnier, who came with a fleet to succor his son, in the hope of recovering Genoa by means of the Castelletto, was so completely beaten at the very landing of his troops that he was compelled ignominiously to return to Provence. When this news reached the kingdom of Naples, John of Anjou became greatly alarmed; nevertheless, he did not abandon his enterprise, but

sustained the war for some time, aided by those barons who in consequence of their rebellion had nothing good to expect from Ferdinand. After many and various incidents the two royal armies came to an engagement, in which John was defeated, near Troia, in the year 1463. But he was less hurt by this defeat than by the defection of Jacopo Piccinino, who went over to Ferdinand. Thus deprived of his forces, John retreated to Ischia, whence he soon after returned to France. This war had lasted four years, and was lost by the negligence of him who by the courage of his soldiers had many times achieved victory. The Florentines took no ostensible part in this war; it is true that they were requested by the ambassador of King John of Aragon, who had come to the throne of that kingdom by the death of Alfonso, to support the cause of his nephew Ferdinand, according to their obligations under the treaty but lately formed with his father, Alfonso. To which the Florentines replied, "that they were under no obligations to Ferdinand, and that "they were not going to assist the son in a war begun by his "father; and as it had been commenced without their knowl- "edge or advice, so Ferdinand must get out of it and finish it without their assistance." The ambassador protested on behalf of his sovereign, the king of Aragon, and claimed the penalty of the obligations, and compensation for damages; and then departed indignant against the republic. Thus the Florentines remained during the whole of that war at peace so far as external affairs were concerned; but matters were by no means tranquil within, as will be shown more particularly in the following Books.

SEVENTH BOOK.

SUMMARY.

1. Connection between the affairs of the other principalities of Italy and the history of Florence. Dissensions that are injurious to republics. Character of such dissensions. — 2. Cosimo de' Medici and Neri Capponi make themselves powerful in different ways. Reform in the elections of magistrates favorable to Cosimo. Discontent of the nobles on account of this reform. — 3. (1458.) The nobles have recourse to Cosimo, but he refuses them his help so as to render himself more necessary. — 4. Tyranny and pride of Luca Pitti and his party. — 5. Death of Cosimo de' Medici (1464). His munificence; his policy. — 6. His eulogy. — 7. The Duke of Milan takes Genoa. Ferdinand of Aragon assures himself, by treachery, of the adverse barons. — 8. Jacopo Picciuino is imprisoned, and dies. — 9. Useless efforts of Pope Pius II. to move the Christians against the Turks (1465). Death of Duke Francesco Sforza (1466). — 10. Conspiracy of Diotisalvi Neroni against Piero de' Medici. — 11. Continuance of the same subject. — 12. Festivities in Florence. — 13. Fickleness of the Florentines with regard to Piero de' Medici. — 14. Niccolo Soderini is elected Gonfaloniere. Great hopes entertained of him, as regards the restoration of tranquillity in the city. — 15. The two parties take to arms. — 16. The great majority of the citizens declare for the Medici. — 17. Reforms of the government in favor of Piero de' Medici. Dispersion of his enemies. Fall of Luca Pitti. — 18. Letter of Agnolo Acciaiuoli to Piero de' Medici. — 19. The Florentine exiles excite the Venetians to a war against Florence. — 20. War between the Venetians and the Florentines (1467), terminated by the peace of 1468. Death of Niccolo Soderini. — 21. Marriage of Lorenzo de' Medici with Clarice d' Orsini. — 22. Sixtus IV. created Pope. His character. — 23. Piero de' Medici tries to check the acts of violence committed in Florence; but is interrupted in his efforts by death (1469). — 24. Messer Tommaso Soderini, a citizen of great reputation, joins the Medici. — 25. Riot in Prato, originated by Bernardo Nardi. — 26. Bernardo has Petrucci, Podesta of Prato, taken prisoner, but releases him. — 27. He is himself taken, and the disturbance is quieted. — 28. Corruption in the city of Florence. Burning of the church of Santo Spirito (1471). — 29. Rebellion of Volterra. — 30. Repressed by arms and by the sack of the city (1472). — 31. Origin of the enmity between Pope Sixtus IV. and Lorenzo de' Medici (1473). — 32. Carlo di Braccio of Perugia attacks the Siennese; but withdraws afterwards by advice of the Florentines (1476). — 33. Conspiracy against Galeazzo, Duke of Milan. —

34. Giovanni Andrea Lampognano, Carlo Visconti, and Girolamo Olgiato kill the Duke in San Stefano; they are all three put to death, the first two by the servants of the Duke, and the latter is decapitated by the public executioner.

1. It may perhaps seem to those who have read the preceding Book that, as a mere writer upon Florentine affairs, I have dilated too much upon the events that occurred in Lombardy and the kingdom of Naples. But as I have not in the past, so I shall not in the future avoid such digressions; for although I have never engaged to write the history of Italy, yet that does not seem to me a reason for omitting to mention all the important events that occurred within that country. For not to narrate them would make our own immediate history less understood and appreciated, especially as it was the actions of the other peoples and princes of Italy that were the most frequent causes of those wars in which the Florentines deemed it their duty to take part. Such was the case with the war between John of Anjou and King Ferdinand, which gave rise to the bitter enmity that sprung up between the latter and the Florentines, and especially between that prince and the Medici family. For King Ferdinand complained that in that war he had not only been unassisted, but that favors had actually been shown to his enemy; and the resentment which he felt in consequence became the cause of some of the greatest evils for Florence, as our narrative will show. Having written of external affairs up to the year 1463, it will be necessary for me to go back several years, so as to be able to relate the internal troubles that occurred in the mean time. But before that, I wish to say by way of argument, as is our wont, that those who believe in the possibility that union and harmony can be preserved in a republic deceive themselves much by this hope. Certainly it is true that some divisions injure a republic and others benefit it; especially are those injurious that engender factions and create partisans; and those are beneficial to a republic that are maintained without factions and partisans. A founder of a republic thus, being unable to prevent dissensions from arising in it, should at least provide against the danger of factions. And for this he must know that there are two ways in which citizens in a republic can achieve reputation and influence; namely, either by public or by private means. Publicly it is achieved either by gaining a battle, taking a town, performing

a mission with zeal and discretion, or counselling the republic wisely and happily. By private ways it is acquired through rendering services to this or that citizen, such as defending him against the magistrates, aiding him with money, procuring for him unmerited honors, and by courting popular favor with largesses and public games and amusements. Such modes of proceeding give rise to factions and partisanship; and just as influence gained by these means is dangerous, so does the former way benefit a republic when unaccompanied by factions, — for then it is founded upon the public good, and not upon private interests. And although it is impossible to provide means for preventing bitter feuds from arising amongst citizens thus grown powerful, nevertheless, not having any partisans who follow them for their own private advantage, they cannot harm the republic, but rather contribute to its benefit. For to overcome their enemies they must devote themselves to the aggrandizement of the state; and above all must they watch each other, so that no one may transgress the limits of the law. The dissensions of Florence have always been accompanied by factions, and therefore they have ever been pernicious; nor did any successful faction ever remain united, except so long as the opposite faction remained active; but when that had been completely crushed, then the dominant faction, no longer fearing and being kept in check by it, and not being controlled within itself by any regulations, became divided in itself and fell to pieces. The party of Cosimo de' Medici gained the ascendency in 1434; but the defeated party being large and comprising many most influential men, the former were for a time kept united and humble by fear, so that they neither committed any errors nor made themselves odious to the people by any wrong. Thus every time the government had need of the people to recover its authority, it always found them disposed to concede to its chiefs whatever Balia or power they desired; and thus in the period from 1434 to 1455 — that is, twenty-one years — the power of a Balia was six times conceded them by the councils.

2. There were in Florence, as we have already several times stated, two most powerful citizens, Cosimo de' Medici and Neri Capponi. Of these Neri was one of those who had acquired his influence by public means, so that he had many friends and but few partisans. Cosimo, on the other hand, having made

his way to his influential position by public as well as by private means, had plenty of both friends and partisans; and as these two men remained united so long as they lived, they always obtained without the least difficulty whatever they wanted from the people; for in all their acts grace was always mixed with the exercise of power. But in the year 1455, Neri having died, and the opposite party being crushed, the government experienced difficulty in resuming its authority. The cause of this was the very friends of Cosimo themselves who were most influential in the state; for they no longer feared the adverse party, which had been crushed, and sought to diminish the power of Cosimo. This disposition gave rise to the dissensions that occurred afterwards, in 1466; so that those who controlled the government proposed in the general councils, where matters of the public administration are openly discussed, that it would be well not to have the powers of the Balia renewed, and to close the election purses, and to have the magistrates drawn by lot from the old Squittini or poll lists. There were two ways for Cosimo to prevent the execution of this design; either to retake the government by force with the partisans and adherents he had, and to put all the others out; or to let things take their course and make his friends comprehend, in good time, that it was not he, but themselves, whom they had deprived of power and influence by the proposed measures. Of these two courses Cosimo chose the latter; for he knew full well that in that form of government he ran no risk, as the election purses were filled with the names of his friends, and he could therefore resume the government whenever he pleased. When the magistrates of Florence were thereupon again drawn by lot, it seemed to the mass of citizens as though they had recovered their liberties; and the magistrates gave their decisions, not according to the will of the most powerful, but according to their own judgment, so that now the friend of one influential citizen was defeated and now that of another; and thus the men who were accustomed to see their houses full of suitors and gifts, now saw them void of clients and of substance. They also saw those become their equals whom they had been in the habit of looking upon as greatly inferior; and those who had been their equals, they now saw their superiors. They found themselves no longer respected nor honored, but often rather jeered and derided;

and the people spoke of them and of the republic openly on the streets and in the piazzas without any respect; so that they soon recognized the fact that they, and not Cosimo, had lost the government. Cosimo pretended not to notice these things, and whatever measures were proposed that favored the people he was always the first to support them. But what alarmed the higher classes most, and afforded Cosimo the greatest opportunity to make them repent of their conduct, was the re-establishment of the Catasto of 1427, according to which the amount of taxes to be laid was fixed by law, and not by the arbitrary will of men.

3. This law having been passed despite of their opposition, and the magistrates appointed for its execution, the nobles assembled and called upon Cosimo to beg him to rescue them and himself from the hands of the people, and to restore to the government that influence which had made him powerful and them respected. To which Cosimo replied that he was willing, but that he wished it done regularly and according to law, and with the consent of the people, and not by violence, of which he did not want to hear in any way. An attempt was accordingly made by them in the councils to have a law passed for the creation of a new Balia, but without success. Whereupon the noble citizens turned to Cosimo and entreated him in the most humble manner that he would agree to a parliament, which he refused altogether, desiring to see them brought to that point that they should become fully sensible of their error. And as Donati Cocchi, who was Gonfaloniere of Justice at the time, wanted to call a parliament without the consent of Cosimo, the latter had the attempt so ridiculed by the Signori that sat with him that Cocchi completely lost his reason and was obliged to be sent home. But as it is never well to let things go until they are wholly beyond the power of control, and Luca Pitti, who was a bold and audacious man, having become Gonfaloniere of Justice, it seemed to Cosimo best to leave the whole management of the matter to him; so that if the attempt should fail, and blame come of it, it might be charged to Luca and not to himself. Luca therefore, in the beginning of his magistracy, proposed several times to the people to appoint a new Balia; but as he could not obtain their consent, he threatened those who sat in the council with insolent and insulting words, to which he soon after added deeds

of like character; for in the month of August, 1458, on the
eve of San Lorenzo, having filled the palace with armed men,
he called the people together in the Piazza and compelled them
by force of arms to consent to that to which they had before
refused their voluntary assent. And having thereupon resumed the government and created a Balia, and then appointed
the chief magistrates according to the judgment and pleasure
of a few, these by way of beginning with terror a government
which had originated in force, banished Messer Girolamo
Machiavelli and some others, and deprived many of the privilege of holding office. This same Messer Girolamo was afterwards declared a rebel for having transgressed the limits of
his banishment; and whilst travelling about in Italy endeavoring to stir up the princes against his own country, he was captured at Lunigiana by the treachery of one of the Signori, and
having been carried to Florence, he was imprisoned and there
put to death.

4. This new government, during the eight years of its existence, was violent and insupportable; for as Cosimo, already old
and wearied and enfeebled by ill health, could no longer personally take an active part in the affairs of government, the
city became a prey to the cupidity of a few of its citizens.
Luca Pitti, in reward for his services to the republic, was made
a noble, and he in return, by way of not being less gracious to
the citizens than they had been to him, ordered that those who
were till then called the Priors of the Trades, should, by way
of preserving at least the name of the substance which they
had lost, be called the Priors of Liberty. He also ordered that
the Gonfaloniere, who until then had his seat on the right
above the Rectors, should henceforth be seated in the midst
of the Priors. And to make it appear as though the Almighty
himself had participated in these doings, he ordered public
processions and solemn offices to be performed in gratitude
to God for the honors restored to them. The Signoria and
Cosimo bestowed rich presents upon Messer Luca Pitti, after
which the whole city vied in making him similar donations;
so that the amount of these gifts was estimated at not less
than twenty thousand ducats. Whence his authority increased
to that degree that it was no longer Cosimo, but Messer Luca
Pitti, who governed Florence. This so filled him with confidence in his power that he commenced the construction of

two palaces, one at Florence, and the other at Ruciano, a place about a mile distant from the city, which were both of royal magnificence; especially the one in the city, which was larger than any other that had ever been built by any private citizen. To complete these palaces, Messer Luca did not hesitate to resort to most extraordinary means; for not only the citizens and private persons made him gifts, and aided him with the material, &c. necessary for these buildings, but even the common people made contributions and lent him their help. Besides this, all the banished, and any one else that had committed murder, or theft, or any other crime that made him amenable to the penalties of the law, found a safe refuge in that palace, provided he would in some way contribute to its erection. The other citizens in the government, if they did not build palaces as Luca Pitti did, yet were neither less violent nor less rapacious than he was; so that if Florence was not impoverished by foreign wars, she was ruined by her own citizens. During this time, as we have said, occurred the wars of the kingdom of Naples, and some which the Pope carried on against the Malatesti in the Romagna, from whom he desired to take Rimini and Cesena, which they held. Pope Pius II. terminated his pontificate in the midst of these enterprises and the preparations for the expedition against the Turks.

5. Whilst Florence continued agitated by her dissensions and troubles, they also broke out in the party of Cosimo in the year 1455, from causes already indicated, but which, as we have narrated, he was enabled to quiet for the time by his prudence. But with the year 1464 Cosimo's illness became so aggravated as to cause his death. Both friends and enemies alike deplored this event; for those who from public reasons did not love him feared that after his decease they would be completely ruined and destroyed; for they had witnessed, even during his lifetime, the rapacity of those whose excesses had been somewhat restrained by their regard for him. Nor had they much confidence in his son Piero; for although he was a good man, yet they judged that, being also in feeble health, and a novice in the government, he might be obliged to have too much consideration for those who controlled the government, and whose rapacity, being now without any check, would in that case become still more excessive. The regret at Cosimo's death was

therefore very general. Of all citizens not of the profession
of arms, Cosimo was the most illustrious and renowned, not
only of Florence, but also of any other republic of which we
have any record. For not only did he surpass all others in
wealth and influence, but also in liberality and sagacity; and
amongst all the other qualities on account of which he became,
as it were, sovereign in his own country, was his exceeding
generosity and munificence. His liberality became much more
manifest after his death; for when his son Piero wished to
ascertain his possessions, it was found that there was hardly
a citizen who held any sort of position to whom Cosimo had
not loaned heavy sums of money. And many times he relieved, unsolicited, the necessities of noblemen so soon as he
became cognizant of them. His munificence is apparent from
the number of public edifices built by him; for in Florence he
erected the churches and convents of San Marco and San Lorenzo, and the monastery of Santa Verdiana; and on the hill
of Fiesole, San Girolamo and the Badia; and in the Mugello
he restored and supplied with new foundations a church of the
Minorite Friars. Besides these, he erected in Santa Croce, in
the Servi, in the Angioli, and in San Miniato the most splendid
altars and chapels, which he supplied, moreover, with costly
vestments and every other necessary for the establishment of
divine service. Besides these sacred edifices must be mentioned his private palaces, of which there was one in the city,
in all respects suitable to so great a citizen, and four without
the city, namely, one at Careggi, one at Fiesole, one at Caffa-
ginolo, and one at Trebbio, each of which was more like a royal
palace than the dwelling of a private citizen. And not satisfied that the magnificence of his edifices should be known in
Italy only, he built also in Jerusalem an asylum for poor and
infirm pilgrims, in the construction of which he expended a
very large amount of money. And although these palaces and
all his other works and acts were royal, and he was like a sovereign in Florence, yet he so tempered his magnificence with
his prudence, that he never transcended the modesty of a civil-
ian. For in his intercourse and conversation, in his servants,
in his equipages, and in his whole mode of living, as also in
the family alliances which he established, he was ever the same
as any other modest citizen; for he knew that any extraordinary display on all occasions excites much more envy than

what these things merit in reality, and that they should therefore be concealed with becoming modesty. And so, when he had to marry his sons, he did not seek alliances with princely houses, but he married John to Cornelia of the Alessandri family, and Piero to Lucrezia de' Tornabuoni; and of the daughters of Piero, Bianco was married to Guglielmo de' Pazzi, and Nannina to Bernardo Rucellai. None either of the princes or civil rulers of his time equalled him in intelligence; whence it came that in a city so liable to change, and a population so variable, he was able to hold the government for thirty-one years. His extreme prudence and sagacity enabled him to foresee evil from afar, and whilst there was still time, either to arrest its growth, or to prepare for it in such manner that in case it should grow it might produce no mischief. Thus he not only triumphed over the ambition of his rivals within the republic, but he overcame even that of many foreign princes so happily and with so much tact that he secured the alliance of all for the benefit of his country, and thus remained equal or superior to its enemies; and whoever opposed him lost both his time and his money, or his state. The Venetians are a striking proof of this, for in union with Cosimo they proved always superior to Duke Filippo; and when separated from him they were beaten and defeated, first by Filippo and then by Francesco; and when they combined with King Alfonso against the Florentine republic, Cosimo, by his credit, so deprived Naples and Venice of money that they were constrained to accept such terms of peace as the Florentines chose to accord them. The many internal and external troubles, then, which Cosimo had to encounter, always terminated gloriously for him and disastrously for his enemies; and thus his power and influence in the city were increased by civil discords within, and the foreign wars added to his power and reputation, so that he was enabled to add to the possessions of the republic the Borgo of San Sepolcro, Montedoglio, the Casentino, and the Val di Bagno. And thus by his virtue and good fortune he destroyed all his enemies and exalted his friends.

6. Cosimo was born in 1389, on the day of SS. Cosimo and Damiano. His early life was full of troubles, as proved by his exile, his imprisonment, and exposure to the danger of death; for, having accompanied Pope John XXIII. to the Council of Constance, he was obliged, after the deposition of the Pope, to

fly in disguise to save his life. But after his fortieth year he lived most happily and prosperously; so that not only those who joined him in his public enterprises, but also those who administered his private wealth in various parts of Europe, participated in his prosperity, whence many families in Florence acquired great riches, as was the case with the Tornabuoni, the Benci, the Portinari, and the Sassetti; and besides these, all those who depended upon his counsel and fortune gained large wealth. Although he constantly spent large sums in the building of churches and in charities, yet he complained sometimes to his friends that he had never been enabled to spend as much in the honor of God but that he should be found a debtor in his books. Cosimo was of ordinary stature, olive complexion, and of venerable presence; he was without great erudition, but most eloquent and full of natural prudence; obliging to his friends, merciful to the poor, profitable in conversation, cautious in counsel, and prompt in execution; and in his sayings and replies he was subtle and grave. Messer Rinaldo degli Albizzi, in the early part of his exile, sent him word "that the "hen was hatching"; to which Cosimo replied, "that she could "hatch but ill, being away from her nest." And when other exiles gave him to understand "that they did not sleep," he said "that he believed it, for he had deprived them of sleep." When Pope Pius II. was laboring to excite the princes of Italy to a crusade against the Turks, Cosimo said "that the Pope was "an old man, and had undertaken an enterprise only fit for a "young man." To the Venetian ambassadors who came to Florence together with those of King Alfonso to complain of the republic, Cosimo uncovered his head, asking them the color of his hair, and when they answered "White," he said, "It "will not be long before your senators will have heads as white "as mine." A few hours before his death, when his wife asked him "why he kept his eyes closed," he answered, "To accus- "tom them to it." After his return from exile some citizens said to him, "that the city was being desolated, and that it was "an offence against God to drive so many good men out of it." Cosimo replied, "that it was better a city should be desolated "than destroyed; that two yards of red cloth would make a "gentleman, but that states could not be governed with rosary "in hand"; which expression gave his enemies opportunity to calumniate him, as being "a man who loved himself more than "his country, and this world more than the next." We might adduce many more of his sayings, but these will suffice.

Cosimo was also a great lover and patron of literary men; and this made him bring to Florence Argiropolo, a Greek by birth and the most learned man of his time, so that he might instruct the Florentine youth in the Greek language and other branches of learning. He supported in his own house Marsilio Ficino, the second father of the Platonian philosophy, to whom he was so much attached that he gave him a property near his own palace of Careggi, so that Marsilio might follow the pursuit of letters with more convenience, and that he himself might with greater facility enjoy his society. Thus his prudence, his wealth, his good fortune, and his whole way of life caused him to be feared and beloved by the people of Florence, and to be in the most extraordinary degree esteemed, not only by the princes of Italy, but of all Europe; thus leaving a foundation for his descendants which enabled them to equal him in virtue and greatly to surpass him in fortune. And the authority and consideration which Cosimo enjoyed in Florence he deserved to have equally throughout all Christendom. In the latter part of his life, however, he experienced great affliction; for of his two sons, Piero and Giovanni, the latter, in whom he had the most confidence, died, and the other was in such infirm health that he was unfit to attend to public or private business; so that, upon being carried through his palace after the death of Giovanni, Cosimo observed with a sigh, "This is too "large a house for so small a family." His great soul also suffered anguish at the thought of not having increased the Florentine dominions by some honorable conquest; and he regretted this the more as it seemed to him that he had been deceived by Francesco Sforza, who, before becoming Duke, had promised him that whenever he should become master of Milan he would undertake the conquest of Lucca for the Florentines, which promise he however never performed. For Count Francesco changed his mind with his change of fortune; and having become Duke of Milan, he wished to enjoy in peace what he had won by war, and would therefore not engage in any new enterprise either for Cosimo or any one else, and was even indisposed to engage in any more wars unless forced to it for his own defence. This was a source of the greatest annoyance to Cosimo, who felt that he had undergone much trouble and expense for the benefit of a faithless and ungrateful man. Besides this, he felt that the infirmity of his body would not permit him to devote himself with his former zeal to either public or private affairs, so that he thought he saw both going to ruin; for Florence was being destroyed by her own citizens, and his private fortune by his agents and his children. All these things caused him much disquietude in the latter part of his life. Nevertheless he died full of glory and great renown, and the city of Florence, as well as all Christian princes, condoled with his son Piero upon his loss. His funeral was attended by all the citizens with greatest pomp; and being interred in the church of San Lorenzo, there was, by public decree, inscribed over his tomb, "FATHER OF HIS COUNTRY."

If, in speaking of the acts of Cosimo, I have followed the example rather of those who write the biographies of princes, and not that of those who write general history, no one need wonder at it; for having been so rare a man in our republic, I felt compelled to speak of him with the extraordinary praises which he merited.

7. At this time, when Florence and Italy were in the above-described condition, Louis, king of France, was involved in a most serious war, which his barons had begun against him, and in which they were aided by the Duke of Brittany, and by Charles, Duke of Burgundy. This war was of such magnitude that King Louis could not think of assisting Duke John of Anjou in his attempt upon Genoa and Naples; and, judging rather that he himself needed the help of others, he gave to Francesco, Duke of Milan, the town of Savona, which had remained in the possession of the French, giving him to understand, at the same time, that he would not oppose Francesco's undertaking the conquest of Genoa, if he desired it. This offer was accepted by Francesco, who, by the influence thus derived from the king's friendship, and the help afforded him by the Adorni, succeeded in making himself master of Genoa. And, not to appear ungrateful for the favors he had received at the hands of the king of France, he sent fifteen hundred horse to his assistance under the command of his eldest son, Galeazzo Sforza. Thus Ferdinand of Aragon and Francesco Sforza remained, the latter Duke of Lombardy and Prince of Genoa, and the former king of the entire kingdom of Naples. And a family alliance having been contracted between them, they considered

how they could establish themselves firmly enough in their respective states to enable them to enjoy them in security during their lives, and dying bequeath them freely to their heirs. They deemed it necessary for this purpose that the king of Naples should make sure of the barons who had offended him in the war of John of Anjou, and that Duke Francesco should destroy the Braccescan party, who were the natural enemies of his family, and who had attained the highest reputation under Jacopo Piccinino; for this Piccinino was now the greatest general of Italy, and, having no state of his own, was to be feared by all who had any dominions, and most of all by the Duke Francesco, who, conscious of the example which he himself had set, seemed to think that he could neither enjoy his state quietly himself, nor leave it securely to his son, so long as Jacopo Piccinino lived. King Ferdinand therefore earnestly endeavored to come to terms with the barons, employing every art for that purpose. He happily succeeded; for the barons saw very clearly that they would be ruined if they continued at war with the king, and were doubtful even of their safety if they trusted and made terms with him; and as men always try to avoid certain evils, it follows that princes can easily deceive persons less powerful than themselves. The barons, seeing the manifest danger of war, put faith in the peace offered by the king; but, having placed themselves in his hands, were afterwards destroyed by him in various ways and under various pretexts. This example alarmed Jacopo Piccinino, who happened with his troops at Sulmona; and to deprive the king of Naples of the opportunity of crushing him, he opened negotiations with the Duke Francesco for a reconciliation through the mediation of some friends. And Sforza, having made him liberal offers, Jacopo resolved to place himself in his hands, and, accompanied by one hundred mounted men, he went to meet him at Milan.

8. (1465.) Jacopo Piccinino had served a long time under the father and with the brother of Duke Francesco, first for Duke Filippo and afterwards for the people of Milan; so that by long intercourse he had made many friends in Milan, and the general good-will of the people towards him had been increased by his present condition. For the fortunate prosperity and present power of the Sforzas had excited much envy against them, whilst adversity and long absence had created with the same people a warm sympathy for Jacopo, and the greatest

desire to see him again. All of which became apparent on his arrival; for there were but few of the nobility who did not go to meet him, and the streets through which he had to pass were thronged with people eager to see him, and who shouted his name and that of his family everywhere. These honors hastened his ruin, for the Duke's apprehensions increased his desire to destroy Jacopo; and to enable him to do so more covertly, he determined to celebrate the nuptials of Jacopo with his illegitimate daughter, Drusiana, to whom he had been for some time affianced. After this Jacopo agreed with the Duke to enter his service, with the title of captain of his forces, and one hundred thousand florins for his maintenance. Having concluded these arrangements, Jacopo went to Naples with his wife, Drusiana, and a ducal ambassador, where he was gladly and most honorably received, and for a succession of days entertained with all sorts of festivities. But having asked leave to go to Sulmona, where he had his troops, he was invited by the king to a banquet in the castle, after which he and his son were thrown into prison, where they were soon after put to death. And thus Italian princes, dreading in others the virtue of which they themselves were destitute, destroyed it; so that from the want of it the country soon after fell into that state of decadence which exposed it to such calamities and ruin.

9. Pope Pius II. had now settled the affairs of the Romagna, and this period of general peace seemed to him favorable for stirring up the Christians to move against the Turks. He adopted for this purpose proceedings similar to those of his predecessors. All the princes promised either money or men, and more particularly King Matthias of Hungary and Duke Charles of Burgundy, who promised to accompany him in person, and were therefore appointed by the Pope as chiefs of the whole enterprise. The Pope was so hopeful that he left Rome and went to Ancona, where he had ordered the whole host of crusaders to assemble, and where the Venetians had promised him vessels for transporting them across to Sclavonia. After the arrival of the pontiff in Ancona, there came together so many people in that city that in a few days all the provisions that were in the city, or that could be had from neighboring places, were consumed, so that all began to suffer from famine. Besides this, there was no money with which to purchase provisions or arms for those that needed them, and neither King

Matthias nor Duke Charles made his appearance. The Venetians sent one of their captains with a few galleys, more for the purpose of making a show of compliance with their pledges than really to transport the army across into Sclavonia. In the midst of all these troubles and disorders, the Pope, who was already old and infirm, died, after which all returned to their homes. The death of Pius II. occurred in 1465, and Paul II., a Venetian by birth, was chosen his successor. It seemed about this time as though all the principalities of Italy were to change their rulers; for Francesco Sforza, Duke of Milan, also died in the following year, after having held the dukedom sixteen years. His son, Galeazzo, was proclaimed his successor.

10. The death of this prince caused an increase of the dissensions in Florence and accelerated their baneful effects. After the death of Cosimo, his son Piero, who fell heir to his father's wealth and state, called to his assistance Diotisalvi Neroni, a man of great influence and highly esteemed by the other citizens, and in whom Cosimo had so much confidence that in dying he recommended to Piero to be guided by Neroni's advice in all matters of state, as well as in the management of his private fortune. Piero therefore manifested towards Diotisalvi the same confidence that Cosimo had done; and as he desired to conform to the injunctions of his father after his death, the same as he had done during his lifetime, he requested Messer Diotisalvi to advise him in relation to his patrimony as well as the government of the city; and told him that, by way of making a beginning with his private business, he would have all the accounts of his assets and liabilities placed in his hands, so that he might judge of the condition of his affairs, and in how far they were well ordered or otherwise; and that then, after having acquainted himself with them, he might advise him in relation thereto according as his prudence might suggest. Messer Diotisalvi promised to use all diligence and good faith in every way. But when the accounts came and were examined by him, he found that matters generally were in great disorder, and impelled more by his ambition than by his love for Piero or by the benefits formerly bestowed upon him by Cosimo, he conceived the idea that it would be easy for him to rob Piero of the credit and state which he had inherited from his father. Messer Diotisalvi therefore advised Piero in a manner that seemed entirely reasonable and honest, but under which his

ruin was concealed. He pointed out to him the disordered condition of his affairs, and how much money would be required to preserve his credit, and with it the reputation of his wealth and his state; and he suggested to Piero that there was no more honest means of re-establishing his disordered finances, than to call in all the moneys which his father had outstanding in the way of loans to so many strangers as well as citizens. For Cosimo, to secure himself partisans in Florence and friends elsewhere, had been most liberal in letting everybody participate in his fortune, so that he had become creditor to an amount neither small nor unimportant. Piero in his desire to restore order in his affairs received the suggestion as a good and honest one; but so soon as a demand for these outstanding loans was made by his order, the citizens resented it as though he wanted to rob them of their own, instead of asking merely for what was his; and they said everything that was ill of him, and calumniated him as an ingrate and a miser.

11. Messer Diotisalvi, seeing the general disfavor and unpopularity which Piero had drawn upon himself by having acted according to the advice which he himself had given him, combined with Messer Luca Pitti, Messer Agnolo Acciaiuoli, and Niccolo Soderini to deprive Piero both of his credit and of the government. They were all actuated by different motives in this. Messer Luca desired to succeed to the government in place of Cosimo; for he had now become so powerful himself that he disdained being subjected to Piero. Messer Diotisalvi, knowing Messer Luca Pitti to be unfit for being at the head of the government, imagined as a matter of course that, when Piero should have lost his place and his influence, the government would undoubtedly in a short time fall into his hands. Niccolo Soderini wished the city to enjoy greater liberty, and that it should be governed solely by the will of the magistrates. Messer Agnolo had a special hatred of the Medici for the following reasons. His son Rafaelle had some time previously married Alessandra de' Bardi, who brought him a very large dowry. Either from her own fault or that of others she had been maltreated by her husband and her father-in-law; whereupon Lorenzo d' Ilarione, a relative of hers, touched by compassion for the young lady, went one night accompanied by a number of armed men and took her from the house of Messer Agnolo. The Acciaiuoli complained of the injury thus done

them by the Bardi, and the case was referred to Cosimo, who decided that the Acciaiuoli should restore to Alessandra her dowry, and it should then be left to her option to return to her husband or not. Messer Agnolo seemed to think that Cosimo had not treated him as a friend in this matter; and as he could not revenge himself upon Cosimo, he resolved to do so upon his son. These conspirators, although each animated by a different private motive, yet gave out to the public that they had but one common object, and affirmed that all they wanted was that the city should be governed by the magistrates, and not merely by the arbitrary will of a few citizens. Besides this the odium of Piero and the reasons for attacking him were augmented by the failure of many merchants at that time, for which Piero was publicly censured, because he had so unexpectedly called in all his outstanding moneys, and had thereby caused these failures, which were a disgrace and injury to the city. To all this it was to be added that Piero was negotiating a marriage between his oldest son, Lorenzo, and the lady Clarice of the house of Orsini, which afforded additional opportunity for calumniating him. For, they said, since he disdains a Florentine alliance for his son, it is evident that he no longer regards himself a citizen of Florence and intends to make himself sovereign of it; for he who will not have his fellow-citizens for relatives must contemplate making them his slaves, and cannot therefore in reason expect that they will remain his friends. The chiefs of this conspiracy seemed to think that they held the victory in their hands, because the greater part of the citizens followed them, being deceived by the cry of Liberty, which the conspirators had taken for their watchword by way of justifying their attempt.

12. Whilst the city was kept agitated by these movements, some citizens who abhorred all civil discord thought it would be well, if possible, to put a stop to them by some novel public entertainments; inasmuch as idle people are apt to become an instrument in the hands of men disposed to sedition. To put an end to this idleness, and to divert people's thoughts from matters of state and give them something else to occupy their minds, they concluded that the year of mourning after Cosimo's death having elapsed, it would be well to offer some amusement to the people of the city; and therefore they ordered two most magnificent festivals, such as had not yet been seen in Florence. One was to be a representation of the nativity and the adoration

of the three Magi who had come from the East guided by a star; which was gotten up with such pomp and magnificence that the preparation and performance of it occupied the whole city for many months. The other was a tournament (for such they call a spectacle that represents a contest between men on horseback), where the first youths of the city should contend with the most renowned cavaliers of Italy. And amongst the most distinguished Florentine youths was Lorenzo, eldest son of Piero de' Medici, who by his own personal bravery, and not by any favoritism, carried off the first honors. After the conclusion of these festivities the citizens reverted to their former thoughts, and each pursued his own projects with more zeal than ever, which gave rise to great differences and troubles, that were much increased by two occurrences: the one was the want of the authority of the Balia, which had expired, and the other the death of Francesco, Duke of Milan. In consequence of the latter the new Duke Galeazzo had sent ambassadors to Florence to confirm the agreements which his father had made with the city; one of which amongst other things provided for the annual payment of a certain sum of money by the Florentines. The leaders of the party opposed to the Medici took occasion to object to this demand, and opposed it publicly in council on the ground that the alliance had been made, not with Galeazzo, but with Francesco, and was cancelled by the death of the latter, and that there was no occasion for its renewal, inasmuch as Galeazzo had not the same ability as Francesco, and therefore they could not expect the same advantages from him; that they had had but little benefit from the former, and would have still less from the latter; and if any citizen wished to employ Galeazzo for his own private purposes, it was contrary to the laws of the republic and to liberty. Piero, on the other hand, pointed out that it would not be wise to forego an alliance so very necessary to them from mere considerations of money, and that there was nothing so beneficial to the republic and to all Italy as their alliance with the Duke of Milan, so that the Venetians seeing them united might not attempt either by a feigned friendship or by open war to injure the duchy. For so soon as they should find that the Florentines were alienated from the Duke, they would take up arms against him; and profiting by his youth and inexperience in the government and want of allies, they could easily win him over either by fraud or by force, and in either case it would be seen that it would lead to the ruin of the republic.

13. Piero's arguments had no effect and were not accepted, and soon the animosities began to show themselves openly. The two parties met nightly at different places, the friends of the Medici in the Crocetta, and their adversaries in the Pieta. Anxious for Piero's ruin, the latter had induced many citizens to sign their names to a list as being favorable to the enterprise. At one of their nightly meetings they discussed particularly the mode of proceeding; for all were agreed that the power of the Medici must be abated, but they differed as to the best way of effecting it. One portion, which was the most moderate, wanted, since Piero's power under the Balia was at an end, that they should watch and oppose his resumption of it; and that being done, all agreed that the government of the city should be left entirely to the councils and the magistrates, and that thus Piero's authority would in a brief period be destroyed; and that it would then be seen that with the loss of his authority and state he would also lose his commercial credit, for his affairs were at that point that, if they were careful not to allow him the use of the public funds, it would inevitably cause his financial ruin; after which he would be no longer dangerous, for a man who falls by his own fault is not sustained by his fellow-men like one who is thrust down by others. Besides, they argued, if no extraordinary attempt were made against him, he would have no grounds for arming himself or to call upon his friends for assistance; and if nevertheless he should do so, it would only injure his cause the more, and would excite such general mistrust of him that it would make his ruin all the easier, and would afford the others better opportunity for crushing him completely. Many others of those assembled were not favorable to this slow mode of proceeding, affirming that time would only benefit Piero, and not them; for if now they were to content themselves with ordinary proceedings, Piero would be in no danger whatsoever, whilst they would be exposed to many; for those magistrates who were his enemies would have to leave him the control of the city, whilst his friends would make him sovereign and ruin them, as happened in 1458;—and if the first suggestion had been made by good men, the present advice was that of wise ones; and therefore it would be best to agree to crush him

now, whilst the minds of men were excited against him; — and that the way to accomplish it was to arm themselves within the city and to employ the Marquis of Ferrara, so as not to be without an army; so that if a Signoria should be drawn that was favorable to them, they might be prepared to avail of it and act decisively. It was resolved thereupon to await the drawing of the new Signoria, and to govern themselves accordingly. Amongst the conspirators was Niccolo Fedini, who had acted as their chancellor, but who, attracted by certain hopes, disclosed all the projects of his enemies to Piero, and gave him a list of the conspirators and of those who had subscribed their names. Piero was alarmed at seeing the number and character of the citizens opposed to him; and having counselled with his friends, he resolved also to prepare a list, and to obtain the signatures of those who were favorable to him. And having put the matter in the hands of some of his most trusted friends, he was surprised to find the minds of the citizens so variable and unstable, that many who had signed the list against him now signed that in his favor.

14. Whilst matters were pending in this state of uncertainty, the time came for the renewal of the supreme magistracy, on which occasion Niccolo Soderini became Gonfaloniere of Justice. It was marvellous to see the crowd, not only of distinguished citizens, but even of the people, who accompanied him to the palace. On his way thither an olive wreath was placed upon his head, to signify that the country depended upon him for her security and liberty. This instance, as well as many others, proves how undesirable it is to accept an important magistracy or principality with extraordinary expectations on the part of the people; for being unable by your efforts to fulfil them, (men ever desiring more than you are able to perform,) you will in the end reap contempt and dishonor. Messer Tommaso and Niccolo Soderini were brothers; Niccolo was the more spirited and enterprising of the two, and Tommaso the more sagacious. The latter being a great friend of Piero de' Medici, and knowing at the same time his brother's disposition, and that he had no other object but the liberty of the city and to establish the government firmly and without injustice to any one, advised him to have no ballotings made, so that the election purses might be filled with the names of citizens devoted to their free institutions; which being done, he would

see the government established and confirmed without disturbance or harm to any one. Niccolo readily adopted his brother's advice, and thus wasted the period of his magistracy in vain efforts, which his friends the conspirators allowed him to do from jealousy, being unwilling that the reform of the government should be effected through the authority of Niccolo, and in the belief that they would yet be in time under another Gonfaloniere. When Niccolo's magistracy came to an end, it became apparent that he had begun many things, but accomplished none; and thus he left his office with much less honor than he had entered upon it.

15. This result strengthened the party of Piero; it confirmed his friends in their hopes, and converted those hitherto neutral into decided adherents. The parties being thus equalized, many months elapsed without any further disturbances. Piero's party, however, steadily grew in power, which aroused his enemies, who conspired together and planned to do by force what they had been incapable or unwilling to do by means of the magistrates when it would have been easy. They resolved therefore to have Piero, who was lying ill at Careggi, assassinated; and for that purpose they caused the Marquis of Ferrara to draw near the city with his troops, so that after Piero's death they might come armed into the Piazza and cause the Signoria to establish a government according to their will. For they hoped that, even if the whole of the Signoria were not favorable to them, yet that those who were opposed to them would be induced to yield from fear. Messer Diotisalvi, the better to conceal his real intentions, often visited Piero, argued with him about the restoration of harmony in the city, and counselled him to effect it. But all these machinations had been revealed to Piero; and, moreover, Messer Domenico Martelli had given him to understand that Francesco Neroni, brother of Messer Diotisalvi, had solicited him to join them, showing him that success was certain and their object all but accomplished. Piero therefore resolved to be the first to take up arms, and availed himself for that purpose of the intrigues of his adversaries with the Marquis of Ferrara. He feigned having received a letter from Messer Giovanni Bentivogli, Prince of Bologna, making known to him that the Marquis of Ferrara was on the other side of the river Albo with troops; and that it was publicly said that he intended march-

ing upon Florence. And thus upon this pretended information Piero took up arms and came to Florence followed by a crowd of armed men. Whereupon all who belonged to his party armed themselves also, and the opposite party did the same, but with less order than the others, who had been prepared for it, whilst Piero's enemies were not yet ready for it according to their plans. Messer Diotisalvi, whose dwelling was next to Piero's, did not feel himself secure there, but went alternately to the palace to counsel the Signori to compel Piero to disarm, and to Messer Luca Pitti to keep him firm to their party. But the one who showed himself more active than all the others was Messer Niccolo Soderini, who took up arms, and was followed by nearly the entire population of his quarter, and went to the house of Messer Luca Pitti, begging him to mount his horse and come into the Piazza to support the Signoria, which was with them, and that this would beyond all doubt assure them the victory. He urged him at the same time not to remain in his house, unless he wished either to be basely crushed by his armed enemies, or shamefully deceived by his unarmed ones, and that presently he would repent not having acted up to his advice, when it however would be too late. And that if he wished the destruction of Piero by war, he could easily accomplish it; and if he wanted peace, it was better to be in a position to dictate the terms than to be obliged to accept such as might be offered. But all these arguments had no effect upon Messer Luca, whose resentment against Piero had been calmed; having been beguiled by Piero with promises of fresh alliances and other advantages, for he had already married one of his nieces to Giovanni Tornabuoni. Luca therefore advised Niccolo to lay down his arms and return home, for it ought to satisfy him to see the city governed by the magistrates, as would be the case; and that both sides ought to disarm, and that the Signoria, the majority of whom were favorable to their party, should be the judges of their differences. Niccolo, being unable to influence Messer Luca Pitti in any way, returned home, having however first said to Luca: "I alone cannot secure the welfare of my city, but I can "foretell the ills that will befall it. The course which you are "taking will cause our country the loss of liberty, and to you "the loss of your power and your substance, and to me and "others the loss of our country."

16. During these disturbances the Signoria caused the palace to be closed, having shut themselves up in it together with the magistrates; and showing favor neither to one nor the other party. The citizens, and especially the adherents of the party of Messer Luca Pitti, seeing Piero armed, and his adversaries not, began to consider, not how they should injure Piero, but rather how they should manage to become his friends. Thereupon the principal citizens, chiefs of the factions, met in the palace in the presence of the Signoria, where all matters relating to the condition of the city and the reconciliation of the parties were discussed by them. And as Piero in consequence of his feeble condition could not be personally present, they all resolved to go to him in his palace, with the single exception of Niccolo Soderini, who, after placing his sons and his affairs in the charge of his brother Tommaso, went away to his villa, there to await the end of the matter, which he regarded as unfortunate for himself and pernicious to his country. When the other citizens had arrived at Piero's, one of them, who had been commissioned to speak for them, complained of the disturbances that had occurred in the city, throwing the blame mainly upon him who had first taken up arms; and, not knowing that this had been Piero, said that they had come to know his wishes, and that if they accorded with the good of the city they were ready to follow him. To which Piero replied: "That it was not he who had first taken up arms that was to "blame for the disturbances, but those who had first given "occasion for arming, and that they would be less surprised "at what he had done for his own safety, if they were to think "more of what their conduct had been towards him; for then "they would see that their mighty conclaves, the signing of "lists, and the negotiations for taking from him the govern- "ment of the city and of his very life, had caused him to arm. "And that the fact that his armed followers had not left his "palace was manifest proof of his having armed only for his "own defence, and not for the purpose of assailing others; and "that he wanted nothing else, and desired nothing so much as "quiet and security for himself, and had never shown the "slightest inclination or desire for anything else. For the "authority of the Balia having ceased, he had never thought "of any extraordinary means of re-establishing it; and that "he was entirely satisfied to let the magistrates govern the

"city if that would content them. And that they ought to
"remember that Cosimo and his sons had known how to live
"and make themselves honored in Florence with or without the
"Balia; and that it was not the house of Medici, but they them-
"selves, who had re-enacted the Balia in 1458, and if they did
"not want it now, no more did he; but that this did not sat-
"isfy them, for he had seen that they believed that they could
"not exist in Florence so long as he remained there, — a thing
"that he never could have believed or thought possible, that
"his friends and those of his father should imagine that they
"could not live in Florence with him, for he had never shown
"himself other than a quiet and peace-loving man." And then
addressing himself to Messer Diotisalvi and his brother, who
were present, he reproached them in words full of gravity and
indignation with the benefits which they had received at the
hands of Cosimo, with the confidence which he himself had
reposed in them, and with their monstrous ingratitude. And
such was the force of his words that some of those present
would have laid violent hands on the Neroni if he had not
restrained them. Piero finally concluded by saying that he
was ready to approve all that they and the Signoria might resolve upon, and that for himself he asked nothing but to live
in peace and security. Many other matters were discussed,
but nothing definite resolved upon, except in a general way
that it was necessary to reform the city and reorganize the
government.

17. The office of Gonfaloniere of Justice was held at that
time by Bernardo Lotti, a man who had not the confidence of
Piero, who in consequence did not deem it proper to attempt
anything so long as Bernardo held that office; which Piero
however deemed of little importance, knowing that Bernardo's
magistracy was nearly at an end. But when the election came
for Signori who were to sit for the months of September and
October in the year 1466, Ruberto Leoni was chosen to the
highest magistracy. So soon as he had taken office, all other
things being prepared, he called the people together in the
Piazza and created a new Balia, composed entirely of adherents of Piero, which soon after appointed the magistracies
wholly in accordance with the wishes of the new government.
All this alarmed the chiefs of the adverse faction, so that Messer Agnolo Acciaiuoli fled to Naples, and Messer Diotisalvi

Neroni and Niccolo Soderini to Venice. Messer Luca Pitti remained in Florence, trusting in the promises made to him by Piero, and in his new relationship with him. Those who had fled were declared rebels, and all the Neroni family were dispersed; Messer Giovanni di Nerone, Archbishop of Florence, to avoid a worse fate, became a voluntary exile to Rome; and many other citizens who suddenly departed were banished to various places. Nor was all this deemed sufficient, but a procession was ordered for the purpose of rendering thanks to God for the preservation of the republic and the restoration of union in the city. During this solemnity some citizens were seized and put to the torture; a part of them were afterwards killed, and the others banished. But in all this great vicissitude of things the most notable example was that of Messer Luca Pitti, who quickly learned the difference between victory and defeat, and between honor and disgrace. His palace, which previously had been visited by the greatest number of citizens, became a perfect solitude. His friends and relatives not only no longer accompanied him in the streets, but actually feared to salute him; for a portion had been deprived of their dignities and others of their property, and all were equally menaced. The superb edifices which he had commenced were abandoned by the builders, the benefits that were formerly showered upon him became changed into reproaches, and the honors heretofore bestowed upon him into infamy. Whereupon many, who for some favor had presented him with costly gifts, now demanded them back as having been mere loans; and others who had been in the habit of lauding him to the skies now blamed him as an ingrate and a man of violence; so that he repented — but too late — not having followed the advice of Messer Niccolo Soderini, rather to die honorably with arms in hand, than to live dishonored amongst his victorious enemies.

18. Those who found themselves expatriated began to think of various means for recovering that country in which they had not known how to maintain themselves. Messer Agnolo Acciainoli however, being at Naples, before attempting any active movement, wanted to ascertain the disposition of Piero, as to whether there was any hope of a reconciliation with him, and therefore wrote him a letter to the following effect: "I smile "at the freaks of Fortune, and how in turn she converts friends "into enemies and enemies into friends. You may remember

"how, during your father's exile, I, thinking more of that act
"of injustice than of my own danger, was subjected to the same
"wrong, and even came near losing my life. Nor have I ever,
"whilst Cosimo was living, failed to honor and support your
"house; neither have I since his death ever had the slightest
"intention of offending you. It is true that your feeble con-
"stitution, and the tender years of your sons, in a measure
"alarmed me; so that I judged it necessary to give such form
"to the government that, after your death, our country might
"not be exposed to ruin. This gave rise to the proceedings
"which were not intended against you, but for the good of my
"country, and which, if erroneous, deserve nevertheless to be
"forgiven on account of my good intentions and my past good
"conduct. Nor can I believe that, inasmuch as your house
"during so long a time has ever found me faithful, I shall not
"now find you merciful, or that all my former merits shall be
"cancelled by a single fault."

Upon receipt of this letter Piero replied thus: "Your smil-
"ing where you are is the reason why I do not weep; for were
"you to be smiling in Florence, I should be crying in Naples.
"I confess that you have been well disposed towards my father,
"but you must admit that you have received much in return for
"it; so that your obligations to us were as much greater than
"ours to you, as deeds are of greater value than words. Having
"thus been well rewarded for the good you have done, you must
"not be surprised now at the just retribution for your evil doings.
"Nor will your love of country excuse you; for no one will ever
"believe that Florence was less loved and its interests less pro-
"moted by the Medici than by the Acciaiuoli. Live, therefore,
"in dishonor where you are, since you have not known how to
"live here in honor."

19. Messer Agnolo, despairing therefore of obtaining pardon, went to Rome, and united with the Archbishop of Florence and the other banished Florentines to do all they could to destroy the credit of the Medici in Rome, in connection with their commercial operations. Piero contended against this with difficulty; still, by the aid of his friends, he thwarted their designs. Messer Diotisalvi and Niccolo Soderini, on the other hand, made every effort to stir up the Venetian Senate against their country, judging that, if the Florentines were involved in fresh wars, they would not be able to sustain their government, which was still

new and was detested. There happened to be at this time at Ferrara Messer Giovan Francesco, son of Messer Palla Strozzi, who, together with his father, had been driven from Florence during the troubles of 1434. He enjoyed very high credit amongst the other merchants, and was reputed exceedingly rich. The new rebels demonstrated to Giovan Francesco the great facility with which they could recover their country if the Venetians were to declare war against Florence, which they supposed the former would readily do, provided a share of the expenses were contributed by themselves, but which otherwise would be doubtful. Giovan Francesco, eager to revenge himself for the old injuries, gave ready ear to their suggestions, and promised to aid such an attempt with all the means in his power. Thereupon they went to the Doge, and complained of their exile, which, they said, " they had to suffer for no other fault than the " desire to have their country governed by equal laws and by the " magistrates, and to prevent a few private citizens from usurp- " ing the authority of the government. They added that Piero " de' Medici and his partisans, who were accustomed to the ways " of tyrants, had treacherously taken up arms, and by deceit " induced them to lay down theirs; and then by fraud and vio- " lence had driven them from their country. And not content " with this, they had availed of the Almighty himself as a means " of crushing many others, who, relying upon the pledges given " them, had remained in the city, and been seized during solemn " and sacred ceremonies and supplications, and imprisoned or " put to death; thus making the Almighty himself a participant " in their treason, which was an impious and nefarious example. " The exiles added that, to avenge these wrongs, they knew not " where more effectually to look for assistance than to the Sen- " ate of that state, which, having always enjoyed liberty them- " selves, ought to have compassion upon those who had lost " theirs. And therefore they appealed to freemen against ty- " rants, and to the pious against the impious; and exhorted " the Senate to remember that it was the family of the Medici " who had robbed them of Lombardy, when Cosimo, contrary to " the will of other citizens, had favored and assisted Francesco " Sforza. So that, if they were not moved by the justice of their " cause, the just hatred and desire for vengeance ought to make " them accede to their request."

20. The whole Senate was greatly moved by these last words,

and it was resolved that their captain, Bartolommeo Colione, should attack the Florentine dominions. The army was got together as soon as practicable (1467), and was joined by Ercole da Este, who had been sent by Borso, Marquis of Ferrara. The Florentines being still unprepared, the enemy in the first attack burnt the Borgo of Dovadole, and did some damage to the surrounding country. But after the expulsion of the party adverse to Piero, the Florentines had formed a new league with Galeazzo, Duke of Milan, and with Ferdinand, king of Naples, and had employed Frederick, Count of Urbino, as captain of their forces. So that, having now re-established their relations with their friends, they cared less for their enemies. Ferdinand sent his oldest son, Alfonso, and Galeazzo came in person, each with a suitable force. They all made head at Castrocaro, a castle belonging to the Florentines, and situated at the foot of the mountains that slope from Tuscany into the Romagna. The enemy meantime withdrew towards Imola. According to the custom of the times, a few slight skirmishes took place, but neither party fairly attacked the other, or laid siege to any place. Neither afforded the other an opportunity for coming to a general engagement, but both, remaining in their tents, acted with extraordinary cowardice. This conduct displeased the Florentines, who found themselves involved in a war that cost much and promised little. The magistrates complained of it to those citizens who had been deputed as commissaries for the conduct of the war. These replied that it was altogether the fault of the Duke Galeazzo, who, having great authority and but little experience, was incapable of devising measures of utility himself and unwilling to listen to those who were able; and that, so long as he remained with the army, it would be impossible to achieve any act of gallantry or movement of advantage. The Florentines, therefore, gave the Duke to understand that they esteemed it of great benefit and advantage to them that he had come personally to their aid; for such a reputation as his was of itself sufficient to alarm their enemies. Nevertheless, they considered his health and the safety of his state of more importance than their own convenience; for with the safety of the former they could hope that all else would prosper, but if that should suffer they would have reason to apprehend all sorts of calamities. They did not, therefore, deem it very safe for him to remain absent too long from Milan, being yet now in the government, and having powerful enemies that were not to be trusted, and who might easily take advantage of his absence to set some plot afoot against him. And therefore they advised him to return to his own state, and to leave a portion of his troops for the defence of theirs. Galeazzo was pleased at this proposition, and returned without further thought to Milan. The Florentine captains who remained in command, being now without any interference, and desirous of proving that they had assigned the true reason for their slow progress, now moved close up to the enemy, so as to bring on a regular engagement, which lasted half a day without either party yielding. Nor were any men killed; only a few horses were wounded and some prisoners taken on both sides. Winter having now set in, when it was customary for all armies to go into quarters, Messer Bartolommeo Colione retired towards Ravenna, the Florentine troops went into Tuscany, and the troops of the king of Naples and the Duke of Milan returned to their respective countries. But as after this attack upon the Florentine state no disturbances had broken out in the city, as had been promised by the Florentine rebels, and as the pay of the hired troops was in arrears, propositions were made for peace, which, after much negotiation, was concluded (1468). The Florentine rebels, therefore, being bereft of all hope, dispersed to various places. Messer Diotisalvi went to Ferrara, where he was received and supported by the Marquis Borso. Niccolo Soderini went to Ravenna, where he lived upon a small pension from the Venetians, and died at an old age. He was esteemed as a just and courageous man, but slow and doubting in his resolves, which caused him to lose the opportunity of victory as Gonfaloniere of Justice, which he strove in vain afterwards to recover as a private citizen.

21. After the conclusion of peace, those citizens who remained masters in Florence seemed to think their victory incomplete unless they overwhelmed, not only their enemies, but all who were suspect to their party, with every kind of injury. They induced Bardo Altoviti, who was Gonfaloniere of Justice at that time, anew to deprive many citizens of their offices, and to banish many others, which increased the power of their party and struck terror into the other. They exercised this power without any consideration, and altogether governed in such wise that it actually seemed as if God and

fortune had given the city up to them as a prey. Piero de' Medici knew little of these things, and could not even remedy that little, being borne down by his infirmities; for he was so drawn together that he was unable to use any of his faculties except that of speech; so that all he could do was to beg and exhort them to conduct themselves according to the laws, and to enjoy the safety of their country rather than its ruin. And by way of diverting the citizens of Florence he resolved to celebrate the nuptials of his son Lorenzo with Clarice d' Orsini, in a most sumptuous manner; and this was done with all the pomp and splendor becoming so great a citizen. Accordingly, many days were spent in a variety of festivities, balls, and representations from antiquity; and for the purpose of displaying still more the greatness of the house of Medici and that of the state, there were added two grand military spectacles, the one representing an open field battle by men on horseback, and the other a siege and the storming of a town; all of which were executed with the greatest order and skill.

22. Whilst these events were taking place in Florence, peace prevailed throughout the rest of Italy, though accompanied with much apprehension of the Turk, who in his wars upon the Christians had taken Negropont, greatly to the discredit and injury of the Christian name. At this time Borso, Marquis of Ferrara, died, and was succeeded by his brother Ercole. Gismondo da Rimini also died: he had been the persistent enemy of the Church, and left his state as a heritage to his son Ruberto, who afterwards became one of the ablest captains in the wars of Italy. Death also carried off Pope Paul; and his successor was Sixtus IV., who had previously borne the name of Francesco da Savona, a man of the lowest origin, but who by his talents had become General of the Order of St. Francis, and afterwards Cardinal. This pontiff was the first to show the extent of the papal powers, and how much of what were afterwards called errors could be concealed under the pontifical authority. Amongst his family were Piero and Girolamo, who were generally believed to be his sons, though he concealed the fact by calling them by names less compromising to his character. Piero, who was a brother of a religious order, was raised by him to the dignity of Cardinal, with the title of San Sisto. To Girolamo he gave the town of Furli, which he had taken from Antonio Ordelaffi,

whose ancestors had for a long time been princes of that state. This ambitious mode of proceeding made Sixtus the more influential with the princes of Italy, who all sought to gain his friendship. The Duke of Milan gave his natural daughter Catherine as wife to Girolamo, with the city of Imola for her dower, which he had taken from Taddeo degli Alidosi. Another alliance was contracted between this Duke and King Ferdinand of Naples, by the marriage of Elizabeth, daughter of Alfonso, the king's oldest son, with Giovan Galeazzo, oldest son of the Duke of Milan.

23. Italy meantime remained pretty tranquil, the chief care of her princes being to observe each other, and by marriages, fresh alliances, and other bonds to secure themselves against one another. Nevertheless during this general peace Florence was greatly afflicted by her own citizens, whose ambition Piero was unable to check, owing to his bodily infirmity. By way of relieving his conscience, however, and to see whether he could influence them by shame, he called all the leaders to his palace, and addressed them as follows: —

"I could not have believed that the time would ever come "when the conduct of my friends would have made me love "and wish for my enemies, and that victory might have been "defeat. For I thought that I was associated with men whose "cupidity had some measure or bounds, and that they would "have been satisfied with living securely and honored in their "country, after having been avenged upon most of their ene- "mies. But I see now how greatly I have deceived myself "for so long a time; and how little I understood the natural "ambition of men in general, and still less yours. For it "seems that you are not content with being the chiefs in so "great a city, and grasping for your small number all the "honors, dignities, and emoluments that were formerly shared "by many citizens. Nor does it suffice you to have distributed "amongst yourselves the possessions of your enemies, or to "load them with all the public burdens, whilst you are ex- "empt from them, and enjoy all the public benefits; but you "must also oppress them with every kind of injury. You "despoil your neighbors of their goods, you sell justice, disre- "garding yourselves all civil judgments; you oppress the peace- "ful and exalt the insolent; and I do not believe that there "are in all Italy so many examples of violence and avarice

"as are to be found in this city. Has our city then given us
"life for no other purpose but to destroy hers? Has she hon-
"ored us so that we may bring dishonor upon her? Has she
"made us victorious so that we may the more effectually work
"her ruin? I protest to you by all that should be most sacred
"amongst good men, that, if you continue to conduct yourselves
"in such a manner that I shall have occasion to regret our vic-
"tory, I will act in such a manner that you shall have occasion
"to repent having misused it."

Piero thereupon sent secretly for Messer Agnolo Acciaiuoli to come to Caffagiuolo, and there talked with him at length about the condition of the city; and there is no doubt that, had not death interposed, Piero would have recalled all the banished to Florence, so as to check the rapine of those within the city. But death prevented the execution of his best intentions; for, borne down with the infirmities of the body and anxiety of the mind, he died in the fifty-third year of his age. His goodness and virtues never could be entirely known to his country, having been almost to the end of his life under the direction of his father, Cosimo de' Medici; and the few years that he survived him were consumed almost wholly by civil contentions, and by his bodily infirmity. Piero was buried in the church of San Lorenzo, near his father, and his obsequies were conducted with all the pomp due to so illustrious a citizen. He left two sons, Lorenzo and Giuliano; and although they inspired every one with the hope of their becoming most useful to the republic, yet their youth caused general misgivings.

24. Amongst the first citizens in the government of Florence, and by far superior to all the others, was Messer Tommaso Soderini, whose sagacity and influence were known not only in Florence, but to almost all the princes of Italy. After the death of Piero de' Medici, Messer Tommaso was looked up to by the whole city, and many citizens called to pay their homage to him at his house, as though he were chief of the state, and many princes addressed him as such by letters. But he was prudent, and knew perfectly well his position and that of the Medici; he made no reply to the letters of the princes, and advised the citizens that they ought to call upon the Medici at their palace, and not upon him. And to show by deed what he had advised in words, he called together the heads of

the noble families in the convent of San Antonio, where he also caused Lorenzo and Giuliano de' Medici to come; and in a grave and lengthy address he spoke of the condition of Italy, of the character and disposition of her princes, and concluded by saying that, "if they wished to live in union and peace in "Florence, secure from internal dissensions and foreign wars, "they must look to these youths, and maintain the renown of "their house; for," said he, "men never complain of that to "which they are accustomed, and although prompt in adopt- "ing anything new, yet they tire of it very quickly. And it "has ever been easier to maintain a government which by "length of time has exhausted envy, than to set up a new "one, which, for a multitude of reasons, may easily be de- "stroyed."

After Messer Tommaso had concluded, Lorenzo arose to speak; and although he was still very young, yet he expressed himself with so much gravity and modesty that he inspired every one with the hope that he would be what indeed he afterwards became. And before the meeting separated, the citizens swore that they would be as fathers to these youths; and they in return pledged themselves to act as sons. Having come to this conclusion Lorenzo and Giuliano were honored as princes of the state, and they continued to act under the advice of Messer Tommaso Soderini.

25. Whilst complete tranquillity, both internal and external, thus prevailed in Florence, there being no war to disturb the general quiet, an unexpected trouble occurred, which was as it were the presage of future calamities. Amongst the families that were involved in the ruin of the party of Messer Luca Pitti was that of the Nardi; for Salvestro and his brothers, who were the chiefs of that family, were first exiled, and afterwards, in consequence of the war against Florence under Bartolommeo Colione, declared rebels. Amongst these was Bernardo, one of the brothers of Salvestro, a young man of ardent and coura- geous temper. Poverty made his exile unendurable to him; and seeing that, in consequence of the establishment of peace, there was no chance of his returning to Florence, he resolved to do something by which to provoke a fresh war. For small be- ginnings often produce great results, especially as men are ever more ready to follow in any movement set on foot by others than to originate one themselves. Bernardo had an extensive

acquaintance in Prato, and still more so in the district of Pistoja, and was particularly intimate with the Palandras, who, although tillers of the soil, yet counted amongst them many men who, like the Pistojans in general, were used to arms and bloodshed. Bernardo knew that they were malcontents, having been ill treated by the Florentine magistrates in some of their quarrels; he moreover knew the disposition of the men of Prato, and their general resentment against the government, which they deemed overbearing and grasping. All this encouraged him in the hope of being able to light a conflagration in Tuscany by making the men of Prato revolt, who would immediately have such large accessions that it would not be in the power of the government to extinguish it. He communicated his project to Messer Diotisalvi, and asked him, in case he should succeed in seizing Prato, what help he might obtain through his intervention from the other princes. Messer Diotisalvi considered the undertaking most perilous, and almost impossible of success. Seeing, however, that at the risk of others he might have another chance at fortune, he advised Bernardo to make the attempt, promising him most certain help from Bologna and Ferrara if he managed to hold Prato for at least two weeks. This promise filled Bernardo with the most sanguine hopes, and he went secretly to Prato (1470), and, on communicating his scheme to some of his friends, he found them most favorably disposed. He met the same readiness and disposition in the Palandras; and, after having agreed upon the time and manner of proceeding, he communicated the whole to Messer Diotisalvi.

26. Cesare Petrucci was at this time Podesta (or governor) of Prato for the people of Florence. It was the custom of the governors of this sort of places to keep the keys of the gates near them; and whenever, especially in periods of tranquillity, any one of the place asked for them, either to go out or to come in, they were readily given him. Bernardo, who knew this habit, presented himself about daybreak, with the Palandras and about a hundred armed men, at the gate leading to Pistoja; and his confederates within, who were cognizant of his movements, had also armed themselves. One of these asked the Podesta for the keys, pretending that one of the inhabitants wished to come in. The Podesta, who had not the least suspicion, sent one of his servants with the keys; and when he was

sufficiently far from the palace, they were taken from him by the conspirators, the gate was opened, and Bernardo with his followers admitted. Having been joined by his confederates, they divided into two bodies. The one led by Salvestro of Prato seized the citadel, and the other, under Bernardo, took the palace, and Cesare Petrucci, with all his family, were put under guard. They then raised the alarm, and went through the place shouting the cry of "Liberty." It was now daylight, and many of the people, hearing this cry, rushed to the Piazza, and, learning that the citadel was taken and the Podesta and his family prisoners, they were astounded and perplexed to know how this could have taken place. The eight citizens who held the supreme authority of the place assembled in their palace to confer as to what was to be done. Bernardo, having gone through the town with his men, and finding that the people did not follow him, upon learning that the Eight were assembled, went to them and explained that the object of his attempt was to liberate them and his country from servitude, pointing out to them how great would be the glory of those who took arms in favor of this cause, and who joined him in this glorious attempt, which would assure them perpetual peace and eternal fame. He reminded them of their ancient liberties and of their present condition, and assured them of certain assistance if they would only hold out for a few days against whatever forces the Florentines might get together. He averred that he had friends in Florence who would rise so soon as they should hear that this place had resolved to sustain his enterprise.

The Eight, however, were not moved by these words, and replied: "That they knew not whether the people of Flor-"ence were free or enslaved, being a matter that did not con-"cern them; but they knew that, as regarded themselves, they "wanted no further liberty than to obey the magistrates that "governed Florence, and at whose hands they had never re-"ceived any wrong that would warrant their taking up arms "against them. And therefore they advised him to restore the "Podesta to liberty, and to leave the place with his men, and "speedily to withdraw from the danger in which he had so "rashly placed himself." Bernardo, however, was not alarmed by these words, but resolved to see whether he could not influence the people of Prato by fear, since arguments had failed to do so. And by way of terrifying them, he resolved to put the Podesta Petruccio to death, and ordered him to be hung at the window of the palace. Cesare was already near the window, with a halter around his neck, and when he saw Bernardo, who was urging his death, he turned to him and said: "Bernardo, "you cause my being put to death, in the belief that the people "of Prato will afterwards follow you; but the result will be "just the contrary, for the reverence which the people of Prato "have for the rectors who were sent here by the people of "Florence is such that, when they shall see the wrong you have "done me, it will excite them to such hatred of you as will "assuredly cause your ruin. It is not my death, therefore, but "rather my life, that can contribute to your success; for were "I to command that which you desire, they would much more "readily obey me than you; and if they were to see me follow "your orders, you would quickly attain the end you have in "view."

Bernardo, who seemed at a loss what course to take, deemed this advice good, and therefore ordered Cesare to go upon the balcony that overlooked the Piazza, and to command the people to obey him. Having done this, Cesare was led back to prison.

27. The weakness of the conspirators was, however, soon discovered. A number of Florentines living in Prato came together, and amongst them Messer Giorgio Ginori, a Knight of Rhodes, who was the first to take up arms against Bernardo, who was running about the Piazza entreating the people to follow him, and threatening them if they refused. Being attacked by Messer Giorgio and his followers, Bernardo was wounded and taken prisoner. This done, it was an easy matter to liberate the Podesta, and to overpower the other conspirators, who, having divided into several small parties, were nearly all captured and put to death. Meantime the report of this affair reached Florence, and being greatly exaggerated, the people were told that Prato was taken and the Podesta with all his family killed, and the place filled with enemies; that Pistoja was in arms, and many of her citizens implicated in the conspiracy. The palace became quickly filled with citizens, who had come together for the purpose of conferring with the Signoria. Ruberto da San Severino, a captain of high repute, happening to be in Florence at that juncture, it was

resolved to send him to Prato with what troops they were able to collect. He was commissioned to approach the place and take particular notice of everything, and to adopt such measures as his prudence might suggest. Ruberto had but just passed the castle of Campi when he was met by a messenger from Cesare Petrucci, who informed him that Bernardo was prisoner and his followers dispersed and killed, and all troubles ended. He therefore returned to Florence, where Bernardo was brought soon after; and, when questioned by the magistrates as to the truth of the affair, which seemed to them most feeble, he said that he had made this attempt because he had resolved rather to die in Florence than to live in exile, and that he wanted his death to be marked by some noteworthy fact.

28. This disturbance having been crushed almost as soon as begun, the citizens returned to their accustomed mode of life, hoping to enjoy without further apprehensions that authority which they had established and confirmed for themselves. This gave rise to those evils in the city which are most apt to be generated in times of peace; for the young men became more dissolute than usual, and beyond measure extravagant in dress, carousings, and all other licentiousness; and being idle they spent their time in gaming, and with women, their chief study being to appear splendidly attired and to be esteemed shrewd and witty in speech, and he who could say the sharpest things to the others was esteemed the cleverest. These evil habits were carried still further through the example of the courtiers of the Duke of Milan, who came with his lady and all his court to Florence, in fulfilment of a vow (1471), and was received with all the pomp and magnificence suitable to so powerful a prince and an ally of the republic. Then was seen a thing which in our day had never yet been witnessed; for it being Lent, when the Church commands us to fast and eat no flesh, this court, regardless of the ordinances of the Church and of God, feasted daily upon meat. Many spectacles were gotten up in honor of the Duke, amongst them one in the church of San Spirito, where was represented the descent of the Holy Spirit upon the Apostles; and in consequence of the many lights on that occasion the entire church was burnt, which was regarded by many as a manifestation of the wrath of the Almighty in his indignation against us for our misconduct. And if the Duke of Milan found in Florence abun-

dance of courtly pleasures and extravagant customs, he left there many more than he found; so that the good citizens deemed it necessary to restrain and put bounds to them by sumptuary laws against extravagance in dress, feastings, and funerals.

29. In the midst of this general tranquillity an unexpected disturbance occurred in Tuscany. Some citizens of Volterra had discovered an alum mine in that territory; and knowing its value, and desiring to find parties who would contribute money for its development and could protect it with their authority, they applied to some Florentine citizens, and gave them an interest in the profits to be derived from it. This matter, as is frequently the case with new enterprises, was at first but lightly esteemed by the citizens of Volterra; but in time they recognized its value, and then, when too late, they wanted to recover the lost profits, which in the beginning they might easily have secured. They began to agitate the matter in their councils, claiming that it was not proper that a mine found upon public property should be worked for private profit. Thereupon they sent ambassadors to Florence (1472), and the matter was referred to certain citizens, who being either bribed by the parties, or because they judged it to be right, decided that it would be unjust on the part of the people of Volterra to deprive their citizens of the fruit of their labor and industry; and that the alum pits in question belonged of right to those individuals who had developed them, but that it would be proper that these should pay a certain yearly sum to the city of Volterra in acknowledgment of her sovereign rights. This decision, instead of diminishing, rather increased the excitement and ill feeling of the people of Volterra, causing much agitation in their councils, as well as throughout the whole city. The people demanded the restoration of what they considered had been taken from them, and the proprietors insisted upon keeping what in the first instance they had purchased, and the enjoyment of which had afterwards been confirmed to them by the decision of the Florentines. In the disputes resulting from this, a respectable citizen of Volterra, called "Il Pecorino," together with many others that had sided with him, were killed, and their houses sacked and burned. And it was with difficulty that the fury of the populace was restrained from putting the Florentine rectors to death.

30. After this first outrage the people of Volterra resolved before anything else to send ambassadors to Florence, who were to give the Signoria to understand that, if they would maintain the ancient privileges of Volterra, they would in return continue their ancient allegiance. The reply to be made to this was discussed at great length. Messer Tommaso Soderini advised "that the Volterrans should be received in "any way they were disposed to return; it seeming to him "most inopportune to light a conflagration so near them that "the flames of it would set their own house on fire; for he "feared the character of the Pope and the power of the king "of Naples, and had no confidence in the alliance of the Vene- "tians, nor in that of the Duke of Milan, not knowing how "much reliance could be placed upon the good faith of the "one or the valor of the other, and remembering the trite ad- "age, *that a lean peace is better than a fat victory.*" On the other hand, Lorenzo de' Medici, thinking the opportunity favorable for displaying the value of his counsel and prudence, and being mainly urged to it by those who were jealous of the authority of Messer Tommaso, maintained that the arrogance of the Volterrans ought to be punished by force of arms; and affirmed that, if they were not corrected in some exemplary manner, it would encourage others to act in a similar manner, regardless of all fear or respect for the Florentine authority. This course was resolved upon, and the answer given to the Volterrans was: "That they must not expect the continuation "of those privileges which they themselves had destroyed, and "that therefore they must submit to the decision of the Sig- "noria or expect war."

The ambassadors having returned with this answer, the Volterrans prepared for defence; they fortified their town, and called upon all the other Italian princes for assistance. But a few only paid any attention to their call, and none but the Siennese and the lord of Piombino gave them any hope of succor. The Florentines, on the other hand, deeming a prompt victory most important, assembled ten thousand infantry and two thousand horse, who under the command of Frederick, lord of Urbino, at once entered the Volterran territory and quickly occupied the whole of it. They then laid siege to the town, which, being situated upon a high and isolated eminence, could only be assailed from the side of the church of San Alessandro. The Volterrans had hired about a thousand soldiers for their defence, who, seeing the bold attack made by the Florentines, lost confidence in their own ability to resist, and were as slow in their defence as they were prompt in daily offending the inhabitants of Volterra by insults. The unfortunate citizens, being thus attacked by their enemies from without, and oppressed by their friends within, despaired of their safety and began to think of making terms. And seeing no better way, they placed themselves in the hands of the commissaries, who at once had the gates opened, and admitted the larger part of the Florentine troops, and then went to the palace where the priors were assembled and ordered them to return to their homes. On their way there one of the priors was in derision stripped by one of the soldiers; and so much more ready are men for evil than for good, that this beginning led to the destruction of the city, which was sacked and pillaged an entire day by the soldiers. Neither women nor sacred edifices were spared, and those who had so illy defended as well as those who assailed her alike despoiled the city of her substance. The news of this victory was received with great joy by the people of Florence; and as this undertaking had originated entirely with Lorenzo, his reputation quickly rose to the highest point. But when Messer Tommaso Soderini was taunted by one of his most intimate friends for the advice which he had given, saying to him, "What say you now since Volterra has been conquered?" Messer Tommaso replied, "To me the place seems rather lost "than won; for if you had received Volterra back by agree-"ment, that city would have proved a source of profit and of "security to you; but having to hold it by force, it will prove "a source of weakness and anxiety to you in time of trouble, "and of injury and expense in time of peace."

31. At this time the Pope, eager to keep the states of the Church to their allegiance, caused Spoleto to be sacked because her internal factions and dissensions had led her to revolt; afterwards he besieged Citta di Castello for having been guilty of a like contumacy. The lord of the latter place was Niccolo Vitelli, who, being on terms of intimate friendship with Lorenzo de' Medici, obtained assistance from him, which, though inadequate for Niccolo's defence, yet was quite sufficient to sow the first seeds of enmity between Sixtus IV. and

the Medici, which soon after produced the most unhappy fruits; and these would not even have been so long in showing themselves had it not been for the death of Fra Piero, Cardinal of San Sisto. For that cardinal had travelled through all Italy, and had visited Venice and Milan, on pretence of witnessing the marriage of Ercole, Marquis of Ferrara, and had sounded the minds of those princes to ascertain how they were disposed towards the Florentines. But upon his return to Rome he died, and not without suspicion of having been poisoned by the Venetians, who feared the power of Sixtus whenever he should choose to avail of the talents and services of Fra Piero. For although of low origin, yet so soon as he became cardinal Piero exhibited such pride and ambition that neither the cardinalate nor even the pontificate seemed sufficient for him; for he did not hesitate to give a feast in Rome that would have been deemed extraordinary even for a king, and for which he expended more than twenty thousand florins. Pope Sixtus IV. being thus by death deprived of this minister, pursued his designs more slowly. But as the Florentines, the Duke of Milan, and the Venetians had renewed their league (1474), and had left it open to the Pope and the king to join it also, Sixtus and the king of Naples also formed an alliance between themselves, leaving it open for the other princes also to become parties to it. And thus was Italy divided into two hostile factions; and every day circumstances occurred that engendered hatred between them, as was the case with regard to the island of Cyprus, which was coveted by the king of Naples, but was seized by the Venetians. This caused the bands of union between the Pope and the king to be drawn still closer together.

At this period Frederick, Prince of Urbino, was looked upon as the most distinguished captain of Italy, and had repeatedly commanded the Florentine forces in their wars. The Pope and the king of Naples, for the purpose of depriving the hostile league of this commander, resolved to win Frederick over to their side. The Pope advised and the king begged him to come and see him at Naples. Frederick complied, greatly to the surprise and displeasure of the Florentines, who believed that he would experience the same fate as Niccolo Piccinino; but the reverse of this happened, for Frederick returned from Rome and Naples laden with honors, and with the appointment as general of that league. Nor did the Pope and the king omit to sound the disposition of the lords of the Romagna and of Sienna for the purpose of securing their alliance, so as to be able by their help the more effectually to damage the Florentines. When the latter became aware of this, they prepared by all available means to provide against the ambitious designs of this league; and having lost Frederick of Urbino, they engaged Ruberto da Rimini as their commander. They renewed their league with Perugia, and formed an alliance with the lord of Faenza. The Pope and the king of Naples alleged as the cause of their enmity against the Florentines, that these wished to detach them from the Venetians, and then form an alliance with these themselves; for the Pope judged that the Church would not be able to maintain her influence, nor the Count Girolamo the states of the Romagna if the Florentines and Venetians were united. On the other hand the Florentines apprehended that the king and the Pope desired to embroil them with the Venetians, not for the sake of securing their alliance themselves, but to be able the more easily to injure the Florentines. Thus two years were passed in these mutual suspicions and jealousies before any actual outbreak took place; and the first that occurred was in Tuscany, though of but slight importance.

32. Braccio da Perugia, whom we have repeatedly mentioned as one of the most distinguished soldiers of Italy, had left two sons, Oddo and Carlo. The latter was still of very tender years at the time of his father's death, and the former had been killed by the people of the Val di Lamona, as we have elsewhere related. But when Carlo afterwards came to a suitable age for military service he was engaged by the Venetians as one of their Condottieri,—partly out of regard for the father's memory, and partly because of the hopes which they had conceived of the young man's abilities. About this time his engagement expired, and Carlo was unwilling to renew it without first trying whether his name and his father's reputation would not enable him to return to Perugia in some suitable capacity. The Venetians readily assented to this, for they knew from experience that every change generally contributed to the increase of their power. Carlo therefore went to Tuscany, and finding the affairs of Perugia complicated by their league with the Florentines, and being desirous that his movements should result in something memorable, he attacked the

Siennese (1476), alleging that they were indebted to him for services rendered by his father to their republic, which claims he wanted satisfied. His attack was so impetuous that he came near overturning their whole state. The citizens, seeing themselves assailed in this manner, and being always ready to credit everything bad to the Florentines, persuaded themselves that it had been done with their connivance, and made great complaints of them to the Pope and the king of Naples. They also sent ambassadors to Florence, who complained of the great wrong done to their city, and demonstrated ingeniously that without assistance Carlo would not have been able to inflict such injury upon them with such entire security to himself. The Florentines protested against this accusation, and declared themselves ready to do everything in their power to induce Carlo to desist from doing the Siennese further harm, and that the ambassadors might use any means they pleased to induce Carlo to discontinue his attack. Carlo complained of this, and pointed out to the Florentines that by failing to support him they had deprived themselves of an important acquisition and himself of great glory; for he promised to give them possession of the place in a short time, seeing the wretched cowardice of the people of Sienna and the insufficiency of their means of defence. Carlo therefore departed and returned to his former employment in the service of the Venetians, and the Siennese, although relieved from this serious danger through the mediation of the Florentines, yet remained full of indignation against them, considering themselves under no obligations to those who had rid them of an evil of which they had themselves been the original cause.

33. Whilst matters between the king of Naples and the Pope and in Tuscany were in the condition related above, an event occurred in Lombardy that was of the greatest importance, and was a presage of the greatest calamities. There was in Milan a certain Cola Montano, a man of great learning and ambition, who taught the Latin language to some of the youths of the first families there. Either from hatred of the evil habits and mode of life of the Duke Galeazzo Sforza, or from some other cause, Cola expressed in all his teachings his detestation of being obliged to live under such a prince; calling those happy to whom fortune had granted the privilege of having been born and living under a republic, and pointing out how all the most

celebrated men had been nurtured in republics, and not under
princes, inasmuch as the former cherish men of merit, whilst
despots try to crush them; for republics profit by the virtue of
others, whilst tyrants fear it. The young men whom he had
taken most into his intimacy were Giovanni Andrea Lampognano, Carlo Visconti, and Girolamo Olgiato. He often discussed with them the vile nature of the Duke Galeazzo, and the
misfortune of those who were subjected to his government, and
so won the hearts and confidence of these young men that he
made them take an oath that, when they should have attained
a suitable age, they would deliver their country from the mis-
rule of this tyrant. The youths, filled with this desire, which
grew with their years, were hastened to the execution of their
design by the habits and mode of life of the Duke, and by the
personal injuries which they had received at his hands. Galeazzo was licentious and cruel, and the frequent display of these
vices had made him most odious; for, not content with debauch-
ing noble ladies, he took pleasure in making it publicly known,
and the mere putting to death of men did not satisfy him unless
he could accompany it with some special cruelty. He was
charged even with the infamous crime of having caused the
death of his own mother; for seeming to feel in her presence
that he was not absolutely master, he bore himself towards her
in such manner that she resolved to withdraw to her estates
near Cremona, which she had received as her dower. But on
her way there she was seized with a sudden violent illness, and
died, which gave rise to the general belief that Galeazzo had
caused her death. The Duke had dishonored Carlo and Girolamo in the persons of their ladies, and had refused to concede
to Giovan Andrea the possession of the abbey of Miramondo,
which had been granted by the Pope to one of his near relatives.
These private injuries increased the determination of these
young men to revenge themselves, and to free their country
from so many ills. They thought that, whenever they should
succeed in killing the Duke, they would be supported, not only
by many of the nobles, but also by the entire people. Resolved
therefore to make the attempt, they had frequent meetings,
which however excited no attention, as their ancient intimacy
was well known. The killing of the Duke was the constant
subject of their discussions; and by way of training themselves
to the act, they practised striking each other in the breast and

sides with the sheaths of the poignards which they intended using in reality. They also talked over the time and place most suitable for success, and concluded that to attempt it in the castle would not be safe; to do it during the chase seemed uncertain and hazardous, and during the Duke's walks through the city difficult and impracticable. They determined, therefore, to kill him at some public show or festival, where they were sure he would come, and where, under various pretences, they might have their friends together. They concluded also, that, in case some of them should for some reason be detained at court, the others should nevertheless proceed to kill the Duke with their weapons and with the aid of some of his armed enemies.

34. The year 1476 was drawing to its close, and the feast of the nativity of Christ was approaching; and, as the Duke was in the habit of going on St. Stephen's day with great pomp to the church of that martyr, the conspirators thought that time and that place would be the best for the execution of their design. On the morning of St. Stephen's, therefore, they made some of their most faithful friends and servants arm themselves, pretending to be going to the aid of Giovan Andrea, who was about to bring water into his grounds by means of an aqueduct, which was being opposed by some of his jealous neighbors. Followed by these armed men, they went to the church, alleging that, before departing, they wanted to obtain the permission of the Duke. They had also caused, under various other pretexts, a number of their friends and fellow-conspirators to meet them at the church, hoping that when the deed was done all these would stand by them and support them in the further carrying out of their enterprise. For it was their intention, after having slain the Duke, to go with these armed followers to that part of the city where they believed it would be easiest to induce the people to rise, and to make them take up arms against the Duchess and the chiefs of the state, judging that the people would be the more ready to follow them on account of the scarcity of provisions, from which they were suffering at the time. For it was a part of their plan to give up to pillage the houses of Cecco Simonetta, Giovanni Botti, and Francesco Lucani, all chiefs of the government, and thereby to secure the support of the people and to restore liberty to them. Having agreed upon the time and place, and steeled their hearts to the

execution of their design, Giovan Andrea turned towards a statue of San Ambrosio, saying, "O patron of this our city, "thou knowest our intentions, and the object for which we are "ready to incur such great danger; favor our enterprise, and "show thereby that injustice is hateful to you." The Duke, on the other hand, before coming to the church, had many forebodings as to his approaching fate. For in the morning he put on a cuirass, as he was often in the habit of doing, and almost immediately took it off again, as though it inconvenienced him, or its appearance displeased him. He wanted to hear mass in the castle, but found that his chaplain had already gone with all the vestments to the church of St. Stephen. Then he wanted the Bishop of Como to celebrate mass instead; but this prelate alleged certain reasonable objections, so that the Duke was, as it were, forced to go to the church. But before doing so, he had his sons, Giovan Galeazzo and Ermes, brought to him, and embraced and kissed them many times, seeming scarcely able to tear himself away from them. But finally he resolved to go, and left the castle, placing himself between the ambassadors of Ferrara and Mantua, and went to the church. The conspirators meantime, by way of exciting less suspicion, as well as to escape from the cold, which was very intense, withdrew to a room belonging to the head priest of the church, who was a friend of theirs. Upon hearing that the Duke was coming, they entered the church, and Giovan Andrea and Girolamo took their position to the right of the church door, and Carlo to the left. Those who preceded the Duke had already come in, when Galeazzo entered, surrounded by a crowd of followers suitable to the ducal dignity on the occasion of so great a solemnity.

The first to move were Lampognano and Girolamo. On pretence of wishing to clear the way for the Duke, they approached him closely, and suddenly drawing their sharp daggers, which they had concealed in their sleeves, they attacked the Duke, Lampognano giving him two wounds, one in the stomach and the other in the throat; Girolamo also struck him in the throat and breast. Carlo Visconti, who had been placed nearer the door, and the Duke having passed ahead of him, could not strike him from the front, and therefore struck him two blows from behind, one piercing the spine and the other the shoulder. These wounds were inflicted upon the Duke so suddenly and quickly that the Duke was down upon the ground before any one was aware of the fact; nor could he do or say anything, except in falling to call once upon Our Good Lady for help. When the Duke was seen stretched upon the ground, a great tumult took place, and many swords were drawn; and, as generally happens on such unforeseen occasions, some fled from the church, and some rushed to the scene of the tumult, without any distinct knowledge as to the cause of it. But those who were near the Duke, and had seen him struck, and had recognized the assassins, pursued them. And of the conspirators, Giovan Andrea, in attempting to escape from the church, got amongst the women, who were there in great numbers, and, as usual, seated upon the ground, so that, becoming entangled in their dresses, he was overtaken by a negro, one of the Duke's grooms, and killed. Carlo was also killed by the bystanders; but Girolamo Olgiato, having got out from amongst the people and the priests, and seeing his associates slain, and not knowing whither to fly, went home to his house, where, however, neither his father nor his brothers would receive him; but his mother, having compassion upon her son, recommended him to a priest, an old friend of their family, who, having disguised Girolamo in his own garments, took him to his own house, where he remained two days, not without hope that some disturbance would take place in Milan that would afford him a chance for escape. But deceived in this hope, and fearing to be discovered in his place of concealment, he attempted to fly in disguise; but being recognized, he fell into the hands of justice, and then confessed the whole organization of the conspiracy. Girolamo was but twenty-three years old, and displayed no less courage in death than he had done by his conduct in this enterprise; for when stripped and standing before the executioner, who, with sword in hand, was ready to strike him, he said the following words in Latin, in which language he was well versed: "*Mors acerba,* "*fama perpetua, stabit vetus memoria facti,*"—"Death is bit- " ter, but fame eternal, and the memory of this exploit will live " forever." The attempt of these unhappy young men was planned with secrecy and executed with great intrepidity; they failed only because those upon whom they relied to aid and defend them did neither the one nor the other. Let this example, therefore, teach princes so to live and so to make themselves respected and beloved that no one may hope for success in any attempt to assassinate them; and let conspirators remember that it is a vain hope to expect the people, however discontented, to follow them or share their dangers.

This event startled all Italy; but those which occurred soon after in Florence caused even greater consternation, for they broke that peace which had endured for twelve years, as we shall show in the following Book, which will have as sad and tearful a conclusion as its beginning will be bloody and horrible.

EIGHTH BOOK.

SUMMARY.

1. Government of the family of the Medici in Florence. — 2. Differences between the family of the Pazzi and that of the Medici. — 3. Conspiracy of the Pazzi, in which Pope Sixtus IV. and the king of Naples are implicated. — 4. Continuation of the same. — 5. Organization of the conspiracy. 6. Execution of the plot. Giuliano de' Medici is killed; Lorenzo saves himself. — 7. The Archbishop Salviati, whilst attempting to make himself master of the palace, is taken and hung. — 8. Fate of the other conspirators. — 9. The dangers to which Lorenzo has been exposed increase the love of the Florentines for him and his power. Punishment of the conspirators. — 10. The Pope excommunicates Florence, and together with the king of Naples makes war upon the republic. Lorenzo speaks to the citizens assembled in the palace. — 11. The Florentines appeal to the future council; and seek the alliance of the Venetians. — 12. The Venetians decline the alliance. Beginning of the war. — 13. Turbulence in Milan. Genoa rebels against the Duke. — 14. The peace negotiations proving unsuccessful, the Florentines attack the forces of the Pope and of the Neapolitans, and drive them back into the Pisan territory. — 15. They invade the territory of the Church, and rout the Papal forces at Perugia (1479). — 16. Victory of the Duke of Calabria over the Florentines at Poggibonzi. — 17. Lorenzo de' Medici resolves upon going to Naples to negotiate a peace with the king. — 18. Lodovico Sforza, called "The Moor," and his brothers, are recalled to Milan. Consequent changes in the government of that state. — 19. Lorenzo de' Medici concludes a peace with the king of Naples, which, however, is not consented to by the Pope and the Venetians. — 20. The Turks attack and take Otranto (1480). — 21. Reconciliation of the Florentines with the Pope. — 22. New method of war in Italy. Discord between the Marquis of Ferrara and the Venetians (1481). — 23. The king of Naples and the Florentines attack the states of the Pope unsuccessfully. — 24. The king of Naples, the Duke of Milan, and the Florentines unite against the Venetians (1482). — 25. Rout of the Venetians at Bondeno (1483). — 26. The league is dissolved (1484). — 27. Discords between the Colonnesi and the Orsini. — 28. Death of Pope Sixtus IV. Election of Innocent VIII. — 29. Origin and state of the Bank of San Giorgio. — 30. War between the Florentines and the Genoese, on account of Serezana. — 31. Capture of Pietrasanta. — 32. War between the Pope and the king of Naples, for the possession of the city of Aquila (1485); terminated by peace (1486). — 33. The Pope, having become

friendly to the Florentines, notwithstanding their having aided the king of Naples in the last war, becomes mediator between them and the Genoese, but is unsuccessful. The Genoese are defeated by the Florentines; they lose Serezana, and give themselves to the Duke of Milan (1487). — 34. Boccolino da Osimo gives the city back to the Pope. Girolamo Riario, lord of Furli, is killed by a conspiracy (1488). — 35. Galeotto Manfredi is killed by the treachery of his wife; she is captured by the people of Faenza, and the government of the city is committed to the charge of the Florentines (1492). — 36. Death of Lorenzo de' Medici. His eulogy.

1. THE beginning of this Eighth Book being between two conspiracies, the one already related and having occurred at Milan, and the other to be narrated and occurring at Florence, it would seem to be proper and in accordance with our usual habit to discuss the nature and importance of conspiracies. This we should gladly have done if the matter could be briefly disposed of, and we had not already treated the subject at length in another place. But having done so, we will now leave it and pass to another, and will relate how, the government of the Medici having overcome all its openly declared enemies, and aiming to obtain undivided authority in the city and to hold a position entirely apart from all the others in the republic, it became necessary that it should also subdue its secret enemies. For whilst the Medici contended with some other families of equal authority and influence, those citizens who were jealous of their power could openly oppose them without fear of being crushed at the very outset of their opposition; for the magistrates having become free, neither of the parties had cause for apprehension. But after the victory of 1466 the whole government became as it were concentrated in the hands of the Medici, who acquired so much authority that those who were dissatisfied with it concluded that they must either submit patiently, or resort to a conspiracy if they wished to put an end to that state of things. But conspiracies rarely succeed, and very often cause the ruin of those who set them on foot, whilst those against whom they were aimed are only the more aggrandized thereby. So that a sovereign who is assailed by such means, if he is not killed, as was Galeazzo, Duke of Milan, (which rarely happens, however,) rises to greater power, and very often becomes bad after having originally been good. For such attempts inspire a prince with fear, and fear brings with it the necessity of se-

curing himself, and this causes violence and wrong to others, whence hatreds are engendered, which in turn often lead to the ruin of the prince. And thus these conspiracies quickly cause the ruin of those who originate them, and in the course of time prove most injurious to those against whom they were directed.

2. (1478.) Italy was divided at this time by two leagues, as we have shown above; the Pope and the king of Naples on the one side, and the Venetians, the Duke of Milan, and the Florentines on the other; and although they had not yet come to actual war, yet every day fresh causes occurred for its breaking out. Above all, the Supreme Pontiff sought on all occasions to injure the Florentines. Thus upon the death of Messer Filippo de' Medici, Archbishop of Pisa, the Pope, in opposition to the wishes of the Signoria of Florence, invested Francesco Salviati, a declared enemy of the Medici, with the archbishopric. And as the Signoria were not willing to give him possession of it, further difficulties resulted. Moreover, the Pope did everything in Rome to favor the family of the Pazzi, and took every occasion to show disfavor to the Medici. The family of the Pazzi were at that time one of the most distinguished in Florence, both by their wealth and nobility. The head of the family was Messer Jacopo, whom the people had created a noble on account of his birth and wealth. He had no children except one illegitimate son; but he had a number of nephews, the sons of his brothers, Messers Piero and Antonio; the sons of the first were Guglielmo, Francesco, Rinato, and Giovanni, and those of the other were Andrea, Niccolo, and Galeotto. Cosimo de' Medici, in view of the opulence and rank of the Pazzi, had given his niece Bianca in marriage to Guglielmo, hoping by this alliance to unite the two families more closely, and to put an end to the hatreds and enmities that were constantly arising from their mutual suspicions. But so uncertain and fallacious are all human calculations, that it turned out just the reverse; for some of Lorenzo's counsellors pointed out to him that it would be most hazardous and adverse to his authority to unite so much wealth and power in the hands of any one citizen; and for this reason Messer Jacopo and his nephews did not obtain those places and dignities, which in the estimation of other citizens they seemed to merit. This was the first thing to excite the anger

of the Pazzi and the apprehensions of the Medici,—and as the one increased, the other grew likewise; whence the Pazzi, on every occasion when they came in competition with other citizens, were not favorably regarded by the magistrates. Francesco dei Pazzi being at Rome, the Council of the Eight, forgetful of that respect which it was customary to observe towards distinguished citizens, compelled him for some slight reason to return to Florence; so that the Pazzi complained of it everywhere in offensive and disdainful language, which only increased the suspicions of the others, and served to bring more injuries upon themselves. Giovanni dei Pazzi had married the daughter of Giovanni Borromei, an exceedingly rich man, and whose entire wealth had descended on his death to his daughter, who was his only child. But his nephew Carlo held possession of some of his property, and, the matter having come to litigation, a law was passed, by virtue of which the wife of Giovanni dei Pazzi was despoiled of her paternal inheritance, which was conceded to Carlo; this wrong the Pazzi ascribed altogether to the influence of the Medici. Giuliano de' Medici often remonstrated on this subject with his brother Lorenzo, saying that he feared that by attempting to grasp too much they would lose all.

3. But Lorenzo in the heat of youth and power wanted to direct everything himself, and wanted to have every one recognize his authority. The Pazzi, on the other hand, proud of their rank and wealth, could not bear to submit to all these wrongs, and began to think of revenge. The first to propose anything definite against the Medici was Francesco, who was more sensitive and high-spirited than the others; so that he resolved either to recover what he had lost, or to lose what he possessed. And as the government of Florence was odious to him, he lived almost entirely at Rome, where, according to the custom of Florentine merchants, he carried on large financial operations. And being intimately allied with the Count Girolamo, they often complained to each other of the Medici, and came to the conclusion that, if they wished to live secure, the one in the enjoyment of his estates, and the other in his city, it would be necessary to change the government of Florence; which they thought however could not be done without the death of Giuliano and Lorenzo. They judged that the Pope and the king would readily agree to this, provided they could

convince them of the facility with which this could be effected. Having once taken up this idea, they communicated the whole matter to Francesco Salviati, Archbishop of Pisa, who being an ambitious man, and still smarting under a recent injury received at the hands of the Medici, readily concurred with them. And after examining as to the best course to be adopted, they resolved, as the best means of insuring success, to draw Messer Jacopo dei Pazzi into their plans, believing that without his co-operation they could effect nothing. For this purpose it was deemed best that Francesco dei Pazzi should go to Florence, and that the Archbishop and the Count Girolamo should remain in Rome near the Pope, so as to be able to communicate the matter to him at the proper time. Francesco found Messer Jacopo more cautious and difficult than he had anticipated; and having so informed his friends at Rome, it was thought necessary to influence him through higher authority. Thereupon the Archbishop and the Count Girolamo communicated the whole matter to Giovan Battista da Montesecco, the Pope's Condottiere, who had a high reputation as a soldier, and was under obligations both to the Pope and the Count. But he pointed out to them the difficulties and dangers of the undertaking, which the Archbishop endeavored to explain away, pointing out in turn the important aid which the Pope and the king of Naples would lend to the enterprise; and, above all, the hatred which the citizens of Florence bore to the Medici, the numerous relatives that would follow the Salviati and the Pazzi, and the facility with which Giuliano and Lorenzo could be killed, they being in the habit of walking through the city unaccompanied and unsuspecting; as also the ease with which the government could be changed after their death. Battista did not entirely believe all this, having heard many of the Florentines speak very differently.

4. Whilst the conspirators were occupied with these projects and discussions, Carlo, lord of Faenza, fell sick, so that his speedy death was apprehended. The Archbishop and the Count Girolamo thought this a suitable occasion for sending Giovan Battista to Florence, and thence into the Romagna, on pretence of recovering certain lands of his of which the lord of Faenza had held possession. The Count therefore commissioned Giovan Battista to seek an interview with Lorenzo, and in his name to solicit his advice as to how best to proceed in

this affair of the Romagna; and to confer with Francesco dei Pazzi and then unitedly to endeavor to persuade Messer Jacopo to come into their views. And to enable Giovan Battista to bring to bear upon Messer Jacopo the authority of the Pope, they caused him, before his departure, to have an interview with the pontiff, who promised to give them all the assistance in his power for their undertaking. Giovan Battista, having arrived at Florence, called upon Lorenzo, who received him most graciously, and advised him most kindly and judiciously in relation to the points he had submitted to him. Giovan Battista was filled with admiration for Lorenzo, having found him to all appearances quite a different man from what had been represented to him; and he judged him to be gentle and wise, and most amicably disposed towards the Count. Nevertheless he wanted to confer with Francesco; but not finding him, as he was absent at Lucca, he had an interview with Messer Jacopo, who was at first quite indisposed to entertain the affair; but before he left him he was somewhat moved by the authority of the Pope, in consequence of which he requested Giovan Battista to go on his trip to the Romagna and return, and said that meantime Francesco would be back in Florence, and they could then discuss the matter more fully. Giovan Battista accordingly went and returned, and after the pretended consultation with Lorenzo about the affairs of the Count, he met Messer Jacopo and Francesco dei Pazzi and succeeded in inducing Messer Jacopo to consent to the enterprise. Thereupon they discussed the mode of proceeding. Messer Jacopo did not think it practicable whilst the two brothers Medici were in Florence, and therefore suggested that they should wait until Lorenzo should go to Rome, as it was generally reported he intended doing; and that then the plot might be carried out. Francesco was pleased at the idea of Lorenzo's going to Rome, but maintained that, even if he did not go there, both brothers might be killed either at some wedding or play, or in church. And as to foreign aid, he thought that the Pope might get troops enough together under pretence of an attempt upon the castle of Montone, there being good reason for taking it from the Count Carlo, on account of the disturbances which he had created in the territory of Sienna and Perugia, which we have related above.

They came, however, to no further conclusion than that Francesco dei Pazzi and Giovan Battista should go to Rome and there arrange everything with the Count and the Pope. The subject was discussed anew in Rome, and finally it was concluded that, the attempt upon Montone being determined upon, Giovan Francesco da Tolentino, one of the Pope's captains, should go into the Romagna, and Messer Lorenzo da Castello into his own country, and that both should hold themselves in readiness, with their own companies and the troops of their respective countries, to act according to the orders of the Archbishop Salviati and Francesco dei Pazzi; that these should come to Florence together with Giovan Battista da Montesecco, and there provide everything necessary for the execution of the plot, for which King Ferdinand, through his ambassador, had promised all needed assistance. When the Archbishop and Francesco dei Pazzi had come to Florence they drew Jacopo, son of Messer Poggio, into their plot, a learned but ambitious youth, and ever eager for novelty. They also drew in the two Jacopo Salviatis, the one a brother and the other a relative of the Archbishop. They furthermore brought in Bernardo Bandini and Napoleone Franzesi, ardent youths, and greatly attached to the family of the Pazzi. Amongst the foreigners who joined besides the above named were Messer Antonio da Volterra, and one Stefano, a priest, who taught Latin to the daughter of Messer Jacopo dei Pazzi. Rinato dei Pazzi, a grave and prudent man, and who well knew all the ills that flow from similar enterprises, did not join in the conspiracy, but rather expressed his detestation of it, and did all that he honestly could do to break it up.

5. The Pope had sent Rafaelle di Riario, a nephew of the Count Girolamo, to the University of Pisa for the purpose of studying the ecclesiastical laws, and whilst still there the Pope promoted him to the dignity of Cardinal. The conspirators deemed it advisable to bring this Cardinal to Florence, so that they might avail of his presence to conceal amongst his retinue such associates as they might need, and who might thus take part in the execution of the plot. The Cardinal came, and was received by Messer Jacopo dei Pazzi at his villa of Montughi, near Florence. The conspirators intended also, by his means, to bring Lorenzo and Giuliano to the same place at the same time, so that they might on that occasion put them both to death. They managed therefore to have the Cardinal invited by them to a banquet at their villa at Fiesole. Giuliano, how-

ever, either from chance or purposely, did not attend this banquet. Having been disappointed in this plan, the conspirators thought that, if they were to invite the Medici to a banquet in Florence, both brothers would surely come. This being agreed upon, Lorenzo and Giuliano were invited for Sunday, April 26, 1478; and the conspirators, confident of being able to kill them in the midst of this feast, convened on Saturday night, and made all necessary dispositions for the execution of their design on the following day. But when Sunday came, Francesco was notified that Giuliano would not appear at the banquet. The chiefs of the conspiracy therefore met again, and concluded that it would not do to postpone the execution any longer; as it would be impossible to avoid discovery, the plot being known to so many. They therefore resolved to kill them in the cathedral church of Santa Reparata, where the two brothers would come according to their custom, especially as the Cardinal was to be there. They wanted Giovan Battista to undertake the killing of Lorenzo, and Francesco dei Pazzi and Bernardo Bandini were to despatch Giuliano. But Giovan Battista refused, either because his feelings towards Lorenzo had become mollified by the intercourse he had had with him, or for some other reason. He said that he would never have audacity enough to commit so great an outrage in church, and thus add sacrilege to treason. This was the beginning of the ruin of their plot. For time pressing, they were obliged to intrust the killing of Lorenzo to Messer Antonio da Volterra and the priest Stefano, who were both by nature and habit entirely unfit for so great an undertaking; for if any act requires boldness and intrepidity, and that resoluteness in life and disregard of death which only great experience can give, it is such an occasion, where it has often been seen that even men experienced in arms and accustomed to blood have had their courage fail them. But having finally decided upon this course, they agreed that the signal for action should be when the priest, who celebrated the principal mass, should take the communion; and in the mean time the Archbishop Salviati with Jacopo di Messer Poggio and their followers should seize the public palace, so that the Signoria either voluntarily or by force would have to act with them after the death of the two young Medici.

6. This arrangement having been determined upon, they went into the church, where the Cardinal had already arrived

with Lorenzo de' Medici. The church was crowded with people, and divine service had already commenced, but Giuliano had not yet come. Francesco dei Pazzi, therefore, together with Bernardo, who had been designated to kill Giuliano, went to his house, and by artful persuasion induced him to go to the church. It is really a noteworthy fact that so much hatred and the thoughts of so great an outrage could be concealed under so much resoluteness of heart, as was the case with Francesco and Bernardo; for on the way to church, and even after having entered it, they entertained him with jests and youthful pleasantries. And Francesco even, under pretence of caressing him, felt him with his hands and pressed him in his arms for the purpose of ascertaining whether he wore a cuirass or any other means of protection under his garments. Both Giuliano and Lorenzo de' Medici knew the bitter feelings of the Pazzi towards them, and their anxiety to deprive them of the government of the state; but they had no apprehensions for their lives, believing that, if the Pazzi were to attempt anything, it would be by civil proceedings and not by violence; and therefore, not being apprehensive of their personal safety, they simulated a friendly feeling for them.

The murderers thus prepared placed themselves, some close by the side of Lorenzo, which the great crowd in the church enabled them to do easily without exciting suspicion, and the others near to Giuliano. At the appointed moment Bernardo Bandini struck Giuliano in the breast with a short dagger which he had prepared for the purpose. After a few steps Giuliano fell to the ground, and Francesco dei Pazzi threw himself upon him covering him with wounds, and was so maddened by the fury with which he assailed Giuliano that he inflicted a severe wound upon himself in one of his legs. Messer Antonio and Stefano, on the other hand, attacked Lorenzo, but after many blows succeeded only in wounding him slightly in the throat; for either their irresolution, or the courage of Lorenzo, who on finding himself assailed defended himself with his weapon, or the interference of bystanders, defeated all their efforts to kill him, so that becoming alarmed they fled and concealed themselves, but being found were ignominiously put to death, and their bodies dragged through the whole city. Lorenzo, on the other hand, together with the friends he had around him, shut himself up in the sacristy of the church.

Bernardo Bandini, seeing Giuliano dead, also killed Francesco Nori, a devoted friend of the Medici, either because of some old hatred, or because Francesco attempted to assist Giuliano. And not content with these two murders, he rushed to seek Lorenzo, so as to make good by his courage and swiftness what the others by their cowardice and tardiness had failed to do; but Lorenzo being shut up in the sacristy, Bernardo could not carry out his intention. In the midst of these violent and tumultuous scenes, which were so terrible that it seemed as though the church itself were falling, the Cardinal took refuge by the altar, where he was with difficulty saved by two priests, until the alarm had somewhat abated, when the Signoria were enabled to conduct him to his palace, where he remained in greatest apprehension until his liberation.

7. There happened at this time in Florence certain citizens of Perugia, whom the violence of faction had driven from their homes; these the Pazzi had drawn into their plot by promises of restoring them to their country. The Archbishop Salviati, who went to seize the palace together with Jacopo di Messer Poggio and his relatives and friends, took these Perugians with him; and having arrived at the palace he left a portion of his followers below, with orders that, upon the first noise they heard, they were at once to occupy the entrance of the palace, whilst he himself with the larger number of the Perugians rushed upstairs, where he found the Signoria at dinner, for it was already late; but after a short time he was admitted by the Gonfaloniere of Justice, Cesare Petrucci. He entered with a few of his followers, leaving the rest outside; the greater portion of these shut themselves up in the chancelry, the door of which was so arranged that, once closed, it could neither be opened from the inside nor the outside without the key. The Archbishop meantime, having entered the hall together with the Gonfaloniere on pretence of having something to communicate to him on behalf of the Pope, addressed him in an incoherent and suspicious manner, so that his language and change of countenance excited such suspicion in the Gonfaloniere that he rushed out shouting, and, meeting Jacopo di Messer Poggio, he seized him by the hair and gave him in charge of two sergeants. The Signoria, having taken the alarm, quickly seized such arms as chance supplied them, and all those who had come upstairs with the Archbishop,

most of whom were shut up in the chancelry and the rest terror-stricken, were either slain or thrown alive out of the palace windows, between which the Archbishop, the two Jacopo Salviatis, and Jacopo di Messer Poggio were hanged. Those who remained below had forced the guard and the gate, and occupied the entire lower floor of the palace; so that the citizens, who upon hearing the alarm had rushed to the palace, could neither give aid nor counsel to the Signoria.

8. Meantime Francesco dei Pazzi and Bernardo Bandini, seeing that Lorenzo had escaped and that the one of them on whom the success of the conspiracy mainly depended was seriously wounded, became alarmed. Bernardo, with the same promptness and courage in behalf of his own safety that he had displayed against his enemies, the Medici, saved himself by flight. Francesco, having returned to his own house, tried to mount on horseback, for it was arranged that they should ride through the city and call the people to arms and liberty; but the wound in his leg and the consequent great loss of blood prevented him. He therefore undressed, and throwing himself naked upon his bed, he begged Messer Jacopo to do what he himself could not. Messer Jacopo, though old and unaccustomed to scenes of violence, yet, by way of a last effort to save their fortunes, mounted a horse, and, followed by about one hundred armed men gathered for this purpose, went to the Piazza, calling for help on behalf of the people and of liberty. But the one having been made deaf by the wealth and liberality of the Medici, and the other being unknown in Florence, his calls remained unheeded by any one. The Signori, on the other hand, who were masters of the upper part of the palace, greeted him with stones and menaces. Whilst hesitating, Messer Jacopo was met by his brother-in-law, Giovanni Serristori, who reproved him for the riot they had occasioned and advised him to return home, as the other citizens had the people's welfare and liberty as much at heart as he. Messer Jacopo, bereft of all hope therefore, and seeing the palace in the hands of the enemy, Lorenzo safe, and the people not disposed to follow him, and being at a loss what else to do, resolved if possible to save his life by flight, and with such followers as were with him in the Piazza he left Florence to go into the Romagna.

9. Meantime the whole city was in arms, and Lorenzo de'

Medici accompanied by many armed men had returned to his house. The palace was recovered by the people, and those who had seized it were all captured and put to death, and the name of the Medici was shouted throughout the whole city; whilst the heads and limbs of the conspirators were paraded on pikes or dragged through the streets, and the Pazzi were pursued by everybody with violent abuse and acts of cruelty. Their houses were already in the possession of the populace, and Francesco was dragged naked from his bed and led to the palace, and there hung by the side of the Archbishop and the others. But it was impossible either on the way there or afterwards to induce Francesco by any degree of maltreatment to say one word of what had been said or done by the conspirators; and fixedly looking in another direction he sighed in silence without one word of complaint. Guglielmo dei Pazzi, brother-in-law of Lorenzo, was saved in Lorenzo's house, both on account of his innocence and through the influence of his wife Bianca. Every citizen, armed or not, called at Lorenzo's house on this occasion to offer him his personal service or his substance; such was the power and public favor which the house of Medici had acquired by their prudence and liberality. Rinato dei Pazzi was living in retirement at his villa when these disturbances occurred. When he heard of the affair, he attempted to fly in disguise, but was recognized on the road and captured and carried to Florence; and although he repeatedly entreated his captors to kill him on the road, yet he could not prevail upon them to do it. Messers Jacopo and Rinato were condemned to death, and executed four days after the attempt upon the Medici. Amongst the many persons that were killed during those days, and whose limbs encumbered the highways, Messer Rinato was the only one that excited commiseration; for he had ever been regarded as a wise and good man, and was known to be free from that pride of which the other members of the Pazzi family were accused. And so that these events might not fail to serve as an extraordinary example, Messer Jacopo, who at first was buried in the tomb of his ancestors, was removed thence, like an excommunicated person, and interred outside of the city walls. And even from there his body was taken and dragged naked through the entire city with the very rope with which he had been hanged; and then, as though unfit to be buried in the earth, the same persons who had dragged the body through the streets of Florence, cast it into the waters of the river Arno, which were at that moment unusually high. A truly memorable instance of the instability of fortune, for a man to fall from such a position of wealth and prosperity, to such a depth of misfortune, ruin, and disgrace. Messer Jacopo dei Pazzi was said to have had some vices, amongst others gaming and swearing, which were compensated for, however, by his many charities, for he gave most liberally to the churches and the poor. It may also be said in his favor, that, on the Saturday preceding the Sunday that was devoted to so many murders, he discharged all his debts, so as to save others from being involved in his misfortunes; and returned with the most scrupulous care to the real owners all the goods which he had in his own and in the public warehouse belonging to others. Giovan Battista da Montesecco was beheaded after a lengthy examination; Napoleone Franzesi escaped by flight from the punishment of death; Guglielmo dei Pazzi was exiled; and such of his cousins as remained alive were imprisoned in the lowest dungeons of the castle of Volterra. All these disturbances being thus ended and the conspirators punished, the obsequies of Giuliano de' Medici were celebrated with general lamentations; for he had possessed as much liberality and humanity as could be desired in any one born to such high fortune. He left a natural son, born a few months after his death, who was named Giulio, and who had all the virtues and good fortune now known to the whole world,* and of whom we shall speak more fully when we come to the affairs of the present day if God spares our life. The troops that had been collected under Giovan Francesco da Tolentino in the Romagna, and under Messer Lorenzo da Castello in the Val di Tevere, and who were already on the march to Florence to support the conspirators, returned home when they heard of the disastrous failure of the enterprise.

10. As the hoped for changes in the government of Florence did not take place, the Pope and the king of Naples resolved to bring about by war what the conspiracy had failed to effect. Both gathered their armies with all possible speed for the purpose of attacking the government of Florence, publishing to the world at the same time that all they wanted of the city of

* This Giulio de' Medici afterwards became Pope under the name of Clement VII.

Florence was that they should remove Lorenzo de' Medici from it, he being the only one of all their citizens whom they regarded as an enemy. The king's troops had already passed the Tronto, and those of the Pope were at Perugia, when the latter, by way of making the Florentines feel his spiritual as well as his temporal power, excommunicated and anathematized them. The Florentines, seeing such large forces moving against them, made the utmost exertions to prepare for their defence. As it was generally reported that this war was particularly aimed at Lorenzo, he resolved before anything else to assemble the Signori in the palace, and with them all the most distinguished citizens, to the number of three hundred, whom he addressed in the following words: "I know not, most excellent Signori, and "you, illustrious citizens, whether to lament with you at the "events that have taken place, or whether to rejoice at them. "Certainly, when I think of the deep deception and bitter "hatred with which I was assailed and my brother murdered, I "cannot but feel overwhelmed with sadness, and lament them "with all my heart and soul. But on the other hand, when I "consider with what promptitude, zeal, and love, and with what "universal accord, my brother was avenged and myself de-"fended, then I not only feel that I have cause for rejoicing, "but actually have an inward feeling of exaltation and glory. "For truly, if experience has shown that I have more enemies "in the city than I had supposed, it has also proved to me that "I have more ardent and devoted friends than I had ever be-"lieved. I am forced, then, to lament with you on account of "the wrongs done to others; but at the same time I must re-"joice because of your kindness to me. But in proportion as "these wrongs were unusual and unprecedented, and the less "they were deserved by us, the more am I constrained to grieve "at them. For consider, O illustrious citizens, to what a de-"gree of ill fortune our house has been brought, that we could "not be secure in the midst of friends and relatives, and not "even in the church itself. Those who have occasion to fear "for their lives generally look to their friends and relatives for "aid; but we found ours armed for our destruction. The "churches usually are a place of refuge for those who are per-"secuted for private purposes or for reasons of state; but "where others look for friendly aid, there we found assassins; "and where parricides and murderers find an asylum, there

"the Medici found their death! But God, who had never be-
"fore abandoned our house, has even now saved us, and has
"taken the defence of our just cause into his own hands.
"What injury have we done to any one to provoke such a de-
"sire for revenge? Truly those who have shown themselves
"such violent enemies of ours had never received any private
"wrongs at our hands; for had we been disposed to injure
"them, they would never have had the opportunity of injuring
"us. If they attribute to us any public wrongs they may
"have suffered, and of which I know nothing, they insult you
"more than us, and this palace and the majesty of this gov-
"ernment more than our house. For it would go to show that
"you have undeservedly wronged your own citizens on our
"account, which is very far from the truth; for you would no
"more have done it than we would have asked it. And who-
"ever will honestly seek for the truth of the matter will find
"that the advancement of our family has ever been by general
"consent, and for no other reason than because we have striven
"to oblige every one with kindness and liberality and with bene-
"fits. If, then, we have treated strangers thus, how can it be
"supposed that we would outrage our own relatives? If they
"were influenced by the desire for dominion, as would seem to
"have been the case from their seizing the palace and coming
"armed into the Piazza, then that of itself shows their detest-
"able ambition and damnable designs, and condemns them. If
"they did it from jealousy and hatred of our authority, then the
"offence was greater to you than to us; for it was you who
"gave us that authority. Certainly the authority which men
"usurp merits hatred, but not that which is gained by kindness,
"liberality, and munificence. And you know that our house
"never attained any rank to which they were not raised by this
"Signoria and your unanimous consent. It was not force of
"arms and violence that brought my grandfather Cosimo back
"from exile, but it was your unanimous desire and approval;
"and it was not my aged and infirm father who defended the
"state against its many enemies, but you defended him with
"your benevolence and authority. Nor could I (being at that
"time, as it were, but a boy) have maintained the rank and
"dignity of my house had it not been for your counsels and
"your favor. Our house never did and never could have
"directed the affairs of this republic, if you, jointly with them,

"had not sustained and directed them. I know not, therefore,
"what reason they could have had for hating us, nor what just
"grounds for jealousy. Let them show hatred to their own
"ancestors, who, by their pride and avarice, lost that influence
"which ours knew how to acquire by the very opposite means
"and efforts. But admit even that the injuries done them by
"us were very great, and that they were justified in seeking our
"destruction, yet this would not justify their attempt to seize
"this palace. Why league themselves with the king of Naples
"and the Pope against the liberties of this republic? Why
"break the long peace of Italy? They have no excuse for all
"this. Let them assail those who have wronged them, but let
"them not confound private enmities with public wrongs. It
"is this that increases our troubles and misfortunes even after
"their defeat; for in their stead come the Pope and the king
"of Naples to make war upon us, which they assert is aimed at
"me and at my house. Would to God that this were true, for
"then the remedy would be prompt and sure; for I should not
"be so base a citizen as to prefer my safety to your dangers,
"but I would infinitely rather avert the danger from you at the
"risk of my own destruction. But as the powerful always
"cover their unjust acts with some less dishonest pretext, so
"have our enemies taken this mode of cloaking their ambitious
"designs. Should you, however, think differently, then I can
"only say that I am in your hands; it is for you to direct me
"or not, as you please. You are my fathers and my defenders,
"and I shall submit at all times with pleasure to your instruc-
"tions, and shall never refuse, whenever it may seem good to
"you, to terminate with my own blood this war, which was
"begun with that of my brother."

The citizens could not refrain from tears whilst Lorenzo spoke; and with the same feelings with which they had listened to him one of their number responded, saying that "the "city of Florence recognized the great merits of himself and "his family, and that Lorenzo might remain of good cheer; "for with the same promptitude with which they had avenged "his brother's death and saved his own life they would assure "him his authority and influence, which he should never lose "so long as they possessed their country." And to make their acts correspond with their words, they provided at once a certain number of armed men to serve as a body guard to Lorenzo, to protect him against insidious attacks of domestic enemies.

11. After that they attended to the preparations for war, getting their troops together and raising large amounts of money. They sent for assistance to the Duke of Milan and to the Venetians, by virtue of the terms of their league with them. And as the Pope had shown himself a wolf rather than a shepherd, and to save themselves from being devoured like guilty ones, they made every effort in their power to exonerate themselves from the charges brought against them. They published throughout all Italy a full account of the treason practised against them, showing the impiety and injustice of the Pope, and how badly he exercised that pontificate which he had wickedly obtained. For he had sent those whom he had raised to the highest prelacy, in company with traitors and parricides, to commit the most atrocious crime within a church, in the midst of divine service and at the very moment of the celebration of the holy sacrament. And then, having failed in the attempt to murder the citizens and change the government of the city and plunder it at his pleasure, he had laid an interdict upon Florence and threatened and insulted her with his pontifical malediction. But, added they, if God be just and violence be offensive to him, then certainly the conduct of his Vicar on earth must greatly displease him; and He would surely permit an outraged people to appeal to him direct, as they were prevented from doing so through the Pontiff. The Florentines therefore, instead of accepting and obeying the interdict, obliged the priests to perform divine service; they called a council in Florence of all the prelates of Tuscany, and appealed to the future council against the wrongs done them by the Pope. On the other hand, the Pope did not lack reasons for justifying his conduct, alleging that it was the duty of the Pope to crush all tyrannies, to oppress the wicked and exalt the good, which he was bound to do by all available means; and that it did not become secular princes to imprison cardinals, hang bishops, murder priests and dismember their bodies and drag them through the streets, and to kill the innocent and the wicked alike without distinction.

12. Notwithstanding all these quarrels and mutual criminations the Florentines restored the Cardinal, whom till then they had held, to the Pope. Sixtus IV. however, regardless of every-

thing, attacked them with his entire forces, and with those of the king of Naples. The two armies, under the command of Alfonso, oldest son of King Ferdinand and Duke of Calabria, with the Duke of Urbino as his general, entered Chianti through the territory of the Siennese, who sided with the enemy. They seized Radda and a number of other castles, devastated the whole country, and then laid siege to Castellina. These aggressions greatly alarmed the Florentines, for they were yet without troops, and their allies were slow in sending forward assistance. Although the Duke of Milan had ordered some sent, yet the Venetians denied their obligation to assist the Florentines in any private affairs; for they argued that, as the war was directed against private individuals, they were not bound under the conditions of their league to render any assistance, as private enmities were not to be defended at the public expense. To induce the Venetians to take a more correct view of the case the Florentines deputed Messer Tommaso Soderini to the Senate of Venice; and meantime they hired troops and appointed Ercole, Marquis of Ferrara, captain of their army.

Whilst these preparations were going on, the enemy pressed Castellina so close that its inhabitants, despairing of relief, surrendered, after forty days' resistance. Thence the enemy turned towards Arezzo, and encamped before Monte a San Savino. But the Florentine army, being now organized and having marched to meet the enemy, took their position within three miles of them, and harassed them to that degree that Frederick of Urbino was obliged to ask for a truce of some days. This was conceded by the Florentines, though so greatly to their own disadvantage that those who had asked for it were much astonished at its having been granted; for a refusal would have obliged them to an ignominious retreat. But having thus gained a respite, they reorganized their forces, so that when the truce expired they took the castle of San Savino in the very face of our troops. Winter having now set in, the enemy retired to the Siennese territory for the purpose of going into convenient winter quarters. The Florentines also went into the most comfortable quarters they could find; and the Marquis of Ferrara returned to his own possessions, having gained small advantage for himself and still less for the Florentines.

13. It was at this time that Genoa became separated from the government of Milan under the following circumstances. After the murder of Galeazzo, his son Giovan Galeazzo being too young to assume the government, dissensions arose between his uncles, Lodovico, Ottaviano, and Ascanio Sforza, and the lady Bona, his mother, each of them wishing to have the guardianship of the young Duke. The lady Bona, dowager Duchess, carried the day in this contention, through the advice of Messer Tommaso Soderini, at the time Florentine ambassador at Milan, and of Messer Cecco Simonetta, who had been the secretary of Galeazzo. Whereupon the Sforzas fled from Milan; Ottaviano was drowned in crossing the Adda, and the others were banished to different places; and with them fled Ruberto da San Severino, who had abandoned the Duchess in these troubles and joined the uncles. The disturbances in Tuscany having broken out soon after this, and these princes hoping in these new events to find opportunities for re-establishing their fortunes, left their places of banishment, and tried each some new means for returning to their country. King Ferdinand, seeing that the Florentines were assisted in their need only by the government of Milan, wanted to deprive them also of this assistance, and therefore resolved to give the Duchess so much to occupy her in her own state that she would not be able to supply any aid to the Florentines. By means of Prospero Adorno and the Signor Ruberto da San Severino, and the rebellious Sforzas, he induced Genoa to revolt against the government of the Duke of Milan. The Castelletto only remained in the possession of the Milanese government; and the Duchess, basing her hopes upon that, sent a large force of men to recover the city; these, however, were defeated. Seeing the danger that might result to the dominions of her son and to herself if this war continued, (Tuscany being at that time all in confusion, and the Florentines, upon whom her sole hopes rested, being themselves in trouble,) the Duchess resolved that, if she could not keep Genoa in subjection, she would at least have it for an ally. She agreed, therefore, with Battistino Fregoso, the enemy of Prospero Adorno, to turn the Castelletto over to him, and to make him sovereign of Genoa, on condition that he should expel Prospero, and show no favor to the rebellious Sforzas. Having concluded this arrangement, Battistino, with the aid of the Castelletto and his party, made himself master of Genoa, and, according to cus-

tom, assumed the title of Doge. Thereupon the Sforzas and Signor Ruberto were expelled by the Genoese, and went with such troops as followed them to Lunigiana. The Pope and the king of Naples, seeing the troubles of Lombardy settled, took occasion, by means of these exiled Genoese, to attack Tuscany in the direction of Pisa, so that the Florentines, by having to divide their forces, might be weakened. And therefore they arranged, winter being now over, to have the Signor Ruberto da San Severino leave Lunigiana with his troops, and attack the Pisan territory. The Signor Ruberto thereupon created the greatest disturbance, taking and sacking many Pisan castles, and devastating the country up to the very walls of the city of Pisa.

14. About this time the Emperor of Germany and the kings of France and of Hungary sent ambassadors to the Pope, who, on their way to Rome, stopped at Florence, and there urged the Florentine authorities also to send ambassadors to the Pope, promising to do their utmost to bring the war to an end by a satisfactory peace. The Florentines, for the sake of proving their real desire for peace, did not refuse to make the experiment; and accordingly they sent ambassadors to Rome, who returned, however, without any result. The Florentines thereupon, having been attacked by one portion of the Italians and abandoned by another, wished at least to secure for themselves the influence of the king of France, and for this purpose sent as ambassador to that king Messer Donato Acciaiuoli, a man very learned in Greek and Latin literature, and whose ancestors had always held a high rank in the city of Florence. But on the way there he died at Milan; whereupon his country, to compensate his family and honor his memory, had him interred with the greatest honors at the public expense, and bestowed upon his sons exemption from taxes, and upon his daughters suitable marriage dowers. Messer Donato was replaced by Messer Guido Antonio Vespucci, a man thoroughly versed in imperial and pontifical matters.

The invasion of the Pisan territory by Signor Ruberto troubled the Florentines greatly, as is generally the case with unexpected difficulties. For having a most serious war upon their hands in the Siennese territory, they hardly knew how to provide for the war in the Pisan country; still they aided the Pisans as far as they could with instructions and provisions. And by way of keeping the Lucchese to their allegiance, so that they might not supply money or provisions to the enemy, they sent Messer Piero Gino di Neri Capponi there as an ambassador. He was received by them, however, with so much distrust, owing to the hatred of the Lucchese to the Florentines on account of former injuries and constant fear, that he ran the risk several times of being killed by the populace. Thus this embassy gave rise rather to fresh animosities than to a new union. The Florentines recalled the Marquis of Ferrara, and took into their pay the Marquis of Mantua; and most earnestly asked of the Venetians the Count Carlo, son of Braccio, and Deifobo, son of the Count Jacopo, both of whom the Venetians conceded to them after much cavilling; for, having made a truce with the Turk, they could make no valid excuse, and were ashamed openly to disregard their obligations under the league. The Counts Carlo and Deifobo came, therefore, with a considerable number of troops, and, uniting these with all that could be detached from the army which under the Marquis of Ferrara was opposed to the forces of the Duke of Calabria, they moved towards Pisa to encounter the Signor Ruberto, who was with his troops near the river Serchio. And although he had made show of an intention to await our forces, yet he did not, but withdrew to Lunigiana, into the same encampment which he had quitted when he entered the Pisan territory. After his withdrawal, Count Carlo recovered all the places that had been taken by the enemy in the Pisan country.

15. The Florentines, being thus relieved of the attacks in the direction of Pisa, concentrated all their troops between Colle and San Giminiano; but there being in that army, in consequence of the accession of the Count Carlo, men who had fought under the Sforzas, and some who had served under the Braccios, the old hostility between them was quickly rekindled, and they would probably have come to an open conflict if they had been allowed to remain together. To avoid therefore this minor evil, it was resolved to divide the forces, and to send one part under the Count Carlo into the Perugine territory, whilst the other part was to stop at Poggibonzi, where they were to establish an intrenched camp, so as to be able to prevent the enemy from penetrating into the Florentine territory. They hoped in this way to oblige the enemy to divide his forces also; for they thought that the Count Carlo would either take

Perugia, where he was supposed to have many partisans, or that the Pope would be obliged to send a large body of troops to defend it. By way of embarrassing the Pope still more, they further ordered that Messer Niccolo Vitelli, who had left Citta di Castello, where Lorenzo, his enemy, commanded, should move upon the place with a sufficient force to drive his adversary out of it, and thus to withdraw it from its obedience to the Pope.

At first it seemed as though fortune would favor the Florentines, for Count Carlo made considerable progress in the Perugine territory; whilst Messer Niccolo Vitelli, although he had not yet succeeded in taking Castello, yet had the superior force in the field, so that he was enabled to pillage the surrounding country without opposition. The troops that had been left at Poggibonzi also scoured the country up to the very walls of Sienna. But in the end all these fine prospects proved to be delusive. In the first place the Count Carlo died in the midst of his hopes of victory; the consequences of his death, however, would have rather benefited the Florentines, if they had known how to take proper advantage of the victory that followed it. For no sooner had the death of Count Carlo become known than the forces of the Church, which had been concentrated at Perugia, became elated with the hope of now being able to crush the Florentine troops; and upon taking the field they established their camp above the lake (Trasimene) within three miles of the enemy. On the other hand Jacopo Guicciardini, commissary of the Florentine army, by the advice of the famous Ruberto da Rimini, who since the death of the Count Carlo was the first and most distinguished captain of the army and who knew the cause of the enemy's confidence, resolved to await him. They came to an engagement by the side of the lake, where the Carthaginian Hannibal had inflicted that memorable defeat upon the Romans, and the pontifical army was completely routed. The news of this victory was received at Florence with universal joy and great praise of the captains; and it would have put an honorable end to the war had not disorders broken out in the army which was at Poggibonzi, and which deranged everything. And thus the good achieved by the one army was wholly destroyed by the disorders in the other. For the troops having taken much booty in the Siennese territory, differences arose in the distribution of it between the Marquis of Ferrara and the Marquis of Mantua; so that it came to a conflict of arms between them. These two captains assailed each other with the greatest violence, to that degree that the Florentines concluded that they could not with advantage keep both, and therefore it was agreed to let the Marquis of Ferrara return home with his troops.

16. The army being thus weakened and left without a chief, and wholly disorganized, the Duke of Calabria, who was with his forces at Sienna, resolved upon an attack, and promptly executed his design. The Florentine troops, seeing themselves assailed, and trusting neither to their arms, nor their superior number, nor to their position, which was exceedingly strong, fled at the mere sight of the cloud of dust, and without even waiting to see the enemy they abandoned to him their ammunition, their wagons, and all their artillery. Such cowardice and lack of discipline were very frequent in the armies of those days; so that the turning of a horse's head or tail would often decide the success or failure of a battle. This rout enabled the troops of the king of Naples to make an immense booty, and filled the Florentines with dismay. For the city had been afflicted not only with the war, but also with a fearful pestilence, which had spread to that degree in the city that most of the citizens, to escape death, had fled to their villas. What made this defeat still more terrible was that those citizens who had fled to their estates in the Val di Pisa and the Val d' Elsa, upon hearing of the rout of the army, rushed at once back to Florence, taking with them not only their families and household things, but even their laborers. It seemed almost as though the enemy might at any moment appear before the city. Those who were charged with the conduct of the war, seeing this general disorder, directed the troops that had been victorious in the Perugine district to abandon the attempt upon Perugia, and to move to the Val d' Elsa, there to arrest the progress of the enemy, who after his victory ravaged the country without opposition. And although these troops had invested Perugia so closely that they expected every moment to succeed in taking it, yet the Florentines were more anxious to defend their own city than to continue their efforts in taking that of others. Thus that army, obliged to forego the fruits of its fortunate successes, was marched to Casciano, a

castle within eight miles of Florence; it being considered that they could not make a stand anywhere else until they should have been joined by the remnants of their defeated army. That portion of the enemy's forces which was at Perugia, being thus relieved by the withdrawal of the Florentines, became more emboldened, and committed daily great depredations in the districts of Aretino and Cortona; whilst the others, who had been victorious under the Duke of Calabria at Poggibonzi, had made themselves masters of that place and of Vico, and had sacked Certaldo; and after these captures and plunderings they laid siege to the castle of Colle, which was then considered exceedingly strong. Its garrison being loyally devoted to the Florentines, it was hoped that they would be able to hold the enemy at bay until the republic could collect her forces again. The Florentines having concentrated all their forces at San Casciano, determined to approach the enemy, who was pressing Colle with all his might, for the purpose of encouraging its inhabitants to hold out. They hoped also that, when their proximity should become known to the enemy, he would have to relax the energy of his assaults upon Colle. Having thus resolved, the Florentines raised their camp at San Casciano, and established it at San Giminiano, within five miles of Colle; and from there they daily harassed the Duke's camp with their cavalry and other light troops. This however did not suffice to relieve the people of Colle, who, being short of all necessaries, surrendered on the 13th of November, to the great displeasure of the Florentines and the greatest joy of the enemy; and especially of the Siennese, who, apart from their general hatred of the city of Florence, had a particular animosity against the people of Colle.

17. Severe winter had now set in, and the weather was too unfavorable for the prosecution of the war. The Pope and the king of Naples, either to encourage hopes of peace or to enable them the more securely to enjoy the fruits of their victories, offered to the Florentines a truce for a term of three months, giving them ten days' time for a reply to their proposition, which was promptly accepted. But as it is always the case that wounds are more keenly felt after the blood has cooled than at the moment of their being received, so it was with the Florentines, whom this brief repose only made the more sensible of

the afflictions experienced. The citizens accused each other openly, and without regard or reserve, of the errors committed in the war, pointing to the useless expenditures and the unjust taxes. These charges circulated not only privately, but were discussed with much bitterness in the public councils, so that one of the citizens made bold to turn to Lorenzo de' Medici, and say: "The city is weary of war, and therefore it is "necessary to think seriously of peace." Whereupon Lorenzo, who was fully aware of this necessity, held counsel with such friends as he deemed most devoted and wise. And seeing that the Venetians were lukewarm and not much to be relied upon, and the Duke of Milan still a minor and himself involved in civil discords, they promptly concluded that it would be best for them to try and better their fortune by new alliances. But they were in doubt as to whether it would be best to throw themselves into the arms of the Pope or the king of Naples.

Having examined the subject on all sides, they decided in favor of an alliance with the king, as being more stable and safe; for the shortness of the lives of the Popes, the changes caused by the succession, the little fear which the Church has of temporal princes, and her lack of consideration in taking sides, were reasons why a secular prince could not entirely trust a Pontiff, nor safely venture to share his fortunes. For whoever might be the Pontiff's ally in war and danger would also have him to share in victory, but in defeat would be abandoned by him; inasmuch as the Pontiff was always sure of being sustained and defended by his spiritual powers and influence. Being satisfied therefore that it would be more advantageous to secure the friendship of the king of Naples, they thought the best and most certain way to obtain this would be through the personal presence of Lorenzo; because the greater the liberality displayed towards the king, the easier it would be to obliterate the remembrance of the past enmity. Lorenzo, having decided to accept this mission, committed the city and state to the care of Messer Tommaso Soderini, who was the Gonfaloniere of Justice at that time, and left Florence in the beginning of December. Upon his arrival at Pisa he wrote to the Signoria in explanation of his departure, who in return, by way of showing him all honor, and to enable him with the more dignity and effect to treat with the king in relation to the peace, appointed him Ambassador of the Florentine republic to the king of Naples, and gave him authority to conclude an alliance with the king upon such conditions as he might deem best for the republic.

18. About this same time the Signor Ruberto da San Severino, together with Lodovico and Ascanio Sforza (upon the death of their brother Ottaviano), made a fresh attack upon the state of Milan for the purpose of recovering the government. Having seized Tortona, and the whole state of Milan being in arms, the Duchess Bona was advised to readmit the Sforzas to their country and to a share in the government, and thereby to put an end to the civil contentions. The author of this advice was Antonio Tassino, a native of Ferrara and a man of low origin, who upon coming to Milan had fallen into the hands of the Duke Galeazzo, who gave him as a valet to his wife. Whether it was on account of his great personal beauty or through some other secret influence, this man Tassino obtained such an ascendency over the Duchess after her husband's death that he almost controlled the government. This so displeased Messer Cecco Simonetta, a man distinguished by his great sagacity and experience in public affairs, that he sought by all means in his power to diminish this influence of Tassino's with the Duchess and others in the government. Tassino observed this, and, by way of revenging himself and of having some one near who would defend him against Messer Cecco, he advised the Duchess to recall the Sforzas from banishment. Without consulting Messer Cecco on the matter, the Duchess acted upon this advice, and restored the Sforzas to their country. Whereupon Messer Cecco said to her, "The "course you have taken will cost me my life, and you the loss of your state." And so it really proved soon after, for Messer Cecco was put to death by order of Signor Lodovico, and, Tassino being after a while expelled from the duchy, the Duchess became so indignant that she left Milan, and resigned the guardianship of her son into the hands of Lodovico, who thus remained sole governor of the Duchy of Milan, which, as will be shown hereafter, proved the ruin of all Italy.

Lorenzo de' Medici had left for Naples, and all parties were enjoying the truce, when suddenly and quite unexpectedly Lodovico Fregoso, by a secret understanding with some of the inhabitants of Screzana, entered that city by stealth with a number of armed men, seized the place, and imprisoned the Florentine governor. This act of aggression greatly incensed the chiefs of the Florentine government, who attributed it altogether to secret orders of King Ferdinand. They complained to the Duke of Calabria, who was with the army at Sienna, that hostilities had been recommenced pending the duration of the truce. He made every effort to prove by letters and special deputies that this affair had originated altogether without the knowledge and consent of his father or himself. The Florentines however regarded their condition as a most alarming one, being without money, and the chief of their state in the hands of the king of Naples, with an old war on hand against the Pope and the king, and a new one with the Genoese, and wholly without allies. For they had no hope of the Venetians, and rather feared the government of Milan, as being liable to change and unstable. The only one hope left to the Florentines was the success which Lorenzo de' Medici might have with the king of Naples in his negotiations for peace.

19. Lorenzo had arrived by sea at Naples, where he was received with great honors and expectations, not only by the king, but also by the whole people; for this great war having had no other object than to crush him, the estimate of his own power had been increased by the magnitude of that of his enemies. Having been admitted to the presence of the king, Lorenzo spoke so ably of the condition of Italy, of the disposition of its princes and peoples, of the good that might be hoped for from peace and of the ills to be feared from war, that the king, after having heard him, was even more astonished by the greatness of his mind, the promptness of his genius, and the solidity of his judgment, than he had been before by Lorenzo's ability single-handed to sustain so great a war. After this the king treated him with still more distinction, and began to think that it would be better to let him return to Florence as a friend rather than hold him as an enemy. He nevertheless detained him on various pretexts from December until March, not only for the purpose of becoming better acquainted with him, but also with the state of affairs in Florence. Lorenzo meantime did not lack enemies in Florence, who would gladly have seen the king keep and treat him as he had done Jacopo Piccinino. And whilst pretending to lament his detention at Naples, they spoke of it

everywhere in the city, but in the public councils they opposed every measure that was favorable to Lorenzo. In this way they spread the report that, if the king detained Lorenzo much longer at Naples, there would certainly be a change in the government of Florence. This caused the king to delay the departure of Lorenzo; but as Florence continued in entire tranquillity, Ferdinand gave Lorenzo leave to depart on the 6th of March, 1479, after having first secured his friendship by every variety of gifts and demonstrations of love, and having concluded between them a treaty of perpetual alliance for the mutual protection of their states. Lorenzo thereupon returned to Florence, greater even than before he left it, and was received by the whole city with the greatest demonstrations of joy, as his noble qualities and fresh services to the state deserved, having exposed his own life for the sake of restoring peace to his country. Two days after his arrival the treaty made between the republic of Florence and the king of Naples was published, according to which they obligated themselves mutually to protect each other's states, and that according to the king's decision all the places that had been taken from the Florentines during the war should be restored to them, and that the Pazzi, who were confined in the tower of Volterra, should be set at liberty, and certain sums of money should be paid at stated periods to the Duke of Calabria.

At the news of this treaty the Pope and the Venetians became greatly incensed; the former because of the want of consideration with which he had been treated in this matter by the king, and the Venetians for similar conduct on the part of the Florentines; for they felt that, having acted together in the war, they ought to have been consulted in the conclusion of peace. When this dissatisfaction became known to the Florentines, every one feared that the peace concluded by Lorenzo would only lead to another and even more terrible war. The chiefs of the government resolved therefore to concentrate the government, and to confine the decisions to a limited number instead of a general council; and accordingly they constituted a council of seventy citizens, whom they invested with all necessary powers for important action. This new institution checked the ardor of those who were anxious for innovations; and by way of establishing their authority the first thing this council of seventy did was to ratify the treaty of peace concluded between Lorenzo and the king, and to appoint and send as ambassadors to the Pope Messer Antonio Ridolfi and Piero Nasi. Notwithstanding the treaty of peace, however, Alfonso, Duke of Calabria, remained with his army at Sienna, assigning as the reason for his not leaving the civil dissensions that agitated that city. The Duke Alfonso was at first encamped at a short distance from Sienna; but these internal discords had reached that point that he had to come into the city to act as arbiter between the contending factions. On this occasion the Duke imposed heavy fines upon many of the citizens; others he condemned to prison, some to exile, and some to death; so that by these severities he excited the suspicions not only of the Siennese, but also of the Florentines, that he desired to make himself sovereign of the city. Florence seemed to be powerless to prevent it, because of the new alliance with the king of Naples, and the resentment of the Pope and the Venetians. This suspicion was entertained not only by the people of Florence, at all times most subtle interpreters of things, but was shared also by the chiefs of the state; and all firmly believed that our city had never before been in such danger of losing its liberties. But God, who in similar extremities has always taken the city of Florence under his special protection, caused an unexpected event, which gave the Pope and the kings as well as the Venetians more important things to think of than the affairs of Florence.

20. The Grand Turk Mahomet had gone with a large military and naval force to besiege Rhodes, and had assailed it already during several months; but although his forces were very numerous and he persevered in the siege with great obstinacy, yet he found that of the besieged still greater, for they defended themselves against his powerful assaults with such bravery that Mahomet was obliged ignominiously to abandon the siege. Whilst returning from Rhodes, a portion of his fleet under Achmet Pacha turned towards Valona; and either because he was tempted by the facility of the undertaking, or because his master had so ordered him, this Pacha, in sailing along the coast of Italy, suddenly landed four thousand men and attacked the city of Otranto, which he quickly took and sacked, putting all the inhabitants to the sword. (1480.) Thereupon, with such means as were most conveniently at hand, he fortified himself in that city and port, and having collected a good body of cavalry he scoured and pillaged the

surrounding country. The king of Naples, hearing of this attack and knowing the power of the assailant, despatched messengers in every direction to make it known, and to ask for help against the common enemy; and in the most pressing manner ordered the immediate return of the Duke of Calabria and his forces from Sienna.

21. Much as this attack of the Turks troubled the Duke Alfonso and the rest of Italy, just so great was the joy it caused to the Florentines and to the Siennese. The latter felt as though they had recovered their liberty, and the former that they had escaped from the danger of losing theirs. This opinion was confirmed by the regrets of the Duke at being obliged to leave Sienna, for he blamed fortune for having, by an unexpected and untoward occurrence, deprived him of the opportunity of making himself master of Tuscany. This same event caused the Pope to change his course; and whilst before he would not listen to any Florentine ambassadors, he suddenly became so affable that he gave ear to any one that would speak to him on the subject of a general peace. The Florentines were assured that, whenever they were disposed to ask forgiveness of the Pope, it would be granted to them. Believing it therefore to be well not to allow this occasion to pass, the Florentines sent ambassadors to the Pontiff.

Upon their arrival in Rome the Pope at first put off, on various pretences, granting them an audience; at last, however, terms were agreed upon between the parties, and their future relations settled, and the respective amounts were fixed which each was to contribute in peace and in war. Thereupon the ambassadors were admitted to the feet of the Pope, who awaited them with great pomp in the midst of all his cardinals. They apologized for the past, attributing it first to an unavoidable necessity, then to the malignity of others, and to the fury and just resentment of the populace. Then they expatiated upon the unhappy fate of those who are compelled either to fight or to die; and they argued that, as men are ever willing to submit to anything to escape death, so they had borne war, and interdicts, and all the ills that follow in their train, for the sake of saving their country from slavery, which in general was the cause of the death of republics. Nevertheless, if under the pressure of force they had committed any fault, they had now come to make amends, and they trusted in that clemency of the Holy Father which, according to the example of the blessed Redeemer, should cause him to receive them in his compassionate arms. To this justification the Pope replied in words full of haughtiness and anger, reproving them for all they had done in the past against the Church. Nevertheless, to act up to the precepts of God, he was willing to grant them the pardon asked for; but gave them to understand that he expected implicit obedience of them, and if they failed in that they would lose, and justly, that liberty which they had now been so near losing; and that those only merited liberty who employed it in good works, and not in evil-doing, for liberty abused injures both itself and others; and to show little respect to God, and still less to the Church, was not the practice of free men; and that it was the duty not only of princes, but of every Christian, to punish such. That therefore he had cause to complain of the past conduct of the Florentines, having by their evil works provoked the war, and supported it by still worse ones; which war had been terminated more by the kindness of others than by any merits of their own. Thereupon the draft of the treaty and the benediction were read; to which, besides the conditions established and agreed upon, the Pope added a clause to the effect that, if the Florentines wished to enjoy that benediction, they should at their expense keep fifteen galleys armed and ready so long as the Turk continued his aggressions upon the kingdom of Naples. The ambassadors complained earnestly of this additional burden, which formed no part of the original conditions of the treaty, but neither prayers nor protestations could induce the Pope to recede from this demand. After the return of the ambassadors to Florence, the Signoria, for the purpose of ratifying the treaty, sent Messer Guido Antonio Vespucci as ambassador to Rome, who had but a short time previous returned from a mission to France. He succeeded by his prudence in obtaining a modification of the conditions of the treaty, so as to make them more tolerable; he also received many favors from the Pope, in proof of his more complete reconciliation to the Florentines.

22. The affairs with the Pope being thus settled, and the departure of the Duke of Calabria from Tuscany having relieved both Florence and Sienna of all apprehensions of the king of Naples, the Florentines availed of the continuance of

the war with the Turk to press King Ferdinand for the restitution of their castles, which the Duke of Calabria upon his withdrawal had left in the hands of the Siennese. The king feared lest the Florentines should leave him in his necessity and declare a fresh war against the Siennese, and thereby prevent him from obtaining the assistance he looked for from the Pope and the other Italian princes; he therefore consented to the restoration of the castles, and thus bound the Florentines to him by these new obligations. It is thus that force and necessity, and not written treaty obligations, cause princes to observe their faith. Florence having recovered her castles, and the new alliance being ratified, Lorenzo de' Medici regained all the reputation and influence of which the war first, and then the peace (whilst there was a doubt as to the king's intentions) had deprived him; for there had been no lack of persons at that time who calumniated Lorenzo openly, charging him with having sold his country to save himself, and that as the castles had been lost in the war, so would their liberty be lost in peace. But now, their castles having been restored to them, and an honorable peace having been concluded with the king, and the republic having regained her ancient power, public opinion changed entirely in Florence, a city ever eager for gossip, and where matters are judged of by their success rather than by the reasons that influenced them; and so they lauded Lorenzo to the skies, saying that it was his sagacity that had enabled them to recover by peace what they had lost by the ill fortune of war; and that his counsels and good judgment had effected more than armies and the power of the enemy.

The attack of the Turk had, however, only deferred the war which was about to break out because of the indignation of the Pope and the Venetians at the conclusion of the peace between Lorenzo and King Ferdinand. But as the beginning of that attack had been unlooked for and had been productive of good, so was its termination unexpected, and proved the cause of great evils. Sultan Mahomet died very suddenly, and dissensions having arisen amongst his sons, the Turkish troops that were in Puglia, being abandoned by their chief, surrendered Otranto to the king. The fear which had kept the Pope and the Venetians quiet having thus been removed, fresh troubles were generally apprehended. On the one side the Pope and the Venetians were leagued together, and with them were the Genoese, the Siennese, and other smaller powers; on the other side were the Florentines, the king of Naples, and the Duke of Milan, who were joined by the Bolognese and many other princes. The Venetians desired to possess themselves of Ferrara, deeming themselves justified in such an attempt, and having confident hopes of success. The ground alleged by them was that the Marquis of Ferrara claimed that he was no longer bound to accept a Venetian vice-governor, nor to purchase any more salt from them, inasmuch as the convention existing between them provided that, after having borne these impositions for seventy years, the city of Ferrara should be relieved of them. To this the Venetians replied, that so long as the Marquis of Ferrara held the Polesine, so long was he bound to purchase his salt from them. And as the Marquis would not submit to this, the Venetians deemed his refusal just cause for war. The moment seemed to them moreover opportune, seeing that the Pope was much irritated against the Florentines and the king of Naples. And by way of assuring to themselves the good-will of the Pope still more, they received the Count Girolamo when he came to Venice (1482) with the greatest demonstrations of honor, and bestowed upon him the privileges of citizenship and nobility, always the highest marks of distinction which they could confer upon any one. By way of preparing for this war, the Venetians levied new imposts and appointed the Signor Ruberto da San Severino to the command of their forces; who having been offended with the Signor Lodovico Sforza, governor of Milan, had fled to Fortena, where he stirred up some tumults, and then went to Genoa, where he was at the time when he was called by the Venetians to be made commander-in-chief of their forces.

23. When these hostile preparations became known to the adverse league, they also set to work to prepare for war. The Duke of Milan chose for his captain Frederick, lord of Urbino, and the Florentines took the Signor Costanzo di Pesaro. For the purpose of sounding the Pope as to his intentions, and to ascertain whether the Venetians had his consent to their attack upon Ferrara, King Ferdinand sent the Duke Alfonso of Calabria with his army across the river Tronto, applying to the Pope for permission for Alfonso to pass into Lombardy to the

assistance of the Marquis of Ferrara, which the Pope absolutely refused; so that the king and the Florentines, no longer doubtful as to the Pope's disposition, resolved to press him with their forces, hoping thereby to constrain him into an alliance with themselves, or at least so to embarrass him as that he should not be able to furnish any assistance to the Venetians. These were already in the field and had begun hostilities against the Marquis of Ferrara, and after having first ravaged the country they next laid siege to Figarolo, a castle of much importance to the possessions of the Marquis. The king and the Florentines having resolved to attack the Pope, Alfonso, Duke of Calabria, made incursions into the country towards Rome, and with the aid of the Colonnesi, who had joined him only because the Orsini united with the Pope, he did great damage in that country. The Florentine troops on the other hand, with Messer Niccolo Vitelli, attacked and took Citta di Castello, drove out Messer Lorenzo, who held it for the Pope, and gave the sovereignty of it to Messer Niccolo.

The Pope thus found himself in the greatest strait, for the city of Rome within was perturbed by factions, and without his territory was overrun by enemies. Nevertheless, like a man of courage, resolved to conquer and not to yield to the enemy, he appointed the illustrious Ruberto da Rimini as his captain, and made him come to Rome, where he had assembled all his armed forces. Sixtus represented to Ruberto how glorious it would be for him to relieve the Church from the troubles from which she was suffering at the hands of the king of Naples, and how great the obligations under which he would lay not only himself but all his successors, and how this would be recognized by all mankind, and even by the Almighty himself. Signor Ruberto, having first reviewed the Pope's troops and examined all his preparations, advised him to organize as much infantry as possible, which was done with the greatest zeal and promptitude. The Duke of Calabria was near Rome, and daily scoured and pillaged the country up to the very gates of the city. This so irritated the people that many of them volunteered to serve with Ruberto in liberating Rome from the presence of the enemy, all of whom the general gratefully accepted. The Duke of Calabria, informed of these preparations, removed to some little distance from the city, thinking that Ruberto would not venture so far out to encounter him; and moreover he expected his brother Frederick, whom his father had sent to him with fresh troops. Signor Ruberto, seeing that his mounted force was nearly equal to that of the Duke, and that in infantry he was greatly superior to him, marched out from Rome in order of battle, and established a camp within two miles of the enemy. Duke Alfonso, seeing the enemy upon him so contrary to all his expectations, judged that he would either have to fight, or to fly as though he had been defeated. Thus constrained as it were by his unwillingness to do anything unworthy of the son of a king, the Duke resolved to fight, and faced the enemy. Each general ranged his troops in the customary order of battle, and the engagement was begun, and lasted until noon. The battle was fought with more courage than any other in Italy for fifty years past; for over a thousand men remained dead upon the field. The result was a most glorious victory for the Church; for the enormous force of Papal infantry so harassed the Duke's cavalry that he was obliged to retreat, and the Duke himself would have been made a prisoner if he had not been saved by a number of Turks who were fighting under his banner. After this victory Ruberto returned triumphantly to Rome, but enjoyed his glory only for a very brief time; for having in consequence of the fatigues of the day drank a great deal of water, he was seized with a dysentery which killed him in a few days. His obsequies were celebrated by the Pope with the greatest pomp and distinction. Immediately after this victory the Pope sent the Count Girolamo against Citta di Castello for the purpose of recovering its possession, and also to make an attempt upon the city of Rimini; for as Ruberto on his death left only a young son, under the charge of his widow, the Pope thought that it would be easy for him to gain possession of that city, in which he would have readily succeeded if the widow of Ruberto had not been protected by the Florentines, who opposed the Count Girolamo so vigorously that he failed entirely, both in his attempt upon the castle and upon the town of Rimini.

24. This was the state of things in the Romagna and in Rome, when the Venetians took Figarolo and passed the Po with their forces. The army of the Duke of Milan and the Marquis of Ferrara were in disorder, for their commander, the Count Frederick of Urbino, had fallen sick, and had himself

transported to Bologna to be cured, but he died there. Thus the affairs of the Marquis were on the decline, and the Venetians became daily more hopeful of getting possession of Ferrara. On the other hand the king and the Florentines made every effort to induce the Pope to come into their views, and not having succeeded in making him yield to the force of arms, they threatened him with the convocation of the council which had already been proclaimed by the Emperor to be held at Basle. The king's ambassadors who were at Rome, and the principal cardinals who were opposed to war, prevailed upon the Pope to think of a general peace, and of the union of Italy. Whereupon the Pontiff, actuated partly by fear and also because he saw that the aggrandizement of Venice would be the ruin of the Church and of Italy, turned to make terms with the league, and sent his nuncios to Naples, where a new league was concluded for five years between the Pope, the king of Naples, the Duke of Milan, and the Florentines; leaving it open to the Venetians also to join it if they so desired. This being accomplished, the Pope sent word to the Venetians to desist from their war upon Ferrara, which the Venetians refused, but rather increased their efforts for the continuance of the war; and having routed the troops of the Duke of Milan and of the Marquis of Argenta, they approached so near to Ferrara that they established their camp in the very park of the Marquis himself.

25. The league therefore thought that there was no time to be lost in sending powerful assistance to that Signor; and accordingly they ordered the Duke of Calabria to proceed to Ferrara with his own troops and those of the Pope (1483). The Florentines likewise sent all their forces there; and the better to regulate the order of the campaign, the league held a diet at Cremona, where were convened the Pope's Legate with the Count Girolamo, the Duke of Calabria, the Signor Lodovico Sforza, Lorenzo de' Medici, and many other Italian princes, who there arranged all the particulars of the conduct of the war. Convinced that there would be no more effectual way of succoring Ferrara than by a powerful diversion, they wanted the Signor Lodovico Sforza to declare open war against the Venetians, in behalf of the Duke of Milan. This he refused to do, fearing to involve himself in a war which it might be impossible for him to stop in his turn. It was resolved, therefore, to move

their entire forces to Ferrara, and to detach four thousand mounted men and eight thousand infantry, who should attack the Venetians, who had only twenty-two hundred mounted men and six thousand infantry. The first thing to do, however, in the opinion of the league, was to destroy the flotilla which the Venetians had on the Po; and having attacked it near Bondeno, they scattered it, destroying over two hundred vessels, and taking prisoner Messer Antonio Justiniano, the Proveditore of the fleet.

Seeing all Italy combined against them, the Venetians, by way of magnifying their reputation, engaged the services of the Duke of Lorraine, with two hundred mounted men; and after the disaster to their fleet, they sent him with a part of their army to keep the enemy at bay, and ordered the Signor Ruberto da San Severino to cross the Adda with the remainder of their forces, and to proceed to Milan, there to raise the cry of the Duke and the lady Bona, his mother. In this way they hoped to stir up a revolution in Milan, believing that the Signor Lodovico Sforza and his government were odious to the people of that city. This attack caused great alarm at first, and roused the whole city of Milan to arms; but in the end it resulted very differently from the expectations of the Venetians, for it caused the Signor Lodovico now to consent to do what at first he had refused. And consequently, having left to the Marquis of Ferrara four thousand horse and two thousand infantry for the defence of his own possessions, the Duke of Calabria, with twelve thousand horse and five thousand infantry, entered the territory of Bergamo, and thence that of Brescia, and after that the Veronese, and devastated almost the entire country belonging to those three cities. The Venetians were utterly unable to prevent this; in fact, it was with the utmost difficulty that the Signor Ruberto succeeded in saving the cities themselves. On the other hand, the Marquis of Ferrara had also recovered the greater part of his territory, for the Duke of Lorraine, who was opposed to him, was unable to resist him, having but two thousand horse and one thousand infantry. And thus during the whole year of 1483 the results of the war were favorable for the league.

26. Winter having passed without any active hostilities, the armies again took the field with the opening of spring. The league had united all their forces for the purpose of more

promptly crushing the Venetians; and if the war had been maintained as in the preceding year, they would easily have taken from the Venetians all the territory they held in Lombardy, for their forces were reduced to six thousand horse and five thousand infantry, whilst the league had thirteen thousand horse and six thousand infantry; for the Duke of Lorraine, having completed his engagement of one year, had returned home. But as it often happens where there are many of equal authority, differences will arise between them that will give the victory to the enemy. After the death of Frederick Gonzaga, Marquis of Mantua, who by his influence and authority had held the Duke of Calabria and the Signor Lodovico Sforza to their engagements, differences began to arise between them, which soon ripened into jealousies. Giovan Galeazzo, Duke of Milan, was now of suitable age to take the government into his own hands; and having married the daughter of the Duke of Calabria, the latter thought that his son-in-law, and not Signor Lodovico Sforza, ought to govern the state; but Lodovico, aware of the Duke's desire, was resolved to prevent his carrying it into effect. So soon as Lodovico's disposition became known to the Venetians, they seized upon the opportunity as a favorable one to enable them, according to their wont, to recover by peace what they had lost by war; and terms having been secretly negotiated between them and Lodovico, they concluded a peace in August, 1484. When this came to the knowledge of the other members of the league, it caused them the greatest dissatisfaction, mainly because they saw that they would have to restore to the Venetians the places they had taken from them, and to leave in their hands Rovigo and the Polesine, which the Venetians had taken from the Marquis of Ferrara, and which would give them almost the same control over the city of Ferrara as they formerly had. Each member of the league seemed to think that they had at great expense made a war, the conduct of which had been creditable to them, but its termination ignominious; for the places they had taken they would have to restore, whilst those they had lost they were not to recover. They had nevertheless to accept the peace, for they were weary of the expense of the war, and were unwilling, on account of the defection and ambition of others, to risk their own fortune any longer.

27. While these events were transpiring in Lombardy, the

Pope, through Messer Lorenzo, besieged Citta di Castello, for the purpose of driving out Messer Niccolo Vitelli, who had been abandoned by the league with the view of conciliating the Pope. During this siege the adherents of Messer Niccolo made a sortie and routed the enemy. Hereupon the Pope recalled the Count Girolamo from Lombardy, and made him come to Rome to re-organize and strengthen his forces, and then to renew the siege of Citta di Castello. But having become satisfied afterwards that it would be better to win Messer Niccolo over by peace than to continue the war, he opened negotiations with him, and reconciled him as best he could with his adversary, Messer Lorenzo. The Pope, however, was influenced to this course more by his apprehensions of fresh troubles than by any love of peace; for he had observed an ugly spirit arising between the Colonnesi and the Orsini. The king of Naples had during his war with the Pope taken the territory of Tagliacozzo from the Orsini, and bestowed it upon the Colonnesi, who were attached to his party. Peace having afterwards been made between Sixtus IV. and King Ferdinand, the Orsini demanded the restoration of their possessions by virtue of the terms of the convention. The Pope had several times signified to the Colonnesi his wish that they should restore the territory in question; but neither the demands of the Orsini nor the menaces of the Pope could induce them to do so, but they rather committed fresh depredations and outrages upon the Orsini. Thereupon the Pontiff, unable to settle the difficulty, united his entire forces with those of the Orsini against the Colonnesi, sacked their palaces in Rome, took and killed those who attempted to defend them, and despoiled them of the greater number of their castles. And thus these troubles were quieted, not by peace, but by the ruin of one of the parties.

28. Tranquillity had not yet been re-established either in Genoa or in Tuscany. The Florentines kept the Count Antonio da Marciano with an armed force on the confines of Serezana, and whilst the war continued in Lombardy these annoyed the people of Serezana by incursions and skirmishes. And in Genoa Battistino Fregoso, Doge of that city, confiding in the Archbishop Pagolo Fregoso, was seized and imprisoned by him, together with his wife and children, whilst Pagolo made himself sovereign of the city. The Venetian fleet also attacked the kingdom of Naples, and had taken Gallipolis and ravaged the

surrounding country. But all these disturbances ceased when
the peace in Lombardy was concluded, excepting in Tuscany
and in Rome; for five days after the proclamation of this peace
Pope Sixtus IV. died, either because he had reached the natural
term of his life, or because his end was hastened by the regret
he felt in consequence of the peace to which he had been so
greatly opposed. Sixtus IV. thus left Italy in peace, which
during his life he had constantly kept involved in war. His
death caused the Romans promptly to rise in arms; the Count
Girolamo retreated with his troops to the castle of San Angelo;
the Orsini feared that the Colonnesi would attempt to avenge
the recent injuries they had inflicted upon them; and the Colonnesi demanded the restoration of their palaces and castles. All
this caused within a few days murders, robberies, and confla-
grations in many parts of the city. But the cardinals having
urged the Count Girolamo to restore the castle of San Angelo
to the Sacred College, and that he should himself retire to his
estates and relieve Rome of the presence of his troops, the
Count, desirous of securing to himself the favor of the future
Pope, obeyed, and restored the castle to the College of Cardinals
and withdrew with his troops to Imola. Whereupon the cardinals being relieved of further apprehensions, and the barons
having no longer the hope of being supported by the Count in
their contentions, the election of the new Pope was proceeded
with. After some debate the unanimous choice fell upon Giovan Battista Cibo, Cardinal of Malfetta, a Genoese, who assumed the name of Innocent VIII. Being an affable and peace-
loving man, he induced the Romans to lay down their arms, and
thus succeeded in pacifying the city.

29. The Florentines could not remain quiet after the peace
of Lombardy; for it seemed to them a dishonor and a shame
that a mere private gentleman should have dispossessed them of
the castle of Serezana. And as the stipulations of the treaty
of peace provided that each party, not only should have the
right to demand back the places they had lost, but even to
make war upon any one who should impede such restoration,
they promptly provided money and troops for the recovery of
Serezana by force. Whereupon Agostino Fregoso, who held
that castle, fearing that he should be unable to sustain so serious an attack with his private forces, made over the place to
the San Giorgio. As I shall have occasion more than once to

speak of the Genoese and of the San Giorgio, it appears to me not out of place here to explain the character of this organization and the usages of Genoa, it being one of the principal cities of Italy. When the Genoese made peace with the Venetians after that most important war which occurred between them some years ago, their republic was unable to repay the large sums of money which she had borrowed from her citizens for the expenses of that war. The republic therefore conceded to these creditors the customs revenues, on condition that each citizen, in proportion to the principal sum loaned by him to the state, should participate in those revenues until their claims were satisfied in full. And to afford these creditors a convenient place for meeting, they assigned to them for that purpose the palace over the custom-house. These creditors thereupon organized among themselves a system of government, appointing a council of one hundred, who should decide upon everything concerning their common interests; and a magistracy of eight citizens as chiefs of the whole, who should carry the resolves of the council into execution. They divided their credits into shares, which they called "Luoghi" (places), and adopted as the title of their whole body the name of San Giorgio.

Having thus organized their government, it happened that the state had further need of money, and had recourse to the San Giorgio for fresh loans. This association, being rich and well managed, was able to supply all the money required; and the republic, on the other hand, in the same manner as they had in the first instance conceded the customs to the San Giorgio, so they now began to pledge their landed possessions for these fresh loans; and thus the requirements of money by the city and the loans made by the San Giorgio went on increasing, until this association had placed under their administration the greater part of the territory and the cities subject to the Genoese government. The San Giorgio governed and defended these, and every year they elected Rectors by public vote, whom they sent to those cities and places without any interference on the part of the state. The result of this was that the citizens of Genoa began to look upon the government as being a tyranny, and withdrew their affections from it, which they transferred to the San Giorgio as being wisely and impartially administered. It also gave rise to the frequent and easy changes in the government of the republic, which at one moment accepted the rule of one of her own citizens, and at another moment that of some foreign prince; whilst the government of the San Giorgio always remained the same. Thus when the Fregosi and the Adorni were contending for the government of the republic, the greater part of the citizens stood aloof, leaving the government a prey to the victor. And when one or the other usurped the government of the republic, the San Giorgio merely required of him an oath strictly to observe the laws of their body, which to this day have remained unchanged. For this association, having arms, money, and a government of their own, their laws could not be interfered with except at the risk of a certain and dangerous rebellion. Truly a rare example, and one which the philosophers, with all the republics they have ever seen or imagined, never thought of, to witness within the same circle, and amongst the same citizens, liberty and tyranny, integrity and corruption, justice and license! for it is this organization alone that preserves within the republic so many ancient and venerable customs. And if it should happen, as in course of time it surely will, that the San Giorgio shall control the city altogether, then will it be a republic more noteworthy even than that of Venice.

30. It was to this San Giorgio, then, that Agostino Fregoso transferred Serezana, which they received most willingly, and at once undertook its defence. They immediately put a fleet to sea, and sent troops to Pietrasanta, so as to cut off all communication with the Florentine camp which had been established near Serezana. The Florentines, on the other hand, wanted to get possession of Pietrasanta, for without it the possession of Serezana would have been of less value, the former lying between the latter and Pisa. But they had no pretext for attacking it unless the inhabitants, or whoever held the place, opposed them in their efforts to take Serezana. And by way of provoking such an act of hostility they sent a quantity of munitions of war and provisions from Pisa to their camp, with but a feeble escort, so that those in Pietrasanta might be tempted by this valuable convoy to capture it. This plan succeeded according to their wishes; for those in Pietrasanta seeing so great a prize before their eyes, promptly seized it. This afforded to the Florentines legitimate grounds for attack-

ing Pietrasanta; and, leaving Serezana aside, they laid siege to Pietrasanta, which, being well garrisoned however, made a stout defence. The Florentines, having placed their artillery in the plain, erected a battery also on the hill above, so as to be able to press the place from that side also. The commissary of the Florentine army was Jacopo Guicciardini. Whilst the siege of Pietrasanta was proceeding, the Genoese fleet took and burnt the castle of Vada; and having landed their troops, they scoured and pillaged the surrounding country. Messer Bongianni Gianfigliazzi was sent against them with a body of horse and infantry, and succeeded in checking their insolence in some measure, so that they could no longer ravage the country with such impunity. But the Genoese fleet continued to annoy the Florentines; it went to Livorno, and attacked the new tower there with pontoons and other contrivances, and battered it for some days with their artillery; but finding that they could make no impression upon it, they ignominiously withdrew.

31. In the mean time the siege of Pietrasanta progressed but tardily, so that the enemy felt encouraged to make an attack upon the battery on the hill, which they captured. This success was most creditable to them, and filled the Florentine forces with alarm to that degree that they came near being thrown into complete disorder, and withdrew to a distance of four miles from the place. The captains, seeing that it was already October, contemplated going into winter quarters and resuming the siege in the spring. When this cowardly conduct became known in Florence, it filled the chiefs of the state with indignation, and they immediately appointed Antonio Pucci and Bernardo del Nero as new commissioners to restore to the army its former valor and prestige. These proceeded at once to the camp with a large sum of money, and stated to the captains the indignation of the Signoria and of the whole city, unless they at once returned with the army to the walls of Pietrasanta; and how they would cover themselves with infamy if so many captains, with so large a force, and having opposed to them only a small garrison, were to fail in taking so insignificant and weak a place. They showed them also the immediate and prospective advantages that were expected from this acquisition, and thus rekindled the courage of all, so that they resolved at once to resume the siege. But before anything else they determined to recover the battery, in the

capture of which it was seen how great an effect can be produced upon the minds of the soldiers by affability and kindness; for Antonio Pucci, alternately encouraging one soldier and promising rewards to another, taking one man by the hand and embracing another, caused them all to rush to the assault with such impetuosity that they carried the battery at the first onset; though unhappily it involved the loss of the Conte Antonio da Marciano, who was killed by a cannonball. This success caused such terror to the besieged that they began to talk of surrendering. Thereupon, with the view of bringing the siege to a still more brilliant conclusion, Lorenzo de' Medici resolved to go in person to the camp; and in a very few days after his arrival the castle of Pietrasanta was taken. Winter had now set in, and therefore the captains deemed it best not to attempt any further operations until spring, especially as the unwholesome autumn air had caused much sickness in the army, and many captains were seriously ill. Amongst them Antonio Pucci and Messer Bongianni Gianfigliazzo not only fell sick, but died, to the great regret of all; for Antonio had won universal favor by his conduct at Pietrasanta.

After the capture of this place, the people of Lucca sent ambassadors to Florence to demand Pietrasanta of them. They claimed it on the ground that it had formerly belonged to them, and that the stipulations of the treaty required the restitution to the original owners of all the places that had been taken by either one or the other party. The Florentines did not deny the conditions of the treaty, but replied that they did not know whether, according to the terms of peace that were in course of negotiation between the Genoese and themselves, they would have to restore Pietrasanta or not; and therefore they could not act in the matter until that point had been settled. And even in case that they should have to restore it, the Lucchese would first have to reimburse them the expenses of the expedition, and to compensate them for the loss of so many of their citizens; and that when they had done that, they might hope to get the place back. The whole winter was consumed in the peace negotiations between the Genoese and the Florentines, which were being carried on through the Pope at Rome; and, as they were not concluded when spring came, the Florentines would have resumed their operations against Serezana had it not been prevented by the illness of Lorenzo de' Medici and the war that had broken out between the Pope and the king of Naples. Lorenzo suffered not only from an attack of gout, which he had inherited from his father, but also from acute pains in the stomach, which obliged him to go to the baths, in hopes of being cured.

82. But the more important reason why the Florentines did not renew their attempt upon Serezana was the war which we have mentioned above, and which had its origin as follows. The city of Aquila, though in part subject to the king of Naples, yet was, as it were, almost free; the Count Montorto was one of her most distinguished citizens (1485). The Duke of Calabria, being with his forces near the Tronto pretending to quell certain disturbances that had arisen amongst the peasants of that neighborhood, but with the real design of subjecting Aquila absolutely to the authority of the king of Naples, sent for the Count Montorto on the pretext of desiring to avail himself of his services in the matter of the disturbances. The Count obeyed the summons without the least suspicion; but upon his arrival he was made prisoner by the Duke and sent to Naples. When this became known at Aquila it stirred up the whole city; the people took to arms and killed the king's commissary, Antonio Concinello, together with a number of citizens who were known to be adherents of his Majesty. And by way of having some support in their rebellion, the Aquileians raised the banner of the Church, and sent deputies to the Pope tendering him the city and their allegiance; and praying him as his own subjects to aid them against the tyranny of the king.

The Pope boldly undertook their defence, for he hated the king for private as well as public reasons. And as it happened that the Signor Ruberto da San Severino (who was an enemy of the state of Milan) was at that moment without any engagement, the Pope appointed him captain of his forces, and requested him to come to Rome as speedily as possible; and solicited at the same time all the relatives and friends of the Count Montorto to rise against the king. The princes of Altemura, of Salerno, and of Bisignano accordingly took up arms against King Ferdinand; who, seeing himself thus suddenly involved in war, had recourse to the Florentines and the Duke of Milan for assistance. The Florentines hesitated at first as to what course to take; but being bound by the terms of their league with the king, they preferred to act in good faith rather than to consult only their own safety and convenience. They engaged the services of the Orsini, and sent all their own troops under the Count of Pittigliano towards Rome in support of the king of Naples, who thereupon organized his forces in two divisions. One, under the Duke of Calabria, he sent towards Rome, who together with the Florentine troops was to oppose the army of the Church; and the other division King Ferdinand himself led against the barons.

This war was carried on by both sides with varying success; but in the end the king proved everywhere victorious; and in the month of August, 1486, a peace was concluded through the mediation of the king of Spain's ambassadors. After these reverses the Pope consented to the peace, being unwilling to tempt fortune any longer. Thereupon all the Italian powers united, excluding however the Genoese, as being rebels to the state of Milan and usurpers of territory belonging to the Florentines. Peace being thus established, the Signor Ruberto da San Severino, who during the war had neither been very faithful to the Pope nor very formidable to his opponents, was ordered away from Rome by the Pope. He was pursued by the troops of the Duke and the Florentines, and finding himself about to be overtaken after he had passed Cesena, he took to flight, and reached Ravenna with less than one hundred horsemen. The remainder of his men in part entered the service of the Duke, and in part were destroyed by the peasants. After the conclusion of peace and his reconciliation with the barons the king caused Jacopo Cappolo and Antonello d' Aversa, together with their sons, to be put to death for having during the war revealed his secrets to the Pontiff.

33. The experience of this war had shown to the Pope with what fidelity and zeal the Florentines adhere to their allies; so that where he had previously hated them on account of the Genoese, and because of the support they had given to the king of Naples, he began now to like them and to show more than ordinary favors to their ambassadors. Lorenzo de' Medici, observing this friendly disposition, encouraged it as much as possible; for he judged that it would add greatly to his influence and reputation if he could add the friendship of the Pope to that which already existed between himself and the

king of Naples. The Pontiff had a son named Francesco, for whom he desired to procure states and allies who should be able to aid him in maintaining such states after his father's death. And there was no one in Italy whose alliance seemed to the Pope safer and more advantageous for his son than that of Lorenzo de' Medici; he managed therefore to have Lorenzo give one of his daughters in marriage to Francesco. Having formed this alliance, the Pope urged the Genoese to cede Serezana amicably to the Florentines; he pointed out to them that they could not hold what Agostino Fregoso had sold, and that Agostino had no right to transfer to the San Giorgio what did not belong to him. But all his efforts to induce the Genoese to give up Serezana proved unsuccessful; to the contrary rather, for, whilst they were negotiating on the subject in Rome, the Genoese armed a number of their vessels, and without the Florentines being in any way aware of it they landed three thousand infantry, who attacked the castle of Serezanello, situated above Serezano, and in the possession of the Florentines, and sacked and burnt the village adjoining it, and then opened a vigorous fire upon the castle with their artillery. This sudden attack was wholly unexpected by the Florentines, who immediately gathered their forces under command of Virginio Orsini at Pisa, and at the same time sent complaints to the Pope that, whilst he was negotiating for peace, the Genoese had renewed the war upon them. They then sent Pietro Corsini to Lucca to keep that city to her allegiance; and also sent Pagolantonio Soderini to Venice to ascertain the disposition of that republic. They furthermore sent for assistance both to the king of Naples and to Signor Lodovico Sforza, but obtained none from either of them; the king saying that he was afraid of the Turkish fleet, and Lodovico delaying on various pretexts. It is thus that the Florentines in their own wars are almost invariably left to themselves, and find no one to support them with the same ardor with which they aid others. Being thus accustomed to it, they were not alarmed on this occasion to find themselves abandoned by their allies. But having raised a large force, they sent it under command of Jacopo Guicciardini and Pietro Vettori against the Genoese, who had established their camp on the upper side of the river Magra.

The enemy meantime pressed Serezanello very hard with

mines and every other means of attack in their power. The
Florentine commissaries attempted to relieve this castle, and
the enemy did not refuse battle; an engagement ensued, in
which the Genoese were defeated, and Messer Luigi da Fiesco
and many other of their officers were made prisoners (1487).
This victory, however, did not frighten the people of Serezana
into thoughts of surrender, but rather disposed them to a still
more obstinate defence, and caused the Florentine commissaries to push their attack with increased vigor; so that both
attack and defence were most gallant. The siege being thus
protracted, Lorenzo de' Medici thought proper to take the
field himself; and having arrived in camp, the Florentine soldiers felt greatly encouraged by his presence, whilst the Sere-
zanese became disheartened, for seeing the persistence of the
Florentines in the attack and the coldness of the Genoese in
rendering them assistance, they surrendered freely and uncon-
ditionally to Lorenzo; and having thus placed themselves in the
hands of the Florentines they were treated with the greatest
humanity by them, with the exception of a few of the principal
authors of the revolt. During the siege Lodovico Sforza had
sent his forces to Pontremoli to make show of coming to the
assistance of the Florentines; but having secret intelligence
in Genoa, his partisans rose against the government, and with
the aid of Lodovico's troops they gave the city to the Duke of
Milan.

34. At this time the Germans commenced a war against the
Venetians; and Boccolino da Osimo in La Marca induced the
town of Osimo to revolt against the Pope, and usurped the government of the place. After many eventful changes he was
persuaded by Lorenzo de' Medici to restore the city to the
Pope, after which he went to Florence, where he lived for some
time much honored, under the protection of Lorenzo. Thence
he went to Milan, where, however, he did not find the same
good faith, for the Signor Lodovico Sforza had him put to
death. The Venetians being attacked were defeated by the
Germans near the city of Trent, and their general, the Signor
Ruberto da San Severino, killed. After this defeat, the Venetians, with their usual good fortune, made a treaty with the
Germans, the conditions of which were so favorable for their
republic that it seemed as though they had been the victors,
and not the vanquished. About this time serious disturbances

also broke out in the Romagna. Francesco d' Orso of Furli, a man of high authority in that city, became suspect to the Count Girolamo, and had been repeatedly threatened by him. Francesco, living thus in constant apprehension, was advised by his friends and relatives to forestall the Count and kill him, and thus by the death of his enemy to ward off the danger from himself. Having resolved to act upon this advice, and his mind being firmly made up to it, Francesco chose as the fittest time for the execution of his design the market day in Furli; for on that day many of his friends, of whose assistance he thought he might avail himself, would come into the city without being expressly sent for. It was in the month of May, when the Italians generally take their supper before dark; the conspirators thought it would be a convenient moment to kill the Count after he should have finished his repast, as he then generally went alone to his room whilst his family were still at table.

Having decided upon this, Francesco went at the appointed hour to the residence of the Count. He left his associates in the antechamber, and having reached the room where the Count Girolamo was, he requested one of the valets to inform him that he wished to speak with him. Francesco was admitted, and finding Girolamo alone he killed him after a few words of pretended conversation; he thereupon called in his associates, and they killed the valet also. The commandant of the place happening to come in at the same time to speak with the Count, he was also slain as he entered the hall with a few attendants. After these murders Francesco and his followers threw the body of the Count Girolamo out of the window, and created a great tumult; and raising the cry of "The Church and Liberty!" they caused all the people to arm, who hated the avarice and cruelty of the Count Girolamo; and having sacked his house they took the Countess Caterina and her children prisoners. The castle only remained to be taken to bring their attempt to a successful termination; but the castellan refused to surrender it. The conspirators therefore requested the Countess to induce him to give it up, which she promised to do provided they would allow her to go into the castle, leaving her children in their hands as a pledge of her good faith. They believed in her sincerity, and permitted her to enter the castle; but so soon as she was inside she menaced

them with death and every kind of punishment in revenge for
the murder of her husband. The conspirators in return
threatened to kill her children, to which she replied, "That
she had the means of getting others." The conspirators
however became alarmed, seeing that they received no support from the Pope, and that the Signor Lodovico Sforza, the
uncle of the Countess, had sent troops to her assistance; they
therefore carried off what they could, and went to Citta di
Castello. The Countess thereupon resumed the government,
and avenged the murder of her husband with every kind of
cruelty. The Florentines upon hearing of the death of the
Count deemed the occasion favorable to repossess themselves
of the castle of Piancaldoli, which some time back had been
taken from them by the Count Girolamo; and having sent
some troops there they recovered that castle, but at the cost
of the life of their most distinguished engineer Cecco, who was
killed on that occasion.

35. Besides these troubles in the Romagna, another of no
less moment occurred in the same province. Galeotto, lord of
Faenza, had for his wife the daughter of Giovanni Bentivogli,
prince of Bologna, who either from jealousy, or from having
been maltreated by her husband, or perhaps from her own
naturally bad disposition, had taken her husband in aversion,
and carried her hatred of him to that point that she resolved
to deprive him of his state and his life. Feigning to be sick,
she took to her bed, having previously arranged that when
Galeotto came to see her he should be killed by some of her
confidants, whom she was to conceal for that purpose in her
chamber. She had communicated her design to her father,
who hoped after the death of his son-in-law to become himself lord of Faenza. The time appointed for the execution of
the plot arrived, and Galeotto entered his wife's chamber as
was his custom. After remaining some time in conversation
with her, his murderers rushed from their concealment and
killed him. The news of Galeotto's death caused great excitement in Faenza; the wife, with her little son Astorre, took
refuge in the castle, and the people rushed to arms. Messer
Giovanni Bentivogli, together with a certain Bergamino, one of
the Duke of Milan's Condottieri, entered Faenza with a number
of armed followers; the Florentine commissary, Antonio Boscoli,
happened to be there also at that time. These chiefs assem-

bled in the midst of the tumult, and were deliberating with regard to the government of the place, when the men of the Val di Lamona, who had rushed in in great number on hearing of the disturbance, attacked Messer Giovanni and Bergamino; they killed the latter and took the other prisoner, and then, raising the cry of "Astorre and the Florentines!" they offered the city to the Florentine commissary. When this affair became known in Florence, it caused general dissatisfaction; nevertheless, they ordered Messer Giovanni and his daughter to be liberated, and took charge of the city and of Astorre in compliance with the wishes of the whole population. Many other disturbances occurred during several years in La Marca and at Sienna, after the main war between the greater princes had been settled. These troubles, however, having been of little moment, I deem it superfluous to relate them. It is true that they were most frequent in Sienna after the departure of the Duke of Calabria, on the termination of the war of 1478; and after many changes, in which the people and the nobles prevailed alternately, the nobles kept the upper hand. The most influential amongst these were Pandolfo and Jacopo Petrucci, who, the one by his sagacity and the other by his courage, became as it were sovereigns of the city.

36. After the successful termination of the war of Serezana, the Florentines lived in prosperous tranquillity until the death of Lorenzo de' Medici, in 1492; for after having established peace by his good judgment and authority, Lorenzo devoted his attention to the aggrandizement of the city and of his own family. He married his eldest son, Piero, to Alfonsina, daughter of the Cavaliere Orsini, and had his second son promoted to the dignity of Cardinal, which was the more remarkable as it was unprecedented, the youth having hardly completed his thirteenth year. This was in fact a ladder by means of which his house was enabled to mount to heaven itself, as indeed it happened in the course of time. He could not provide equally good fortune for his third son, as he was still too young when Lorenzo died. Of his daughters, one was married to Jacopo Salviati, another to Francesco Cibo, and a third to Piero Ridolfi; but the fourth, who, by way of keeping the family united, had been married to Giovanni de' Medici, her cousin, died. In his commercial affairs, however, Lorenzo was very unfortunate; for through the irregularity of his agents, who managed his affairs, not like

those of a private individual, but of a prince, the greater part of his private fortune was consumed; so that he was obliged to call upon his country to aid him with large sums of money. In consequence of this he gave up all commercial operations, and turned his attention to landed property, as being a more safe and solid wealth. He acquired large possessions in the districts of Prato and Pisa, and in the Val di Pesa, and erected upon them useful and elegant buildings, not like a private citizen, but with truly royal magnificence. After that he directed his attention to extending and embellishing the city of Florence, in which there was still much vacant land. Here he had new streets laid out and built up with houses, whereby the city was greatly enlarged and beautified. And to secure greater quiet and security within the state, and to be able to resist and combat its enemies at a greater distance from the city, he fortified the castle of Firenzuola, in the mountains towards Bologna; in the direction of Sienna he began the restoration of the Poggio Imperiale, which he fortified in the most complete manner. Towards Genoa he closed the road to the enemy by the acquisition of Pietrasanta and Serezana. Besides this, he maintained his friends the Baglioni in Perugia with subsidies and pensions, and the same with the Vitelli in Citta di Castello; and in Faenza he kept a special governor; all of which measures served as strong bulwarks to the city of Florence.

In peaceful times he often entertained the people with various festivities, such as jousts, feats of arms, and representations of triumphs of olden times. He aimed to maintain abundance in the city, to keep the people united, and the nobility honored. He had the greatest love and admiration for all who excelled in any art, and was a great patron of learning and of literary men, of which his conduct towards Cristofano Landini and Messer Demetrius the Greek furnishes the strongest proof. For this reason the Count Giovanni della Mirandola, a man of almost supernatural genius, was attracted by the magnificence of Lorenzo, and preferred to establish his home in Florence rather than in any other part of Europe, all of which he had visited in his travels. Lorenzo took the greatest delight in architecture, music, and poetry; and many of his own poetic compositions, enriched with commentaries, appeared in print. And, for the purpose of enabling the Florentine youths to devote themselves to the study of letters, he established a university in the city of Pisa, where he employed the most eminent men of all Italy as professors. He built a monastery for Fra Mariano da Chianozzona, of the order of St. Augustine, who was a most admirable pulpit orator. And thus, beloved of God and Fortune, all his enterprises were crowned with success, whilst those of his enemies had the opposite fate. For besides the conspiracy of the Pazzi, Battista Frescobaldi also attempted his assassination in the church of the Carmine; and Baldinatto of Pistoja tried the same at his villa. Each of these, together with their accomplices, suffered the most just punishment for their nefarious attempts.

Thus Lorenzo's mode of life, his ability and good fortune, were recognized with admiration, and highly esteemed, not only by all the princes of Italy, but also by those at a great distance. Matthias, king of Hungary, gave him many proofs of his affection; the Sultan of Egypt sent ambassadors to him with precious gifts; and the Grand Turk gave up to him Bernardo Bandini, the murderer of his brother. These proofs of regard from foreign sovereigns caused Lorenzo to be looked upon with the greatest admiration by all Italy; and his reputation was daily increased by his rare ability, for he was eloquent and subtle in speech, wise in his resolves, and bold and prompt in their execution. Nor can he be charged with any vices that would stain his many virtues, though very fond of women, and delighting in the society of witty and sarcastic men, and even taking pleasure in puerile amusements, — more so than would seem becoming to so great a man, so that he was often seen taking a part in the childish sports of his sons and daughters. Considering, then, his fondness for pleasure, and at the same time his grave character, there seemed as it were united in him two almost incompatible natures. During his latter years he was greatly afflicted with sufferings from his malady, the gout, and oppressed with intolerable pains in his stomach, which increased to that degree that he died in the month of April, 1492, in the forty-fourth year of his age. Neither Florence nor all Italy ever lost a man of higher reputation for prudence and ability, or whose loss was more deplored by his country, than Lorenzo de' Medici. And as his death was to be followed by the most ruinous consequences, Heaven gave many manifest indications of it. Amongst these was that the highest pinnacle of the church of the Santa Reparata was struck by lightning, so that a large part of the pinnacle fell to the earth, filling every one with terror and amazement. All Florence then, as well as all the princes of Italy, lamented the death of Lorenzo; in proof of which there was not one who did not send ambassadors to Florence to express his grief at so great a loss. And events very soon after proved that they had just cause for their regrets; for Italy being deprived of Lorenzo's counsels, no means could be found to satisfy or check the ambition of Lodovico Sforza, governor of the Duke of Milan. From this, soon after Lorenzo's death, there began to spring up those evil seeds of trouble, which ruined and continue to cause the ruin of Italy, as there was no one capable of destroying them.

END OF VOL. I.

University Press: John Wilson & Son, Cambridge.

www.ingramcontent.com/pod-product-compliance
Lightning Source LLC
Chambersburg PA
CBHW031955300426
44117CB00008B/768